I0815445

SPYING ON STUDENTS

MAKING THE MODERN SOUTH

David Goldfield, Series Editor

SPYING ON STUDENTS

THE FBI, RED SQUADS, AND STUDENT ACTIVISTS IN THE 1960s SOUTH

GREGG L. MICHEL

LOUISIANA STATE UNIVERSITY PRESS
BATON ROUGE

Published with the assistance of the V. Ray Cardozier Fund

Published by Louisiana State University Press
lsupress.org

Manufactured in the United States of America
First printing

DESIGNER: Michelle A. Neustrom
TYPEFACE: Whitman
PRINTER AND BINDER: Sheridan Books, Inc.

Portions of this book first appear as "Surveilling the Memphis Movement: Police Spying in Memphis, 1968–1976" in the *Journal of Southern History*, v. 87, no. 4, Nov. 2021: 673–710.

Jacket photograph: Student protestors at the University of South Carolina, May 1970. Photo by Ed Tilley. The State Newspaper Photograph Archive, Richland Library, Columbia, SC. Background text: Memo from the San Antonio FBI office with the text of a letter it planned to send anonymously to the parents of an antiwar activist. Records of the Federal Bureau of Investigation.

LIBRARY OF CONGRESS CATALOGING-IN-PUBLICATION DATA
Names: Michel, Gregg L., author.
Title: Spying on students : the FBI, Red Squads, and student activists in the 1960s South / Gregg L. Michel.
Other titles: Making the modern South.
Description: Baton Rouge : Louisiana State University Press, [2024] | Series: Making the modern South | Includes bibliographical references and index.
Identifiers: LCCN 2024002134 (print) | LCCN 2024002135 (ebook) | ISBN 978-0-8071-8222-2 (cloth) | ISBN 978-0-8071-8287-1 (epub) | ISBN 978-0-8071-8288-8 (pdf)
Subjects: LCSH: United States. Federal Bureau of Investigation—History—20th century. | College students, White—Political activity—Southern States—History—20th century. | Domestic intelligence—Southern States—History—20th century. | Police patrol—Surveillance operations—History—20th century. | Student movements—Southern States—History—20th century. | Southern States—Race relations.
Classification: LCC LB3610 .M44 2024 (print) | LCC LB3610 (ebook) | DDC 378.1/98109750904—dc23/eng/20240207
LC record available at https://lccn.loc.gov/2024002134
LC ebook record available at https://lccn.loc.gov/2024002135

for Rhonda, Halle, & Jeffrey

If you could not accept the past and its burden there was no future
. . . for only out of the past can you make the future.

—ROBERT PENN WARREN, *All the King's Men*

CONTENTS

ACKNOWLEDGMENTS

I OWE A DEBT OF GRATITUDE to the many people who helped me get this book over the finish line. It is with profound appreciation that I take this opportunity to thank them for their support and encouragement.

From the outset of my research, I knew I would face a challenge gathering sources for a book focused on surreptitious and often illegal government surveillance. But thanks to the guidance and direction provided by numerous librarians and archivists, I was able to locate many of the sources that inform this book. I especially wish to thank Gerald Chaudron and the Special Collections staff at the University of Memphis Library; G. Wayne Dowdy and the librarians in the Memphis and Shelby County Room of the Memphis Public Libraries; Ken Fieth and staff at the Metropolitan Government Archives of Nashville–Davidson County; the librarians who manage the Civil Rights Collection of the Nashville Public Library; the staff at the LBJ Presidential Library; and the archivists in the Vanderbilt University Special Collections and Archives. A special thank you to Shari Salisbury and the late Rita Wilson, librarians at my home institution, the University of Texas at San Antonio (UTSA), who helped me identify and access important source materials over the many years I worked on this project.

I extend my thanks to several historians and scholars who have supported and assisted my research. They include Christina Greene, who, years ago, generously shared with me FBI files she had collected on the Southern Student Organizing Committee, a collection that persuaded me that the sources existed for me to write this book. Marc Perrusquia also shared with me his large trove of files on surveillance in Memphis that he had acquired as a result of his lengthy lawsuit against the FBI to gain access to files about Ernest Withers's work as an informant. These materials were crucial to the story I tell about Memphis; it is not hyperbole to say I could not have written about Memphis without Marc's support. Michael K. Honey has been a steadfast supporter as I worked on this book, providing timely guidance, trenchant criticism, and consistent enthusiasm. As the foremost historian on Memphis in the civil rights era, his encouragement gave me boosts of confidence at several critical junctures. Leta McCollough Seletzky, whose book on her father, Marrell McCollough, a key figure in the Memphis Police Department's surveillance operations in the 1960s, was published as I was finishing this book, helpfully pointed me to additional resources that enrich this study. Finally, I extend my deep appreciation to Brett Bursey for always making himself available to talk about his experience in South Carolina, an experience many people would probably be happy to forget. Though he is not a historian, he has always expressed interest in preserving the historical record. And thanks to Brett for allowing me to use the photo of him, which is my favorite picture in the book.

The historians at UTSA are friends as much as they are colleagues. They inspire me with their teaching, their scholarship, and their ability to balance the two. I have benefited from their personal and professional support for many years. I particularly thank for their support Kirsten Gardner, Wing Chung Ng, Jack Reynolds, and Catherine Clinton. Thanks also to the UTSA College of Liberal and Fine Arts for providing important research funding for my work.

At LSU Press, I have profited from the guidance of editor in chief Rand Dotson. With a light touch and seemingly infinite patience, he gave me the time I needed to complete the manuscript. David Goldfield, editor of the Making the Modern South series, has championed this book from the moment we first spoke about it, quickly seeing its potential for the series. I am grateful for his support and honored for this book to be included in the series. Elizabeth Gratch did a masterful job copyediting the manuscript, saving me from numerous stylistic faux pas and other assorted missteps. Any remaining errors and inaccuracies are my own.

I save my final thanks for my family. My sister, Randi Michel Felberbaum, and her husband, Kenny, and children, Alex and Dylan, have sent long-distance love and positive energy that helped keep me going through the long years of research and writing. My mother, Barbara Michel, has been a source of support and love throughout, always asking how the work was coming and saying how proud she was of me. She even moved to San Antonio as I was finishing the book, ostensibly to be near family but also, I'm sure, to keep an eye on me. Two men who did not live to see the publication of this book were never far from my mind as I worked. My father-in-law, Irwin Katzman, was one of the most intellectually curious people I ever knew, and his wide interests were an inspiration as I ranged far and wide in my research. My father, Dr. Stephen L. Michel, was a model of selfless dedication and hard work throughout his life, someone who never let his long workdays as a surgeon compromise time with his family. He taught me about everything from ballgames to books, and he showed me how to be a man and a father.

I dedicate this book to my wife and children. Halle and Jeffrey have grown from toddlers to young adults over the course of this project. Their own journeys and experiences continually remind me that the history we write today will shape the world they inherit. Rhonda Michel is my partner in all things. She is my biggest advocate, most honest critic, and most important source of support. She picks me up when I'm down and does not hesitate to put me in my place when I deserve it. Most of all, as the person who knows me best, she has pushed, when needed, and cajoled, when necessary, to help me finish this book. For this and everything else, I am grateful to her. She is, and always will be, the only story I tell.

SPYING ON STUDENTS

INTRODUCTION

JACQUE SROUJI WAS A BIT PLAYER in the long-running saga over the mysterious 1974 death of Karen Silkwood, a lab technician in a plutonium fuel production facility run by energy giant Kerr-McGee in Crescent, Oklahoma. Silkwood was on her way to meet a *New York Times* reporter with evidence of alleged lax safety protocols at the facility when her car smashed into a culvert and plunged off a rainy road. Her death was ruled an accident, but suspicions of foul play emerged: there was evidence she may have been run off the road, and the papers she carried with her to substantiate her allegations were never recovered from the accident scene. Over the next decade, the story of her death and its unusual circumstances was a subject of national media attention. Silkwood herself became a divisive figure. To some, including the makers of the Oscar-nominated film *Silkwood*, she was a courageous whistleblower who was martyred for calling out the dangers of nuclear energy years before the Three Mile Island nuclear meltdown. To others, she was a fanatical, publicity-hungry activist who had stolen nuclear fuel from the plant in a desperate ploy to fabricate evidence against the company.[1]

Nashville-based Jacque Srouji was one of Silkwood's critics. In a book she wrote about nuclear power, she devoted a full chapter to Silkwood, calling into question her credibility and disparaging her as a drug-addled, emotionally unstable, unfit mother who sought to frame her employer with lies and untruths. In 1976, a congressional investigation into the case uncovered that Srouji had a "special relationship" with the FBI that enabled her to gain access to confidential documents related to the case, documents that the bureau had not turned over to Congress. A firestorm ensued. Srouji was summoned to testify before a congressional subcommittee, was deposed in litigation connected to the case, and was fired from her job as a copyeditor for the *Nashville Tennessean* newspaper. Srouji was uncomfortable in the public spotlight, and she proved to be an unreliable narrator of events in which she participated, changing her testimony, shifting her story, and forgetting crucial details. Her story sparked outrage—from the congressional subcommittee, which wanted to know what was in the documents she saw and why the FBI had withheld them from Congress, and from her boss, John Seigenthaler, a former official in the Kennedy Justice Department and at that time the editor of the *Tennessean*, who was incensed that he appeared to have an FBI informant on his staff. Less examined in the coverage was how Srouji had connected with the FBI in the first place.[2]

Srouji's ties to the FBI dated to 1963 or 1964 and her first job as an eighteen- or nineteen-year-old reporter on the civil rights and student movement beat for the staunchly conservative *Nashville Banner*.[3] Student activism was on the upswing in the early 1960s throughout the United States, and Nashville had emerged as a vibrant center of civil rights activism. John Lewis, Diane Nash, Marion Barry, Bernard Lafayette, and other students from the city's Black colleges and universities had spearheaded one of the first sit-ins of the era, and the Nashville students played a key role in the founding of the Student Nonviolent Coordinating Committee (SNCC); one of their own, Marion Barry, won election as the first chairman of the group that would become the most consequential student civil rights group of the decade.[4] White students in the city also began to stir in the early 1960s. Anti-segregation protests developed among students at Vanderbilt University, Scarritt College, and Peabody College (officially, the George Peabody College for Teachers), and Nashville became home to the Southern Student Organizing Committee (SSOC), a group that brought together progressive white students on campuses across the South.[5] As a young white woman in Nashville, Srouji was well positioned to cover the movement for the *Banner*. Moreover, she was clearly in sync with the paper's hostility to the civil rights and student movements, a hostility that flowed down from the office of James "Jimmy" Stahlman, the paper's arch segregationist editor. Sometimes able to blend in with the crowd at protests or persuade activists to confide in her by implying sympathy for their causes, Srouji wrote articles that were critical of student activists, their lifestyle, and the issues they supported. Stahlman liked her stories, and he encouraged her to share information she had gathered in her reporting with local FBI agent Lawrence Olson Sr., to whom he introduced her. Over her time at the *Banner*, Srouji shared notes, photographs, and other material with Olson. A decade later, Olson was stationed in Oklahoma City, and Srouji reached out to her old contact for assistance as she worked on the Silkwood case.[6]

The revelation in 1976 that Srouji had served as an informant for the FBI while working as a journalist occurred shortly after explosive congressional investigations revealed that the FBI, the Central Intelligence Agency, and other federal agencies had operated wide-ranging and abusive surveillance programs that targeted a broad spectrum of American citizens, mostly on the Left, for their political views. A common tactic in these programs was to utilize media sources to spy on activists and to spread malicious rumors about them, and Srouji's exposure was a clear example of such work; in fact, hers was the first relationship between a reporter and the FBI to be exposed in the wake of the congressional investigations.[7] More generally, their relationship fit with a broader pattern of surveillance executed by public safety officials in the South in the 1960s. Law enforcement at all levels, including the FBI but also state investigative agencies and internal security units in metropolitan police departments, monitored, investigated, and harassed leftist student activists. At a distance of several decades, Srouji's collaboration with Olson may seem unusual given its focus on white students in Nashville who constituted a small and decidedly non-menacing component of the larger movement. But the fact that there were white students at all in this mid-South city who aligned themselves with Black civil rights activists and supported other leftist causes surprised, unnerved, and concerned local officials, who worried that the students' activism presaged broader disruptions to the social order. These authorities welcomed any help they could get, which made Srouji's assistance valuable.

Srouji was one of numerous individuals in the South who participated in surveillance operations against white students in the region. Paid informants, friendly journalists, and school administrators were among those who spied on student activists. Security and police officials invested significant resources—time, capital, labor—in surveillance programs aimed at white students. They infiltrated the students' organizations, spied on their meetings, disrupted their activities, exacerbated tensions among the students themselves, and sowed discord with students' families and their schools. Their tactics ranged from the passive reading of alternative newspapers in an effort to identify activists and leaders—whom they pejoratively referred to as "ringleaders"—to blatantly illegal and unconstitutional actions such as warrantless spying on individuals for their putatively subversive views rather than any lawbreaking activity. On a personal level, the surveillance could have devastating consequences: student targets experienced family ruptures, expulsion from school, and arrests. Its impact on organizations could be equally consequential, derailing their activities and hobbling their ability to attract support.

Student activists around the nation endured official harassment and surreptitious surveillance in the 1960s. Major metropolitan areas outside of the South that were home to tens of thousands of young people crowded onto college campuses were sites of concerted campaigns by local police and federal agents to prevent student activists from gaining traction and inducing other students to join their groups and protests. As student protest activity exploded, first around Black civil rights and the United States' growing military involvement in Vietnam and then women's rights, university reform, and drives for equality for other marginalized and oppressed groups, organizations such as the Students for a Democratic Society (SDS), the American Indian Movement (AIM), the Mexican American Youth Organization (MAYO), the Puerto Rican Young Lords, the Black Panthers, and various women's liberation groups became targets. New York, Chicago, Seattle, Los Angeles, Minneapolis, and San Francisco were among the cities in which authorities conducted intensive and frequently extralegal surveillance of student protesters and implemented programs that went beyond mere monitoring to include acts of repression and violence. A surge of counterintelligence campaigns undertaken by law enforcement agencies was an enduring legacy of the rise of student protests of the 1960s. The surveillance of southern activists fit with this national trend.[8]

African Americans, not whites, bore the brunt of police surveillance and harassment in the South of the 1960s. From the infiltration of civil rights groups by police informants to the FBI's well-known surveillance of Martin Luther King Jr. and other Black leaders to episodes of police violence that resulted in the deaths of unarmed Black students in Orangeburg, South Carolina, in 1968 and Jackson, Mississippi, in 1970, the historical record is replete with examples of brutality and surveillance directed at Black dissenters. Black civil rights protesters and activists, and even those who merely sympathized with calls for racial equality, endured abuse and harassment from law enforcement at all levels of government that extended over decades. White student activists simply did not suffer comparable abuse. Yet the fact that they were subjected to wide-ranging, intrusive, and illegal surveillance highlights the pervasiveness of the surveillance regime. Moreover, it illustrates how little room there was for dissent in the South. White students who advocated for civil rights, organized opposition to the Vietnam War, or embraced the stylings of the counterculture appeared as threats to the established order, an order based on segregation and elite domination of political and economic power. Such fears did not seem merely hypothetical, alarmist, or fantastical to authorities given the unrest on college campuses around the country.

As white students revolted against the status quo, most notably but by no means only at the University of California, Berkeley, and Columbia University, southern authorities sought to choke off such disruptions in the South. State actors' use of surveillance against white students was part of the drive to suffocate dissent in the region. Officials would not tolerate any divergence from conventional norms or mainstream views, let alone criticisms of the white supremacist sociopolitical order or questioning the virtue of the war in Southeast Asia. The authorities' use of spycraft and surveillance techniques against citizens exercising their constitutional rights makes clear that law enforcement saw no threat as too small or insignificant. Just as revealing, the surveillance regime highlighted the fragility of the status quo. If organizing by white students could inspire a government-wide crackdown, then perhaps the established order was more brittle than it appeared and social and political change was actually possible in the region.

White student activists could be found across the region in the 1960s, from large public universities to small religious or liberal arts colleges. In 1964, forty-five white student activists, hailing from fifteen schools in ten southern states, came together in Nashville to create the Southern Student Organizing Committee, which would emerge as the most significant organization of white activists in the South in the second half of the decade. From 1964 until its demise in 1969, the loosely organized group connected leftist students on campuses throughout the South with one another, providing them with an organizational home as they worked to support civil rights, build opposition to the war, encourage gender equality on their campuses, and advocate for the rights of workers and unions in a region where organized labor struggled to make gains. SSOC sponsored workshops and meetings, published a widely distributed magazine and numerous other pamphlets and newsletters, and sent "campus travelers" to schools to support organizing efforts. The group especially focused on drawing white student support through an approach that emphasized their southern roots, making the case that as a white southerner in a region soaked with racial violence, one could advocate for racial reform while still maintaining pride in one's heritage and history. SSOC was close to SNCC—some of its founders had participated in the Black student–led group—and maintained ties to the northern-based SDS, the leading antiwar student group in the country. These ties, along with SSOC's promotion of causes that were anathema across much of the white community in the South, brought the group to the attention of law enforcement and domestic security officials. To them, SSOC represented a dangerous threat: an organization of white students with ties to radical groups that promoted extremist ideologies and tactics, raising the prospect that SSOC had the ability, and the desire, to instigate destabilizing student protests.

The government agencies and law enforcement units that surveilled white student activists in the South represented a cross section of public safety authorities. At the federal level, the Federal Bureau of Investigation led the effort to repress student activism. The FBI's campaign against white southern students was part of its notorious, expansive drive to decimate leftist organizations and activists across the country in the post–World War II era. Led by J. Edgar Hoover, a culturally conservative, hardened racist who used his political savvy to curry support with the nation's top leaders during his nearly fifty-year tenure as FBI director, the bureau deployed tactics from the unsavory to the illegal in its effort to cripple student activism. Its actions against white students in the South were akin to its work against the larger student activist formations in the major metropolitan areas of the Northeast, Midwest, and West Coast. The smaller numbers of white southern student activists did not shield them from the bureau's campaign of surveillance and harassment. State-level investigative bodies also monitored and disrupted the work of white students in their states. To these state-level actors, the advent of white student activism was a new and startling development that they interpreted as an existential threat to established norms and elite control. Protest against the war or in favor of desegregation could quickly spiral out of control, they feared, and thus justified a sharp response. At the most local level of public safety, police departments in the South implemented their own programs to undermine student activism in their communities. Domestic internal security units—so-called Red Squads, given their initial formation to pursue suspected communists earlier in the century—surveilled, harassed, and attacked campus-based activists as well as collaborated with their state and federal peers to create an interlocking web of surveillance to hinder the ability of student activists to build support for their causes. White southern student activists who opposed the war, flouted community norms, and worked alongside their Black friends for racial reforms stood out to public safety officials not merely as curiosities but as harbingers of the dangers that awaited southern communities if student activism was to take root and spread.

While authorities may have considered their work against student activists to be a prudent response to a dangerous threat, their campaign was problematic for several reasons. First, the effort highlights officials' conflation of political dissent with subversion and disloyalty. Their actions exposed both their contempt for dissent and their view that opposition to the war in Vietnam or support for Black equality constituted a serious and credible threat to domestic security. Conceptualized in this way, student activism was a threat to be neutered by any means necessary. Warrantless surveillance, false flag operations, unmerited investigations of individuals' personal lives and financial affairs, and arrests based on trumped-up or manufactured charges were regular tools law enforcement authorities believed they were justified in using to blunt student activism. Second, officials often exceeded their agencies' mission in their headlong drive against students. The FBI's counterintelligence programs dispensed with any pretense of law enforcement aims when the bureau used its powers against individuals whose only "crime" was to assemble with others and to express their views on the issues of the day. Similarly, police and state investigators did not bother to conceal the fact that students' political views and lifestyle choices were the basis for turning the power of the state against them.

Third, by seeking to criminalize dissent, the surveillance regime had a chilling effect on the exercise of constitutionally protected rights. The Supreme Court had warned of this peril in 1963, when it ruled that surveillance would discourage citizens from exercising rights cherished by all Americans.[9] The Senate committee that investigated abuses by the FBI and other federal agencies made a similar point: "No citizen should have to weigh his or her desire to express an opinion, or join a group, against the risk of having lawful speech or association used against him. . . . What some suspected and others feared has turned out to be largely true—vigorous expression of unpopular views, association with dissenting groups, participation in peaceful protest activities, have provoked both government surveillance and retaliation."[10] Fourth, once established, surveillance regimes became nearly impossible to dislodge. In part, this was because they operated in secret, not just immune from public scrutiny but hidden from those with supposed authority over them. Only a small circle of officials typically knew of the activities of police department Red Squads, while Hoover's FBI operated with virtually no oversight from the executive branch officials to which it nominally reported. These programs also endured because of the self-justifying logic that underlay their very existence. If they faced a multifaceted, devious, and unrelenting adversary, then only a continuously expanding and ever-vigilant response could safeguard the community and the nation. Moreover, "mission creep" came to define the programs, as they gradually expanded their focus to target seemingly benign activities, such as attending a meeting, subscribing to a leftist magazine, or merely being acquainted with someone already under investigation. As they vacuumed up ever increasing amounts of information, the data collected stood as unquestionable proof of the value of the programs. And this served to insulate them bureaucratically from challenges to their budgets or staffing levels. Surveillance administrators had every incentive to trumpet their programs' supposed successes to further entrench them within the administrative order.

Finally, perhaps the most significant problem with the domestic surveillance regime was that it was wholly ineffective and counterproductive. The vast expenditure of time and treasure, labor and resources, to surveil student activists and gather data on their activities failed to generate evidence of subversion or disloyalty. Time after time, counterintelligence officials and police investigators discovered through their spying that the students they had set their sights on were not doing the bidding of foreign interests or seeking the violent overthrow of the American government. Instead, they found that the activists they surveilled were sincerely committed to extending democracy and freedom to all Americans, to opposing American imperialism in all its forms, and to promoting a vision of the common good that threatened the white supremacist order. Yet the absence of evidence of subversion not only did not end the surveillance but became motivation to look harder, probe deeper—it was testimony to the deceptive and dangerous practices of the nation's adversaries and thus became justification for further surveillance. By such logic, the battle against extremism and subversion would never end; any victory was a temporary respite in a never-ending fight.

White southern students appear infrequently in the works of scholars who have examined the surveillance of the 1960s and 1970s. The unmasking by the media and Congress of the FBI's multiyear campaign of surveillance and harassment of American citizens and the release of the voluminous files the agency maintained has resulted in a vast literature on FBI misdeeds. Important and innovative works, including David Garrow's *The FBI and Martin Luther King, Jr.*, Kenneth O'Reilly's *Racial Matters*, and Athan Theoharis's *Spying on Americans* concentrate on the FBI's pursuit of Black civil rights activists in the South and white antiwar radicals elsewhere in the country while making only glancing reference to the bureau's campaign against white students in the South.[11] Similarly, white southern activists are absent from studies of CIA spying, such as Angus Mackenzie's *Secrets* and John Prados's *The Family Jewels*.[12] They also receive scant attention in the few scholarly works that consider surveillance activities undertaken by local and state forces. More than three decades after its publication, Frank Donner's *Protectors of Privilege* remains the only monograph focused on police Red Squads. Donner rarely considers the South, though, concentrating instead on police activities in northern and western cities.[13] The historical literature overlooks state efforts to surveil and repress white southern activists as well. Thanks to the opening of its files in the 1990s, only the Mississippi State Sovereignty Commission (MSSC) has received significant coverage from historians, and their works focus almost exclusively on the agency's campaign of surveillance and violence against African American civil rights activists in the state.[14]

Spying on Students thus offers a unique perspective on the surveillance state and the social movements of the civil rights era. It reveals the breadth and depth of federal, state, and local government entities' efforts to short-circuit white student activism in the South. It demonstrates that authorities' war on dissent extended beyond campaigns against African Americans and white northern radicals to also include work designed to repress white activists in the South. By documenting the authorities' sustained surveillance of white students in the region, it makes clear that officials perceived these students to be a threat to community peace and thus justified abusive and invasive tactics to frustrate their activities. Indeed, the counterintelligence operations initiated against white students reveal that authorities considered them a menace. As such, exposing the authorities' attention to white activists helps render visible young whites in the South as something other than opponents of social change or as indifferent to the movements of the era. White students in the South were active in civil rights, antiwar, and other organizing efforts throughout this era, and law enforcement officials certainly saw their efforts as dangerous and impactful. This work, then, offers fresh insights on the commitment of white activists in the South to social change as well as government efforts to strangle this activism before it could threaten the norms and conventions of the white supremacist order that continued to hold sway in the region.

This work's examination of white students' activism should not be construed as minimizing the contribution of Black students to the movements of the era. The Student Nonviolent Coordinating Committee, the Black Panthers, and campus-based groups of Black students around the country defined and shaped much of the activism of the era. Instead, the emphasis on white students here reflects the breadth of the state's surveillance apparatus. White students were an active presence in the movements of the day and thus became targets for government repression. It is also important to recognize that authorities perceived white and Black students as operating separately from one another. The FBI and local law enforcement agencies distinguished between white and Black students, coding the former as antiwar and New Left adherents and the latter as racial agitators and extremists. Such distinctions guided anti-activist operations. Moreover, as the 1960s progressed and calls for racial exclusivity radiated out of the civil rights movement, ties between white and Black students frayed. Interracial alliances and collaborations lost their appeal, particularly to Black youth, who sought to align themselves organizationally and intellectually with other Black activists. As historian Doug Rossinow has written, "The lines of political identity separating white radicals from activists of color were quite real and important during the 1960s, and we elide those boundaries at risk of distorting the past."[15] Although Black and white students may have shared similar ideals and goals, they often identified differently and worked through different organizational entities.

As a study of government surveillance of social and political activists, this work faced a significant challenge from the outset: locating source material of surveillance operations that often were secretive and hidden. Police departments, for example, are not in the habit of sharing with inquiring historians evidence of their counterintelligence work, if such material even survives after more than a half-century. Moreover, some agencies were known to have destroyed evidence of surveillance activities to shield their programs from exposure and themselves from public censure and possibly legal action. Interviews with participants in domestic security operations are unlikely to be available as well. Few officers and agents survive to this day. Those who do, and are interested in talking about the past, often have memories that have been greatly diminished by the passage of time. More commonly, I have found, they are uninterested in revisiting the surveillance programs in which they participated, choosing to ignore my requests to speak or lashing out at me for the supposed bias of my work. As one law enforcement operative wrote me, "I am not interested in contributing to any liberally edited publications."[16] This paucity of source material has created a lacuna in the literature of social movements. As one scholar put it in a reference to federal officials that was equally applicable to those at other levels of government, "The U.S. government's systematic destruction and withholding of documents related to its intelligence programs has produced a massive historical and cultural erasure in both academic and popular U.S. history."[17] I am hardly the first scholar to confront this issue, and I have benefited from the work and generosity of others who have meticulously labored to make surviving collections of government files available to me and the broader community of scholars. But because this book's focus on student activists in the South is not one that has received attention from historians, I have cultivated a unique set of source documents.

At the federal level, I have used Freedom of Information Act requests to gain access to thousands of pages from the FBI's files that document its pursuit of student activists across the South. My initial request grew out of research I had conducted for my book *Struggle for a Better South: The Southern Student Organizing Committee, 1964–1969*. Aware of the FBI's well-known animus toward the New Left, I wondered if the group had captured the bureau's attention. In fact, it had. While some of these documents were part of the bureau's notorious COINTELPRO programs against civil rights and antiwar activists, others existed as part of other bureau programs to monitor suspected subversives. These records are flush with evidence of the bureau's fears of communist infiltration of the southern movement and its scheming to surveil and undermine southern students' efforts to build support for progressive causes on their campuses. At the state level, I have made extensive use of the surviving records of the Mississippi State Sovereignty Commission, by far the most significant state agency in the region tasked with a surveillance mission. The commission's records, which initially were slated for destruction and then later survived a legal challenge to being made public, provide broad evidence that state authorities directed surveillance and harassment of white student activists in the state. The MSSC records are a treasure trove. They are also unique; there is no other extant collection of records compiled by the investigative agencies of other southern states. This highlights an important consideration for this study, namely, that existence of records shaped the locales on which this book focuses. Thus, Mississippi gets attention thanks to the perseveration of the MSSC's files. So do Oklahoma and South Carolina because documentary evidence of surveillance survives in those states. Of course, one should not interpret the absence of records as meaning a locality did not conduct surveillance, only that the files providing the granular details of an agency's activities do not exist.

Access is an equally important issue for research into the work of intelligence units within southern police departments. Records of Red Squad activities generally do not exist or long ago were purged by police departments anxious to jettison evidence of illegal spying when the post-Hoover era political climate made such activities cause for censure and condemnation. Whether it be evidence of a counterintelligence unit's surveillance activities or documents related to internal discussions about police brutality cases, police departments have no incentive to preserve, let alone share, evidence of potential wrongdoing, thereby rendering invisible in the historical record activities that were unethical, unconstitutional, and illegal.[18] For this study, I have managed this challenge by focusing on Red Squads that operated in two localities—coincidentally in the same state, Tennessee—where I discovered evidence of their surveillance activities. In Memphis, that meant the records from a 1970s lawsuit that accused the police department of spying on activists. In Nashville, it meant stitching together evidence from disparate public records on the department's repressive surveillance work. These were not the only southern police departments to operate Red Squads. Richmond, for example, had an active unit, and fragmentary evidence of its work appears in FBI documents discussing collaborations between the two law enforcement agencies. But the documentary record of Red Squad activities in Richmond and elsewhere in the region is limited, offering only occasional glimpses of their work. In Memphis and Nashville, a fuller, richer evidentiary record reveals the diverse set of surveillance tactics that Red Squads deployed in a drive to throttle student activism in these cities.

This book is organized into four chapters that detail the wide-ranging, intensive campaign by federal, state, and local governments to surveil and harass white student activists in the South. Chapter 1 examines the work of investigative units within the sprawling federal bureaucracy, most notably the FBI but also the Central Intelligence Agency and Army intelligence. Acutely sensitive to student dissent, federal officials strived to undermine the activities of student groups nationally. The FBI played the most important role in this effort. Prodded by Hoover to lash out at student activists wherever they appeared, the bureau developed a range of programs to counter and disrupt student activists in the South, just as it did elsewhere. The apogee of the bureau's efforts was COINTELPRO–New Left, a campaign begun in 1968 that authorized agents to use mundane and trivial tactics, such as reading New Left publications, as well as those that were unsavory and illegal, such as warrantlessly surveilling targets and sending anonymous letters to friends and family. Despite the fact that white student activists in the region were often loosely organized and fewer in number than in other parts of the country, their very existence stood as a challenge to the existing order, a threat that authorities believed they needed to contain before it metastasized.

Intelligence units operated by state governments added to the web of surveillance that white activists encountered. Authorized by state legislatures and governors that saw student protesters as a direct challenge to the social order, state investigative agencies deployed similar tactics as federal authorities in their effort to cripple civil rights and New Left activism. Chapter 2 examines the surveillance activities of several of these state agencies to show how they not only collaborated with local and federal law enforcement but developed their own programs to monitor and disrupt student activism in their states. The chapter explores the surveillance activities of an executive-level intelligence agency in Oklahoma, the state police in South Carolina, and the legislatively authorized Mississippi State Sovereignty Commission. Opposition to the Vietnam War by white students galvanized the Oklahoma and South Carolina officials' work, as they feared that students' anti-draft and antiwar activities could become the leading edge of a wave of dissent that would wash over campuses there. The Sovereignty Commission was equally unnerved by antiwar activism but also was broadly attuned to dissent on racial matters, which often was its overriding concern given the swelling civil rights activism there. Each of these agencies operated as a key part of the machinery of repression in their state, a tool deployed by law enforcement to suppress dissent before it could garner broad student support and thereby threaten the very order of society.

Complementing federal and state officials' work and demonstrating the breadth and depth of the surveillance campaign against white student activists were the activities of intelligence units operating within metropolitan police departments. Chapters 3 and 4 turn attention to two such units. Chapter 3 focuses on the Memphis Police Department's Red Squad. The Memphis police had a long history of spying on activist networks and using the vast powers at their disposal to intimidate and abuse dissidents. Memphis's Black civil rights activists took the brunt of this harassment. But as the Vietnam War, the demands of organized labor, and the radicalization of the civil rights movement after Martin Luther King Jr.'s assassination intensified social unrest in Memphis in the late 1960s, white student dissenters also emerged as a target of police surveillance. The Memphis Red Squad, backed by the city's political leadership, moved to crack down on activists at Memphis State University, local high schools, and wherever else activism sprouted. The spying went on, undetected and hidden from the public, for more than a decade until it was exposed in the media. In response, the police, with the mayor's blessing, hastily, and unsuccessfully, tried to burn all the records to keep them out of the hands of the American Civil Liberties Union (ACLU), which was preparing to sue the city. The resulting litigation revealed how little tolerance there was for dissent in Memphis and, ultimately, resulted in a court-ordered consent decree that banned the Memphis police from surveilling citizens engaged in constitutionally protected activities.

Nashville's Red Squad is the subject of chapter 4. The police unit's clandestine work to cleanse the city of dissent belied the image of a moderate and pragmatic Nashville that business and political leaders sought to project. The Red Squad aggressively moved to undermine dissent wherever it appeared. Increasingly, that meant on college campuses and against students. While dissent had been common at the predominantly Black Fisk and Tennessee State Universities, it also grew during the 1960s at the largely white schools in the city, including Vanderbilt University and Scarritt College. The Nashville students were the driving force behind the creation of SSOC in 1964 and, for the next five years, played a leading role in the organization. Throughout this time, the Nashville Red Squad conducted a campaign of intimidation and harassment of the white activists. They photographed them at meetings, collaborated with the FBI to track their movements, and worked with informants to gather information about their plans. In 1969, hounded by the Nashville police and other law enforcement and beset by internal problems that the surveillance exacerbated, SSOC disbanded. Unlike in Memphis, the Nashville police never faced rebuke for the Red Squad's activities.

It may seem like government surveillance of white student activists in the South was an exercise in overkill, that the intensity of the effort was vastly disproportionate to the challenge posed by students. But there is meaning in the mismatch between threat and response. The sharp government retort to student organizing demonstrates officials' worries about the potential for widespread student unrest to destabilize the sociopolitical order. As such, it suggests that the status quo they sought to protect was weaker than it appeared. Indeed, it was; the movements of the era, beginning with the Black-led civil rights movement, chipped away at the old norms and standards of the white supremacist order. This order would eventually crumble, but not without a fight from its staunchest defenders. Their clandestine efforts are an important, if understudied, component of the movements of the era. For white student activists in the South, government surveillance added to the challenges they faced as they sought to grow their organizations and build support among other students. Revealing the surveillance campaigns allows for a fuller assessment of the movements themselves. It also exposes the way in which those who held political power used it to stifle dissent. Writing about the broader student movement of the 1960s, historian Beverly Gage has said: "There is no separating law enforcement from politics. To understand the history of the New Left, we must also understand the inner workings and political influence of its greatest adversary."[19] Domestic security and investigative units in the South operated in a political environment conducive to surveillance of political organizing. Well funded and bureaucratically entrenched, they built their efforts around the idea that dissent of any type could be the opening salvo of an attempt to overturn the established order. The myriad tactics they deployed against student activists showed their contempt for dissenting views and exposed their fear that the activism of white students constituted a credible threat to domestic tranquility.

1

FEDERAL SURVEILLANCE

J. EDGAR HOOVER WAS OBSESSED with the activism of college students. The longtime director of the Federal Bureau of Investigation was a staunch anticommunist who saw himself and his agency as vital bulwarks against communist-inspired insurgency in the United States and protectors of the nation's social and political order. In the fourth decade of his tenure at the helm of the FBI as the 1960s started, Hoover had watched with increasing alarm as one segment of society after another rose up to demand their rights, protest injustice, and agitate for change. In response, he mobilized the bureau as never before to surveil, harass, and disrupt the work of activists he considered extremists and subversives. Chief among them, of course, were civil rights advocates, starting with Martin Luther King Jr. and extending deep into the ranks of SNCC, the Southern Christian Leadership Conference (SCLC), the Black Panthers, and a range of other organizations. Throughout Hoover's tenure as director, and intensifying as the civil rights movement gathered steam in the 1950s and 1960s, the bureau schemed and plotted, both overtly and covertly, to derail the movement and harass and surveil the Black activists who led it. Hoover attacked King relentlessly, calling him the "most notorious liar in the country" and labeling him a communist and anti-American extremist. The rest of the bureau followed his lead. Officials up and down the organization, from Hoover's close associates in Washington to field agents in far-flung locales, worked to discredit Black activists, thwart their organizing efforts, and even facilitate violence against them. In a particularly revealing example of the bureau's antipathy toward Black activists, one of its informants played a vital role in the Chicago Police Department's murder of Black Panthers Fred Hampton and Mark Clark. Fed tactical details by the informant about the apartment where they resided, the police executed an early-morning raid and killed the two men as they were startled awake. For his work, Hoover awarded the informant a bonus payment.[1]

Hoover also increasingly focused on the white college students drawn to action by the racial justice movement and, especially, the spiraling conflict in Vietnam. At too many schools, he believed, cowed administrators and leftist faculty coddled students and acquiesced to their demands. The surge in student activism—from large marches in the nation's biggest cities to isolated demonstrations in small college towns, from teach-ins at major public research universities to draft card burnings at tiny liberal arts colleges—frustrated and angered Hoover. Capturing his sense of grievance and dismay was his awkward, condescending "Open Letter to College Students," which the FBI distributed to United Press International for wide circulation in 1970. While paying lip service to the value of dissent in a democratic society, Hoover devoted the bulk of the letter to lambasting student activists as extremists who sought to corrupt other students, destroy their campuses, and tear down the American social order. New Leftists, he charged, peddled poisonous views and distorted ideas and promoted violence and nihilism: "They ridicule the flag, poke fun at American institutions, seek to destroy our society. . . . They have no rational, intelligent plan for the future either for the university or the Nation." The New Left, thus characterized as a potent threat to the nation, had to be stopped, by whatever means necessary. Hoover's FBI would take the lead in this campaign. But it was not alone.[2]

Intelligence, national security, and law enforcement officials across the sprawling federal bureaucracy developed a strong interest in the protest activities of college students in the 1960s. Broadly charged with protecting the country from foreign threats and domestic unrest, these agencies took aim at the nation's campuses as student protest swelled in support of civil rights and in opposition to the Vietnam War. In the context of the Cold War, the officials who guided these agencies, encouraged by the nation's top political leaders, readily suspected that student activists were doing the bidding of America's enemies, and they believed it was their duty to uncover the activists' foreign ties and to thwart their plans.

Presidents Lyndon Johnson and Richard Nixon shared a similar perspective on student protests, and they pushed their underlings in the security apparatus they controlled to reveal the foreign connections that they were certain underlay student activism. Angered that protests and demonstrations were distracting from their agendas and hurting them politically, they insisted that security officials use their considerable powers to investigate student groups and activists. Presidential support helped accelerate the surveillance activities undertaken by federal agencies. These efforts intensified over the latter half of the 1960s. While the FBI's campaign to stamp out activism and protests of all types zeroed in on the white New Left, military intelligence, the Central Intelligence Agency, and the National Security Agency launched or expanded programs designed to counter student activism and identify the communist ties of activist groups and individuals. Their programs were deeply intrusive and often illegal, and they shocked the nation as enterprising journalists and brave citizens revealed them, one by one, in the early 1970s. The resulting furor led to presidential and congressional investigations in 1975—the "Year of Intelligence"—that exposed the sordid details of federal intrusion into the private affairs and political views of American citizens.[3]

White student activists in the South were among those targeted in federal surveillance programs. While officials may have been more acutely concerned with Black civil rights activists throughout the county and white New Leftists on the nation's two coasts, they also turned their sights on activists at the overwhelmingly white campuses in the South, particularly in response to antiwar activity. That they did so reflected a worldview that conflated political dissent with disloyalty and subversion. Federal law enforcement and national security officials considered student activists a credible threat to the status quo even on campuses where activists were few in number and in locales that were hardly in danger of being overrun by radicals. But small numbers did not so much suggest insignificance as they did potential, sprouts of activism ready to burst forth and spread like a toxic weed throughout the campus and community. Officials therefore always had to be on guard, prepared to counter the slightest hint of dissent or political activism that could destabilize the established order.

THE CIA AND ARMY INTELLIGENCE

The Central Intelligence Agency was a key component of the federal surveillance machinery. In violation of its charter, which defined its mission as protecting American interests overseas and prohibited the agency from engaging in domestic intelligence or law enforcement activities, the agency developed a multipronged counterintelligence campaign to spy on and disrupt the work of domestic activists starting in the 1950s and continuing for over twenty years. Tactics the agency had used overseas were now deployed on American soil, as the agency tampered with mail, intercepted telegrams, and monitored phone calls in cryptically named programs such as Project Lingual, Project Shamrock, and Project Minaret. Ostensibly aimed at surveilling foreign sources or identifying the foreign connections of domestic activists, the projects, in fact, targeted Americans for surveillance. The CIA's domestic counterintelligence work intensified in the mid-1960s, after *Ramparts* magazine embarrassed the agency by exposing its secret work with Michigan State University in support of the South Vietnamese government and its two decades of clandestine funding of the National Student Association, a program intended to ensure that students in this national organization promoted U.S. interests when attending international meetings. The CIA responded to these revelations by digging for dirt on *Ramparts* and then, in 1967, creating a new unit, the Special Operations Group within the Counterintelligence Division, to investigate not just *Ramparts* but hundreds of underground newspapers. It also sought information on ties between student activists and foreign actors, including Soviets, Chinese Communists, and Cuban radicals. A few months later, the agency launched Project Resistance with a goal of identifying and gathering information about students and groups involved in antiwar activities. In 1968, the agency joined the two programs under the umbrella project known as "Operation CHAOS," which employed a staff of more than fifty people at its peak in 1970 and represented more than 20 percent of the entire counterintelligence staff. Using informants and undercover agents to infiltrate campus groups and sharing information with the FBI and local police, the agency over the next several years opened investigative files on more than 10,000 American citizens and indexed the names of more than 300,000 Americans in its computer systems.[4] Spying on Americans proved not merely incidental to the agency's activities but was an intentional focus of CIA operations.

The CIA strained to filter its domestic intelligence work through its internationalist agenda. Repeatedly, though, domestic activists emerged as the focal point of the agency's work. It used its vast resources to gather information on activists and organizations, sent agents undercover to college campuses, and produced reports for the White House that analyzed the student antiwar movement. One 1968 report, *Student Dissent and Its Techniques*, focused on antiwar activism among American students, with a particular emphasis on Students for a Democratic Society, while a notorious 1969 study, *Restless Youth*, so blatantly violated the agency's charter's prohibition on domestic intelligence work that a cover memo emphasized the need for secrecy to avoid the "considerable notoriety" that would result if the report were exposed. As CIA director Richard Helms put it when he sent an updated version of the report in early 1969 to Henry Kissinger, the assistant to the president for National Security Affairs in the new Nixon administration, "It would prove most embarrassing for all concerned" if the report were leaked, given its discussion of the American student movement.[5]

The agency was aggressive in its cultivation of informants. In late 1969, the Office of Security sought to recruit individuals who could infiltrate the student movement as a means of establishing their radical bona fides—what the agency called "reddening" or "sheepdipping"—prior to being sent overseas on intelligence assignments. Between 1970 and 1974, eleven agents served in this capacity, and though the agency insisted any intelligence gathered on domestic activities would be incidental to the foreign focus of this work, these agents did, in fact, collect information on the activities of student groups in the United States, which the agency subsequently sent to the FBI. Some of these agents became deeply involved in the organizations they joined, with one providing his handler minutes from meetings and another becoming an officer in the group he joined.[6]

Operation CHAOS also deployed its own agents, approximately thirty total, between 1969 and 1972. The FBI referred some of them to the agency, while CIA agents recruited others. The reports produced by the CHAOS-controlled agents, one government review concluded, were "often highly detailed," and "all names, organizations, and significant events were then indexed in the Operation's computer." Three of these CHAOS-recruited agents had a history in the activist movements, making them especially valuable as agents. The CIA used all three to collect intelligence about the activities, plans, and goals of specific domestic activist groups, and the agency shared the information with the FBI. Including reports from these agents, Operation CHAOS officials sent more than five thousand reports to the FBI based on its own intelligence-gathering work in the United States.[7] The Senate Select Committee to Study Governmental Operations with Respect to Intelligence Activities, known as the Church Committee, ultimately concluded that this high-level coordination between the two agencies confirmed that "a major purpose of CHAOS activity in actual practice became its participation with the FBI in the Bureau's internal security work."[8]

The CIA's domestic spying was a national endeavor, but documenting the specific times and places of its activities is difficult, given that much of the documentary record remains inaccessible to researchers.[9] Nonetheless, it is clear that CIA's interest in the student movement took it to all parts of the country and led it to focus on dozens of organizations, including SNCC, SDS, Women's Strike for Peace, and the American Indian Movement. While one can surmise that the agency focused especially on activities in and around Washington, DC and on the two coasts—places of intense student activism—it is highly likely that the white New Left in the South also was subject to CIA surveillance. Indeed, it would defy logic were it not to have garnered CIA attention. Student activism anywhere was problematic, and its presence in the South would have stood out as especially notable given that activist formations were less common in the region than elsewhere in the country. Additionally, the shear breadth of the CIA surveillance campaign—monitoring hundreds of alternative newspapers, keeping an eye on numerous college campuses—meant that southern activists were just as likely to be the focus of CIA surveillance as others. And the CIA's strong relationship with the FBI and local police departments allowed it to benefit from the work of bureau agents and Red Squads that were active in the South, just as they were elsewhere in the nation. According to the head of the CHAOS program, the FBI was sending the CIA more than one thousand reports per month by mid-1970.[10] Many, no doubt, came from agents across the South. As the Church Committee concluded, "In any ordinary sense of the word, the CIA had 'collected' a great deal of information in the United States about Americans, which was systematically maintained in files on those persons and used in the CHAOS program."[11]

In addition to the CIA, the U.S. military deployed its vast resources to surveil student activists in the 1960s, often without civilian oversight or authorization. The army was the service branch that developed the most intrusive and far-reaching domestic intelligence program during the era. While the army had long run intelligence operations to protect personnel and installations, it drastically broadened its work in the 1960s to focus on domestic dissidents. Initially, it justified this work on the grounds that intelligence regarding domestic activists would enable the army to prepare for potential civil unrest it might be called on to quell. But as the decade progressed, army intelligence, working through what one scholar called a "hydra-headed bureaucracy," gathered information regarding the views and actions of civil rights and antiwar activists and groups that were unconnected to any potential army action.[12] At its zenith, army intelligence agents fanned out around the country to monitor and infiltrate groups. The army did not distinguish among dissenters nor utilize a clear or consistent definition of dissent. In a political culture that labeled all dissenters as radicals and all opponents of the status quo as dangerous extremists, the army considered surveillance a vital tool to protect national security. Yet the army's counterintelligence activities yielded little actionable evidence. North Carolina senator Sam Ervin, who led a subcommittee investigation of army surveillance after Christopher Pyle, a former intelligence officer, exposed it in 1970, blasted the army's program as "ill-defined" and its assessments to be "worthless and unsubstantiated." Although the army shamelessly tried to obscure and downplay the surveillance, including by concealing and even destroying records of its activities, enough evidence survived that, combined with testimony from those involved, allowed Ervin to conclude that army surveillance constituted "a clear and present danger to the privacy and freedom of thousands of American citizens." An effort begun as a way to plan for urban unrest or identify foreign involvement in American politics inexorably bled into surveillance of constitutionally protected rights. As Ervin concluded, "Army intelligence, in the name of preparedness and security, had developed a massive system for monitoring virtually all political protest in the United States."[13]

Army domestic intelligence work, known by the acronym CONUS—Continental United States Intelligence—was in actuality the work of different organizational units. Loosely connected and often in competition with one another, these groups frequently overlapped in their efforts. The most significant of the army intelligence units was the United States Intelligence Command (USAINTC), based at Fort Holabird in Baltimore. USAINTC was established in 1965 and operated through seven Military Intelligence Groups (MIGs) situated across the country. The MIGs, in turn, oversaw regional and subregional offices so that by the end of the 1960s, USAINTC maintained a network of more than three hundred offices deploying approximately fifteen hundred agents. Their work intensified and expanded in the wake of the racial confrontations and urban unrest of 1967. On the theory that greater intelligence was needed to thwart future problems, MIGs throughout the country trained their attention on activists because they could be sources of disruption in their communities. This put civil rights and antiwar protesters in their crosshairs. Significantly, MIGs filtered all dissent through the lens of civil unrest; what was a peaceful demonstration now could be a precursor for more disruptive or violent action in the future. This fear of unrest—whether agitation over racial inequities or protests against the war—justified intrusive and invasive counterintelligence operations against student activists, whom army investigators conceptualized as agitators and militants, perhaps with foreign connections.[14]

Like their counterparts elsewhere in the federal intelligence bureaucracy, army investigators vacuumed up an avalanche of information on their targets. Newspapers and magazines were low-hanging fruit in the intelligence-gathering effort, as they were plentiful and easy to obtain. While intelligence offices openly subscribed to a range of national and local publications, such as the *Wall Street Journal* and *New York Times*, they sought to conceal their subscriptions to underground newspapers and alternative publications by routing them through PO boxes outside the military bases. In Virginia, for example, the intelligence office used a PO box in Alexandria belonging to the fictitious "R. Allen Lee Associates" as a cover for its subscriptions to New Left publications. The army's extensive collection of publications formed an important part of its intelligence files. Whether they were a valuable resource, though, is debatable. They likely were more useful as retrospective rather than prospective sources; these sources documented past actions more reliably than future plans. Moreover, the dizzying array of alternative publications and seemingly byzantine factional disputes, oft-changing leadership, and shifting priorities among New Leftists was unlikely to yield useful intelligence to army officials, who were on the whole not steeped in the politics of the New Left or familiar with its rhetorical excesses. Nonetheless, in 1969 and 1970, the army opened investigations of fifty-three different alternative publications.[15]

Beyond newspapers and magazines, army intelligence received a significant amount of material from local police and FBI offices. Christopher Pyle, the army whistleblower, remarked during his testimony before Ervin's subcommittee that "in 1969, especially, the Intelligence Command seemed to have been a dumping ground for FBI reports." But army agents also conducted their own surveillance operations to gather material. This ranged from collecting the publications and flyers of activist groups to infiltrating activist organizations in order to spy on suspected subversives. As a result, each MIG around the country had its own files on suspected individuals and organizations. The one located at Fort Sam Houston in San Antonio, for example, maintained 120,000 card files on so-called personalities of interest.[16] In an effort to manage all of the information that was flooding the USAINTC, army officials, according to Pyle, "hit upon the idea of mug books as a convenient way to disseminate its information on potential 'troublemakers.'" Formally called *The USAINTC Identification List*, it was, in practice, a blacklist of people to be monitored and targeted. Consisting of six volumes with detailed entries on more than one thousand people, it was, in one scholar's estimation, "encyclopedically over-inclusive . . . inaccurate, paranoid, and irrelevant." The Counter-Intelligence Analysis Branch (CIAB) within the army bureaucracy provided the MIGs with even more information, most notoriously its two volume *Compendium*, which was a collection of profiles of groups and individuals categorized as "left wing," "right wing," or "racial." Its official, mind-numbingly bureaucratic title, *Counterintelligence Research Project, Persons and Organizations of Civil Disturbance Unrest*, obscured the invasive nature of the project. It was, as one analyst later said, "pure domestic intelligence of political activities . . . [that] had no bearing whatsoever on the execution of the Army's civil disturbance function." Together, the mug book and the *Compendium* stood as evidence of army intelligence's close cooperation with other domestic surveillance agencies: FBI reports heavily informed the *Compendium*. And while army investigators compiled four of the mug volumes, CIAB received the other two from the Alabama state police.[17]

The surging antiwar movement and the metastasizing civil rights struggle sharpened army intelligence's focus on Black activists and white college students. In the South, army agents surveilled Martin Luther King Jr.'s funeral, the development of the Poor People's Campaign, and the Southern Christian Leadership Conference as well as suspected Black activists across the region. Agents in North Carolina had instructions to monitor "'any suspicious black man' and find out what he was doing and who he was." In Atlanta, in the months after King's assassination, agents spied on the African American–dominated sanitation workers' union, including infiltrating meetings.[18] All the MIGs also kept close tabs on the college campuses in their areas, monitoring antiwar activity and occasionally participating surreptitiously in demonstrations. They often relied on local police and campus officials for tips and information. In Winston-Salem, North Carolina, for example, security officials regularly met with army domestic intelligence as well as monitored groups on campus, such as the Afro-American Society, and shared information with army investigators.[19] SDS was a frequent target of surveillance by army intelligence units given its high profile. But the army also focused on the Southern Student Organizing Committee, the Nashville-based group of white student activists in the region. As SSOC expanded its antiwar organizing and gained adherents on campuses throughout the South, it drew attention from army intelligence. Ralph Stein, a former domestic intelligence analyst for the army who, like Christopher Pyle, testified before the Senate investigative committee, identified SSOC as one of the "Left wing and antiwar" groups under army surveillance. Seemingly routine and ordinary demonstrations garnered military surveillance. When SSOC planned to hold an antiwar rally at the University of Miami in March 1968, army domestic intelligence took note, as USAINTC included the event in its weekly intelligence summary, which it distributed to units not just in the United States but around the world.[20]

Army intelligence was sensitive to the slightest provocations, actions, or statements that veered from established norms or conventions. Antiwar views among southern students, no matter how innocuously expressed, made one a target for army surveillance because such expressions of dissent contrasted with the patriotic, pro-military stance that characterized many communities. Thus, in 1965, the MIG based in Oklahoma City surveilled the handful of antiwar protesters who turned out regularly to demonstrate at the federal courthouse.[21] But it was not just the war that attracted the army's attention. Agents in the Fayetteville, North Carolina, area, near Fort Bragg, monitored a progressive group within a local Presbyterian church because they had discussed whether violent revolution was a possibility in the country. One intelligence official later expressed incredulity that such talk could land one on an army watch list, especially because, as he put it, "even President Nixon makes extensive use of the concept of 'revolution.'" Surveillance of the group revealed the church members' commitment to uplifting the downtrodden—the churchgoers discussed how the group "might be involved in providing information and other services for poor people seeking low cost housing under Federal programs"—but no evidence that revolution was in their plans.[22]

Opposition to the war among the troops was of particular interest to the army's domestic intelligence units. Investigators carefully monitored soldiers suspected of harboring antiwar views. Because they believed soldiers would seek to conceal antiwar sympathies, investigators cast a wary eye on activities they deemed suggestive of a dissenting view on the war. At Fort Bragg, for example, intelligence operatives attended an ecology program meeting in the base library to observe soldiers who were participating in it presumably because, the agents believed, an interest in ecology suggested a progressive political orientation that would include opposition to the war. They also routinely surveilled off-base meetings of GI antiwar groups, giving particular attention to coffeehouses. Throughout the South, coffeehouses near military installations served as meeting places that nurtured dissent about the war. In a relaxed and informal setting, community members, students, and soldiers could come together to discuss the war and support one another's opposition to it. Army officials considered the coffeehouses a threat to troop unity and morale, and intelligence officials worked to undermine them. They recruited informants to report on the coffeehouses, and they deployed young intelligence agents, who could readily blend in with the other young servicemen at the coffeehouses, to infiltrate the venues. Army intelligence investigated and surveilled seventeen coffeehouses in 1969 and 1970 alone, including Fun, Travel, and Adventure near Fort Knox in Kentucky, Oleo Strut near Fort Hood in Texas, and the UFO Coffeehouse near Fort Jackson in South Carolina.[23]

The full scope of the army's domestic intelligence work will never be known because the army destroyed or refused to release or declassify many of its files. Yet the files that did survive and that congressional investigators were able to pry out of the army bureaucracy confirm that the army engaged in political intelligence work that far exceeded its mission and its expertise. Despite the file destruction and effort to conceal records, a conservative estimate is that the army maintained records on more than 100,000 people, not counting duplicate files held by various units. "At root," Frank Donner, perhaps the foremost student of the American domestic intelligence infrastructure, concluded, the army's domestic intelligence operations were "forms of aggression against legitimate political expression."[24] Senate investigators put it more bluntly: the army, using a "vacuum-cleaner approach . . . . was collecting, disseminating, and storing amounts of data on the private and personal affairs of law-abiding citizens." The tragedy of the army's work was not only that it infringed on individuals' constitutional rights but that, as the Senate analysis concluded, its "vast collections of fragmentary, incorrect, and irrelevant information—composed of vague conclusions and judgments and overly detailed descriptions of insignificant facts—could not be considered 'intelligence' by any sense of the word. . . . In fact, it was merely wasting time, money and manpower, and infringing on the rights of the citizens it was supposed to be safeguarding."[25]

THE FBI AND THE SOUTH

"The FBI regards campus spying as a near sacred obligation," Frank Donner wrote in 1968. The FBI's focus on college campuses derived from its campaign against the New Left. The campus was the soil from which the New Left grew, and any attempt to control or stop it required engaging with students at the nation's colleges and universities. The bureau, unsurprisingly, gave considerable attention to schools on the two coasts that had well-deserved reputations for student activism around the war, civil rights, and other progressive issues. But the "G-men" also trained their sights on colleges and universities in the South. Indeed, no school was safe from the bureau's prying eyes. Agents roamed southern campuses, both overtly and covertly; collaborated with school officials to identify activists and gather information that could be weaponized against them, such as who they fraternized with and where they worked; and sent informants to insert themselves into activist groups not just to collect information but to disrupt activities and create discord among the activists. Operating on the assumption that it faced a devious, dishonest, and insidious adversary, J. Edgar Hoover and his team believed they were justified in using secretive, intrusive, and even illegal tactics to stop student activists. It did not matter if a campus was home only to a handful of loosely organized activists. From the bureau's perspective, all were an extremist threat; any constellation of activists had the potential to grow and become a menace to the broader campus and community. For southern activists, seemingly innocuous actions, such as forming a study group on the war or hosting a visiting speaker on American foreign policy, could earn them FBI attention because such activities, in the bureau's view, could be the first step in radicalizing students and turning them against their schools and country. As Hoover put it in his letter to college students, New Leftists sought to indoctrinate students "in a mood of negativism, pessimism, and alienation toward yourself, your school, your nation."[26]

In addition to their political and ideological orientation, the cultural attitudes and behaviors of student activists repulsed Hoover and his team. To conservative and tradition-bound bureau officials, starting with Hoover, the stylings of the New Left were dangerous, frightening, and incomprehensible. They recoiled from the activists' lifestyle choices—their style of dress, casual drug use, and profanity-laced speech (and writings)—and were offended by their blithe dismissal of the older generation as hopelessly reactionary. Hoover condemned the New Left for its "depraved nature and moral looseness," and he considered New Left students to be moral failures who sought to spread their poisonous attitudes and ideas to their peers.[27] In his letter to college students, Hoover repeatedly charged New Leftists with trying to corrupt students by leading them to disrespect American institutions, starting with their families. "They'll encourage you to lose respect for your parents and the older generation," he wrote. "This will be one of their first attacks, trying to cut you off from home."[28]

The bureau's interest in white student activists dated to the first years of the 1960s and intensified in 1968, with the launch of COINTELPRO–New Left, a program that directed agents around the country to surveil white student activists and devise counterintelligence actions to disrupt their activities. COINTELPRO—shorthand for "counterintelligence program"—was the bureaucratic basis for FBI covert and, occasionally, overt actions against a range of individuals and organizations it deemed a threat to national security or domestic tranquility. Beginning in 1956 with a focus on the U.S. Communist Party(CP), the bureau created twelve COINTELPROs over the next dozen years that trained attention and resources on perceived threats. Thus, the bureau created COINTELPRO–SWP Disruption Program in 1961 on the Socialist Workers Party, COINTELPRO–White Hate Groups in 1964 on the Ku Klux Klan and other white supremacist groups, and COINTELPRO–Black Nationalist–Hate Groups in 1967, which targeted a broad range of civil rights and Black nationalist groups, including the Black Panther Party, the Student Nonviolent Coordinating Committee, and the Southern Christian Leadership Conference.[29] The COINTELPROs were the apogee of the FBI's domestic security operation in the Hoover era and the most significant cause of furor when the operations were exposed in the 1970s. The COINTELPROs wreaked havoc in the lives of those targeted and did enormous damage to the bureau's reputation, damage that reverberated for years to come.

The FBI's domestic security work was rooted deep in the organization's history. Founded as the Bureau of Investigation in 1908, it investigated German nationals during the World War I era and was at the center of the antiradical hysteria that followed the war's end. A young J. Edgar Hoover, as head of the Justice Department's Radical Division, led the drive against communists and other suspected radicals, which included the notorious Palmer Raids. Hoover kept the bureau involved in anti-communist work once he ascended to director in 1924. Over the next decade, Hoover proved to be a master political and public relations operative, burnishing the bureau's image as the nation's supreme crime-fighting agency—nabbing gangsters and presenting the bureau as the model of police efficiency and professionalism—while continuing to target radicals and supposed subversives. Its domestic security operations ramped up in the 1930s and World War II years. In 1936, Franklin Roosevelt authorized the bureau, now renamed the Federal Bureau of Investigation, to investigate communists and fascists in the United States, and in 1939, he gave the bureau authority over all federal domestic intelligence operations. Hoover wasted no time going to work, as he ordered agents to conduct surveillance and gather information on putative radicals throughout the country, especially in government, the media, and labor unions. The bureau conducted most of this work secretly, shielded from public scrutiny and without meaningful bureaucratic oversight. This gave Hoover immense power to shape the domestic security infrastructure. Under his leadership, the bureau added agents by the hundreds and grew its budget by millions, with significant portions of both directed toward domestic security investigations. With virtual carte blanche for domestic security work, Hoover's FBI used tactics ranging from the unsavory to the illegal to investigate a widening array of alleged subversives, a group that came to include not merely those suspected of ties to foreign governments but individuals and groups expressing views that diverged from mainstream thought and ideas.[30]

The COINTELPROs were the clearest manifestation of the bureau's approach to dissent. Each COINTELPRO trained the bureau's significant resources on groups and people whose political views clashed with Hoover's notions of propriety and ideas about the social and political order. A fear of communism undergirded these programs and reflected Hoover's obsession with the Communist Party. An unreconstructed anticommunist from his earliest days in government, Hoover saw the red menace lurking in every social and political movement of the 1950s and 1960s. His long history fighting communism shaped his view that one always had to be on guard. Communists were wily and deceitful and required the bureau's diligent attention, regardless of how many communists actually existed in the country. As Hoover told President Dwight Eisenhower's cabinet in 1958, "The loss of CP membership makes no difference—size has little relation to the importance of the CP's mission."[31]

Communism was central to the FBI's interest in white southern students. The participation of white students in civil rights actions in the region, from campaigns to desegregate campuses to community-based efforts to oppose segregation in public facilities in the wake of the 1964 Civil Rights Act, brought them to the attention of local FBI agents, who viewed such activism through the prism of communist infiltration. The creation of SSOC in the spring of 1964, an organization born of the civil rights struggle and with ties to groups and individuals the FBI believed had communist ties, invited further bureau scrutiny. As the southern movement expanded to encompass other causes, most notably the war in Vietnam, more students gravitated to SSOC, SDS, and other New Left formations. The launch of COINTELPRO–New Left served to formalize the bureau's counterintelligence efforts in the South, just as it did elsewhere. In the South, though, the program was entwined with local and state law enforcement drives to shore up the white supremacist order. The white activists and organizations that challenged the racial status quo endured surveillance and harassment by an interconnected network of local, state, and federal law enforcement. The FBI led this work.

As a leftist organization in a region where white supremacy reigned and dissent of any type made one suspect, SSOC was an obvious target for the FBI. The group first drew the attention of the bureau in the summer of 1964, three months after its creation, as a result of its ties to the Southern Conference Educational Fund (SCEF), the civil rights organization Hoover long had accused of having communist ties. Anne and Carl Braden, who led the group, had suffered bureau harassment for years, and their strong support for SSOC immediately cast suspicion on the new student group. After the New York FBI office mentioned SSOC in a June 1964 memo on "Communist Influence in Racial Matters," the special agent in charge (SAC) of the Atlanta FBI office wrote to FBI headquarters and several other offices around the South that it had learned from a confidential source that SSOC relied on SCEF for funding and that the Braden-led organization had played a role in the group's formation.[32] He included with the memo information about SSOC's founding, a list of officers, and its mailing list, a valuable document for identifying students associated with the new group and one suggesting that the agent already had sources with access to this important information. All of this material, the SAC wrote, should help "determine whether in the future a Cominfil investigation of SSOC should be authorized," using the acronym for "Communist Influence," the bureau's program to investigate communist sympathizers. Two weeks later, Hoover ordered just such an investigation. In a memo addressed to the SAC of the Memphis FBI office, which had jurisdiction in SSOC's home base, Nashville, the FBI director called for a review of information in the office's files in an attempt to determine "the extent of influence of the SSOC by the members of the Southern Conference Educational Fund" and, by extension, whether SSOC members were fellow travelers or communists themselves.[33] But after two and a half months, the Memphis SAC reported that the office could not definitively determine SSOC's political orientation, and he asked for approval to start a "discreet investigation" in order to make "an accurate determination of the organization's true character." Notably, he labeled his memo "Cominfil—Southern Student Organizing Committee (SSOC) Internal Security—C," the first instance in which *SSOC* appears in the FBI's elaborate and complicated classification system under the "Internal Security–Communist" designation. The director consented to the request, and given the group's involvement in civil rights activity, advised, "You should also consider the possibility that this group may be a racial-type organization."[34]

In early 1965, the Memphis SAC submitted a sixty-two-page report to headquarters and seventeen other field offices. Based on information gleaned from SSOC publications and reports from informants in Nashville, Atlanta, and New Orleans, it offered a detailed discussion of SSOC's brief history and identified those involved with the group. But the report did not conclude that communists had infiltrated SSOC, a point Hoover noted in his response. Crucially, though, he did not consider SSOC absolved of communist ties. Rather, he said that the bureau would await the results of investigations by other field offices into the "subversive nature [of] individuals connected with this organization" before reaching a conclusion about the group's orientation.[35] So directed, FBI offices around the region investigated SSOC, monitoring its activities, cultivating informants to access the group's meetings, and surveilling students involved in the organization. But these investigations, too, failed to confirm that SSOC was a communist group or that communists had infiltrated or controlled it. SSOC activists, the Memphis office reported in August 1965, were "active in racial matters and civil rights groups" but did not have "subversive backgrounds." Many also were members of SDS, and the Memphis SAC raised the possibility that SDS might one day take over SSOC. But without evidence of communist ties, the Memphis office closed its Cominfil investigation of SSOC. "If information is subsequently received which would alter the present situation, the Bureau will be promptly advised, along with appropriate recommendation," the SAC wrote.[36]

The conclusion of the Cominfil investigation did not end the bureau's surveillance of SSOC. In late 1965, agents in Little Rock, Oklahoma City, and San Antonio reported on SSOC's involvement in a student conference at the University of Arkansas, and in early 1966, the Memphis office wrote to headquarters that Klansmen in the Nashville area were casing the SSOC office, which one Klansman called a "love nest," with the intent of harassing the students who were part of what the Klan considered a communist, interracial organization, a perspective aligned with the FBI's own view.[37] SSOC's growing profile on southern campuses heightened the bureau's suspicions about the group. As SSOC gained adherents in the region and attracted support—and publicity—for its work in support of civil rights and, increasingly, against the war, the bureau gradually reconsidered and then reversed its decision to terminate its investigation of the group. The Memphis office led the way in this effort. In June 1966, the Memphis SAC recommended opening a new investigation on SSOC, arguing that the group "has gained considerable money from sources yet unknown and is becoming a major power among southern student groups in the areas of poverty programs, civil rights, anti-war movement and related areas." Initially, headquarters did not believe this constituted sufficient evidence to justify a new investigation. Moreover, Hoover and his leadership team recognized that investigating SSOC would take the bureau on to numerous southern campuses and risk exposure of informants and the methods the bureau used. "The possibilities of embarrassment to the Bureau are too great," they warned.[38]

The Memphis office tried again a few months later to interest headquarters in SSOC, and this time it succeeded. The difference was that the office supported its request with a five-page memo outlining SSOC's recent activities that highlighted its ties to supposedly communist and antiwar organizations, ranging from the Southern Conference Educational Fund and the Communist Party to Students for a Democratic Society and the Nashville Committee for Alternatives to War in Vietnam. SSOC's work with the latter group to hold a

"Peace Fast" at Nashville's War Memorial Building the previous summer was a brazen display of antiwar sentiment that garnered media attention, prompted a counter-demonstration, led to numerous arrests, and was monitored by the bureau. The Southern Student Organizing Committee, the Memphis SAC wrote, "has been expounding views similar to those prevalent among the various new left groups regarding anti-war and social change." The memo proved persuasive, and in November 1966, headquarters authorized Memphis "to conduct a discreet investigation" of SSOC.[39]

The Memphis office immediately sent a memo about SSOC to twenty-four field offices, most in the South, and in subsequent weeks, these offices issued their own reports on the group, circulating them to their colleagues around the region.[40] In a bureau culture that prized aggressive surveillance, the growing paper trail on SSOC undoubtedly motivated agents to focus on the group. Headquarters blessed a new investigation, and agents knew they were expected to act. Additionally, no agent wanted to be an outlier, neglecting to take steps that their peers had taken. Thus, over the coming months, field offices in Atlanta, Richmond, Jacksonville, New Orleans, Charlotte, Columbia, and elsewhere called on their regular contacts and sources to search out information about the group. At the University of Virginia, home to a vibrant group of SSOC activists, a source provided agents in the Richmond office with personal information about students involved in the group. In Little Rock, a source in the Motor Vehicle Bureau identified the owners of vehicles whose license plates agents had provided. Offices outside the region participated as well, as those in Detroit, Boston, and New York scoured their files for information on individuals with SSOC connections.[41] Agents shared their reports widely, distributing them not only to FBI offices but to other law enforcement and investigative bodies, including military intelligence. In one common occurrence, the Richmond SAC sent a report on SSOC to the Richmond office of the Secret Service, the 109th Military Intelligence Group, and the Office of Special Investigations as well as to the U.S. Naval Investigative Service Office in Norfolk. By distributing its reports across the law enforcement spectrum, the bureau further ensnared SSOC in the federal surveillance regime.[42]

SSOC's antiwar activities increasingly captured the bureau's attention. When three members of the group in Nashville tried to block President Johnson's motorcade as he departed the Tennessee capital after delivering a speech in March 1967, the Memphis office produced a detailed report that it shared with military intelligence, the Secret Service, and the U.S. Attorney's Office in Nashville. Cartha DeLoach, the number three official in the bureau, also kept abreast of the investigation.[43] Actions in subsequent months kept SSOC on the FBI's radar. They included the Peace Tours, teach-in like events that took SSOC activists to white-dominated campuses; a demonstration at the University of Georgia to protest an appearance by Vice President Humbert Humphrey; picketing of the Cobb County, Georgia, plant of defense contractor Lockheed Aircraft Corporation during its Armed Forces Day open house; and a protest at the Atlanta Selective Service office as part of national "Stop the Draft Week" in October 1967. Agents monitored these events and investigated participants, gathering data from informants, cooperative school officials, and local government agencies.[44]

SSOC's association with SDS, a regular target of FBI surveillance, also heightened the bureau's interest in the group. Agents frequently noted in their communiqués that SSOC was a fraternal organization of SDS, implying that SSOC therefore posed a similar threat to the established order. Officials already suspicious of SSOC because of its amorphous connections to SCEF increasingly saw its ties to SDS as confirmation that radicals and militants comprised the southern group. In September 1967, Charles Brennan, an official in the bureau's Domestic Intelligence Division, told his boss that SSOC leaders had "subversive backgrounds," thereby justifying the ongoing investigations of the group.[45] In December 1967, the director's office sent a memo to seventeen southern field offices, instructing them to investigate SSOC and its leaders if they were not already doing so. The impetus for the directive was the bureau's assessment that "SSOC has been following the SDS line" on the war and campus reform issues and that "known Communist Party members are actively participating" in the group. What headquarters called SSOC's "fraternal closeness with SDS and Communist Party influence within its leadership" illustrated Hoover and his team's fixation on supposedly subversive elements in the New Left.[46]

The allegation that SSOC had communist ties was not new; it had been the basis for the FBI's initial focus on SSOC. But in 1967, with antiwar actions surging around the nation as the American war effort deepened, SSOC's ties to

SDS and its actions against the war seemed especially ominous to the bureau. In reality, SSOC's connections to SDS were tenuous at best, and the group hardly maintained the type of formal organization the bureau assumed. The notion of a command-and-control structure within SSOC or that it operated with cadres taking orders from a central committee was laughable given the group's loose organization, fluctuating level of support, and the independence that campus groups maintained from one another. Yet this was the model the bureau believed SSOC and other New Left organizations employed, hence, the memo's instruction to the offices to "set forth in detail the complete organizational structure of SSOC together with the identities of officers and functionaries on the chapter and national levels. . . . [and] the subversive affiliations of the officers and other members of the chapter." Moreover, the leadership expected the field offices to develop informants to investigate SSOC. Attuned to the bad publicity that could arise if bureau agents or their charges were caught spying on college students, especially after the exposure of the CIA's secretive funding of the National Student Association earlier in the year, the memo acknowledged that "establishing complete coverage is going to confront you with the need to operate discreetly in a sensitive and delicate area." But reflecting the urgency of the situation, field agents that did not yet have "live informant coverage in a particular chapter" should take steps "to develop such coverage."[47] Although the bureau had curtailed its use of campus informants after the CIA scandal broke, this turned out to be merely a brief pause. Before 1967 was out, the FBI was again authorizing the recruitment of campus informants, and the instruction to deploy informants against SSOC students was part of this reversal.[48]

Hoover's memo prompted offices around the South to sharpen their focus on SSOC. After reviewing the memo, the Jackson office, for instance, announced that it "has reopened [its] file on SSOC," and Little Rock agents said they were working with informants to monitor "the formation of any SSOC chapter" in its jurisdiction—in fact, they had been using informants since 1965 to follow the group. In Charlotte, the FBI special agent in charge explained that it had "excellent informant coverage of the Duke University Chapter of SSOC" through a student who was a member of the group.[49] Agents elsewhere also kept tabs on the organization. Even where SSOC did not have an organizational presence, SACs revealed in their replies to Hoover that they had investigated students known to have participated in SSOC activities. The Mobile office, for example, reported that although SSOC did not have a chapter in the area, a member of the group's executive committee came from nearby. The office subsequently investigated this individual, including contacting his or her mother "under suitable pretext at her residence" in order to obtain contact information for the student.[50] The agents' reports also highlighted the close working relationship FBI offices maintained with university officials and local police departments' intelligence units, or Red Squads. Given the sensitivity of placing agents on campus, the FBI offices relied on their networks of local officials to supplement and enhance their own coverage of student activists. Campus officials, such as university police officers and school administrators, were a vital source of information on activist students. At the University of Virginia, for example, the assistant dean of students and the director of security, who was a former FBI special agent in charge, were key sources for the bureau.[51] Additionally, agents regularly received tips from city police departments. In New Orleans, the Red Squad tracked SSOC and other activist groups in the city and shared the information it gathered with the local FBI office. And in Miami, the FBI received information on SSOC from a confidential Red Squad source as well as an undercover city police officer who had infiltrated several local groups with ties to SSOC.[52]

Unsurprisingly, the Memphis office submitted the most detailed report in response to the director's memo. Over 105 pages, the Memphis agents cataloged the group's activities in the region over the past year, detailed its associations with groups and individuals already assumed by the bureau to be subversive, and made the case for confirming that SSOC, too, was a subversive, if not communist, organization. The Memphis report is a revelatory document. On one level, it reflects the bureaucratic maneuverings of agents determined to highlight their contributions to the battle against extremism that Hoover and his leadership team had prioritized. Memphis may not have been Washington, DC, New York, or Los Angeles, but it was not a sleepy backwater where nothing happened. The report, then, could be read as the Memphis office's effort to justify the campaign it had agitated for since 1965. Once headquarters consented to an investigation of SSOC, it was in the Memphis office's interest to demonstrate that the group constituted a threat and thus merited the bureau's attention.[53] On another level, the report details the breadth and depth of the bureau's surveillance efforts against a group that remained a lightly organized, regional organization. In 1967 alone, the Memphis office utilized forty-three different informants in its surveillance of the group, including students at area colleges. One source, possibly a student, absconded with the group's membership and mailing list on a visit to SSOC's Nashville headquarters, and a portion of the Memphis report is devoted to listing the contact information of participants in a recent SSOC meeting. The Memphis agents also used informants to access SSOC's financial records. After acknowledging that such information "can be obtained only by the issuance of a subpoena duces tecum," the report lists detailed information about SSOC's banking activities provided not by a court order but by a confidential source who worked at First American National Bank in Nashville, where the group had accounts. "During the first eleven months of 1967," agents reported, "$40,981.81 was deposited to SSOC checking account." Though redacted in the records released by the bureau, the report included the sources of the group's funds, the salaries of employees, and its savings account information. It also had access through the bank employee to records from the United States Trust Company and Manufacturers Hanover Trust Company that enabled them to trace the origins of checks drawn from accounts at these institutions for SSOC. The implication of the bureau's financial surveillance was that SSOC was flush with cash that it had received from like-minded organizations that were using the group to promote their anti-American, extremist agenda on southern campuses.[54]

Guilt by association was a theme of the Memphis document. The report emphasizes SSOC's connections to a who's who of leftist and progressive organizations—Students for a Democratic Society, the Southern Conference Educational Fund, the Student Nonviolent Coordinating Committee , the Socialist Workers' Party, and of course, the Communist Party. The evidence of such ties was often flimsy. The first item highlighting SSOC's "Connection with the Communist Party" was that the group subscribed to the *People's World*, the CP newspaper, and that this paper once ran an article about SSOC's antiwar activities in Nashville. SSOC's connections with SDS and SCEF were more substantive, and the report lists some of the ways in which the groups collaborated on projects and programs, with its ties to SCEF occupying the most pages in the report. As an indication of the bureau's proclivity to transform the innocuous into the suspicious, the report highlighted a reading list provided by SCEF that appeared in a SSOC publication. Entitled *Books for People Who Want to Know How Things Run,* it recommended Marx's *Capital*—an obvious red flag for the bureau—but also scholarly works such as Gabriel Kolko's *Wealth and Power in America,* Leonard W. Levy's *Jefferson and Civil Rights,* and W. E. B. Du Bois's masterpiece, *Black Reconstruction in America.* That such works could be cited as evidence of SSOC's radicalism shows the bureau's eagerness to tie the group to supposedly radical and un-American views.[55]

SSOC's involvement in the antiwar movement raised its threat profile to the bureau. Throughout the country, opposition to the war grew as more American troops joined the conflict and the nation's involvement in the war deepened. Martin Luther King Jr. denounced the war in 1967, Eugene McCarthy emerged as a peace candidate to challenge Lyndon Johnson for the 1968 Democratic presidential nomination, and the Tet Offensive in early 1968 undermined Americans' support for the conflict. For SSOC and other student groups, the war became a potent organizing tool. The Memphis office took notice. Its report highlighted SSOC anti-draft activities, its sponsorship of Peace Tours around the region, its role in organizing protests against the war, and the high-profile trip SSOC chairman Tom Gardner made with other student leaders to Czechoslovakia in 1967 to meet with representatives of the National Liberation Front and the North Vietnamese government.[56] Seemingly unremarkable items took on a sinister pall to agents inclined to see opposition to the war as subversive. In April 1968, Memphis agents reported that SSOC's main publication, the *New South Student,* had published "scurrilous remarks relative to president Lyndon B. Johnson." The offending comments voiced by young men from Kentucky were merely criticisms of Johnson and the war, some expressed in profane language but none unusual or threatening. So worried were the agents that they shared the document with the Secret Service detail in Nashville.[57] FBI offices beyond Memphis also reported on SSOC's antiwar work. Agents' reports, memos, and urgent teletypes routinely directed attention to student activism around the war, much of it coordinated and supported by SSOC. These included antiwar protests organized by the

Miami SSOC group; a protest against Dow Chemical, the maker of napalm, at the University of Arkansas; the picketing of the Armed Forces Induction Centers in Raleigh and Charlotte; and a demonstration against an appearance at the University of Georgia by Secretary of State Dean Rusk.[58] SSOC's work to build opposition to the war on southern campuses stood as damning evidence against the group to the FBI.

COINTELPRO–NEW LEFT

The spring of 1968 was a turning point in the bureau's campaign against New Left groups. Protests against the war and the draft intensified around the country, bringing new attention to student activists. In April, the bureau was caught flat-footed when antiwar protests and a student strike engulfed Columbia University, shutting down the school and drawing national attention. To Hoover and other bureau leaders, the Columbia crisis represented a failure of leadership by university officials unable to control their campus. More broadly, the events at Columbia stood as proof to the bureau that unchecked student activism threatened the foundations of American higher education. Columbia galvanized the bureau to take a stronger response to student activists. The result was COINTELPRO–New Left. Like other COINTELPROs, this one operated in secrecy as it worked to decimate the white New Left. Over the three years of its existence, COINTELPRO–New Left initiated hundreds of counterintelligence operations against white student activists, making this COINTELPRO, in one scholar's estimation, the "most fully developed counterintelligence effort initiated under the COINTELPRO banner."[59]

The driving force behind COINTELPRO–New Left was William Sullivan, a longtime bureau official who had risen to become the assistant director over the bureau's Domestic Intelligence Division. Brash, ambitious, an effective player of bureau politics, and a strong advocate of counterintelligence actions against suspected domestic radicals, Sullivan oversaw the development of several of the COINTELPROs of the 1960s. An aggressive opponent of the civil rights movement, he urged strong actions to counter and discredit it, and he likely was the author of the notorious anonymous 1964 letter to Martin Luther King Jr. that threatened to expose him as an adulterer, castigated him as a fraud and a moral degenerate, and not so subtly invited him to kill himself.[60] In style and substance, the New Left offended him just as it did Hoover, and he knew that Hoover would be sympathetic to an effort to expose student activists as communist dupes or stooges. The Columbia protests prompted Sullivan to act. "After the Columbia riot," he wrote in his memoir, "the New Left was fair game."[61]

On May 9, 1968, one of Sullivan's top aides, Charles D. Brennan, explained the rationale for the new COINTELPRO in a memo to his boss. "Our Nation is undergoing an era of disruption and violence caused to a large extent by various individuals generally connected with the New Left," Brennan wrote. "Some of these activists urge revolution in America and call for the defeat of the United States in Vietnam. . . . . With this in mind, it is our recommendation that a new Counterintelligence Program be designed to neutralize the New Left and the Key Activists." Like COINTELPROs that already existed, Brennan explained that "the purpose of this program is to expose, disrupt, and otherwise neutralize the activities of this group and persons connected with it."[62] The next day, Hoover formally launched COINTELPRO–New Left. "Effective immediately, the Bureau is instituting a Counterintelligence Program directed against the New Left movement and its Key Activists," he wrote to SACs around the country. Two weeks later, the director wrote to the fifty-nine field offices requesting that each provide headquarters with the names of New Left groups and their "ringleaders" in their jurisdictions and that they develop specific actions to undermine them. "Every avenue of possible embarrassment must be vigorously and enthusiastically explored," Hoover stressed.[63] This was hardly the crime fighting for which the bureau had made its name under Hoover's early leadership. Instead of pursuing gangsters and organized crime, it was going after college students whose political views and social activities offended Hoover and his minions. COINTELPRO–New Left would thus be the most political of all the COINTELPROs. As the Church Committee concluded, "Few Bureau programs better reflect 'pure intelligence' objectives which extended far beyond even the most generous definition of 'preventive intelligence.'"[64]

SSOC and SDS were among the five dozen groups that agents identified as New Left organizations in their areas in response to Hoover's memo, and they sent headquarters ideas for ways to weaken them and disrupt their activities. Their suggestions informed an early-July memo from the director outlining counterintelligence actions to use against New Left targets. The two-and-a-half-page memo is a concise summary of steps the field offices would take to combat the New Left over the next three years. The proposed tactics included spreading propaganda and misinformation through the preparation of fake leaflets designed to denigrate and discredit New Left groups; leaking negative information or sending anonymous criticism of activists to students' family members, officials at their schools, and friendly journalists; and sowing discord among the groups themselves by surreptitiously questioning leaders' commitment to the cause, accusing some of being informants, or criticizing their personal relationships. The director advised his agents that no opportunity should be lost to criticize, mock, or humiliate New Leftists. Agents, for example, should send to school officials and legislators articles from the underground press that "show the depravity of the New Left. . . . Articles showing advocation of the use of narcotics and free sex are ideal." "Ridicule," he wrote, "is one of the most potent weapons which we can use." Appalled by what he called the "scurrilous and depraved nature of many of the . . . activities, habits, and living conditions representative of New Left adherents," Hoover urged agents to use anonymous letters to publicize student activists' behavior—drug use and sexual immorality, especially—to parents and college administrators and to encourage local police to conduct drug raids as a means of attacking and weakening these organizations. Above all, Hoover encouraged his agents to be creative in their work. As he put it in concluding the memo, COINTELPRO–New Left "must be approached with imagination and enthusiasm if it is to be successful."[65]

Field agents could not move fast enough for Sullivan or Hoover, who anticipated that New Left activity would intensify with the start of the new school year in the fall of 1968. A memo to the field offices in the summer excoriated them for not yet taking action against the student activists. "I have reminded you time and again that the militancy of the New Left is escalating daily," the memo thundered. "Unless you recognize this and move in a more positive manner to identify subversive elements . . . this type of activity can be expected to mount in intensity and to spread to college campuses across the country. This must not be allowed to happen and I am going to hold each Special Agent in Charge personally responsible to insure that the Bureau's responsibilities in this area are completely met and fulfilled."[66] "Each office will be expected," the director declared in another communiqué, "to afford this program continuous effective attention in order that no opportunity will be missed to destroy this insidious movement."[67]

The hurdles to success for the bureau, however, were significant. For starters, the FBI never defined what made a group or individual part of the New Left. Was it a stance on the war? An attitude toward authority? A perceived curiosity about communism? A call for violent action? More often, it was merely a label applied to those who espoused or embraced causes and attitudes that seemed un-American to Hoover and his team. According to one bureau missive, the New Left had "no definable ideology" but was characterized by "strong Marxist, existentialist, nihilist, and anarchist overtones."[68] Another acknowledged that the New Left was not a group but a "loosely-bound, free-wheeling, college-oriented movement."[69] Such imprecision made it difficult to measure success or, for that matter, to even know who the adversary was. Moreover, it encouraged field agents to be expansive in identifying potential targets because it was not difficult to find groups or students who fit the bureau's vague description of the New Left. Critically, that meant agents trained their attention on views and ideas, stylings and behaviors, that struck bureau officials as unconventional or nonconforming. The threat New Leftists posed, in other words, emanated not from acts of violence or actual subversion, which were rare—though the bureau, of course, highlighted New Left violence when it occurred—but from their political views, alternative lifestyle, and cultural forms.

Additionally, as an ever-evolving constellation of groups and individuals that shared overlapping yet distinct priorities and interests, the New Left was not necessarily vulnerable to counterintelligence tactics that the bureau had honed in an earlier era against a very different adversary, the Communist Party. Unlike the CP, the New Left was not a rigidly hierarchical organization with cadres taking orders from leaders or pursuing clear goals. To combat the New Left required the FBI to monitor groups large and small around the country, each with its own rotating cast of student leaders. SDS may have been the most prominent New Left organization, but it did not in any sense "lead" the movement. As a result, the bureau could not simply discredit, harass, or neutralize SDS leaders and expect to decapitate the movement. Hoover, Sullivan, and other top officials were always drawn to—seduced by, even—the celebrity certain activists had achieved. Yet their relentless campaigns against such individuals, from Martin Luther King Jr. to SNCC's Stokely Carmichael to SDS's Bernardine Dohrn, had little effect on the broader movements of which they were a part. Finally, in its pursuit of the New Left, the bureau encountered a cultural chasm that was too wide to bridge. Agents, quite literally, did not speak the language of student activists, nor did they look like them in their dress or act like them in their mannerisms. This made it difficult for agents to get close to the activists as well as challenged them to develop counterintelligence actions, such as fake letters and news releases, that appeared authentic and not obvious frauds.

Agents thus faced a range of difficulties as they responded to headquarters' push for a campaign against the New Left. But as the director's memos made clear, headquarters expected fast action and documented results; Hoover and his team were uninterested in the nuances that distinguished New Left groups from one another or the finer points of leftist critiques of the war. As a result, agents pursued a wide range of groups and individuals. In the South, this made SSOC an obvious target. Its presence on campuses throughout the region created the appearance to the bureau of a group with a long reach and dedicated following. COINTELPRO–New Left prompted agents to turn their full arsenal of counterintelligence tactics on the group in an effort not only to monitor the organization but to disrupt its activities, intimidate its student supporters, and make it a pariah on southern campuses by creating the impression that the group was radical and un-American. These tactics included running disinformation campaigns to promote distrust among the group's leaders; encouraging selective law enforcement against activists; planting stories in the news media or collaborating with sympathetic journalists to smear the organization; and surreptitiously sending letters to activists' families, friends, and employers as a means of "outing" them and creating discord in their personal lives. The fact that several offices reported that there was little activity by SSOC or other New Leftists in their area was irrelevant to the bureau's planning as headquarters made clear that the potential threat of New Leftists required steadfastness and vigilance.

The starting point for investigations of New Left organizations was the mundane but important task of reading the group's published material—in the case of SSOC, its monthly magazine, the *New South Student*, and a variety of pamphlets, newsletters, and reprints. Agents across the South secretly subscribed to SSOC publications, read them closely, and shared them with each other and headquarters. The Memphis FBI office, for example, surreptitiously received SSOC materials at a post office box under the name "Jay Hervie."[70] The group's writings provided agents a window into the organization and an opportunity to identify reasons to consider the group subversive, and agents filled their reports on the group—some running dozens of pages—with summaries, quotations, and even verbatim reproductions of SSOC publications. This literature review made clear that SSOC, like the vast majority of other activist formations, neither promoted nor participated in violent actions, thus removing one rationale for the bureau to surveil it. Agents instead used the leftist ideology and countercultural views they discovered in the publications as the basis for investigating it as subversive. Agents dutifully reported on seemingly every reference they found in a SSOC publication to the Bradens, SCEF, SDS, or other putative extremists. Similarly, they drew on the publications to highlight what they considered to be the activists' scandalous behavior, from the celebration of recreational drug use to scatological humor, all to demonstrate that the group posed a threat to the American way of life.

While jokes about G-men in wing tips and crew cuts trying to infiltrate activist groups may have been apocryphal, the reality was that agents had to rely on others to get close to student activists since they stood little chance themselves of inconspicuously fitting in alongside college students. The bureau thus particularly valued human intelligence sources, and agents worked hard to cultivate them, especially with the inauguration of COINTELPRO–New Left. "Confidential sources," in the parlance of the bureau, were defined as individuals who provided information to the FBI that they had access to by virtue of their status or position, such as being an employer or landlord.[71] School administrators routinely served as confidential sources for agents investigating New Left students in the South. As antiwar activism surged, agents relied increasingly on campus security officials, deans of students, and registrars for insights into New Left activity on campuses and for information about the identities and backgrounds of student activists. Agents' reports routinely reference campus sources they described as reliable, trustworthy, and long-standing conduits for information about New Left activity at their schools. At the University of Virginia, for example, agents reported in May 1968 that one unnamed administrator was closely monitoring the SSOC chapter on campus and credits this official with prompting the administration to declare it would not tolerate activities that disrupted classes or campus operations. Similarly, in 1969, agents in North Carolina relied on information provided by the Central Records Office at Duke to determine the enrollment status of an SSOC activist in the area.[72]

Distinct from confidential sources were informants recruited to infiltrate activist groups. The use of "the paid and directed informant is the most extensively used technique in FBI domestic intelligence investigations," the Senate Committee that investigated the FBI in the 1970s found."[73] It was certainly a commonly used tactic in COINTELPRO–New Left. While individual students or faculty occasionally approached field offices to report on New Left activity, more commonly the FBI sought to discreetly identify and train students to serve as its eyes and ears in activist groups. This was sensitive work, for as Hoover and his team knew, it would make headlines were it to come out that the bureau was recruiting students to spy on their peers. Given the transitory nature of the student population, the headquarters pressured field agents to continuously refresh their informant ranks. "It is . . . recognized that with the graduation of senior classes, you will lose a certain percentage of your existing student informant coverage," headquarters told SACs in early 1969. But "this decreasing percent of coverage will not be accepted as an excuse for not developing the necessary information." Field offices were already prioritizing informant recruitment by 1969. Some indirectly gained access to student informants through local Red Squads that managed their own informants. Others developed recruitment programs tailored to the student population in their area. In Richmond in 1968, the SAC reported "that sons and daughters of Bureau personnel are often students at pertinent colleges in the Richmond Division and would be very helpful in furnishing the desired information." Similarly, the SAC in Charlotte wrote to headquarters in 1968 that it had devised a plan "to identify former military intelligence officers who are returning to school and who might be utilized in these areas [as informants]."[74]

Agents' reports on SSOC and other activist groups repeatedly drew on information provided by informants who had embedded themselves within New

Left groups and built relationships with student activists. Thanks to their access, informants kept their handlers abreast of planned protests and provided them with the names of students involved in the activities as well as those of casual participants who perhaps attended a meeting or a demonstration. In North Carolina, for instance, agents in Charlotte depended on the reporting of a student informant who had joined the SSOC chapter at Duke to stay informed of the group's activities on campus. In Jackson, the FBI office relied on informants to report on activist students at Millsaps College, and they used this information to shape their counterintelligence efforts. In Birmingham, the reporting of a local informant alerted agents to potential SSOC organizing activities and led them to open an investigation into suspected New Leftists in Birmingham and Tuscaloosa, home to the University of Alabama. And in Richmond, agents relied on no fewer than nine informants to surveil and gather information on SSOC activists at the University of Virginia and Lynchburg College.[75]

The curious case of Don Cole illustrates how individuals who could insinuate themselves into activist groups contributed to surveillance campaigns. The son of a prominent real estate agent and builder, Donald F. Cole was a native of Ridgeland, Mississippi, just north of Jackson. As a high school student in 1964, Cole came to the attention of the local sheriff for his participation in anti-segregation demonstrations in Canton and for speaking positively about communism in school. The sheriff considered him a "racial agitator," and he spoke with Cole and then his father in an effort to pressure him to change his ways. He also reported Cole to the Mississippi State Sovereignty Commission, the state's infamous agency that sought to enforce segregationist norms and disrupt activism of any type in the state, which proceeded to open a file on him. He attended school briefly at Millsaps College, where he quickly earned a reputation for promoting outlandish ideas, such as encouraging antiwar men to get drafted so they could go to Vietnam and defect to the Viet Cong and handing out pro-communist materials that were sure to alienate white Mississippians. Although he soon departed Millsaps and began working at hardware stores in Jackson and Ridgeland, he remained involved in a variety of groups, including SSOC, Progressive Labor, SDS, SCEF, the Communist Party, and the Young Peoples Socialist League. He also became involved with the FBI, a relationship kept secret from the Sovereignty Commission, which continued to monitor him. Cole's evolution from civil rights sympathizer to FBI informer was a well-kept secret, and it is unclear what caused him to, in effect, switch sides. But over several years, Cole spied on activist groups for the FBI, which undoubtedly valued his connection to these organizations. The activists who knew Cole had harbored suspicions about him. Ken Lawrence, who knew Cole from a Marxist study group they both participated in, thought his political views were particularly shallow and uninformed—"bumper sticker slogans," he put it—but that activists valued his participation in protest actions because he helped increase their numbers. Not until 1974 did it come to light that Cole was an FBI source, when he revealed his informant activities to a former girlfriend, who promptly exposed him to the other activists. Until then, he had served as a conduit for information about student activists that informed COINTELPRO–New Left.[76]

WHITE ACTIVISTS IN THE CROSSHAIRS

While agents typically relied on others to provide up-close and real-time information on student activists, they deployed a range of other tactics to fulfill Hoover's guidance to disrupt and discredit the New Left. Sometimes agents overtly surveilled activists as a form of intimidation, for example, by openly taking notes at off-campus protests without any effort to conceal their identity or jotting down license plate numbers on vehicles parked outside meetings. Little Rock agents in 1968, for instance, monitored an antiwar protest in the city and a demonstration before the Arkansas-Baylor football game in Fayetteville against the continued segregation of the football team. In Jackson, agents sought to intimidate SSOC activists at Millsaps by interviewing them about their activism. Some of the students refused to talk with the agents, but others clearly were rattled to be contacted by the agents and either denied or minimized their involvement in the group.[77] More commonly, agents operated surreptitiously. Secrecy and obfuscation afforded the bureau plausible deniability in operations intended to damage the public perception of student activists and raise the personal costs of participation for the students themselves. Such tactics proliferated with the advent of COINTELPRO–New Left and fueled—as well as reflected—the repressive atmosphere that existed in many southern communities, where dissent was unwelcome and advocacy of progressive causes deemed threatening.

Southern agents worked through multiple channels to foment disapproval of student activists. One common approach was for agents to create and distribute anti–New Left propaganda in order to tarnish student activists' reputation on campus and discourage others from joining with them. In late 1968, agents in the Richmond office proposed posting a flyer on the University of Virginia and Virginia Commonwealth University campuses that attacked SSOC as un-American and too close to SDS. Attributed to "A Group for Liberal Student Government," a fictitious organization, and occasioned by the appearance of a sign with four-letter words in the window of a "head shop" in Richmond, the flyer warned students that SSOC, like SDS, has "never opposed a communist program" and "resorts to filth and obscenities to express its opposition to American ways of life." While headquarters ultimately did not approve the flyer, judging it too risky to ask agents to post it on the campuses, it illustrated the bureau's effort to stigmatize New Left students as, in the flyer's words, "loud and smelly minorities" that promoted "depravities" to "undermine American institutions and loyalties."[78] In a similar vein, the Jackson SAC believed it could use a drawing of someone wearing a swastika that appeared in an unnamed New Left publication to dampen Jewish support for the New Left. The agent proposed sending the drawing to a prominent Jewish community leader in Jackson with a note that read: "Thought you might be interested. It appears this group has turned Anti-Jew. . . . This group bears watching."[79]

To reach an audience beyond the campus community, agents cultivated friendly news media sources in local communities by feeding reporters tips about unconventional, putatively subversive, or illegal activity by New Leftists. SSOC was one of the many groups the FBI targeted.[80] Mainstream southern newspapers, with their conservative orientation and typically all-white staffs, catered to an audience that embraced the status quo and needed little encouragement to dislike the New Left. In Jackson, local FBI agents found a willing partner in the city's two main dailies, the sister publications the *Jackson Daily News* and the *Jackson Clarion-Ledger*. The staunchly segregationist newspapers, the largest in the state, formed part of the bulwark against social change in Mississippi. The newspapers regularly and vitriolically lambasted civil rights and antiwar activists as communist dupes, un-American radicals, and amoral freaks. This made them valuable allies to the FBI. The newspapers, the special agent in charge of the Jackson office wrote to headquarters, "have been highly praiseworthy of the accomplishments of the FBI and are very anti-Communistic in their articles." As the Jackson office contemplated counterintelligence operations against the small New Left presence in the city, the agents saw the newspapers as a useful tool for denigrating the student activists.[81]

Their conduit was Jimmy Ward, who wrote the Covering the Crossroads column in the *Jackson Daily News*. Agents had funneled information to Ward before, and they considered him to be, one memo noted, "discreet, trustworthy, and reliable."[82] When New Left activists in the city launched an alternative newspaper, *The Kudzu*, in the fall of 1968 that criticized law enforcement, opposed the Vietnam War and draft, and flouted the norms of mainstream society by promoting free love and glorifying drug use, the agents encouraged Ward to write an exposé about the new publication. A critical article about *The Kudzu* would draw attention to the depravity of the New Left and, if it named the students involved in the publication, the SAC wrote headquarters, would bring pressure "to bear upon the parents of the students responsible for the printing of [*The Kudzu*] and membership in SSOC in view of the fact the 'political climate' in Mississippi is of a conservative nature and communities in the state would not tolerate any formation of any 'New Left group' on any other college campuses within the state." Headquarters endorsed the proposal and, as it did in other locales, sent the field office anti–New Left material—the pamphlet *Students for a Democratic Society, Front Runner of the New Left* and the article "Campus or Battleground? Columbia Is a Warning to All American Universities," which appeared in the financial newspaper *Barron's*—to pass along to the columnist to ensure he took a jaundiced view of *The Kudzu*.[83]

Ward was more enthusiastic about the story than the bureau had anticipated, "exhibit[ing] unusual interest in literature furnished by the Bureau," according to the SAC. The journalist believed that *The Kudzu* was "of vital interest to the residents of Mississippi," the Jackson SAC reported, "and he personally would write the article concerning New Left activities in the United States and in the State of Mississippi." In fact, Ward wrote seven separate articles based on the materials the agents sent him, including one that directly quoted the "Campus or Battleground?" article. Ward sent the articles to the agents "to edit and review," which they did, and soon after, his columns began appearing in the paper, each one running above the fold on the front page.[84] The columns appeared to have the intended effect. Ward informed the FBI that "he had received numerous telephone calls and letters from throughout the State of Mississippi which were all favorable toward the series of articles." Moreover, according to the FBI's confidential sources, the articles had created deep concern among local SSOC activists, with many worried that "physical harm may be done" to them as a result of the newspaper publishing their names. The columns were an unqualified success from the SAC's perspective, and he wrote headquarters that the office "will continue to be alert for opportunities to confuse and disrupt the New Left activities in the State of Mississippi."[85] Ward gave the office another opportunity to do so early in 1969, when he proposed writing a history of the New Left that highlighted its "subversive affiliations," which the American Legion would finance and distribute to colleges and high schools around the state. Headquarters gave its blessing to the project and sent a dozen additional articles critical of the New Left to the local office to furnish to Ward in order to assist in his effort.[86]

The Mississippi office's collaboration with Jimmy Ward was similar to tactics the bureau deployed elsewhere in nation in response to Hoover's order to develop counterintelligence actions against the New Left. The New Left in Mississippi, though, would not seem to merit much attention at all from the FBI since, the local office noted, it consisted of a grand total of eight students in an SSOC chapter at Millsaps. Chicago SDS this was not. Yet the bureau treated the group as a serious potential threat because in the logic of its national security analysis, any dissident activity could be the harbinger of serious disruptions to come. In the South, where segregation remained deeply entrenched and it took only the slightest hint of nonconformity to become suspected of radicalism, the emergence of any leftist group was alarming. An eight-member group in a community otherwise bereft of white student activism was thus not just notable but worrisome. The argument in "Campus or Battleground?"—the article on the events at Columbia in 1968 that the bureau shared with Ward and other friendly media sources—that the New Left was a "revolutionary movement which aims to seize first the universities and then the industries of America" resonated strongly with agents in the South. Hence, authorities could not ignore any New Left formation because all of its participants drank from the same poisoned ideological well. And the bureau could justify virtually any tactics to neutralize student activists as necessary preventive measures to lance the threat before it metastasized.[87]

To that end, the bureau sought to weaken New Left groups from within by stoking tensions and exploiting disagreements among activists. Hoover encouraged agents working on COINTELPRO–New Left to take every opportunity to promote distrust and factionalization in New Left groups. As he put it in his July 1968 memo to agents, "the instigating of or the taking advantage of personal conflicts or animosities existing between New Left leaders" ought to be a key tactic used against activist groups.[88] Southern agents used this tactic against SSOC. In Mississippi, the Millsaps SSOC group was the focus of a concerted bureau campaign of harassment and disinformation. As COINTELPRO–New Left got underway, the Jackson field office devised a plan to send a letter from a "Disenchanted Millsaps SSOC member" to the Nashville-based chairman of SSOC, Tom Gardner, attacking the chapter's leader, David Doggett, as insufficiently committed to the cause and insinuating that he was only looking out for himself. Such a plan stood little chance of success. Doggett was widely respected in SSOC for having helped build and sustain the chapter at Millsaps and weathering continual harassment for his efforts. Nonetheless, the Jackson agents proposed an action to smear him after a demonstration at the U.S. Marine and Naval Reserve Station in Jackson. "Dear Tom," the agents wrote, "I thought you should know something about . . . our leader in Jackson. [Doggett] makes a lot of noise but I noticed something funny about his actions at the picketing. . . . [H]e held back while we had to stick our necks out. He was afraid of a trap by the police and was afraid to be arrested. . . . Good old [Doggett] has his hand on everybody's back pushing them up front." The Jackson agents believed the letter could "discredit [Doggett] with the National SSOC Officers and show dissension in [the] Millsaps College chapter."[89] But when they sought approval for the letter, headquarters responded by suggesting a different tactic. Fearing that a successful campaign could lead to Doggett's "replacement by a stronger leader," Hoover's team counseled that a "better approach to disrupt the Millsaps College Chapter of SSOC might be through a word-of-mouth campaign . . . pointing out his [Doggett's] timidity, thereby undermining his leadership and possibly causing the disbandment of the Chapter."[90]

The following year, the Jackson agents went after a different Millsaps SSOC activist, Cassell Carpenter. Her involvement in SSOC had brought her to the agents' attention. But they also found it noteworthy—and troubling—that she "has been instrumental in getting college women interested in the Women's Liberation Movement in Mississippi," highlighting the bureau's ready conflation of any activism or beliefs that diverged from the norm as a reason for concern. Moreover, the agents strategically targeted her because she had grown up in the privileged, segregated environment of elite Natchez, where her father was a banker and she had been Queen of the Natchez Pilgrimage in 1966. "She has always boasted of her background," the Jackson SAC alleged, without offering any evidence, and this "has had an effect on the youth in Mississippi in that they have a tendency to idolize her due to her wealth." The Jackson agents proposed sending a letter to "a New Left leader"—perhaps Doggett, the chapter leader, or Gardner, the chair of SSOC—that attacked her for being more interested in her new boyfriend than in the movement. Signed by "Riverside Rievers," the letter begins by stating, "We are for and very much interested in your New Left Movement, against the close [*sic*] society." It then complains that Carpenter and her boyfriend don't contribute anything to the movement. "Are they in it for free love? For their own personal motives, or what? Let's get rid of these two and get on with the program."[91] Headquarters endorsed the plan but did not think it went far enough to denigrate her, and encouraged the SAC to "fully consider other measures for neutralizing her. Since her family appears to hold a position of social prominence in the Natchez area, adverse publicity might be effective if such can be obtained securely." A few weeks later, the Jackson agent reported that the letter appeared to have had the intended effect. There had been a "'shake-up' in the New Left Movement in Jackson," he wrote, and Carpenter had left the city to return home to Natchez before leaving the state altogether.[92]

The personal repercussions for Carpenter were precisely the type of outcome the bureau desired when it targeted individual activists. Just as agents hoped to fuel conflicts within New Left groups that would lead some activists to disengage, they also sought to provoke crises in individuals' personal lives that would pull them away from the movement. Hoover long had argued that the lifestyle of student activists could be a potent weapon in this effort. His antipathy for the cultural stylings adopted by many in the New Left was well known in the bureau. He frequently disparaged the appearance of student activists, taking personal offense at the way they looked, acted, and spoke. The casual celebration of drug use, openness about sexual experimentation, and rejection of mainstream norms and conventions incensed him further. The grafting of a cultural critique onto a political one created new opportunities for the bureau to damage the New Left. Students could be attacked for their lifestyle choices as a proxy for their political stances, and Hoover and his team encouraged agents to ridicule, mock, and condemn the activists' cultural practices as a valuable component of their counterintelligence planning.[93]

Agents perhaps did not need much prodding to focus on the nonconformist ways of the New Left, as they regularly made pejorative comments about how New Leftists appeared and acted. In a report on a 1968 SSOC conference in Mississippi, for example, Memphis agents took pains to offer unflattering physical descriptions of the attendees and make insidious comments about their backgrounds. Among the descriptions: "white male, Greek or Jewish appearance . . . long black hair, and acne scars on his neck"; "tall white male, wearing a planters hat and handle-bar mustache, who is the 'hippy' type"; "white female, Jewish-looking girl"; "white male . . . wearing rimless glasses, with short 'Hitler' type mustache, pudgy with a big stomach."[94] Agents also were attuned to events or gatherings that fit with the bureau's narrative that the New Left was awash in immorality and contemptuous of community standards. Of course, a reading of virtually any underground publication could provide evidence for such a perspective given that profanity and frank discussions of sexuality ran alongside political diatribes and social commentary. But organized events offered particularly useful ammunition for the bureau to illustrate the New Left's offensiveness. Festivals and music concerts were a rich target for bureau ridicule for this reason. In 1968, for example, the Jackson office sent an urgent teletype regarding a "Love-In" at Riverside Park. "A six member psychodelic [*sic*] hippie band from New Orleans" performed for approximately 120 people ("all white youths"), including "about thirty hippies." SSOC activists from Millsaps were in attendance, selling copies of their antiestablishment publication, *The Kudzu*. The event was a peaceful and, as advertised, fun-loving occasion; "no incidents occurred and no arrests made," the office reported, and the crowd dispersed before 7:00 p.m. But it drew the bureau's attention because it symbolized the appearance of the counterculture in Jackson. Events and ideas that had started on the two coasts had migrated to the heartland. If a love-in and alternative newspaper could appear in Mississippi, could violent extremism and anti-American radicalism be far behind?[95]

Agents furnished negative information about the students' lifestyle and political activities to their parents in the hope that they would then compel their children to change course. Undoubtedly, many did not approve or even know about what their children were doing while away at school. This made them important potential allies for the bureau if they could be made aware of their children's activities. Hoover and his team wanted to make sure they knew. When a student was arrested at a demonstration or their involvement in a protest was "accompanied by the use or engagement in an obscene display," a memo to agents instructed, "This information is to be promptly incorporated into an anonymous letter which can be directed to his parents. Where a photograph or other evidence is available to substantiate information in the letter, it should be made part of the mailing."[96] Armed with this information, bureau officials hoped parents would clamp down on the students. "By mailing anonymous letters," Charles Brennan wrote to William Sullivan, the activities of some of these students may be "restricted thus depriving the New Left of some of its force."[97]

A plan by the Little Rock office highlighted a typical approach. In 1968, the SAC targeted a woman who had attended SSOC meetings and participated in antiwar activity in the area. The agent proposed sending an anonymous letter to the woman's parents that seemingly sympathized with them for having a rebellious daughter while insinuating that she was an embarrassment to them and that her behavior reflected their failure as parents. "I am sure that you have long been aware that your daughter . . . has been running around with a group of 'beatniks,' many of whom have been arrested for possession of marijuana and for involvement in illicit drug traffic," the letter, signed by "A sincere and concerned friend," states. "I felt this was none of my business and it was so well known by everyone that you were probably doing the best you could with an uncontrollable child." The letter then turned to its main point, exposing the woman for lying to her parents by telling them she and her boyfriend had married when they "have been going around Little Rock openly bragging about the fact that they are not married. . . . I feel that you would want to know about this sinful and immoral behavior." The SAC hoped that the letter, though it ignored her political activities, would inspire her parents to "take some action to disrupt [her] involvement in 'New Left' activities . . . and possibly disrupt other activities of the LR [Little Rock] SSOC."[98] Headquarters, though, did not approve the letter. Revealingly, its concern was not with its tone or content and certainly not with its anonymity but, rather, that the agent had not made clear what role the woman played in SSOC. "While this proposal might be effective, it is not felt her New Left leanings have been sufficiently established," the director wrote to the SAC. The bureau, thus, had no objection to an anonymous letter attacking a student for her personal relationships, only that her New Left credentials had not been confirmed.[99]

Agents also fed information to local law enforcement regarding alleged drug offenses by student activists. Hoover considered such collaborative efforts to be a particularly fruitful line of attack on the New Left. "Since the use of marijuana and other narcotics is widespread among members of the New Left," Hoover averred in his July 1968 memo to agents, "you should be alert to opportunities to have them arrested by local authorities on drug charges."[100] The Memphis office embraced this approach in its work against SSOC. "This group is vulnerable through the rigid enforcement of local, State, and Federal laws in that the individual staff members may from time to time violate the various laws such as parking, traffic, narcotics, and with increasing frequency the Selective Service laws," the Memphis SAC wrote to headquarters. "Memphis is continually alert to any indications that these individuals are engaged in any unlawful activities and will promptly submit any such indication to the responsible law enforcement agency."[101]

This type of interagency collaboration was an important element of COINTELPRO–New Left. FBI agents in the South regularly shared information they had collected with state investigative offices and local police departments, which, in turn, passed along tips they had gathered in their own efforts to undermine New Left groups. These law enforcement agencies were just as keen as the FBI to repress New Left activity. The Richmond SAC noted in 1969 that his office "continues to be in . . . close liaison with the Richmond Police Department and its Intelligence Squad which has a very active interest in disrupting New Left activities in Richmond, namely, that of the Southern Student Organizing Committee." The FBI agents "pointed out to the Intelligence Squad what seemed to be ways in which the City of Richmond could take action . . . on grounds of disorderly conduct, obscenity, acts against the dignity of the community." The FBI also approvingly noted that the Richmond Vice Squad's effort to "crackdown on drug abuse" meant that "SSOC members, as well as anyone who might appear in a hippie-type dress, receive far from a friendly welcome in the Richmond area." The police attention had hindered New Left activity in the city, the FBI agent noted, by causing "fear of arrest and harassment by local authorities, as well as all forms of law enforcement."[102]

While the Richmond FBI office cheered on the police department's efforts, agents in Little Rock more proactively coordinated with the police. In July 1968, an informant reported that a local SSOC leader was known to use and sell marijuana at her residence. The SAC relayed this information to the Little Rock Police Department, which subsequently executed a search warrant that led to her arrest as well as that of four other people, two of whom were SSOC members, all for possession of marijuana.[103] The field office considered the operation a resounding success because it "resulted in the complete neutralization and disassociation" of the SSOC leader from activists in the city; after her arrest, she was expelled from school and left Little Rock to return to her family.[104] In Texas and South Carolina, the bureau targeted coffeehouses that had sprung up in the vicinity of important military bases. Similar to army intelligence, the FBI agents sought to undermine support for these venues in any way they could. Agents in San Antonio ran a counterintelligence operation against activists it had identified as patrons of the Oleo Strut coffeehouse near Fort Hood. In early 1969, they sent an anonymous letter to the parents of one person who was "connected" to the coffeehouse and who, the letter claimed, participated in "'pot' parties" at the residence he shared with a woman.[105] In South Carolina, agents in Columbia collaborated with local police to surveil and harass the proprietors and customers at the UFO Coffeehouse. Located near Fort Jackson, the coffeehouse was a salon-type gathering place for opponents of the war, including students from the University of South Carolina (USC) and military personnel from the base. Hoover considered coffeehouses to be a significant enough threat that he singled them out in his directive to agents in July 1968. Alleged drug use was the focus of his critique. Because marijuana and other drugs would "probably be utilized by individuals running the coffeehouses or frequenting them," he wrote, "local law enforcement authorities should be promptly advised whenever you receive an indication that this is being done."[106] Thus, in addition to asking the Internal Revenue Service and state revenue office to investigate if the coffeehouse was paying its entertainment tax—it was—and tasking informants to take and destroy stacks of antiwar, New Left, and underground publications from the coffeehouse, which prompted the owners to start asking people to pay for what they took, agents provided tips drawn from informant reports to the Columbia Police Department and Richland County Sheriff's Office that led to the arrest of eighteen people on drug or disorderly conduct charges in 1969. The arrests fueled efforts by local authorities to shut down the coffeehouse as a public nuisance, which it succeeded in doing in 1970.[107]

In the spring of 1969, SSOC collapsed amid internal tensions and the meddlesome intervention by factions within SDS. SSOC's disbandment, however, did not initially stop the FBI's campaign against the group out of concern that it could be revived. Agents expressed particular worry about a resurgence of SSOC at Furman University in Greenville, South Carolina, which had hosted one of the group's most vibrant and active chapters. When agents learned from an informant that the Furman students were planning to restart the chapter on campus in the fall of 1969, they received headquarters' approval to confidentially contact school officials to let them know SSOC no longer existed. Armed with this information, school administrators could deny recognition of the group as an official campus organization, thus limiting its ability to radicalize other students.[108] Agents elsewhere in the region saw SSOC's demise as an opportunity to further stoke tensions within the New Left. In Richmond, agents spent months honing an anonymous letter to send to New Left publications, purportedly from an SSOC staff member, that castigated SDS for its role in SSOC's collapse. It did not matter that organized New Left activity had diminished in Richmond without SSOC's presence; at the same time the agents were working on the letter, they noted that, as they put it in one memo, "organized New Left activities within the Richmond Division have reached an all-time low in view of the fact that Southern Student Organizing Committee (SSOC) no longer exists." The disappearance of one foe did not mean the threat posed by the New Left had been resolved. The key was to keep up the pressure, to continue "to take aggressive steps" against the New Left. The fictitious letter the Richmond office drafted would serve this purpose by "continuing to foster unrest in the southern portion of the United States with SDS" and "continue to cause factionalism in the New Left."[109]

Headquarters' response when one southern field office sought to stop its surveillance of SSOC highlighted the importance the bureau attached to continuing to surveil New Left groups in the South after SSOC collapsed. The FBI office in Knoxville earned Hoover's ire when it reported in mid-1969 that it was ending its counterintelligence campaign against New Left groups in the area due to lack of activity. Headquarters responded by unequivocally rejecting the Knoxville office's assessment of student activism: "In view of the serious violence which occurred on campuses during the last academic year, many of which were spontaneous, and in view of the fact that there has been no evidence whatsoever to substantiate the conclusion that the New Left's efforts on the Nation's campuses are abating, you should not close out this Program in your office." It was imperative to remain vigilant because it was only a matter of time before a new wave of campus protests erupted. "During this period of abated activity by the New Left," the Director's Office advised, "you should prepare for and seek new ways of arresting the attacks by the New Left which will, in all probability, develop during the coming academic year." The Knoxville office got the message, and over the next year, as student activism picked up on campus, it continued its surveillance efforts with a focus on the "30 to 50 hippie-type individuals . . . causing all the discontent on the UT campus."[110] SSOC's dissolution, then, was a momentary victory that ultimately required heightened surveillance to detect the next manifestation of New Left activity in the region. The campaign to destroy the New Left was never-ending.

COINTELPRO–New Left exacted a significant toll on the white student movement in the South. The bureau's campaign of harassment and disruption raised the cost of participation to students inclined to support movement causes. For SSOC, the most important organizational expression of white student activism, COINTELPRO–New Left battered the group and contributed to its collapse by exacerbating tensions among the activists and undercutting its ability to grow and ultimately survive. Although it was a small regional group comprised of loosely connected activists on campuses scattered around the South that eschewed the type of provocative actions and radical ideology that characterized New Leftists elsewhere, SSOC stood out in the South for its focus on white students. To the FBI, the group had the capacity and the interest in stirring campus unrest and destabilizing southern communities and therefore required monitoring and disruption.

More broadly, white southern student activists like those involved in SSOC represented a direct rebuke to the established order. Their opposition to the military misadventure in Southeast Asia and their wholehearted support of the Black-led civil rights movement marked them as radicals and nonconformists in a region where white dissent was an anomaly and drew attention from federal officials who readily equated dissent with disloyalty. That the activists were relatively few in number compared to those elsewhere in the nation did not exempt them from official harassment or deep and intrusive surveillance. For federal authorities determined to contain student dissent, their small numbers suggested not ineffectualness or weakness but, rather, the potential for dangerous growth: today's handful of student activists would become tomorrow's mass movement if authorities allowed activism to continue unchecked. Hence, it was vital—imperative, even—to turn the state's surveillance machinery against the activists in a desperate effort to undermine student activists and shore up support for the established order.

The secret surveillance campaigns undertaken by federal officials against New Leftists unraveled in the 1970s as journalists, whistleblowers, and activists exposed the extralegal and often sordid details of the drive to discredit and diminish the student movement. In April 1971, after activists brazenly broke into the FBI office in Media, Pennsylvania, and made off with COINTELPRO files, J. Edgar Hoover ended COINTELPRO–New Left and all the other COINTELPROs as well. With the theft, Hoover well understood that the bureau could no longer ensure that COINTELPROs would remain secret, though he would be dead for nearly two years before information about them blew up in the press in 1974.[111] The revelations about the FBI's misdeeds, along with *New York Times* journalist Seymour Hersch's exposure of the CIA's domestic spying operation and former army captain Christopher Pyle's unmasking of military intelligence's counterintelligence work, prompted congressional investigations that tarnished all of the agencies and led to wide-ranging reforms that clipped their ability to conduct domestic intelligence.

The publicity that attended the discovery of the federal surveillance operations shined a bright light on the FBI, CIA, and other agencies. It also diverted attention from surveillance campaigns unleashed at other levels of government. In the South, agencies embedded in state governments had devised and implemented their own programs to surveil and undermine the work of student activists that echoed the federal efforts. State-led campaigns against student activists, in some cases dating back to the 1950s and continuing into the 1970s, further restricted the space in which activists had to work in the South and subjected students to intensive and often overlapping counterintelligence programs.

2

STATE SURVEILLANCE

"ATTACHED IS A COPY of the report which we discussed verbally . . . along with attachments of the resolution dissolving SSOC," Kenneth W. Fairly, an assistant to Mississippi governor John Bell Williams, wrote on June 11, 1969, to officials in the Mississippi Highway Patrol, Mississippi National Guard, and Mississippi State Sovereignty Commission. Three days earlier, the Southern Student Organizing Committee had voted to dissolve itself at an acrimonious meeting held at the Mt. Beulah Conference Center near Edwards, about twenty-five miles outside Jackson. Fairly, who the governor had tasked with organizing an investigative group focused on student activism and illegal drugs, had learned of the meeting thanks to the work of an informant who had attended part of the multiday gathering. The informant, David Davidson, was generally inept. Attempting to pass himself off as someone interested in getting involved in student activism, he left the meeting the first night because he had to be at work at six o'clock the next morning, and when he returned the following evening—after first drinking a quart of beer—he was turned away and told to come back in a couple days, when the meeting would be over but he could talk to those who remained about how to get involved in the student movement. When he returned as instructed, the activists permitted him to observe the discussion and the vote to dissolve the organization. Not that he understood it much, as he was oblivious to the dynamics and meaning of the internecine battle over the group's fate. This hardly mattered, though, to Fairly, who was pleased with Davidson's work and happy to make him available to his colleagues for future assignments. He only asked them to keep "his name in extreme confidence and treat it as classified information."[1]

Fairly's interest in SSOC's last days and his assumption that others in the law enforcement infrastructure would have an interest as well, was indicative of the attention government officials paid to white student activists in the region. State investigative agencies were a vital component of the surveillance regime in the South, joining federal forces and police Red Squads to provide another layer of surveillance to monitor and disrupt student activism. The agencies themselves came in different flavors, from highway patrols to ad hoc committees created by political leaders for the express purpose of spying on activists. But they shared an antipathy to student activism and a commitment to quashing any perceived challenges to the segregationist system, patriotic devotion to the American military, or the conservative, mainstream values of the community. While the state surveillance units focused especially on African American activists, they also devoted time, attention, and resources to surveilling the activities of white students involved in social justice causes as well as nonconforming counterculturalists. They monitored their protests, sent informants to gather intelligence on their plans, and collaborated with federal authorities and local police—for example, tipping off police about potential drug violations and sharing information with FBI agents. They were acutely sensitive to any sign of dissent. As a result, subscribing to an alternative newspaper or patronizing a coffeehouse could land one on a watch list just as readily as attending a protest against the war or joining a civil rights organization. Actions that on their face seemed innocuous appeared to authorities as causes for concern, as a dangerous precursor to more serious problems. To state investigators, like their local and federal peers, no threat was too small for concern. They could not take the chance of ignoring what appeared trivial because the trivial could carry in it the seeds of destruction.

State officials' pursuit of what often were small bands of activists shows the depth of intolerance for dissent that existed in the region. White student activists constituted a threat not because of their size or the scope of their activities but because they contained within them the potential to metastasize into a threat to the established order. The lesson that state officials took from disruptions that plagued campuses elsewhere in the nation was that unrest would spiral out of control quickly if not immediately suppressed. It was incumbent, therefore, to maintain close surveillance of campuses in order to be prepared to respond quickly to any hint of disruption. Driven by the fear of impending doom, state officials went to work.

We may never know the full extent of such efforts given the paucity of surviving records. As time passed and these agencies lost funding, became inactive, and were dissolved, state officials made little effort to preserve their files, and over time, many disappeared, either through the routine purging of state records or intentionally destroyed by officials to conceal illegal or unethical conduct. In Alabama, for example, archivists suspected that the files of the state's investigative agency were far from complete when only six cubic feet of records arrived at the state archives after years of legal wrangling. "This commission was in existence for fifteen years," one archivist said. "It's our belief there was material purged from these files before the case went to court."[2] Yet the records of state surveillance activities that do survive paint a damning portrait of state-funded efforts to attack citizens for exercising their constitutionally protected rights to assemble peacefully and to voice their opinion on issues of the day.

The Mississippi State Sovereignty Commission is by far the most well-known, oft-cited, and frequently studied of the state agencies that organized against progressive reformers, owing to the survival of its files and extent of its surveillance activities. Mississippi's reputation as a state hostile to racial reform and liberal policies, as a place where the influential regional network of segregationist civic leaders known as the Citizens' Council was born and where governors led the charge to defend white supremacy by any means necessary, and as home to some of the most violent episodes in civil rights movement history, ensures that the state looms large in studies of the era. But Mississippi was not the only state to train its power on activists, and to focus only on the Magnolia State's misdeeds and deviousness is to miss the breadth of surveillance activities that government entities around the region initiated. From its four immediate neighbors—Louisiana, Arkansas, Tennessee, and Alabama—to those farther afield, such as South Carolina, Florida, Oklahoma, and Texas, state leaders launched campaigns to disrupt, discredit, and derail protest activity. White campus activists found themselves in the crosshairs of these campaigns. While perhaps not as viscerally threatening to state leaders as Black Power advocates, white students who organized to oppose the draft and the war, trafficked in the rhetoric of anti-capitalism and political radicalism, or challenged authority on their campuses in the myriad ways students did during the era became subjects of state surveillance efforts. Regardless of their tactics, their goals, or their numbers, white students' activism posed a threat to the status quo. It was another example to white political leaders and elites—as if one were needed—that the world they knew was under assault. The threat to the established order was all too real, dramatized by the upheaval in faraway places like New York and Berkeley but also occurring closer to home, in Austin and Jackson, Nashville and Columbia. Such upheaval was to be expected unless authorities acted with dispatch and urgency, creativity and ruthlessness, to upend protest efforts before they even began.

Across the South, the burgeoning civil rights movement and the broader push for social change in the 1950s and 1960s prompted state legislatures and governors to invest state resources in efforts to surveil and undermine the forces that threatened the racial status quo or the political and social conventions of the era. The manifestation of their efforts took varied forms. The Georgia Bureau of Investigation and the North Carolina State Bureau of Investigation explicitly modeled themselves on the FBI. The Louisiana State Police's Criminal Bureau of Identification, the investigative unit within the Tennessee Department of Safety, and the South Carolina Law Enforcement Division vested investigative authority in existing state law enforcement agencies. The Alabama Legislative Committee to Preserve the Peace and the Florida Legislative Investigation Committee, better known as the Johns Committee after its chairman, Charley Johns, were created by legislative acts and controlled by state lawmakers. The notorious House Un-American Activities Committee (HUAC) was an inspiration for the creation of the Louisiana Joint Legislative Committee on Un-American Activities, the Kentucky Un-American Activities Committee, and other so-called Little HUACs in the South. And several states sought to shore up their defenses against progressive assaults by establishing brand-new state agencies, including sovereignty commissions in Alabama, Arkansas, Louisiana, Mississippi, and Virginia and a secret unit housed in the state military office in Oklahoma.[3]

Opposition to racial reform, resistance to what white lawmakers often characterized as federal intrusion into state affairs, and a conviction that communists were at the center of protest activity served to underlay state investigative work. State officials justified their surveillance activity as a necessary pillar to uphold peace, order, and prosperity in the community. To be sure, the battle to preserve segregation and white control was central to their work and usually the motivating factor for their creation in the first place. But as time passed and the perceived threats multiplied—demands for student rights, opposition to the draft and Vietnam War, surging drug use on college campuses—state agencies expanded their work. No longer were they focused solely on civil rights and African American activists but now also trained their attention on the growing number of white students involved in protest activities, New Left organizations, and countercultural formations.

State authorities' intolerance of dissent was grounded in the same fears that impelled local and federal intelligence units to pursue white activists. As protest activity swelled around the country and campuses on both coasts experienced significant disruption and unrest, state investigators worried that their community would be next unless they clamped down on dissent in whatever form it emerged. What had happened elsewhere was a warning sign, a portent of what was to come if they did not proactively move against dissenters and nonconformists on campuses. State agencies deployed the full range of counterintelligence tools in their work, from monitoring activists to infiltrating student groups to planting false information in an effort to sow discord among activists. The state leaders behind these efforts evinced not only a contempt for their own citizens but a deep insecurity about the socioeconomic, racial, and political arrangements because only through repression of dissent could they be preserved.

OKLAHOMA AND THE OFFICE OF INTERAGENCY COORDINATION

The border state of Oklahoma was far from the coastal enclaves where campus activism seemed endemic. But that distance did not insulate the state's overwhelmingly white, conservative electorate from fears that leftist activists were poised to assault the state's institutions of higher learning and, more broadly, Oklahomans' cherished way of life. These were not new concerns in Oklahoma. In 1939, the state's governor charged that faculty at the University of Oklahoma (OU) were teaching communist propaganda and ought to be fired. Soon after, the state senate established a committee to investigate possible communist activities in the state, including among students and faculty at both the University of Oklahoma and Oklahoma State University (OSU). The committee, modeled after the House Un-American Activities Committee and known as one of the "Little Dies Committees," after HUAC's chair, Martin Dies of Texas, concluded that communists were working to spread their ideology throughout Oklahoma and that they had successfully established a foothold in all parts of the state. The fact that the committee did not identify any communists at OU or OSU did little to assuage concerns that the campuses were ripe breeding grounds for foreign ideologies. Over the next two decades, as political conservatism hardened in Oklahoma and the state became a bastion of evangelical anticommunism, the state's colleges and universities remained suspect in the eyes of political leaders. In 1968, in the wake of small-scale antiwar organizing—including a protest that the SDS chapter at OU organized against an appearance in Oklahoma City by Selective Service System head Gen. Lewis B. Hershey—Governor Dewey Bartlett used his executive authority to create the Office of Interagency Coordination (OIC), a secret agency to gather, evaluate, and disseminate "information related to civil disorders" to law enforcement agencies. In practice, the OIC focused its efforts exclusively on civil rights and antiwar activities, primarily at the state's colleges and universities. With little oversight and no public accountability, the OIC quickly compiled files on thousands of individuals and organizations, much of it of dubious quality and accuracy. Led by James DeFrates, a retired army lieutenant colonel, the OIC operated with neither the consent nor knowledge of the state legislature for two years, until its exposure in the state press garnered negative national publicity and brought an ACLU lawsuit. The exposure of the agency prompted Bartlett's successor as governor, David Hall, to unilaterally order the destruction of the OIC's files. The loss of the files in Oklahoma short-circuited the brewing legal case and thus prevented a full accounting of the state's actions.[4]

Fear was the driving force behind the OIC's creation. The twin worries that small-scale protests on campuses in the state would spin out of control or that radicals from elsewhere would instigate unrest in Oklahoma prompted the governor's decision to establish the new intelligence office. By the mid-1960s, small groups of leftist students had organized Students for a Democratic Society chapters at OU and OSU, and they and other like-minded students began to speak out and protest against the war. Black students around the state also had organized protest actions to draw attention to racial inequities and to push for civil rights reforms. Though these groups and actions were small compared to what was taking place elsewhere in the country—the University of Oklahoma's SDS chapter had approximately a dozen students and Oklahoma State University's all of three—they were conspicuous in a state where student dissent rarely had occurred in recent years. Equally, if not more, concerning was the possibility that the actions and rhetoric of student activists outside the state would inspire Oklahoma students to rebel on their own campuses. These "outside agitators" were beyond the reach of Oklahoma authorities, which made it all the more important to monitor their activities so as to be prepared should Oklahoma students respond favorably to them.[5]

The emphasis on preparedness was a common trope that surveillance advocates called on to defend their snooping. It was also a means to cast surveillance activities in the most innocuous terms possible by framing them as a way to keep law enforcement informed of potential disruptions to daily life in Oklahoma. Just as the FBI and local Red Squads characterized their activities as vital to preserve peace and tranquility, so did the OIC's defenders. Governor Bartlett told one interviewer in 1970 that "good intelligence, good information" was the reason why Oklahoma had experienced little unrest. OIC head James DeFrates justified the agency's surveillance work as providing crucial information that helped law enforcement plan for crowd control and even manage traffic jams as a result of large or provocative gatherings. In reality, though, the OIC, like other state-sponsored intelligence agencies, was not a neutral planning agency but a government unit established to monitor and discredit the work of perceived threats to the state—supposed political radicals, racial and ethnic minorities, and organizations that opposed the war, supported racial reforms, or promoted other progressive causes.[6]

Bartlett and DeFrates believed leftist activists required the state's attention because they were the ones who could cause unrest and tension. The latter term, though vague and imprecise, was one that DeFrates often invoked as a rationale for state action against student activists. The OIC, he explained, existed "to find the possibility of tension" and then to prepare to defend against it because "rising tensions . . . may lead to disorder."[7] Those on the political Left were the cause of this tension, according to DeFrates. Consequently, "Oklahoma law enforcement agencies must be constantly prepared to cope with individuals/organizations engaged in dissident activities." No matter how fleeting one's connection to an activist group, individuals could still find that the OIC had added their names to its files. As DeFrates told one news organization, a person's name could appear in the OIC files because "you might be affiliated with an organization . . . any type of organization."[8]

The OIC was the culmination of Governor Bartlett's increasingly worried efforts to insulate Oklahoma from protest activity that, by 1968, seemed to be surging around the country. Racialized police violence across the urban North and the widespread unrest that swept through the nation after Martin Luther King Jr.'s assassination heightened the sense of foreboding. The relative quiet of Oklahoma campuses only served to heighten fears that they were ripe targets for student activists. After King's murder, Bartlett deployed DeFrates to gather information about the Poor People's Campaign, which had made a brief stop in the state on its way to the nation's capital. He also created "Operation Sooner Able" to plan for potential civil unrest should Oklahoma cities face disorder similar to what other cities recently had experienced. The OIC built on and formalized these efforts. With its creation, the governor now had at his disposal an agency devoted exclusively to monitoring the leftist activists and organizations officials deemed troublesome or threatening.[9]

In some respects, the OIC proved to be an amateurish operation. With only four or five employees, it lacked the staff to conduct investigations and instead relied on information largely gathered from news sources.[10] Most of this information focused on happenings outside Oklahoma, unsurprisingly, because that's where most of the action took place. DeFrates wrote weekly summaries that he drew from news accounts in both mainstream and alternative publications and that the OIC distributed to law enforcement groups around the state. Sprinkled into his summaries were references to Oklahoma-specific activities, ranging from the benign—a gathering of the Council of Five Civilized Tribes, for example—to the mundane, such as the activities of a peace candidate in the campaign for a congressional seat. The information he provided was often replete with errors, inaccuracies, and wild misinterpretations. In one glaring example, he claimed that Oklahoma student groups that used the term *Afro-American* in their names were tied to the Black Panthers. He also asserted that the Panthers were created by the Student Nonviolent Coordinating Committee and the Revolutionary Action Movement (RAM) and that all of these groups likely had communist ties.[11] In other instances, he erroneously claimed that SDS chapters and African American groups at OU and OSU were connected organizations, and he drastically inflated the number of students involved in SDS; rather than the seventy students he claimed were part of the group at OU and OSU in 1968 or 1969, the actual number was closer to fifteen or perhaps twenty at the two institutions combined. So off base were many of the OIC's accusations that OU president J. Herbert Holloman, who met several times with DeFrates and Bartlett about their concerns for potential campus disturbances, dismissed the agency's claims as unreliable and inaccurate. In one instance, after DeFrates sought to raise suspicions about a professor on the Norman campus, Holloman recalled that "the information concerning the faculty member of Oklahoma University [*sic*] was so patently ridiculous to me, that I paid little heed to it."[12]

To say the OIC was amateurish, though, is not to suggest it was harmless. As OU president Holloman had discovered, it tracked students and professors, creating files on them and thousands of other people suspected of subversive ties or activities. It sent disparaging information and allegations of concern to campus officials in hope of prompting a crackdown on suspected radicals. It assigned cameramen to photograph protesters at demonstrations and occasionally hired part-time investigators to collect information on targets. It collaborated with the FBI and local police departments, providing them with reports on the agency's "findings." DeFrates personally visited police departments across the state to encourage them to send information to the OIC that he could then circulate through his weekly reports, in that way amplifying local issues into statewide concerns. All of this activity may have led to the blacklisting of individuals whose names were in the OIC's files, as allegations surfaced that students who had engaged in protest activities could not find jobs or were rejected by colleges. In one 1970 case, a female student at one school was "near a nervous breakdown" after college officials showed her parents the file on her, including photographs of her participation in a vigil after the shooting deaths of students at Kent State University.[13]

By 1970, the OIC had amassed several thousand "incident reports" and files on approximately eight hundred organizations and six thousand individuals, a third of whom were Oklahomans; the rest were "'known troublemakers such as Angela Davis'" from elsewhere, according to one news account quoting an OIC official, likely DeFrates.[14] As the number of files the OIC maintained mushroomed, DeFrates developed a process for managing all of the information he had gathered. The system he created contributed to the OIC's bureaucratization, a means of making its work seem routine and ordinary—just another function of state government rather than a secretive and intrusive surveillance regime. His system was not always intuitive or easy to understand. For instance, it included incident reports and incident summaries, and individuals could be listed in one but not the other, which determined whether their names were indexed and thus incorporated into the larger filing system. To allow for cross-referencing, the files were arranged in multiple ways—by name, geographic area, subject matter, and news clipping number, the latter determined by the labor-intensive process of cutting articles out of newspapers and pasting them to sheets of paper. Equally complicated was the process DeFrates devised for assessing the information the OIC gathered. The source of the information was evaluated on an A–F scale, while the information itself received a rating on a 1–6 scale, meaning that each item had a double rating. Crucially, low ratings—that is, a rating indicating that a source was unreliable or that the information could not be verified—did not prevent the OIC from adding the names of individuals and organizations to the files and thus marking them as potential sources of trouble.[15]

By housing the Office of Interagency Coordination in the state's Military Department and not formally establishing it through a proclamation process that would have produced a public record of its creation, the governor hid the agency from legislators and citizens alike. But this also meant the OIC lacked a dedicated source of funds. Instead, it was allocated a portion of the state National Guard's budget, amounting to approximately twenty-seven thousand dollars, virtually all of which, DeFrates claimed, went toward the reports he prepared. This was not enough to keep up with the information flowing into the agency nor to manage the filing system DeFrates had created. In 1970, DeFrates and the governor sought to increase the OIC's budget by applying for a grant administered by the Law Enforcement Assistance Administration (LEAA), which the Omnibus Crime Control and Safe Streets Act of 1968 had established to support local and state law enforcement. DeFrates sought LEAA support to enhance the OIC's operations. LEAA funding, DeFrates wrote in the grant application, would enable the OIC to add the personnel and equipment necessary to "increase the volume of essential information" it gathered and provided to local police departments. Without more staff, he warned, the vast trove of information the agency collected could not "be fully evaluated and updated for further use by law enforcement agencies."[16]

Student activism loomed large in DeFrates's characterization of the challenges to peace and security in Oklahoma. He stressed in the application the need for information on student activists despite the fact that the state was far from the centers of campus unrest. Although Oklahoma had experienced "a minimum of violence connected with civil disorder," DeFrates invoked the law enforcement shibboleth that "the absence of violence does not discount the potential of violence which exists in various cities and on college campuses throughout the state." Antiwar groups, labor organizers, and Black student organizations all appeared in Oklahoma and, by their very existence, constituted a threat, in DeFrates's estimation. He dwelled on these groups and their activities, counting on the fact that like-minded law enforcement officials would understand the threat such groups posed to law and order. "There are ten colleges/universities which have active black student organizations," he wrote, and on at least three campuses these organizations made "racial type demands for changes" and "supported these demands with demonstrations." In addition, "other activist/dissident organizations on campus at colleges/highschools [*sic*]" had appeared, including those organizing opposition to the Vietnam War.[17] To create the impression that law enforcement faced an onslaught of protest and activism, he attached to his application forty newspaper clippings about protests and demonstrations that had taken place recently in the state. These ranged from a peace vigil at OU to antiwar and civil rights demonstrations at the University of Tulsa to protests surrounding a sanitation workers' strike in

Oklahoma City.[18] All of this activity, DeFrates asserted, meant that "the potential for rising tensions which may lead to civil disorder exists in Oklahoma" and thus required police departments to "be constantly aware of individuals/organizations involved in dissident type activities." He invoked the violence that had plagued the nation's cities in recent years to remind his readers that it would not take much to spark a crisis in Oklahoma that "could have an impact on the population equivalent to those experienced nationwide in 1967–68." The OIC would play the key role in law enforcement preparedness by providing "timely information pertinent to civil disorders." And because disorder was always possible, it was vital that the OIC serve as a sentinel, always on guard for any hint of dissent as dissent could quickly turn to disorder.[19] DeFrates was persuasive; the LEAA made two grants to the OIC: one, for $18,347, for personnel and office materials, and another for communication equipment.[20]

Despite the federal support, the OIC was out of business barely six months later. While Bartlett and DeFrates had shielded the agency from public view for nearly two years, eighteen days after it received the LEAA awards, Tulsa newspaper reporter Mike Flanagan exposed the clandestine agency after obtaining one of DeFrates's weekly summaries. In a front-page article in the *Tulsa Daily World*, Flanagan revealed that the OIC was a secret agency that was "keeping tabs" on citizens and sharing information with local police. The weekly report Flanagan reported on, drawn mostly from newspapers, combined information about national events, such as a Black Panther meeting in Philadelphia, with Oklahoma-based activities, including the work of the Oklahoma City National Welfare Rights Group. The report also mentioned the activities of the independent congressional candidate Kenneth Kottka, who "is circulating a mimeographed paper asking Oklahomans to write to their congressmen and express their views on the proposed McGovern-Hatfield amendment called 'the amendment to end the war.'" Kottka, an OU graduate student and former CIA agent who was running on a peace platform for the seat in Oklahoma's Fourth Congressional District, was of interest to the OIC, DeFrates vaguely explained to the reporter, because law enforcement was "concerned with 'some of the organizations' that might be involved" in his campaign.[21] The exposé led to a raft of coverage in the local and national press, culminating in a segment in a December 1970 episode of *First Tuesday*, an investigative news show on

NBC, in which Bartlett and DeFrates defended the OIC, which the program gave the more catchy name of "Sooner CIA" in reference to its location within the state's Military Department.[22]

In addition to having the OIC thrust into the glare of the national spotlight, the Oklahoma ACLU sued the governor, DeFrates, and other state officials in federal court on behalf of two individuals whom the agency had tracked: Kottka, the congressional candidate, and biochemist Earl Mitchell, the faculty advisor to the Afro-American Society at OSU and the president of the Stillwater NAACP chapter. Kottka said that the press coverage of the OIC's surveillance of him had cost him volunteers and financial support. Moreover, he said, "it is difficult for me to explain to people why a former Central Intelligence Agency employee . . . who has been cleared almost to the highest levels for security clearance, has a file maintained on him by a State Intelligence Agency." Mitchell, whose work with Black students made him an OIC target, vehemently objected to DeFrates's contention that the mere existence of Black student groups constituted a threat to peace and safety: "As the faculty advisor to one of these black student organizations I specifically deny that they constitute a potential for violence and such statements are made without foundation."[23]

Attorney Stephen Jones led the ACLU lawsuit. Jones was a disaffected Bartlett campaign worker and speechwriter—and himself the subject of an OIC file—who recently had resigned from his law firm in Enid, Oklahoma, rather than decline to represent an OU student arrested for displaying a Viet Cong flag. The suit charged that the OIC surveillance activities violated constitutionally protected rights of speech and assembly, and it called for the files to be destroyed. The plaintiffs accused the agency of seeking to "cast a pall over lawful political protest," arguing that the OIC sought to "harass and intimidate plaintiffs and to deter them from exercising their constitutionally protected right to political protest and to dissent from governmental policies."[24] "This is the essence of plaintiffs' First Amendment claims," they wrote in another filing. "When the military arm of government acts upon constitutionally protected political expression in a manner which can only burden that expression it constitutes an infringement of First Amendment rights."[25] While Bartlett defended the agency in the press—telling the *New York Times*, "So long as I am Governor, I will use all the resources at my command to protect the rights of all citizens including the right to dissent, to fight civil disorders on campus or anywhere, to fight drug abuse, and to fight crime in all forms"—his days as governor were numbered. David Hall, Bartlett's opponent in the 1970 election, won a narrow victory after a campaign in which he had derided the OIC as a "super snooper group." Once in office in January 1971, he abolished the agency, and after he and two staffers cursorily reviewed a few files—including one on him—he ordered them destroyed. In this, he was in alignment with Jones, who had pressed for the files' destruction in the lawsuit. On his orders, his staffers burned the more than six thousand files the OIC had collected.[26]

State surveillance against activists on the prairies of Oklahoma was testament to the concerns and fears among state officials about the views and, more importantly, intentions of nonconformists of all types. Oklahoma police authorities were no different than their peers across the nation's southern tier in seeking to clamp down on dissent wherever it threatened political or social stability. In the states of the former Confederacy, where segregation was under assault and the Vietnam War was galvanizing student opposition, governments mobilized to defend the status quo. Whereas Oklahoma established an executive branch office to lead investigative efforts, other states conferred this authority on existing state law enforcement agencies. Such was the case in South Carolina.

SOUTH CAROLINA AND THE STATE LAW ENFORCEMENT DIVISION

From antebellum Fire-Eaters like Robert Barnwell Rhett to arch segregationists like Strom Thurmond, the Palmetto State had a long history of aggressively defending white supremacy. In the 1960s, as the civil rights movement pressed for gains throughout the state, police agencies worked to thwart their campaigns, both implicitly, by allowing vigilantes and white mobs to descend on nonviolent demonstrators, and explicitly, by using force to disperse and repel protesters. In February 1968, in the most notorious incident in the state's civil rights history, highway patrolmen fired into a crowd of African American students on the South Carolina State University campus in Orangeburg who were protesting segregation at a nearby bowling alley, killing two students and a high schooler waiting for his mother to get off of work. The "Orangeburg Massacre," as the shooting became known, followed by the acquittal of highway patrolmen on federal charges of using excessive force and the arrest, conviction, and imprisonment of SNCC activist Cleveland Sellers on fabricated charges of inciting the incident, revealed that the state would neither hesitate to use force nor be held accountable when it resorted to violence against perceived threats to the established order.[27]

The growing anti–Vietnam War movement became another state target as students increasingly took up the call to oppose the war. White students, in particular, were drawn to the cause. While South Carolina police authorities did not unleash violence against them as they had done against the Black students in Orangeburg, they did work to undermine the antiwar movement in the state. From the perspective of state leaders, the surge of student protest activity, particularly in the late 1960s, intensified their fears that the unrest on campuses elsewhere in the country was seeping into South Carolina. So deep were the concerns that the General Assembly's Committee to Investigate Communist Activities in South Carolina made college campuses the sole focus of its work because the "proliferation of mass membership organizations portrays a potential for violence and subversion that endangers the internal security of this State and Nation." The threat such groups posed not just to the campus but to the state necessitated a decisive and firm response from state officials, according to the committee. After consulting with FBI officials and surveying the scope of campus activism nationally, the committee concluded in its 1971 report that "vacillation, equivocation, indecision and amnesty have proved to be inadequate administrative weapons to deal with campus lawlessness. Such action can only be interpreted by the students as weakness." Instead, the committee counseled, students who disrupted campus life "should be punished swiftly, equitably and justly."[28]

The State Law Enforcement Division (SLED) played a key role in the state's work to monitor, discredit, and undermine the work of activists in the state. Originally created during the Depression years to enforce the state's liquor laws, SLED's portfolio expanded in 1947, when lawmakers also tasked it with providing assistance to local, state, and federal law enforcement. This assistance could take many forms, such as technical support to under-resourced police departments and intelligence gathering in collaboration with the state highway patrol or the FBI. Additionally, SLED had authority, in the words of the *South Carolina Legislative Manual,* "to make special investigations upon instruction of the Governor."[29] Such broadly worded authority allowed SLED wide latitude to undertake investigations of activists and dissenters. J. P. "Pete" Strom, a folksy and politically astute lawman, led the division in the 1960s. A native of rural McCormick County, near the Georgia border, where his father was sheriff and where he worked as a deputy, Strom joined SLED in 1947 and was appointed its chief in 1956, a position he would hold under eight governors until his death in 1987. Known to many as "Mr. Law Enforcement" and the "J. Edgar Hoover of South Carolina"—he did, in fact, know Hoover—Strom played a key role in modernizing and professionalizing law enforcement in South Carolina by raising standards for training and introducing new technologies into crime fighting in the state, such as polygraph tests and forensic and chemical analyses of crime scenes.[30] His many supporters credit him with being a fair-minded and moderating force who helped prevent civil rights conflicts from spiraling into violent melees, as happened elsewhere in the region. They celebrated him for working to weaken the Ku Klux Klan in the state, helping maintain the peace when Clemson University and the University of South Carolina desegregated in the early 1960s, and defusing a potential confrontation when civil rights demonstrators picketed George Wallace's arrival in Columbia in 1964. Yet he was hardly an ally of civil rights activists, and he remained a staunch defender of segregation so long as it was the law of the land. Moreover, his agents, though not directly involved in the Orangeburg Massacre, were deeply implicated in the state's response, and he closely consulted with highway patrol officials and the governor throughout the crisis. He also maintained an expansive network of informants across the state. In one observer's words, his was "one of the most heralded 'informer' networks in law enforcement." This network was a tool Strom could activate against perceived subversives, an ill-defined category that, by the late 1960s, could include Black nationalists, countercultural students, and antiwar activists.[31]

By the late 1960s, college students throughout the country were speaking out and demanding changes on everything from curricular matters to the Vietnam War. Students sought a more relevant, meaningful education connected to the most important issues of the day, and they sought respect from administrators who, too often, treated them as charges to protect rather than as young adults capable of contributing to the decisions that affected their lives. In loco parentis policies that gave school officials the role of protector of students were a particular source of agitation for students, who bristled at policies that limited the hours they could be off campus or restricted who could be in their dorm rooms. The gendered nature of these rules, which almost always focused on restricting the autonomy of college women, heightened the sense of grievance among students. Their efforts to dismantle these policies, captured by the term *university reform*, intersected with the growing antiwar movement, as students questioned the fairness of the draft, the morality of allowing military recruiters on campus, and the appropriateness of hosting Reserve Officers' Training Corps (ROTC) units. When school officials prohibited antiwar speakers from appearing on campus, as they did with increasing frequency, the connection between "university reform" and the war became jarringly obvious to students across the political spectrum.

South Carolina students, like those across the nation, organized and demonstrated to express their opposition to the war and unhappiness with how college administrators treated them. The Southern Student Organizing Committee, the region's leading group of progressive white students, made inroads on campuses across the state, including Clemson University, Furman University, Winthrop University, and the College of Charleston. The group had three staff members in South Carolina who traveled to these and other campuses to help coordinate and support antiwar and university reform activity. In 1968, the group brought to South Carolina its Peace Tour, events in which activists spoke on campuses to educate students about American foreign policy and encourage their opposition to the war in Vietnam. Local SSOC chapters and activists helped galvanize protest activity on their campuses. At Clemson, SSOC students focused on ending regulations on women's activities and also held a peace vigil. At Furman, where a particularly robust movement sprouted after the formation of an SSOC chapter in 1967, students protested compulsory chapel, marched through downtown Greenville after the Orangeburg Massacre, and successfully led a broad-based student uprising that forced school officials to rescind a speaker ban that prevented student groups from inviting Black nationalists and antiwar activists to campus. And at the University of South Carolina in Columbia, students in AWARE, a campus group that united SSOC and SDS students, led a December 1968 march of more than one hundred people, including soldiers from nearby Fort Jackson, to the state capital in opposition to the war.[32]

The growing assertiveness of students on issues of concern to them, especially the war, was an unwelcome development in the eyes of Strom and other state leaders. To them, displays of opposition to the war were unpatriotic and evidence of anti-American sentiment. Because of its status as the state's flagship campus, the officials were uniquely sensitive to antiwar activities at USC. In 1967, for instance, Strom directed SLED agents to forcibly remove student demonstrators from the site of a ceremony bestowing an honorary law degree on Gen. William Westmoreland, the commander of U.S. troops in Vietnam.[33] The prospect that USC students were organizing against the war in such close proximity to Fort Jackson, where the army conducted basic training, deeply worried law enforcement officials. The opening of the UFO Coffeehouse in January 1968 catalyzed these fears. Run by antiwar activists, the coffeehouse was a gathering spot for students, activists, and Fort Jackson soldiers seeking camaraderie with others who dissented from the shibboleths about the war. The coffeehouse embarrassed and scandalized officials with its open embrace of the counterculture and its criticisms of the war. "We don't want it in town," the chief of detectives in the Columbia Police Department told a *New York Times* reporter, undoubtedly irked by the seeming incongruity of the coffeehouse's setting. "We feel it is a bad influence on our youngsters. There are people with whiskers. Some wear sandals. . . . We think these coffeehouses are a Communist front." Its close proximity to Fort Jackson made it a target for base and city leaders, who cooperated to monitor and harass the business on a nightly basis, seeking any pretext for disrupting its operations. Base leaders stationed military policemen outside the coffeehouse to interrogate soldiers who sought to enter in an effort to intimidate them, and on at least one occasion, MPs entered the coffeehouse and ordered the uniformed soldiers present to leave. Police arrested people for loitering outside the business and used the city's noise ordinance to shut down musical acts, part of the effort to "check them every night to see if we can get something on them," in the words of Columbia's police chief. A military policeman and an undercover SLED agent regularly acted as patrons of the coffeehouse in order to monitor the business. Finally, in early 1970, after two years of harassment, city officials forced the coffeehouse to close and charged the owners with running a public nuisance. In response, antiwar USC students opened a UFO in Exile location on campus, a move that intensified police surveillance and harassment of students.[34]

AWARE was at the forefront of much of the antiwar activism on campus in the late 1960s. The student group, which functioned as a joint SSOC-SDS organization, promoted civil rights and university reform in addition to advocating resistance to the war. The group's activism had waxed and waned over time, but in 1968, it entered a sustained period of high-profile activism under the leadership of Brett Bursey. Bursey was new to USC in 1968. He had grown up in a military family and spent most of his high school years in Beaufort, South Carolina, where the family lived at the Marine Corps Recruiting Depot on Parris Island, before starting his college career at the University of Georgia. In Athens, he became involved in SSOC, joining protests against the racist governor, Lester Maddox, and participating in civil rights and antiwar actions. After leaving Georgia and spending a short time back in Beaufort, he moved to the University of South Carolina, where he served as a "campus traveler," one of the paid SSOC staff members in the state who traveled to other schools to build support for progressive causes. At USC, he also quickly became active in AWARE and was elected the group's chair in 1968. As head of the group, he organized provocative actions, including holding "White Awareness Week" to help white students understand that "Black Power is a democratic, political, social, and economical necessity," as he told *The Gamecock*, the USC student newspaper; attempting to protest President Richard Nixon's appearance in Columbia, the state capital, in 1969, an action for which he and several other AWARE members were arrested; and holding a rally in the Horseshoe, the historic center of campus, to protest the war.[35] Most notoriously, at a February 1969 AWARE protest against the use of Confederate imagery and symbols on campus and at the statehouse, he burned the Confederate battle flag outside the university president's house, an act for which he was arrested and charged with desecrating the flag in violation of state law.[36]

The flag burning and other actions made Bursey a marked man. The FBI surveilled him, compiling a file that eventually ran several thousand pages.

Pete Strom and SLED also kept close watch of Bursey, subjecting him to constant harassment and surveillance. An agent was assigned to follow him and did so conspicuously so that Bursey knew he was being watched. Bursey at one point discovered listening devices hidden in the wall of his home. To Strom and other officials, such as John Foard, the solicitor in Richland County, Bursey constituted a genuine threat to the social order. They feared that his call to "bring the war home" and promote progressive causes would instigate unrest on the USC campus. In the wake of the Columbia University student uprising in 1968, the dangers of unrest seemed all too real. Bursey may have been just one person and AWARE only a small group, but their potential to sow discord seemed more than hypothetical to state officials and thus justified intrusive action to discredit them and disrupt their plans.[37]

The State Law Enforcement Division took the lead, assigning an agent to go undercover to infiltrate AWARE and monitor Bursey. SLED had the perfect agent for this task: Jack Weatherford. The oldest of seven children whose father was an army sergeant stationed in Vietnam in the late 1960s, Weatherford was a South Carolina native who graduated high school in Columbia and earned a bachelor's degree in political science from USC in 1967. By 1969, he was back on campus taking classes toward a master's in sociology while also in the employ of the state. His law enforcement work began in 1968 with Richland County, and in the summer of 1969, SLED hired him to work undercover to keep watch on campus activists. It is unclear when or how he trained for his position as an undercover agent. In an interview with *The State* (Columbia, SC) newspaper in 1988, he was evasive on this question, saying, "I just kind of eased into it." An unnamed SLED agent, however, said Weatherford was induced to work for the state to avoid being charged in a drug bust in which he in some way was involved. In fact, his first assignments were focused on drug investigations.[38] He also was the SLED agent assigned to monitor the UFO Coffeehouse.[39] But tracking campus activists was his main task so as to alert law enforcement officials of any plans for violent protests. That he reported directly to SLED chief Pete Strom suggests the importance officials attached to Weatherford's work. For state leaders, the lesson of the Orangeburg Massacre was that they needed to be better informed about potential eruptions of student protest. As Weatherford explained: "The governor was extremely concerned that not happen again. I was to keep any eye out for that kind of trouble, and with young people it tended to center around campus. There was a real fear there would be more violence."[40]

Weatherford was not the only agent on campus, a SLED official later acknowledged, but his position as a student created a unique opportunity to get close to Bursey and other activist students.[41] His long hair, casual attire, and seeming commitment to civil rights and antiwar issues helped him forge ties with the activists. His appearance at the UFO in his undercover role only strengthened his progressive bona fides. So, too, did his participation, captured by a local television news team, in a march through downtown in January 1970 to protest the coffeehouse's closing.[42] At Pete Strom's direction, Weatherford quickly became involved in AWARE, and by early 1970, he and Bursey were cochairs of the group.[43] Bursey himself continued to stir controversy. Although he was no longer a student, he remained active in AWARE and was a frequent presence on campus. In late 1969, the university took the extraordinary step of banning him from campus for violating university rules, including the unauthorized distribution of antiwar materials and moving furniture from the Russell House student center to the Horseshoe for a meeting. Such violations were an obvious pretense for trying to keep from campus someone school officials considered a threat to stir unrest or provoke violence. *The Gamecock*, not known for its liberal positions, saw right through the ban, editorializing that barring Bursey from campus "smells more of a scared administration than one acting in the best interest of students."[44]

Weatherford's proximity to Bursey gave SLED its best opportunity to gather information on AWARE's plans and disrupt its work. It also gave Strom and his team the chance to get Bursey, whose reputation as an agitator had not diminished despite the campus ban. Weatherford's access meant he could funnel information quickly to his SLED handlers about any potentially illegal activity on the part of AWARE or Bursey. Given Bursey's history of confrontations and arrests during protest actions, it seemed only a matter of time before there would be another incident. That moment arrived in March 1970 as student activists around the country participated in National Anti-Draft Week, organized by the New Mobilization Committee to End the War in Vietnam, or New Mobe. In Columbia, *The Gamecock* discerned little visible activity beyond a small USC Mobe group's declaration that it would flood local draft boards with information and material in an effort to gum up the selection process. The newspaper, though, was unaware of what Bursey had planned.[45]

Bursey sought to directly confront the system by holding a protest at the Selective Service office in Columbia, about a half-mile from the Horseshoe. He initially planned a guerrilla theater–type action in which costumed demonstrators would affix a note to the door of the draft board declaring it a health hazard. But haphazard and late planning scuttled this idea. Instead, Bursey and others planned a nighttime assault on the office to ensure that the group conducted some type of activity before the end of National Anti-Draft Week.[46] Such actions had become increasingly common nationally by 1970, spurred by the publicity garnered by Daniel and Philip Berrigan, Catholic priests and antiwar activists, who destroyed draft files at Selective Service offices in Maryland in 1968 and 1969.[47] "The planning and implementation was pretty quick," Bursey recalls. Several of the activists met at Gantt's Grill near campus late one afternoon and then reassembled at a friend's house around midnight.[48] Then, in the early-morning hours of March 20, Bursey and three others—Weatherford; Greg Merrick, another undercover agent; and friend Danny Bolder—drove in Bolder's car to the draft office on Gervais Street. While Bolder waited in the car, the others crept up on the building that housed the office and set to work. They splattered red paint and graffitied peace slogans on the exterior walls—Bursey spelled out "Hell No We Won't Go" and "Peace," while Weatherford added "Now"—and Merrick threw paint and a brick through the office window. Attached to the brick was a missive Bursey had written that reflected the alienation and disenchantment that many student antiwar protesters had come to feel by 1970: "Amerika, you have become a monster, a self-destructive monster that thrives upon war, racism, and desperation, a monster that grows fat by consuming the sons and daughters of humanity. There is no amount of damage we could do here that would be commensurate to the death and destruction wielded by the Selective Service System in the name of Amerika." The vandalism caused several hundred dollars' damage. It was a "perfectly executed plan in the wee hours of the morning except for one minor exception," Bursey's attorney later quipped. "They had brought a SLED agent with them."[49]

Weatherford had told Pete Strom beforehand of the impending attack, and law enforcement officers were present in the building when the protesters arrived. But the officers neither interrupted the attack nor detained the activists because the protesters had remained outside the building, never trying to enter the Selective Service office. Later that day, acting on information Weatherford had provided Strom, six plainclothes policemen burst into an AWARE meeting in the USC student center and arrested Bursey. To help Weatherford maintain his cover, they arrested him too. The two were charged and later indicted for malicious injury to property, and Bursey also was charged with carrying a tear gas weapon. The police subsequently questioned Merrick and Bolder but did not charge them (they interviewed Merrick, an agent himself, to help protect his identity). Bursey had no idea that Weatherford was an agent. Given his experience with surveillance during his time as an activist in South Carolina, he assumed that authorities were watching him, and after the arrest, he gathered that one of the participants had informed on the group. He was certain, though, it was not Weatherford. Bursey had never doubted Weatherford's commitment to the cause. From his long hair and beard to his radical politics, including applying to break the American travel ban to Cuba as part of the Venceremos Brigade, Weatherford seemed every part the antiwar activist. Moreover, in the months between the arrests and the trial, scheduled for late July, Weatherford had kept up appearances. He acted like a defendant. He retained counsel, met with Bursey and his attorney, and participated in crafting a defense, including seeking to sever his case from Bursey's.[50]

The effort to preserve Weatherford's undercover status reflected his value to South Carolina authorities. Pete Strom expected Weatherford to continue his work after the arrest. Strom, in fact, ensured that solicitor John Foard, who was prosecuting the case, knew Weatherford was a SLED agent, and Foard helped arrange for Weatherford's legal counsel as part of the effort to protect his identity. Inexplicably, however, Strom allowed Weatherford to take a vacation to Hilton Head Island with other agents shortly before the trial commenced. While there and in the company of other agents, he encountered one of Bursey's friends, thus jeopardizing his status for future operations (although word of this encounter did not reach Bursey). Additionally, Foard wanted Weatherford to testify to ensure Bursey's conviction. Foard was outspoken in his disdain for student activists and openly criticized the USC administration for seeming to tolerate it. Bursey's trial was an opportunity to get the ringleader. "We've got enough evidence, but I want to cinch this," he recalls telling Strom. "I don't want to take a chance." The pressure from Foard combined with concern that Weatherford's cover had been blown led Strom to reluctantly approve Foard's request that Weatherford testify in open court.[51]

It was not until the trial commenced that Bursey realized he had been betrayed. Indeed, Bursey had not even expected to see Weatherford at his trial. The night before, his attorney, C. Rauch Wise, asked Weatherford not to be in the courtroom. Weatherford wished Bursey luck, though he also encouraged him to flee the state, telling him, Bursey remembers, "You better leave or they'll hang you."[52] Bursey declined the advice. When Weatherford entered the courtroom the next day as the state's first witness, Bursey recalled a year later, with "his blue jeans, long hair, and a shit eating grin; . . . my mind was totally blown." And not just his. "Freaks went flying out the doors as if someone had yelled fire!" Bursey recalled about the reaction of his friends who had come to the trial to support him. "Pig Weatherford had something on nearly every longhair and revolutionary in the courtroom."[53] Weatherford's betrayal stung Bursey. "I don't think I have been more hurt or more shocked," he said. "I thought that we had a basis of trust that had developed between us while we had known each other. I trusted him implicitly." Wise protested the calling of a surprise witness and repeatedly moved for a mistrial based on his inability to craft an effective defense of his client when faced with such a stunt. The judge rejected his requests, and Weatherford proved to be a devastating witness. He acknowledged that he was a SLED agent assigned to report to Strom directly on Bursey, and he detailed the events of March 20. Bursey testified in his own defense, but given Weatherford's eyewitness testimony, the conclusion of the trial was a foregone conclusion: the jury returned a guilty verdict, and the judge handed down an eighteen-month sentence. Rauch Wise remembers being pleasantly surprised that the jury deliberated as long as it did—fifty-eight minutes; he figured the case was a slam dunk because of Weatherford's testimony. When he thanked a juror afterward for taking so long to deliberate, the juror remarked that many on the panel "'didn't think it was fair'" that Bursey was the only one charged given that Weatherford had participated in the action as well.[54]

For Bursey, the conviction was the conclusion of a tumultuous few months. Seven weeks after his arrest for the Selective Service vandalism, USC students, like many others across the nation, boycotted classes and held demonstrations in outrage over the shooting of unarmed students at Kent State University who were demonstrating against Richard Nixon's surprise announcement of the expansion of the war into Cambodia. Bursey, who was on the edge of the protests since he had been banned from campus, was nonetheless targeted by Strom, who had him arrested and held in solitary confinement for several days. This arrest followed by the conviction on the earlier charges made clear to Bursey the extent to which the state would go to stop him. Shortly after his release on bond as the case was on appeal, he fled the state and went underground before being apprehended in Texas and returned to South Carolina to serve his sentence. He later sued Weatherford and Strom in federal court under the Civil Rights Act for violating his constitutional right to a fair trial and effective counsel because Weatherford had participated in trial planning meetings with Bursey and his attorney. The case went all the way to the Supreme Court, which overturned an appellate court decision in Bursey's favor. In a cramped and narrow seven-to-two decision, the high court ruled that the Sixth Amendment "does not establish a *per se* rule forbidding an undercover agent to meet with a defendant's counsel" and that Weatherford had not shared with the prosecution anything he had learned from the meeting with Bursey and his attorney. Justices Thurgood Marshall and William Brennan dissented, with Marshall writing, "I cannot join in providing even the narrowest of openings to the practice of spying upon attorney-client communications."[55]

The trial brought an abrupt end to Weatherford's career as an undercover operative, and within two months, he had left SLED altogether to focus on his academic work. His exposure as an agent created difficulties for him, he later recalled; some students refused to attend class with him, and bomb threats were made to the buildings where his classes were held.[56] While Weatherford had not intended to unmask himself in the case, he seemed to think doing so was justified in order to uphold the law. Indeed, he rationalized his undercover work on the grounds that his deceptions were in the service of protecting academic freedom and legitimate forms of dissent. He believed, he later wrote in the student newspaper, that "it was necessary that I be as far within as possible the activities of those individuals who were felt to pose the greatest threat to this community" in order to protect the rights of political dissenters and others "advocating change." His was a law enforcement role, he insisted, one of "simple vigilance against legal infractions," and he hoped the campus community would not view "his presence as having been one of 'spying' on faculty or compiling files on student activists." Such self-serving justifications elided the fact that SLED had dispatched him to USC precisely to spy on students and track the activists, particularly Bursey, who had proven to be a particular irritant to Strom and others.[57]

The loss of Weatherford may have cost SLED the services of an important undercover agent, but Weatherford was just one cog in the surveillance system that authorities had put in place to monitor activism at the University of South Carolina. Other SLED agents were embedded on the campus, and the agency also gained insights from informants. The FBI office in Columbia had agents at work on campus as well. "There were so many" undercover agents from across law enforcement focused on USC, John Foard said, according to one of Bursey's attorneys in a later legal action, that he "didn't know who was working for whom."[58] Additionally, the FBI kept busy hatching plans to harass the activists, including feeding the local police information gleaned from bureau sources about "pot parties," which agents hoped would lead to the arrest and expulsion from school of activists and troublemakers.[59] The threat that students activism posed demanded such interventions in the view of law enforcement. Protesting against the war or defacing the local draft office were all the proof they needed that activists were bent on destroying the status quo on campus and in Columbia. It did not matter that their numbers were small. To Strom and the rest of the law enforcement apparatus in the state, not to take action would be a dereliction of duty, an abdication of their responsibility to protect the community when confronted with what they considered a direct assault on the community's standards, norms, and way of life. Bursey's proclivity for drawing attention through provocative actions and statements made him an obvious target. But rather than seeing him as an outlier, SLED saw him as the tip of the iceberg, the canary in the coal mine, who represented the dangers of what was to come in Columbia and thus justified surveillance and harassment to eradicate the threat he represented.

THE MISSISSIPPI STATE SOVEREIGNTY COMMISSION

As it did in so many other ways during the civil rights era, Mississippi's mobilization to counter student activists stands out for its scope and intensity. The state took a unique approach to this work. Unlike Oklahoma, which established an executive-level agency, or South Carolina, which relied on the work of law enforcement agencies, Mississippi utilized a legislatively authorized, quasi-independent body to combat activists. The Mississippi State Sovereignty Commission was a crucial cog in the machinery of repression in the southern state most hostile to progressive activism of any type. Thanks to the work of future governor William Winter, who in 1977 persuaded state legislators to preserve the commission's files—"there is too much historical value in these records to destroy them without giving historians some way to interpret this era of our history," he said—and the court-ordered decision to open the files to the public in 1998, historians have mined these records to expose the vast, deep, and invasive work of the commission.[60] Its work against Black activists has rightly garnered the most attention, as the MSSC cooperated with the Citizens' Council to harass and monitor activists, utilized paid and unpaid informants to monitor and disrupt civil rights activity, and collaborated with the FBI to attack and discredit civil rights organizers. But the MSSC also worked to undermine white activists in the state, efforts that the scholarship on the commission largely has overlooked. The drive against white student activists expands our understanding of state-sanctioned repression in Mississippi because it demonstrates just how little room for dissent existed in the Magnolia State. No one in Mississippi was safe from the harassment or surveillance that defined the state's work to preserve the status quo and defend white supremacy.[61]

The MSSC was established in 1956 with a mission, according to its founding legislation, to "perform any and all acts deemed necessary and proper to protect the sovereignty of the state of Mississippi, and her sister states, from encroachment thereon by the Federal Government." Fear of racial integration inspired the commission's creation. Born in the crucible of the Cold War, the MSSC saw communism and civil rights as intertwined threats. It was an article of faith to segregationist everywhere that communists lurked behind civil rights activists. In such a reading of the movement, civil rights activists were, at the least, unwitting stooges of their communist overlords or, at worst, fellow travelers or committed communists conspiring to destabilize the region by disrupting the white supremacist social order. African Americans bore the brunt of the MSSC's anti–civil rights work, though the commission also trained attention on white civil rights supporters whom the commission tarred as communists or outside agitators. Civil rights activists, along with meddlesome federal officials who sought to promote integrationist schemes, threatened the state's sovereignty. In a sign of the importance the state attached to the work, the governor served as ex-officio chairman, and the attorney general, speaker of the state house, and president of the state senate served as ex-officio members.[62]

A small group of staff members conducted the actual work of the state's Sovereignty Commission. Led by a general director, the commission employed a public relations director, investigators, and clerical staff. The first directors had strong political backgrounds; Ney Gore and Maurice Malone, his successor, were state representatives. Albert N. Jones, who the arch segregationist governor Ross Barnett appointed director in 1961, had a law enforcement background to buttress his political ties, as he came to the commission after a long career as a sheriff and more than a decade as president of the Mississippi Sheriff's Association. The commission drew its investigative staff from the ranks of law enforcement. Leonard C. Hicks, the first investigator, was a former sheriff and head of the state highway patrol, and Zack J. Van Landingham, the second investigator hired, was a nearly three-decade veteran of the FBI who had served a stint as Director J. Edgar Hoover's administrative assistant. Undoubtedly drawing on his experience in the bureau, Van Landingham developed the elaborate filing system that would endure throughout the commission's existence. With a dozen classification categories, ranging from "Civil Rights–Violence" and "Criminal Cases" to "Race Agitators" and "Integration Organizations"—a thirteenth category, "Subversion," was added later—the system he designed sought to bring coherence and organization to the material the commission both collected and produced. In addition to the files, Van Landingham implemented an index card system meant to capture information from the files in catalog form, making information easier to find. By 1960, the system had resulted in the creation of five thousand index cards cataloging information from five hundred files.[63]

The Sovereignty Commission lived up to its reputation as the state's "segregation watchdog" during the Barnett administration, from 1960 to 1964. As the civil rights struggle intensified, the commission launched investigations into myriad groups and activists it deemed a threat to the "Mississippi Way of Life." It conducted surveillance, deployed informants, spread misinformation through its collaborators in the press, supported white supremacist groups that used violence against civil rights supporters, and shared information with the FBI and similar agencies in other states. In fact, Erle Johnston, the commission's director in the mid-1960s, believed the commission "operated like a little FBI." Its investigators played a key role in this work. While Van Landingham left the commission after clashing with Barnett, three new investigators joined the fold: Tom Scarbrough, Andy Hopkins, and Virgil S. Downing. All three had law enforcement backgrounds: Scarbrough was a sheriff and then public safety commissioner in charge of the state highway patrol; Hopkins was a criminal investigator in the Hinds County Sheriff's Office and also had served as chief investigator in the highway patrol; and Downing was a former Hinds County constable. With support from the top of state government and guidance from the commission's director, the investigators helped turn words of opposition into actions of resistance in the face of a surging civil rights movement.[64]

Increasingly, white students came into the commission's crosshairs for their support for civil rights. The Freedom Summer campaign of 1964 was a watershed event in this regard. White college students' high-profile participation in this campaign for voting rights and equal treatment made them a Sovereignty Commission target. From the moment these students assembled for training at Western College for Women in Oxford, Ohio, the commission closely monitored them. Two informants, young African Americans posing as volunteers, joined the training and then traveled to Mississippi with the others.[65] The white students who hailed from northern and western schools were of particular concern to the Sovereignty Commission, as many came from elite institutions and had received favorable press attention for their involvement. The focus on these students intensified after two of them, Michael Schwerner and Andrew Goodman, along with James Chaney, a Black volunteer from Meridian, Mississippi, went missing in the state at the start of the summer. Their disappearance and the eventual discovery of all three bodies in a shallow grave almost two months later received an avalanche of media coverage and brought a massive FBI investigative operation to the state. While the murders captured national attention and kept a spotlight on the non-southern students, it also obscured the significant involvement of white students from Mississippi and other southern states. These students did not receive gushing media tributes for their work or big send-offs as they departed for the summer. But their participation did not go unnoticed, least of all by the Sovereignty Commission.

The Southern Student Organizing Committee was the vehicle through which most of the white southern college students joined Freedom Summer. SSOC's primary focus during the summer was to build white support for civil rights in Jackson, Greenville, Meridian, Vicksburg, and the communities along the Gulf Coast. The White Folks Project, as it was known, involved twenty-five white students, three-quarters of whom were southerners. While some never left Jackson, approximately twenty of the white volunteers fanned out across the state. The work was hard going, as they found little sympathy for civil rights within the local white communities. Even among those inclined to be supportive, fear of provoking unwanted attention deterred people from aligning with the activists. The project's lack of success did not shield it from the commission's attention. From the segregationists' standpoint, a campaign undertaken by southern whites that aimed to relax white opposition to Black equality was just as audacious as bringing "outside agitators" to the state to stir up trouble. Consequently, the commission tracked the white students who participated in the project just as it monitored other white activists who participated in Freedom Summer. Investigators compiled a list of the students involved in the White Folks Project and researched their background, an effort fueled by an informant's surreptitious removal of a file with summer volunteers' applications even before Freedom Summer began.[66]

The commission considered its informants to be an indispensable asset. Erle Johnston said informants helped the commission learn "what militant civil rights workers were saying, doing, or—more important, planning. It was this advance information that enabled us to avoid violent confrontations."[67] The commission intensified its focus on SSOC early in 1965, thanks in large part to the effort of one of its informants. Edgar Downing was a McComb native who by the 1960s resided in Long Beach, California, where he worked as a welder. A former communist, he had left radical politics behind and fashioned himself into a freelance informant devoted to exposing those who advocated for causes he considered subversive or radical. He took a particular interest in the Free Speech Movement and campus unrest at the University of California at Berkeley, traveling hundreds of miles from his home in Southern California to photograph demonstrations and make reports on what he observed. His work there apparently led him to the civil rights movement in Mississippi. In late 1964, he reached out to the Sovereignty Commission to offer it information about "communist activity in Mississippi," and over the next few years, he submitted reports and sent photos to the commission of Berkeley activists, including Bettina Aptheker, Jo Freeman, Mario Savio, and Steve Weissman, some of whom had participated in Freedom Summer or other civil rights activity in the state.[68]

Downing was a curious and eccentric figure, and the commission staff was intrigued but wary of him. "Edgar Downing has the appearance of a civil rights worker," one investigator wrote of him, "as he is usually dirty and shoddily dressed and in the midst of racial trouble in Pike County and other places in Mississippi—taking photographs that he does not identify and later attempts to peddle to law enforcement agencies." He appeared to drive frequently from California to Mississippi, where he would set himself up in various hotels in McComb, sometimes camping in the lobby or making use of hotel photocopiers to duplicate his materials.[69] Investigator Tom Scarbrough met Downing for the first time in December 1964 at the Pike Hotel in McComb, where Downing was staying. Scarbrough was in awe to find Downing's hotel room filled with copies of leftist publications, some dating to the 1930s. "He has done a magnificent job of preserving and keeping all of this material together," Scarbrough wrote after the visit. But none of it was organized, and it was overwhelming in volume; his hotel room was so filled with old magazines and newspapers that "if the door had not opened out in to the hall, it is doubtful we could have gotten into this room." Scarborough was dubious that much of the material was of any value to the commission, and he was dumbfounded at how Downing managed to work. "I do not see how this poor fellow can sustain himself and spend as much time as he apparently spends in wagging around with him all over the country 500 or 600 pounds of old newspapers and magazines which contain only maybe a short item on the subject matter in which he is interested for his files."[70] But the investigators' skepticism about Downing did not stop them from accepting material he sent them or funding his activities.

The commission's director, Erle Johnston, personally authorized payments to Downing, typically of about one hundred dollars each, in response to Downing's urgent pleas for funds to support his efforts, including ninety dollars for a tape recorder to surreptitiously record conversations.[71]

SSOC was one of the organizations about which Downing supplied information to the commission. His portrayal of the group as communist dovetailed with the commission's interest in what Johnston called "subversives who operate in Mississippi and participate in so-called civil rights activities."[72] In February 1965, in his first apparent communication to the commission about SSOC, he called it a "communist front" that he had been following "for some time now." He had been to Nashville recently, SSOC's home base, and made contact with someone who provided him with material he was forwarding to the commission: a few SSOC publications and a purloined letter sent to SSOC organizer Ed Hamlett. He claimed to have contacts on the group in Atlanta and Auburn, and he identified a friend in Houston, Rev. T. Robert Ingram, the segregationist founder of the city's Saint Thomas' Episcopal School, "who is in this fight against Communism who is in a beautiful position to infiltrate this group."[73] A few days later, Downing was back in McComb meeting with the city's mayor, Gordon Burt, and called Scarbrough from the mayor's office to tell him about an upcoming SSOC meeting in Houston and that he was traveling there to arrange for someone to attend the gathering. Presumably, he was thinking of Ingram, though it seems improbable that the anti-integrationist minister would be welcome at an SSOC meeting. Moreover, reflecting Downing's own confusion, the meeting to which he referred was not an SSOC one but, rather, a seminar sponsored by the American Friends Service Committee and the Ecumenical Institute to bring together Mississippi activists and Houston college students. Nonetheless, he had contacted the Houston Police Department's intelligence division to provide information about the upcoming meeting, and he shortly thereafter contacted the Atlanta police to make sure authorities were aware that SSOC was soon to hold a meeting in that city as well.[74]

Downing remained focused on the Southern Student Organizing Committee over the rest of his time informing for the Sovereignty Commission. He regularly collected SSOC publications and seemed to scour an impressive range of newspapers for articles on the group; he provided the commission with clippings of articles from the *Atlanta Constitution*, the *Memphis Commercial Appeal*, the *Nashville Banner*, and the *New Orleans Times-Picayune*. In 1967, Erle Johnston wrote that Downing had personally delivered to the commission's office a trove of documents on SSOC—photos, pamphlets, newsletters, news articles. Downing did not stay long in Jackson, as he went on to Atlanta and Montgomery, he wrote to Johnston, "for picking up other material and information concerning SSOC and other organizations." With this new batch of material, he was headed to Washington, DC, where Congressman William Tuck of Virginia, a member of the House Un-American Activities Committee, had arranged for Downing to meet with a committee investigator. And later that year, Downing sent the commission a fifty-seven-page, single-spaced, handwritten report on SSOC, much of it transcriptions of publications and news articles about the organization.[75]

Despite the investigative staff's reservations about Downing and his methods, they readily accepted as fact that SSOC was a subversive organization that merited watching. The commission supplemented Downing's materials with other records it gathered of its own accord so that by 1967, its director, Erle Johnston, could remark, "We have in the office a very voluminous file on SSOC, its pamphlets, its policies, and its connections with subversive individuals and groups."[76] The Sovereignty Commission believed SSOC publications revealed crucial information about the group and its plans, and it went to elaborate means to acquire them. In 1964, it enlisted a Jackson resident named John Kochtitzky to subscribe to the "publications of communist front organizations," Johnston wrote in a report on the commission's activities that year. "We wanted a name that sounded 'Russianish,'" Johnston said, apparently so as not to raise suspicions. Kochtitzky proceeded to subscribe to SSOC publications, among many others, and the commission reimbursed him for a post office box he rented to receive the materials.[77] Johnston, who alerted other officials that Kochtitzky was working on behalf of the commission and should not be considered suspect because of the mail he received, considered Kochtitzky's work invaluable, writing that "he rendered a great service in helping the Sovereignty Commission to build a file on subversives."[78] In 1967, the commission initiated a similar arrangement with Mike Smith, a reporter with the *Jackson Daily News*, after Kochtitzky stopped his work. The commission already had a relationship with Smith, as it had fed him information that he had used in news articles. Smith willingly assumed the role Kochtitzky had played, renting a post office box, subscribing to publications such as *Ramparts, Southern Patriot,* and the decidedly un-radical *Harvard Crimson.* He also received payments for "services rendered," though it is unclear if this was merely reimbursing him for the costs he incurred or actual compensation for his efforts.[79]

The material it had gathered, both from informants and on its own, persuaded the commission staff that SSOC was a dangerous, radical organization in league with communists and Black revolutionaries. Not that the commission needed much persuading. In many respects, its perspective on SSOC was prefigured, shaped by the staff's own commitment to white supremacy and the segregationist order on which it was built. The commission could only perceive SSOC, an organization that challenged the structure of Mississippi society, as a threat. Investigator Andy Hopkins articulated this perspective in a report on the group he drafted in 1967. He concluded, "It is the purpose of the SSOC and related civil rights groups, as well as the Communist Party, to cause a revolution in the USA as soon as possible."[80]

The suggestion that SSOC and its compatriots on the Left sought revolution aligned with the segregationists' view that civil rights was inextricably linked to subversion. Indeed, over time, the MSSC increasingly expanded its focus beyond civil rights to include what it considered other elements in the revolutionaries' playbook, particularly anti–Vietnam War activism and countercultural activities, ranging from promoting drug experimentation to celebrating sexual freedom. In August 1966, Johnston formalized this expanded approach by requesting and receiving approval from the commission's leadership, including the governor, to concentrate on "subversive individuals and organizations that advocate civil disobedience."[81] The commission's emphasis on subversion ensured that more scrutiny would fall on white students who, like their peers elsewhere, increasingly focused on issues that the commission conflated with subversion. MSSC investigators did not have to look far for unsettling examples of what it considered subversive behavior: just a short distance from its office in Jackson, student protest activity was growing at Millsaps College.

The war, civil rights, and the counterculture mixed together to fuel activism and unrest at Millsaps, a small, Methodist, liberal arts college in the city. The Black-led civil rights movement first inspired the activism of a contingent of Millsaps students and led them to form a SSOC chapter, which became the group's most visible and active one in the state. Led by David Doggett, a Mississippi native whose father, Blanton Doggett, was a Methodist minister who served on the school's board of trustees, the Millsaps students quickly landed on the commission's radar. Its records contain numerous newspaper clippings on the students' activities, with individuals' names underlined by commission staff and occasional notations to "index [the] names" in the files. In fact, all of the Millsaps activists had files in the MSSC records. The highly visible role that Doggett played seemed particularly to irritate the commission. Erle Johnston labeled him "the chief agitator at Millsaps," and investigators kept close track of his activities. Doggett's Mississippi roots endowed him with greater power and authority and thus made him more of a threat. The commission could not simply dismiss him as an outside agitator or accuse him of being a radical carpetbagger. As a result, the investigators devoted significant time and attention to Doggett and this small but resilient group of activists.[82]

In the spring of 1967, Doggett and fellow Millsaps student Lee Makemson led a march of approximately twenty white students through downtown to protest the killing of Jackson State Student Benjamin Brown by National Guardsman during a protest on campus. In addition to startled onlookers, the protesters encountered an informant for the commission, most likely Edgar Downing. The informant took photos of the marchers and gathered information about them, which he then forwarded to Johnston, who, in turn, shared them with the governor's office.[83] The alternative newspaper the Millsaps activists started in 1968 also drew scrutiny from the commission. Created by Doggett and fellow Millsaps student Everett Long, *The Kudzu* was redolent of the underground press of the era, mixing progressive politics with counterculture stylings. *The Kudzu* filled its pages with articles and graphics that lampooned the status quo, celebrated the hip, and castigated conservative politics. The paper's orientation became clear in the first issue, which, besides carrying stories on the FBI and the tumultuous Democratic National Convention in Chicago, featured articles on Jefferson Airplane and Bob Dylan. *The Kudzu* scandalized official Jackson and quickly earned the attention of the MSSC.

That Doggett and others Millsaps activists led the paper heightened the Sovereignty Commission's concern. The commission studiously collected copies of the newspaper, used an informant to report on activities among the staff, and worked with the Jackson police to try to prevent the distribution of the paper around the city, including arresting *The Kudzu*'s staff for trying to hand out the paper at local high schools. The police also sought to frame the staffers on drug possession charges after an informant, possibly Don Cole, the FBI informant, planted a bag of marijuana in the newspaper's office.[84]

The Sovereignty Commission also joined with the Mississippi Highway Patrol in surveilling and disrupting youth festivals that *The Kudzu* hosted in the spring and fall of 1969 at the Mt. Beulah Conference Center, outside of Jackson, a frequent site for meetings and activities of social and political activists in the state. Billed as the "Mississippi Youth Jubilee," the events fused the hip and the radical. As *The Kudzu*'s announcement of the April gathering explained, the Jubilee would include three days of musical performances, poetry, and politics, including workshops on "the draft, guerilla theater, women's liberation, students' rights, and black power." Such a description undoubtedly raised the suspicions of investigators who read about it in *The Kudzu*. At the April event, which drew several hundred people, highway patrolman set up roadblocks at which they stopped vehicles approaching the gathering and took down the names and addresses of the festivalgoers and searched some people's cars. The Sovereignty Commission monitored the gathering as well, with "a Mr. McLain of the 'State Investigative Committee,'" *The Kudzu* reported later, entering the property several times, including with plainclothes officers driving unmarked cars. After the last incursion, the festival participants used their cars to block the officers from leaving the property unless they agreed not to return without a warrant. They refused, but the students allowed them to depart so the festival could continue. Later, a small fire broke out on the property that appeared to have been deliberately set. While its origins were mysterious, people suspected "right-wing or police agents" had started it, with attention focused on "three unfriendly strangers" whom people had encountered right before the fire broke out. The authorities' sharp response to *The Kudzu* and their harassment of Jubilee attendees highlighted how little space there was for dissent in this bastion of southern conservatism. To glamorize marijuana or promote sexual freedom, let alone advocate for racial reform, was intolerable to those who defended the Mississippi Way of Life and justified turning state power against its creators and advocates.[85]

The commission's focus on subversives accelerated after 1968 with the inauguration of a new governor and turnover on the commission's staff. As governor, John Bell Williams hewed closely to the segregationist policies of his predecessors and added to them a strong anti-crime, law-and-order stance. A component of this effort was to crack down on student unrest, and Williams tasked the commission with investigating "campus student disturbances and use of drugs . . . [at] state operated schools."[86] The campaign against drug use was a way to pursue political dissenters by other means. Rather than targeting them for their political views, the commission used drug charges to try to undermine their work.[87] The new commission director, whom Williams appointed in 1968, fell in line with this work. William Webster "Webb" Burke was the first head of the Mississippi Highway Patrol in 1938 and went on to a long career as an FBI special agent before coming out of retirement from law enforcement to lead the commission. Burke brought on three new investigators: C. Fulton Tutor, an army veteran and former sheriff; James M. Mohead, an air force veteran and former policeman; and Edgar Fortenberry, also a former policeman and veteran of the FBI. As the investigators fanned out across the state, they incorporated anti-subversive work into their agenda to counter activities that, as Burke vaguely put it, "tend toward destruction of state institutions and traditions."[88]

The commission's effort to root out subversion and illegal drug use made targets of the state's two largest and most prominent public universities, the University of Mississippi and Mississippi State University. School officials cooperated with the commission's work. Burke reported that the commission regularly shared information with "the Presidents, Deans of Student Affairs, and Chiefs of Security, in all of the State colleges and universities." The commission also utilized "confidential source coverage" to maintain "very close observation" on activists and organizations, including SDS, the Black Panthers, the ACLU, and others.[89] Among the network of informants the commission utilized at Ole Miss was Charles Lamar Neill, whose father was the first neurosurgeon in the state and a professor at the university's medical school. Neill's work was coordinated and managed by Security Consultants, Inc., one of the several private detective firms retained by the commission over the years to recruit informants to infiltrate activist organizations. In December 1968, H. A. Gusack, Security Consultant's president, met with Neill's father and Governor Williams to "discuss the many problems that have arisen on the campuses of the universities in Mississippi, in reference to narcotics traffic and radical student movements, which have tended to cause disruption of campus administration." Security Consultants would deploy the younger Neill in what Gusack euphemistically called "a fact finding program" to gather information at Ole Miss.[90] Over the next months, Neill befriended activist students, attended gatherings of leftist groups, and provided regular updates to Gusack, who dutifully filed reports with the Sovereignty Commission that emphasized the threat student activists posed.

While Gusack perhaps played up the student threat out of a desire to invest his company's work with significance and ensure the continuation of its contract with the state, doing so also reflected the overheated, fear-based sense of state leaders; the threat from subversives demanded covert campaigns, sting operations, and surveillance activities. In Gusack's words, Neill worked to "target" individuals for supposed friendship as a means to "establish channels" for learning about activists' "operations" and about students "who appeared to be interested in overthrowing the administration." Through 1969 and into 1970, Gusack's reports, based on information from the confidential source at Ole Miss, detailed activists' gatherings, with particular emphasis on drug use.[91] Neill, the likely source of this information, even went so far as to win election to the board of directors of the Mississippi Chapter of the ACLU, a position from which, Gusack said, he could gather information on this putatively subversive organization.[92]

The commission worked to contain and suppress student dissent at Mississippi State as well. Investigator Fulton Tutor regularly monitored campus activities and stayed in close contact with the school's head of security, who typically reported that the campus was quiet. In early 1970, the two men scoured the bulletin boards at the campus YMCA in search of flyers from radical organizations but found none. When dissent did break into the open, it often caught the commission by surprise. In 1969, Webb Burke wrote to a National

Guard official to complain that the commission had not been kept informed about the potential for protests surrounding a talk on campus by Gen. Maxwell Taylor. The lapse in communication was worrisome to Burke, and he pledged to reaffirm that security leaders at all campuses understood the importance of providing the MSSC with timely information about potential unrest.[93]

The previous year, the Sovereignty Commission had responded sharply in response to an article in the Mississippi State student paper critical of the commission itself. The article condemned the MSSC for defending "the Mississippi tradition of bigotry and reaction, while harassing and intimidating those who are outspokenly opposed to the 'official viewpoints,'" and it insinuated that "there is reason to believe that certain students on this campus are picking up some extra coins by acting as informers."[94] The article set off alarms at the highest levels of government. The governor's office sent a copy to the Sovereignty Commission, and Burke promptly checked with campus security for information about whether Pat Coughlin, the author of "this very derogatory article . . . is the type of individual who could be contacted and talked to." Burke and Tutor then paid a visit to Coughlin at the newspaper's offices and, in Burke's recounting of the meeting, leaned hard on the student, insisting that the commission's work was all aboveboard and legal. Without a trace of irony, Burke said they "pointed out in detail that not one single part of [commission] activity involved infringement upon any persons' rights regardless of race, color or creed. It was also made quite clear that no part of the activity of the Sovereignty Commission could possibly be considered unlawful in any respect." If the young columnist still had not gotten the point, Burke went on to make clear that "Mr. Coughlin was advised that in any investigation conducted by the Sovereignty Commission only legal and ethical tactics are employed," including the "use of individual sources of information"—that is, informants. Coughlin seemed to sincerely appreciate the visit, Burke thought, and he smugly concluded "that there will be no distribution of this type of report in the future."[95] And just in case Coughlin developed second thoughts, Burke wrote him two days later to thank him for his time and to press his point: "I do want you and the staff there to know that activities of the Commission are completely within the law and in no way infringe upon the rights of any individual."[96] Hypersensitive to criticism, the MSSC reacted to the article with the same intolerance for dissent that persisted throughout the Sovereignty Commission's existence.

In this, the commission was similar to police, state investigators, and FBI officials across the region. Their common fears of revolt, whether from Black activists or white radicals, undergirded the surveillance regimes they imposed in their jurisdictions. The Sovereignty Commission served as a model and inspiration to officials in neighboring states. When Alabama created its own Sovereignty Commission in 1964, Mississippi's commission was glad to offer guidance and support.[97] The Mississippi body was also central to efforts to pool information and coordinate surveillance activities among state investigative agencies. Informally, the agencies traded information with one another.[98] More formally, in 1966, the Southern Association of Investigators initiated a program to gather information about groups throughout the South "whose purpose or programs might cause breach of the peace or pose problems for law enforcement." The association would use the reports to "provide a liaison [*sic*] of information between the investigative groups in member states." The first report included discussion of a number of activist organizations—the Student Nonviolent Coordinating Committee, the National Association for the Advancement of Colored People, Students for a Democratic Society, the Southern Student Organizing Committee, and the Southern Christian Leadership Conference—noting about the SCLC's most well-known figure, "King's halo is begining [*sic*] to tarnish."[99] In 1968, the Sovereignty Commissions of Mississippi, Alabama, and Louisiana joined together to create the short-lived Interstate Sovereignty Association. Representing Mississippi at the founding meeting were two members of the Sovereignty Commission and William Simmons, the unctuous, bitingly racist leader of the Citizens' Council. The association, which took as one of its purposes the collection of information about "Communistic influences, narcotics traffic, subversive activities and pornographic literature" at high schools and on college campuses in the states, met only three times before becoming defunct.[100]

More fruitful was the Sovereignty Commission's collaboration with police officials and the FBI. The commission regularly shared information gathered from its informants with FBI agents in Jackson as well as with the Internal Revenue Service and staff in the offices of Senators James Eastland and John

Stennis, both avowed defenders of segregation.[101] And the commission regularly funneled to Mississippi law enforcement reports it had received from informants such as Charles Neill about drug activity on campuses. Similarly, the commission was the beneficiary of surveillance conducted by the FBI and local police. Erle Johnston recalled that the commission relied on sheriffs around the state for tips and leads. "We tried to maintain a liaison with the sheriffs, asking them if they have any people in the county who were new and strangers, if they could find out who they were and let us know, and we'll see whether or not they are people who already have a past history of turbulence and stirring people up."[102]

The Sovereignty Commission's efforts to neutralize individuals it considered a threat to the established order epitomized the work of state investigative bodies in the South as they sought to respond to the rise of student activism in the region. No group or activist formation was too small or disorganized to merit watching because, officials believed, the disruption and turmoil that had embroiled campuses and communities elsewhere made clear the danger of allowing such activism to go unchallenged. Their view of what constituted activism was exceptionally broad—it encompassed actions as diverse as attending a protest and subscribing to an alternative newspaper—indicating their concern that resistance could boil up from any number of sources. And it was not merely actions that troubled officials but attitudes and beliefs, which could be hard to deduce but which officials sought to determine nonetheless. State Sovereignty Commissions, "Little FBIs," "Little HUACs," and legislative investigative committees all shared a common goal: to smother dissent wherever it appeared; to monitor and harass, cow and intimidate, those who fomented dissent, merely sympathized with leftists causes, or sought to live unconventionally; and to drive these individuals off campus and out of the community, much as Brett Bursey had experienced in South Carolina.

State domestic intelligence authorities joined forces with federal officials to tighten the web of surveillance that surrounded white student activists in the South. Police departments across the region made their own contributions to this effort as well. Police leaders and officers in the streets shared with their federal and state peers an antipathy for student activism and, given their deep community roots, had the considerable local knowledge on which to build surveillance campaigns. Police surveillance made clear that law enforcement and domestic security units throughout government considered white activists a threat that, if left unaddressed, risked further destabilizing the social order of southern communities. As a result, the space in which students could maneuver free of the prying eyes of government officials continued to shrink as officials desperately sought to contain student activism. The rise of a police surveillance operation in Memphis in the 1960s shows just how far police officials were willing to go in their drive to staunch student activism.

Founding SSOC members at the first meeting in Nashville, April 1964 (seated on floor, *left to right*): Dan Harmeling, Harry Boyte, Sue Thrasher, Cathy Cade, and Marjorie Henderson; (top row, *left to right*) Sam Shirah, Jerry Gainey, Roy Money, Gene Guerrero, Ed Hamlett, Jim Williams, John Shively, Bob Potter, Bob Richardson, and Marion Barry Jr. Photo by Gunter's Studio. Carl and Anne Braden Papers, Wisconsin Historical Society, WHI-24492.

William Sullivan, assistant director for Domestic Intelligence in the FBI, testifying before the President's Commission on Campus Unrest in 1970. At his side is Charles D. Brennan, another key official within the bureau's Domestic Intelligence Division. FBI Brennan Sullivan 1970 ID 700723010. AP Photo.

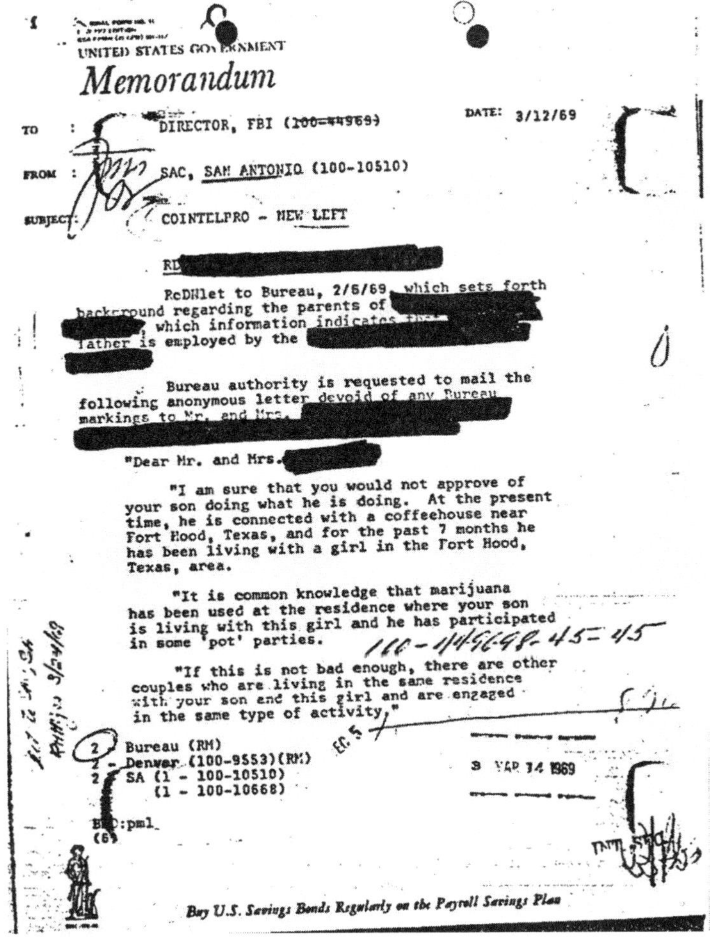
UNITED STATES GOVERNMENT

Memorandum

TO : DIRECTOR, FBI (100-449698)

DATE: 3/12/69

FROM : SAC, SAN ANTONIO (100-10510)

SUBJECT: COINTELPRO - NEW LEFT

RE

ReDNlet to Bureau, 2/6/69, which sets forth background regarding the parents of , which information indicates that father is employed by the

Bureau authority is requested to mail the following anonymous letter devoid of any Bureau markings to Mr. and Mrs.

"Dear Mr. and Mrs.

"I am sure that you would not approve of your son doing what he is doing. At the present time, he is connected with a coffeehouse near Fort Hood, Texas, and for the past 7 months he has been living with a girl in the Fort Hood, Texas, area.

"It is common knowledge that marijuana has been used at the residence where your son is living with this girl and he has participated in some 'pot' parties.

"If this is not bad enough, there are other couples who are living in the same residence with your son and this girl and are engaged in the same type of activity."

100-449698-45-45

2 - Bureau (RM)
2 - Denver (100-9553)(RM)
2 - SA (1 - 100-10510)
(1 - 100-10668)

B:pml
(6)

MAR 14 1969

Buy U.S. Savings Bonds Regularly on the Payroll Savings Plan

Memo from the San Antonio FBI office with the text of a letter it planned to send anonymously to the parents of an antiwar activist involved with the Oleo Strut coffeehouse near Fort Hood.

Millsaps College students protest the death of Jackson State University student Ben Brown with a march through the city in 1967. The photo, taken by a Sovereignty Commission informant, identifies some of the students as Doug Rogers, Mike Gwinn, David Atwood, and Alex Valentine. Mississippi State Sovereignty Commission, May 1967, SCRID no. 3-11-0-25-4-1-1-cph, ser. 2515. MSSC Records Online, 1994–2006. Courtesy of the Archives and Records Services Division, Mississippi Department of Archives and History.

— Chief Photographer Will Peters

You won't?

This was written on the side of the Richland County Selective Service building. Two USC students were charged with damaging the building with bricks and paint.

Graffiti painted on the building that housed the Selective Service office in Columbia, SC, in March 1970. Courtesy of University of South Carolina Archives.

South Carolina Law Enforcement Division officers arresting Brett Bursey during a May 1970 demonstration at the University of South Carolina after the killing of student protesters at Kent State University. *The State*, September 29, 1988.

South Carolina Law Enforcement Division undercover officer Jack Weatherford participating in a 1970 protest in Columbia, SC, over the closing of the UFO Coffeehouse. Moving Image Research Collections, University of South Carolina.

An editorial cartoon from the *Memphis Commercial Appeal,* September 14, 1976, mocking Mayor Wyeth Chandler and police chief W. O. Crumby about the destruction of the Domestic Intelligence Unit's files after their existence became known. © Bill Garner—USA TODAY NETWORK.

Frank Holloman, director of Fire and Police in Memphis, starting in 1968. © Fred J. Griffith—USA TODAY NETWORK. Reproduction courtesy of the Memphis and Shelby County Room, Memphis Public Libraries.

Before the police broke it up and arrested them, Nashville peace activists held a five-day fast at the city's War Memorial Auditorium to protest the bombing of Hanoi and Haiphong in 1966. *Southern Patriot*, August 1966.

John Sorace, head of the Nashville Intelligence Division, and Robert Hill, his deputy, preparing to testify before a Senate Judiciary Committee hearing about the unrest in the city following Stokely Carmichael's appearance in 1967. They were joined by police chief Bryce Kinnamon of Cambridge, MD; Capt. George Campbell and Lt. Daniel Hennessey of the Plainfield, NJ, Police Department. Racial Unrest Hearing ID 6708020190. AP Photo / Henry Griffin.

UNITED STATES OF AMERICA

Congress of the United States

To Joe Bogle

1111 - 17th Avenue, South

Nashville, Tennessee, **Greeting:**

Pursuant *to lawful authority, YOU ARE HEREBY COMMANDED to appear before the* Subcommittee on Internal Security of the Committee *on* the Judiciary *of the Senate of the United States, on* Thursday, October 16, *19*69 *at* 10:00 *o'clock* a. *m., at their committee room* 2300 New Senate Office Building, Washington, D. C., *then and there to testify what you may know relative to the subject matters under consideration by said committee,* pursuant to S. Res. 366 approved by the 81st Congress-2d, as amended and extended, and S. Res. 46 agreed to February 17, 1969, and to produce and bring with you the following located in any part of the above address, room section or part thereof, or with your control, or custody, or within (continued on attached sheet)

Hereof fail not, *as you will answer your default under the pains and penalties in such cases made and provided.*

To U. S. Marshal *to serve and return.*

Given *under my hand, by order of the committee, this* 1st *day of* October, *in the year of our Lord one thousand nine hundred and* sixty-nine

James O. Eastland

JAMES O. EASTLAND. U.S.S.
Chairman, Committee on

your means to produce:

1. Records, financial and otherwise, documents, of the Southern Students Organizing Committee, (S.S.O.C.).
2. Correspondence and copies thereof, bank statements, checkbooks and/or stubs of the said Southern Students Organizing Committee, (S.S.O.C.).
3. Membership lists, rosters and records, and
4. All other documents and records of the said S.S.O.C. either located at the above address, or any part thereof, or within your control, or custody, or within your means to produce.
5. The activities of S.S.O.C. or any member thereof.

Subpoena that the Subcommittee on Internal Security of the Committee on the Judiciary sent to several SSOC activists in 1969 demanding that they appear before the subcommittee and turn over records of the organization.

3

MEMPHIS

ERIC CARTER WANTED TO ENSURE he had a clean police record. A former U.S. Marine who had served in Vietnam in the late 1960s, Carter had returned to his hometown of Memphis in 1970 to attend Memphis State University, where he became friendly with other student veterans. Like him, many of his friends had grown disenchanted with the war. These students, perhaps two dozen in number, acted on their beliefs by forming a chapter of Vietnam Veterans Against the War (VVAW) and participating in antiwar demonstrations in the city. Occasionally, VVAW members were arrested during such activities, though not Carter. But when he learned that one VVAW friend was actually an undercover police officer sent to spy on the group and another, who Carter knew was a policeman, confided that the police had numerous surveillance pictures of him in their records, he became concerned that the Memphis Police Department (MPD) might have information that could derail his aspirations to become a lawyer. So, in August 1976, Carter wrote to Memphis police chief W. O. Crumby asking to see any material the police had collected about him. In fact, the police did have a file on Carter—and on thousands of other citizens and organizations, collected over a decade by an intelligence unit that operated outside of normal controls and was kept hidden from public view and government oversight.[1]

Carter's request ultimately caused the existence of the police files to tumble into public view and touched off a mad scramble in the department over how to respond. After stalling for two weeks, the police destroyed Carter's file rather than show it to him. When the local press exposed this police action, police officials conferred with Mayor Wyeth Chandler, who, upon learning about the scope of the intelligence program for the first time, ordered all the files destroyed and the intelligence unit dissolved. But the destruction of the files, which included informant accounts, surveillance photos, and undercover officers' reports, did not put the matter to rest. City council and the *Memphis Commercial Appeal* newspaper criticized the mayor and police for their actions, and the American Civil Liberties Union filed suit, accusing the police of spying on citizens in violation of constitutionally protected rights. As the lawsuit, *Kendrick v. Chandler*, progressed, deposition testimony from former intelligence officers and the discovery of intelligence files that had survived the purge painted a picture of a police department that methodically surveilled perceived political radicals. To avoid the spectacle of a trial that would divulge its secrets in open court, city officials sought to settle the lawsuit, and in 1978, they reached a groundbreaking agreement with the ACLU in which Memphis became the first city in the nation to prohibit police from conducting surveillance of purely political activities.[2]

Although personal concerns had prompted Eric Carter to act, his inquiry created a civic crisis because it revealed that the police had engaged in an extensive and sustained program of political surveillance against progressive activists and groups. This surveillance was rooted in the long, aggressive, hostile, and racialized history of police practices in Memphis. Dating to the 1930s, the MPD had worked to cripple labor organizing campaigns and hobble civil rights drives, and it did not hesitate to resort to violence to suppress activists of all types. In the late 1960s, the intensification of the civil rights movement—best symbolized by the fusion of labor and civil rights goals in the 1968 strike by city sanitation workers—and the development of anti–Vietnam War activism, led the MPD to formalize and institutionalize its surveillance activities through the creation of a dedicated surveillance unit, the Domestic Intelligence Unit (DIU). The DIU developed its own administrative practices that bureaucratized its work, most notably the creation of an elaborate system of files on the targets of surveillance. These files proliferated over the years as the DIU kept close watch on activists in the city. By the time the mayor ordered the files destroyed, they filled ten filing cabinets and contained information on organizations as disparate as the VVAW, Black Panthers, NAACP, Memphis State University Student Government Association, and various small communist groups. To get rid of the records, the DIU officers threw them into one hundred large garbage bags and formed a "bucket brigade" to move them from the DIU office to a police vehicle that transported them to a city incinerator, where they were covered in old motor oil and turned to ash. When curious reporters asked what was going on, the intelligence officer overseeing the covert action said the documents being burned were "just old newspapers."[3]

The depth and the persistence of the spying in Memphis reveal the fragility of the status quo and the fear and paranoia that gripped city officials. These fears had multiple roots, both local and national: a fear of rising Black nationalism in the post-King era, represented nationally by the Black Panthers and locally by the Invaders, a small, motley group of young, outspoken, and brash activists; horror at the prospect of student revolt and antiwar activity in the wake of the Columbia University takeover in 1968 and the student strike that followed the Kent State shooting in 1970, a strike that drew support at Memphis State; an increasingly outdated perspective that viewed dissent through the prism of the Cold War and considered protests and demonstrations to be the tools that outside agitators, fellow travelers, and Communist Party faithful used to tear at the fabric of American society; and encouragement from the FBI in the inflammatory language FBI director J. Edgar Hoover used to condemn activists, the harsh tactics he ordered his agents to deploy against them, and the close ties maintained between the Memphis FBI office and the MPD. Police surveillance in Memphis, then, was prefigured; it would have been more surprising had the leadership backed away from such tactics. In Mayor Chandler's words, the surveillance was undertaken "because of the fear of the times," implicitly blaming the activism of the late 1960s for the surveillance that began well before that and persisted into the mid-1970s, outlasting the FBI's multifaceted COINTELPRO campaign. To the MPD, no threat was too small, no person or group too obscure, for attention.[4]

The political intelligence work of the MPD was not atypical of metropolitan police departments in the 1960s and 1970s. Police investigative and intelligence units, commonly known as "Red Squads" for their pursuit of political radicals, traced their origins to the radical hunting of the Gilded Age and Progressive eras. Their efforts expanded with the anticommunist campaigns of the 1950s and their targeting of a broad range of leftists in the 1960s and 1970s.

The Cold War imperatives that gave these units their mission remained intact even as the putative threat of domestic communism receded and their targets shifted to civil right activists, New Left students, and antiwar protesters.[5]

To police officials, the rising threat that dissent posed, whether in the form of Black nationalists, antiwar radicals, or supposed communist sympathizers, fueled fears of chaos and even revolution. Eric Carter's discovery that the police had maintained a file on him indicates the breadth and depth of the post-1968 surveillance, years in which the police spied on a wide range of activists in civic, religious, and student groups. The surveillance was routine and regular, embedded in the police department's organizational structure yet kept apart administratively to ensure its secrecy, a step that at least implicitly acknowledged the dubious legal grounds for such work. Moreover, the survival of some of the files—overlooked by the police in their haste to destroy the records—along with the deposition testimony in *Kendrick v. Chandler,* compelled the city to negotiate a settlement. As an extension of the power structure in Memphis, the police used their surveillance power to control, curtail, and disrupt activity that could imperil the political, social, or economic status quo. Driven by a fear of dissent and concern that peaceful protest activity, no matter how benign, could morph into a direct challenge to conventional norms and ideals, the police executed a sustained surveillance program that did not end until it was exposed.

THE RISE OF POLICE SPYING IN MEMPHIS

"Nashville," a character in Peter Taylor's novel *A Summons to Memphis* remarks, "is a city of schools and churches, whereas Memphis is—well, Memphis is something else again. Memphis is a place of steamboats and cotton gins, of card playing and hotel society." Born as a crossroads to facilitate the trade in cotton and slaves, Memphis was a rough-and-tumble town that blended urban cosmopolitanism and rural traditionalism. The Bluff City's strategic location on the Mississippi River and role as a commercial center for the Mid-South region made it a vital component in the cotton economy and the sixth largest city in the country in 1860. During the Civil War, Memphis was a magnet for runaway slaves and a target for Union forces, who occupied it starting in 1862.

By the end of the war, the city was a stew of federal troops, northern workers, German and Irish immigrants, and a surging freedmen population, fifty of whom died at the hands of white assailants, including police officers, in an 1866 riot that was one of the worst episodes of racial violence during Reconstruction. Whites regained control of municipal government in 1879, ushering in decades of unalloyed white power. The subsequent growth of the city's industrial sector, represented by new Ford, Fisher Body Works, Firestone, RCA, and Swift factories, solidified white economic power, as whites had access to the best jobs, while African Americans were limited to the lowest-paid and least-skilled positions. The apotheosis of white rule occurred during the first decades of the twentieth century, when Edward Hull "Boss" Crump ran the Democratic political machine that controlled the city. His critics condemned his domination of public life in Memphis, but the city's white residents celebrated his leadership and ability to keep taxes low, attract business investment, and ensure racial tranquility.[6]

Crump's iron-fisted control of Memphis afforded African Americans space for limited economic development and a measure of political rights, so long as they did not threaten white dominance. Beale Street, scorned by whites as a den of iniquity, developed as the heart of the Black community and its commercial hub, home to a diverse set of businesses ranging from banks to bars, brothels to theaters. Unlike in other urban areas of the South, African Americans regularly participated in the electoral process during the Crump years. Crump tolerated Black voting, paying the poll tax for "dependable" Black voters and expecting them to cast ballots for his candidates. He also supported Black education, backed the development of parks in Black neighborhoods, and provided city jobs to African Americans, positions that won him some Black support. But his generosity was premised on Black accommodation to total white control, and he steadfastly opposed any racial reform efforts, prompting A. Philip Randolph to call him the "Memphis political boss who out Hitlers Hitler."[7] As Crump declared after President Harry Truman's 1948 speech in support of civil rights, "I would be willing to go to jail and stay there the balance of my life rather than abide by [civil rights]."[8]

The city's shifting demographics after the Civil War resulted in an Irish-dominated police force, and positions in the police department, awarded through patronage, became a tool for cementing Irish political support for white elite rule. The police department served as an extension of white business and political interests and an enforcer of Jim Crow laws. It suppressed opposition to the Crump machine, used arrests and violence to undermine unionization drives at the city's large industrial employers, and took little interest in serving or protecting the Black community. Clifford Davis, the police and fire commissioner in the 1930s, was a member of the Klan, while Joe Boyle, who succeeded him in the 1940s, bluntly stated that the role of the police was to ensure Memphis remains "'a white man's country.' . . . Any negro [*sic*] who doesn't agree to this better move on.'"[9] By midcentury, the force remained lily-white, poorly educated, and lightly trained, with many officers hailing from the surrounding rural counties, where anti-Black violence was routine.[10] Consequently, it maintained a well-deserved, fearsome reputation for abuse and brutality among Memphis's Black residents. Officers regularly invaded Black homes and businesses, assaulted unsuspecting individuals, and abused political dissenters and Congress of Industrial Organizations organizers. During the "Reign of Terror" of 1940, the police surveilled and harassed Black businessmen and community leaders and raided Beale Street establishments in a campaign to intimidate the growing Black opposition to the Crump machine. For decades, the police euphemistically used the term *John Gaston turban* for suspects, typically African American, whom police had beaten with nightsticks and who needed treatment at John Gaston Hospital. As the Black diplomat and scholar Ralph Bunche remarked, "The only connection Negroes have had to the Memphis police force has been Negro heads colliding with the nightsticks in the hands of white policemen"[11]

The police also did the bidding of agricultural interests. They used arrests for idleness and vagrancy to deter African Americans from seeking better-paying industrial jobs in Memphis and push them into the cotton economy of nearby rural counties in West Tennessee and Arkansas, where planters were in dire need of labor. The police did not hesitate to use force in this work. As LeMoyne College professor Collins George wrote to the national NAACP office: "Police enter any colored cafe at any time to paw over the patrons in search of God-knows-what. Negroes are stopped on the street, cursed, beat, kicked; they are pulled off of street cars for the dire offense of not rising to give the very last seat in the car to a white, and likewise arrested if they dare to make any audible comment about it."[12]

Despite police opposition, racial justice efforts gained steam with the fracturing of the Crump machine following his death in 1954 and the rise of a strong NAACP chapter. Without Crump as a unifying force, white political leaders fought for control of city government and became divided over whether, or how, to accommodate growing Black demands to end police brutality and efforts to elect Black officials.[13] More important, a resurgent NAACP, along with an eruption of civil rights activism among high school and LeMoyne and Owen College students in the early 1960s, prompted disruptive and successful protests against segregated public accommodations. Demonstrations at downtown lunch counters and restaurants prompted their desegregation and a commitment from business owners to hire Black staff, while protests and NAACP-led litigation achieved the desegregation of Memphis schools, libraries, parks, and the zoo. Black labor activism, which had been tamped down during the 1950s but never completely stopped, gained new momentum in the 1960s, with organizing campaigns developing among factory, service, and municipal workers, including sanitation workers protesting inhumane working conditions. Additionally, white students at Memphis State University and Southwestern College (later Rhodes College), a small liberal arts school in the city, became involved in the Memphis freedom movement. They joined with Black students to demonstrate in support of the 1964 Civil Rights Act, picketed segregated businesses, and participated in a bold "kneel-in" campaign to desegregate the prominent Second Presbyterian Church. By 1965, the Vietnam War also had captured student interest, and opposition to it began to stir at Memphis State and other schools. The flowering of progressive activism posed a threat to the narrative of racial tranquility and economic progress that white political leaders sought to project, and the Memphis Police Department played an increasingly important role in the defensive effort to shore up and preserve white hegemony in the city.[14]

Police harassment and abuse were the most obvious manifestations of official hostility to activist causes in Memphis. But the police also used surveillance and spying to restrain activism and gain intelligence on civic groups. By the mid-1960s, the MPD had created the Inspectional Bureau, a dedicated office for handling surveillance work. While the bureau's creation formalized police spying in Memphis, important developments in 1967 and 1968 prompted the police department to expand its surveillance activities.[15] In 1967, a growing anti–Vietnam War movement in Memphis added to establishment concerns about racial tensions in the city and spurred the MPD to turn attention to white students questioning the war. Students and faculty at Memphis State University were at the forefront of the activities, and they quickly earned the attention of both the FBI and the MPD. In April 1966, Ernest Withers, the famed civil rights photographer who also was an FBI informant, photographed the approximately forty participants in an antiwar march through the city organized by MSU students and faculty, a march the Memphis FBI office had learned about from a tip from the MPD.[16] The next month, the FBI reported on a melee at Memphis State when antiwar students met resistance while trying to distribute copies of an alternative newspaper, *Logos*.[17] Both the MPD and the FBI also monitored a series of weekly silent peace vigils in 1967 involving participants from MSU and Southwestern. Held downtown on Saturdays in front of the Memphis Federal Building and in Court Square, they involved war opponents walking the sidewalks with placards and signs. Lt. Eli H. Arkin of the Inspectional Bureau was assigned to keep watch on the vigils. Dressed in plainclothes, he observed the vigils and photographed the participants in an effort to identify the organizers.[18]

A confluence of local and national events in 1968 prompted the MPD to intensify its surveillance work. The sanitation workers' strike that began in February was a focal point. Police operations began immediately, spearheaded by the Inspectional Bureau. An undercover officer infiltrated planning meetings in the strike's first days, and the police had informants and officers reporting on meetings throughout the strike. The police also photographed strike demonstrations, sought to identify strike supporters from license plates on vehicles outside meetings, and obtained financial information on strike leaders in search of compromising information. Once Martin Luther King Jr. became involved, the Inspectional Bureau monitored his activities as well, and throughout the strike, it shared information with the Memphis FBI office.[19] For a police department obsessed with controlling Black activism and enforcing segregationist norms, it could only understand the strike as a weapon of racial discord. Writing in a report after the strike, Lieutenant Arkin declared that the purpose of the strike was to capitalize on "a growing Negro Activist movement within the City." "Memphis," he wrote, "had been chosen as a Target City, not only by the Unions, but also by Civil Rights leaders to be used as proving ground for their own interests."[20] The strike, in fact, originated with the Memphis workers themselves, who were responding to the inhuman and often degrading conditions of their work.

Especially worrisome to the police was the involvement in the strike of the Invaders, a loosely organized, Black Power–inspired group that injected a new level of militancy into the Memphis civil rights struggle. Along with Black student groups at LeMoyne, Owen, and MSU, it worked under the auspices of the Black Organizing Project (BOP), an umbrella group that celebrated Black culture, encouraged a more confrontational stance toward white power, and promoted autonomy for Black communities. The Invaders, though, stood out from the other groups. Named after a science fiction television program about aliens who masqueraded as ordinary humans to threaten society, it drew support from large numbers of young, disaffected youth in the city and cultivated a radical and militant image; its slogan was "Damn the Army, Join the Invaders," and many of its supporters took to wearing military-style jackets with INVADERS emblazoned on the back.[21] Despite the group's lack of structure, many young people found its combination of racial pride and demands for change appealing. Even its more militant stances, including saying that Memphis needed a "good riot" and distributing a how-to guide for making Molotov cocktails, brought it notoriety and support. Some Invaders may have crossed the line from violent rhetoric to violent actions, such as intimidation, extortion, and arson against opponents, but that did little to dampen youth enthusiasm for the group, even as it confounded the NAACP and church leaders who traditionally had set the tone, pace, and agenda for the movement in the city.[22]

The Invaders and the BOP unsettled white officials, who feared they would radicalize African Americans and precipitate racial violence, and the police quickly began surveilling those associated with the groups, including brothers Richard and Charles Laverne Cabbage, Coby Vernon Smith, John Burl Smith, and Calvin Taylor. Their Afrocentric stylings, talk of Black Power, opposition to the war, and unapologetic rhetoric of confrontation heightened police scrutiny, which only intensified after the Invaders became involved in the sanitation strike. The police infiltrated the group (as did the FBI) and conducted a regular campaign of surveillance and harassment of the activists, monitoring their meetings, raiding their homes, and subjecting them to beatings and arrests. The situation became so bad that in early 1968, several of the Invaders took the unusual step of meeting with the Memphis FBI agents William Lawrence and Howell Lowe to explain the group's goals and agenda and to complain about MPD harassment.[23] This had no discernible impact; police and FBI surveillance continued. To law enforcement, the Invaders were an anathema. They were, a 1969 police report concluded, "a group of young Memphis Blacks who adopted a philosophy of hatred of the white race, hatred of the capitalistic system, and hatred of all constituted legal authority, particularly law enforcement agencies."[24]

While the strike and the emergence of the Invaders were Memphis-specific events that inspired police surveillance, national policy developments legitimized and encouraged such police activity. Federal commissions, notably the President's Commission on Law Enforcement and Administration of Justice (1966) and the National Advisory Commission on Civil Disorders (1968)—the Kerner Commission—recommended that local police departments establish and strengthen intelligence units. The Kerner Commission deemed this strategy particularly important because its investigation revealed that police had been unprepared for the urban unrest of 1967. It therefore recommended that police departments around the country develop their intelligence-gathering capabilities to head off future episodes of potential civic disorder: "An intelligence unit staffed with full-time personnel should be established to gather, evaluate, analyze, and disseminate information on potential as well as actual civil disorders. . . . It should use undercover police personnel and informants."[25] Equally important was the Law Enforcement Assistance Administration (LEAA), created by Title I of the Omnibus Crime Control and Safe Streets Act of 1968. The LEAA, according to one assessment, "provided substantial support funding for local police departments to set up and operate intelligence divisions, grants for surveillance equipment, computerization of subversive files, and intelligence training."[26]

THE DOMESTIC INTELLIGENCE UNIT AND THE INVADERS

The increased federal support for police intelligence work coincided with the 1968 appointment of former FBI man Frank C. Holloman as the new director of fire and police in Memphis. A native of Itta Bena, Mississippi, and a twenty-five year veteran of the bureau, including time working directly with Hoover as the inspector in charge of his Washington office and several years as the special agent in charge of the Memphis office, Holloman was a no-nonsense lawman and intelligence enthusiast whose political conservatism aligned with that of the city leadership.[27] Holloman owed his appointment as the top public safety official in the city to Henry Loeb, who had recently won election to his second (nonconsecutive) term as a mayor by dominating the white vote after running as an opponent of racial reform and an advocate of law and order.[28] Holloman had been on the job in Memphis for only six weeks when the sanitation strike began, and he, with Loeb's support, encouraged the police to monitor strike activities and closely track the Invaders. "A good, efficient intelligence bureau" was vital, he later remarked, for police to effectively manage and control the city.[29] To that end, the Inspectional Bureau deployed at least eight officers, including those working undercover, as part of its surveillance efforts during the strike. Later in the year, the MPD moved all of its intelligence operations from the Inspectional Bureau, which existed as part of Internal Affairs, into a new, stand-alone intelligence branch, the Domestic Intelligence Unit. The DIU existed outside the normal MPD organizational structure and came to report directly to the chief of police and the director of fire and police. In an effort to preserve the secretive nature of its work, the DIU, by 1969, had relocated from police headquarters to a satellite building that also housed the Uniformed Division and thus facilitated the collection of information from the officers who worked the streets. Additionally, the DIU took custody of the intelligence files the Inspectional Bureau had created and expanded them dramatically over the next several years. As W. E. Routt, an assistant chief who oversaw the unit initially, wrote in a memo to police chief Henry Lux, the DIU's "present focus on local subversion, disorders, civil rights activist activities, and Union and Negro coalition activities, keeps it fully occupied and increased staffing can be foreseen for the Bureau."[30]

Memphis police officials offered a range of justifications for the DIU's ever-increasing workload. They frequently argued that surveillance kept the police force informed so it could head off criminal activity or violent action and thereby protect Memphians from those who threatened peace and security. In deputy chief of police George W. Hutchinson's words, police intelligence was designed "to help us try to prevent any rioting in this city," a comment that aligned with FBI agent William Lawrence's remark that "our primary purpose was to determine whether or not any group had or initiated any potential or actual violence. . . . We had a duty to protect the country as best we could through finding out those who were potentially or actually dangerous."[31] Intelligence officers also explained that the surveillance alerted police about planned marches and rallies so that police could assign appropriate manpower to ensure public safety. This was a curious argument to advance especially during the months of the sanitation strike, when rallies and marches were well publicized in order to encourage turnout. Additionally, the police maintained that outside agitators, long a trope in white southerners' conceptions of activism, sought to infiltrate local groups and use them as launchpads for their extremist goals. Hutchinson argued that "rogues" sought to "infiltrate" local groups "to get an opportunity to do a little looting or a little disturbance and give the police a bad time." From this perspective, the threat of extremist infiltration was constant and thus justified close monitoring of any organization or protest action. As Hutchinson bluntly put it, "The fact that it's a peaceful demonstration doesn't mean that it's going to be peaceful. There is the fact that an outside element can always come in."[32] Or as Capt. Patrick Ryan explained, "You never knew from one minute to the next what may happen or what a certain group may align itself with, and the possibility was there that they may become disruptive or cause action to be taken by the Police Department."[33]

Such ex post facto explanations obscure the reality that the police surveilled individuals and groups for their political and social views. Beliefs and viewpoints the police considered objectionable, rather than the prospect of criminal activity, underlay the DIU's choice of targets. Intelligence officers acknowledged as much.[34] Eli Arkin, who led the DIU, later defended its work by saying that the unit only wanted to focus on those it considered regular participants in activists causes—not because they had engaged in criminal conduct but because the police interpreted the very act of protesting as a threat. "If they were constantly coming down there," he remarked about the 1967 peace vigils, "then that particular person was of interest to the Memphis Police Department, not only for his own safety but for the safety of the citizens of the City of Memphis, and it behooved us to know who they were and what they were doing."[35] More generally, Patrick Ryan conceded that every peaceful political demonstration about civil rights or the war had at least a theoretical potential to lead to illegal activity and therefore was an appropriate subject of concern for the DIU. "I mean, you might could look at something for a good while and not have criminal activity involved," he said, "but there is always the possibility that there was going to be, or indications that there could be, criminal activity."[36] By this logic, merely attending a demonstration marked one for police surveillance.

Such an approach made the Invaders a prime police target in the aftermath of the sanitation strike and the assassination of Martin Luther King Jr. The group's unabashed Black nationalism and embrace of Black Power particularly infuriated the police, which blamed the group for a Black Power–infused riot at Carver High School in 1968—several Invaders were charged and convicted of incitement—and for their role, limited as it was, in the takeover of administration buildings by students at LeMoyne-Owen College and Memphis State in 1968 and 1969, respectively.[37] The group's open rejection of moderation, dialogue, and reconciliation in favor of assertive demands and menacing rhetoric frightened a police department already on edge. The national situation heightened police concerns. Eli Arkin both captured and stoked police fears in a 1968 memo, "Summary of the Plans of Black Extremists in the United States of America (Taken from Newspapers, and Sources Known to This Bureau)." After starting with a quotation from SNCC leader and Black Power advocate H. Rap Brown—"'We must move from resistance to aggression, from revolt to revolution. . . . May the deaths of '68 signal the beginning of the end of this country'"—Arkin wrote, "It's going to be a long and violent summer, if plans being discussed by Black extremists materialize." Arkin offered a superficial and hyperbolic overview of Black organizing work, which he summarized as planning "guerilla warfare, firearms training, take-overs of college administrations, assassinations of public figures, arson, 'blackouts' of cities, bank robberies, and chaos in the cities."[38] Frank Holloman fueled this sentiment a few months later in a confidential presentation to the local media outlining the extremist forces arrayed against the police. Entitled "The Badge Speaks"—likely a not-so-subtle rejoinder to the "Afro-American Brotherhood Speaks: Black Thesis, Black Power," distributed earlier in the year by Charles Cabbage and his confederates in the BOP—Holloman painted a picture of a besieged and overwhelmed department facing violent, radical militants while the wider community remained apathetic and unconcerned. "What is happening to Memphis!" handwritten notes on the presentation asked, capturing police anger and frustration.[39] Police would not remain passive, Holloman made clear; they would meet any threat head-on. As he told one white civic group in the summer of 1968, any "lawlessness" by local Blacks will prompt a police response in which "we'll knock them on their ass."[40]

In its campaign against the Invaders, the DIU collaborated with agents in the Memphis FBI office, who were just as keen on monitoring the group and disrupting its activities. FBI agents William H. Lawrence, Hugh Kearney, and Howell S. Lowe directed the bureau's anti-subversive work in Memphis, which included managing a network of informants and confidential sources. Lawrence, who had worked in the Memphis office since the 1940s and won commendation from Hoover for his work in apprehending the fugitive Communist Party official Junius Scales in 1954, was the key figure linking the two law enforcement agencies. By his own account, Lawrence helped the MPD establish its intelligence operations, and he and the other agents maintained close professional and personal ties to the officers in the DIU. Eli Arkin of the DIU socialized with Lawrence and the others, joining them for lunch occasionally and playing on the bureau's bowling team. And the FBI agents had ready access to the DIU files. Patrick Ryan recalls that Howell Lowe was permitted to access the files without the special approval normally needed for someone outside the unit to see the materials.[41]

In their pursuit of the Invaders, the DIU and the FBI routinely conducted joint interviews of targeted individuals, a step that undoubtedly heightened tensions and anxiety for those they pursued. They also regularly shared information they had developed independently. The DIU, in fact, exchanged information with a number of federal investigative bodies, including Army

Intelligence, the investigative unit at the Internal Revenue Service, the Secret Service, and Immigration and Naturalization Service. But its relationship with the FBI was the deepest. FBI files from the Memphis office are filled with references to the MPD's intelligence operations. Lawrence, for example, frequently noted in memos on the Invaders that he was reporting information forwarded by the MPD, and he later testified before Congress that the MPD had provided him with updates during the sanitation strike. Similarly, the MPD received information from the bureau's agents. In a time-tested strategy that bureau agents across the country deployed, the Memphis office regularly informed the MPD of any actionable offense, no matter how trivial or insignificant, by individuals it monitored. The police would use this information, such as allegations of marijuana possession or expired vehicle registrations, as the basis, if not the pretext, for citations and arrests. In 1968, the Memphis agents approvingly noted that the police, by acting on the information, were putting a significant strain on their targets' financial resources.[42]

The police and FBI also strived to undermine the work of federally funded War on Poverty programs in Memphis that employed Invaders or BOP activists. Worried that Black militants were using these programs to advance a radical agenda, the DIU and FBI agents in Memphis worked in tandem to get these activists fired and the programs defunded. They had at least the implicit support of the city's white political leadership; Congressman Dan Kuykendall, Mayor Henry Loeb, and city councilman Wyeth Chandler deplored the Black activists' participation in the projects and questioned the value of the programs themselves. Chandler, for example, challenged the purpose of the Neighborhood Organizing Project (NOP), planned for the summer of 1968 to educate young African Americans about their own history and culture. With the Invaders in mind, he asked how "the teaching of Black history, Black art, and Black culture in this project could help the apparently unemployable."[43] The FBI office sent a long memo to the Office of Economic Opportunity, which funded War on Poverty projects, accusing the NOP of being ineffectual and staffed by subversives who also were drug pushers. The DIU, in a letter signed by police chief Henry Lux, damned the activists as Black Power radicals and informed the Washington administrators that several of the workers had been arrested in a drug raid of Invader and NOP staffer John Smith's apartment, which served as the Invaders' primary meeting place. "Since members of the Black Organizing Project were basically unemployed until the summer Project known as Neighborhood Organizing Project was formed, it was found that the money received from NOP had been used to fund BOP operations and in part purchase the marijuana and . . . drugs." With a wink and a nod, the letter concludes, "Hoping the above information will be of some assistance to you." Indeed, shortly afterward, the local War on Poverty office fired the NOP staff and shuttered the program.[44]

Both the DIU and the FBI gathered intelligence about the Invaders from informants—private citizens who had volunteered information about the group or had been recruited to do so. The Invaders had among its core activists at least a half-dozen individuals who reported to law enforcement. The FBI managed at least five informants, including Ernest Withers, who photographed the activists and regularly betrayed them in reports he made to Lawrence. Withers also was instrumental in pursuing Charles Cabbage for draft evasion. His reports to Lawrence that Cabbage wanted to pursue conscientious objector status prompted Lawrence to tell the Selective Service Board that Cabbage was a Black Power radical and subject of an FBI investigation, helping doom his appeal and leading to his arrest, conviction, and sentencing to more than four years in prison in May 1969 (he also was convicted on charges of firearms possession and burglary).[45]

The DIU occasionally received information about the Invaders from local Memphians who had contacted the MPD with complaints or concerns that ultimately found their way to the intelligence bureau. For instance, during the sanitation strike, a white woman phoned the police to report "a large number of carloads of negroes sitting in the Northgate Shopping Center, and the Frayzer Shopping Center," most with out-of-state plates. She "stated the reason she had called was because she had never seen this many negroes [*sic*] in the Frayzer area and this was upsetting to her."[46] More commonly, the DIU gained information from a shadowy network of informants it cultivated. According to Eli Arkin, informants were individuals the police considered reliable and trustworthy and who had a proven record of providing accurate information. Perhaps surprisingly, the DIU unsuccessfully tried to entice Coby Smith, a BOP founder, into becoming an informant. While Smith never flipped, the

DIU managed a number of informants in the group. Because the police records about informants were destroyed with the rest of the files, it is impossible to know how many confidential sources the police used. But it appears it was a considerable number. In the fall of 1968, for example, the DIU reported that informants had worked a staggering 336 hours that September. The tracking of hours suggests that many of them were paid for their work. While, again, records of payments do not survive, the DIU maintained a fund of up to ten thousand dollars out of which it paid informants.[47]

The DIU also deployed Black undercover police officers against the Invaders. Unlike informants, whose reporting could be episodic and whose accuracy and reliability were always open to challenge, undercover intelligence officers were inherently trustworthy sources. Moreover, in an overwhelmingly white department that frequently faced accusations of brutality and harassment in the Black community, African American policemen were a valuable asset for tracking Black activists. The DIU first assigned Black officers to monitor the Invaders during the sanitation workers' strike. By posing as students or workers, these officers, including Marrell McCollough, Tyrant Moore, and Donald Pigford gathered valuable information about the group.[48] McCollough was the most important and effective of the undercover officers. Known to the Invaders as "Max" and as "Agent 500" to his DIU colleagues—the undercover officers were code-named "Agent 500," "Agent 501," and so on—McCollough was a twenty-three-year-old native of Tunica, Mississippi, who had served three years as a military policeman in the army before attending the police academy in Memphis and becoming a patrolman in December 1967. He had been on the police force for just ten weeks when officials sent him undercover, in February 1968, to report on a strike meeting and then, two weeks later, assigned him to infiltrate the Invaders, which the police worried would radicalize the strikers. With a cover as a warehouseman at a local electrical repair business and a part-time student at Memphis State, McCollough became a trusted figure in the Invaders, assisted at least in part by the fact that his 1967 Volkswagen Fastback made him the only one in the group with a car. He became the group's "Minister of Transportation" and remained undercover in the group for over a year, participating in its activities while phoning in almost daily reports to his DIU colleagues.[49]

McCollough was an effective impostor. Wearing his hair in an Afro and regularly accompanying Oree McKenzie, Coby Smith, John Smith, Lance "Sweet Willie Wine" Watson, and others associated with the group, he was considered a dangerous radical by police officers who did not know he was undercover. "He did such a fine job, that he had half of the men on the department that would have given their eye teeth to have locked him up," one officer who was in the know, Frank Kallaher, recalled in 1970. "He called us pigs, he called us names that you've never heard of. He played it to the hilt."[50] His involvement in the group was wide-ranging. During the sanitation strike, he joined Invader leaders at the Lorraine Motel for discussion with Martin Luther King Jr. and his staff, and he was present at the motel when King was gunned down—McCollough is kneeling over the gravely wounded civil rights leader in the famous *Life* magazine photograph taken moments after he was shot.[51] He helped organize the drug raid of John Smith's apartment, was at the Carver High School walkout that resulted in charges against several Invaders, and was the driver when a few Invaders went in search of vacant houses to burn down.[52] After the strike, he reported on meetings between the Invaders and union organizers as the groups discussed possible collaborations.[53] The DIU regularly shared McCollough's reports with the local FBI office.[54] The Memphis SAC, Robert G. Jensen, said the reports were "of inestimable value to this office," and J. Edgar Hoover even lauded the work against the Invaders in the aftermath of the drug raid. He encouraged the Memphis office not just to rely on the MPD's efforts but to "consider possible counterintelligence measures to neutralize this group," and he gave approval for the agents to monitor phone calls, access bank records, and develop other means of disrupting the group. Hoover apparently was unaware that the Memphis FBI office already was targeting the Invaders, but Lawrence and the others no doubt welcomed his support.[55]

McCollough remained undercover with the Invaders until April 1969. The circumstances by which his assignment ended are murky. Eli Arkin, who oversaw his work in the DIU, suggested that the police reassigned McCollough in anticipation of his testifying in a case against the Invaders, testimony that Arkin says never happened.[56] One of the Invaders also may have exposed McCollough's identity.[57] This is quite plausible because his identity may not have been as secure as he and the DIU thought. Charles Cabbage told congressional investigators in 1978 that he suspected McCollough was a police spy given "his manner, his availability . . . popping out of nowhere, with no background. . . . I was rather close to a state of being paranoid because of the pressure put on us by the police department, so I just immediately interpreted him as being a plant." John Smith testified that another activist told him that McCollough worked for the police. Cabbage and Smith said that the group had discussed what to do and decided that expelling him "would have been a mistake," according to Cabbage. Instead, Smith explained, they decided that "the best thing to do was to just keep him. If we ran him off they would only send someone else."[58] Whatever the case, McCollough left the Invaders but continued to work with the DIU on monitoring leftist activists and working on narcotics cases until the CIA hired him and he departed Memphis in 1974.[59]

Donald Pigford and Tyrant Moore followed McCollough as undercover officers assigned to the Invaders. Pigford joined the MPD in September 1968, after having served three years in the U.S. Air Force, some of that time as a base patrolman. He may have been Agent 501; his appointment to the force coincided with references to this agent in surviving DIU records. FBI reports on the Invaders also noted Pigford by name, though not as an agent—an April 1969 memo identifies him as the Invaders' business manager.[60] Moore, too, began to appear in FBI reports on the Invaders in the months after his June 1969 hiring by the police, and as with Pigford, the FBI did not appear to know he was an undercover officer.[61] Although Pigford and Moore remained involved with the Invaders into 1970, by mid-1969 the DIU campaign of intimidation, harassment, and arrests had severely weakened the group. Invader Louis Welch glumly remarked in early 1969 "that since the assassination of Martin King more than 60 young Black men and women have been jailed, more than half a million dollars in bond have been assessed, and almost every man labeled by the local news media as a 'black militant' has been thrown into jail."[62] Others had moved away, been inducted into the army, or awaited trial on other charges. Marrell McCollough told the local FBI office in July 1969 "that for all practical purposes the Invaders have ceased to exist." "He said the Invaders have never been an effective group," SAC Jensen continued, but "were basically phony, criminally intent and petty in their actions."[63] Nearly a decade later, McCollough downplayed the threat they posed, telling a congressional committee that the Invaders were just a noisy group spouting militant rhetoric. It was "a lot of young people getting together, making violent statements and doing a lot of violent talk but actually committing no acts of violence."[64] The distance of years and the collapse of the civil rights movement perhaps colored McCollough's recollections. The group did engage in criminal activity, as he himself had witnessed. But it was never the threat to the social order that the police believed. Its militant rhetoric, though, led the police to brand it a dire threat to the community and to channel significant resources toward decimating it.

THE DOMESTIC INTELLIGENCE UNIT EXPANDS

The DIU's success against the Invaders affirmed the MPD's commitment to intelligence work, and the unit grew in size, gained new assignments, and saw its budget increase as a result of this success. However, its structure and policies often lacked coherence and were beset by inefficiencies and uncertainties that suggested a hurried, haphazard process of development. The numbingly complex filing system the unit developed is a prime example. There were subject files, files on groups and individuals, and files on informants that were stored apart from the others in an office safe. When an informant filed a report, an officer would place it both in the informant's file and in the file of the group or person being surveilled, meaning there would be multiple copies of the same report. The unit also developed a numbering system that categorized files by subject area—for example, "Communism," "Black"—each with unique numerical identifiers. Eli Arkin, who oversaw the process, said that by 1976, the list of codes ran at least eight legal-sized pages long. To manage the ever-growing number of files, the unit created an index card system to serve as a finding aid for the actual files themselves. Each time an officer added new material to a group's or person's file, he noted it on the corresponding index card. Arkin gave an example: if he observed and could identify someone who participated in a demonstration, he would note their name in the report he made; "after that was typed the secretary would then go down a list of names in there and a card would be made out with your name on it and that particular report would be placed in . . . the master file [on you]. . . . Your name on your index card that she made out would also have the file that was in plus the page number that your name appeared in that report."[65]

The amount of work this created was staggering. In late 1968, Arkin pleaded to his supervisor for more administrative support. "Though the Intelligence files are growing, there is much work that needs to be done on them, and a full time clerk, cleared for confidential work, would prove invaluable."[66] When the DIU at one point lost one of its two secretaries, it was nearly impossible for the one who remained to keep the files up-to-date. "There were not enough hours in the day for her to keep up with this," Arkin said. Indeed, the process of managing the files was time-consuming and confusing, and the result was a file system that officers found difficult to use. As a frustrated Arkin explained: "It was "a very laborious job to go through the files and try and sift out things and still do your daily work. . . . There was talk as to how we could streamline our files. They were getting quite large."[67] The size of the files and the penchant for detailed and thorough recordkeeping echoed the FBI's practice with its COINTELPRO files and the Mississippi State Sovereignty Commission with its records.[68] And the very fact that the MPD had created such an elaborate filing system highlights how law enforcement fetishized files and records. The MPD's struggle to track activists may seem silly or amusing as well as futile and pointless. But the banality of the bureaucratization of intelligence gathering should not obscure the widening net the unit was casting to surveil and monitor citizens whom it considered subversives. What historian Kenneth O'Reilly said about the FBI intelligence gathering was equally true of the DIU's: "They would pretty much take everything. . . . If you don't collect it in the first place you don't have a chance of using it later. That's what a police state does."[69]

The intelligence bureau's management of its informants and undercover officers reflected a similar complexity and inefficiency. The manner in which reports from these individuals ended up in files suggest the children's game of telephone. For starters, neither informants nor undercover police officers used recording devices when conducting surveillance, which meant that they relied on their memory when they reported to the DIU, usually by phone. Eli Arkin insisted that those reporting information were good at remembering things they overhead, especially if it was critical; Agent 501, in particular, he said, "had a very good mind for retention."[70] For its part, the DIU did not even have the capability to record phone calls—other than holding up a cassette tape recorder to the phone handset, which was rarely done—so the officer who received an intelligence report by phone made notes on the call. The officer then placed these handwritten notes directly in the appropriate files unless he needed to first ask a unit secretary to transcribe them before filing.[71] The accuracy of such reports is difficult to gauge, but based as they were on memory, they do not inspire confidence. Moreover, although the DIU professed a desire to protect informants' identities, as the practice of having them phone in their reports rather than deliver them in person reflects, the unit risked revealing their identities by insisting that those who were being paid sign a receipt—to be placed in their file, of course—indicating they had received payment. Because they were paid in cash, they had to meet with their DIU handler in order to receive payment, making them vulnerable to exposure.[72] The DIU was also sloppy about concealing the names of its undercover officers in the files. Marrell McCollough, for example, appears in DIU documents as "Max," "Agent 501," and "Marrell McCollough."[73] This inconsistency ensured McCollough's exposure to others beyond the MPD because the police frequently circulated reports with his name to the FBI, military intelligence, and others.

The DIU pursued its work with a zeal that was rooted in fears that community well-being depended upon the police's ability to frustrate the designs of racial militants and radical activists. The professed worries about civic unrest masked the real concerns—the disruption of the economic status quo, the challenge to white supremacy, and social and cultural upheaval—and were self-justification for the DIU to take increasingly aggressive action against those it saw not as political dissenters but as enemies of the people. The police, by this view, were all that stood between the peace-loving people of Memphis and those bent on causing chaos and crisis in the city and whose actions legitimized—necessitated, in the DIU's views—tactics that ranged from the blatantly illegal to the comically trivial against an ever-growing list of threatening actors.

Intelligence officers pried into the personal and financial histories of those it suspected of subversive activity. Without warrants, they obtained credit reports and histories, academic records, and phone logs of targets from their contacts within a range of private businesses, public institutions, and government entities. In 1969, for instance, DIU detective Jerry Davis, conducted a background check on an African American doctor who had come under DIU suspicion. Davis reported that checks with other law enforcement agencies showed the doctor had a clean record. He learned from Consumer Credit that the doctor carried debt on his Bank America credit card and had balances at Sears and Levy's department stores. Through contacts at the phone company, he discovered that phone calls had been placed from the doctor's residence to several Mississippi locales as well as to New York.[74] Not all targets were Memphians. In mid-1968, the assistant police chief with oversight of intelligence directed Davis to dig for dirt on two New York journalists who were coming to Memphis to make a documentary film on the newly formed Memphis Search for Meaning Committee, the group led by Memphis State professor David Yellin and his wife, Carol Yellin, a former *Reader's Digest* editor, that over the next several years conducted oral histories and collected documentary material that would form the core of the most significant archival collection on the sanitation strike. Reflecting an unfamiliarity with world geography, Davis reported that one of the journalists was "a citizen of Tanzania, South Africa" who had overstayed a student visa. Working with immigration authorities in New York, Davis gained access to the journalist's immigration file and learned that he would claim political asylum if immigration authorities sought to deport him. Davis suggested that the immigration angle would be worth pursuing and approvingly noted that "the Immigration Department stated that they would work with us in any way that they could on him."[75]

After the sanitation strike, the DIU routinely expanded the number of groups and individuals it surveilled. In late 1968, when the American Federation of State, County and Municipal Employees (AFSCME) local led a strike of hospital workers, the vast majority of whom were African American, the DIU monitored it closely. Undercover officers—Agent 500 and Agent 501—infiltrated strike meetings, and other officers watched the strikers when they gathered outside hospitals or participated in demonstrations. Wary that the hospital strike was, in Arkin's words, an "instant replay of the Sanitation Strike, and the strategy used" of transforming a labor dispute into a civil rights cause involving the larger Black community, the DIU was particularly attuned to the presence of radical activists, including Invaders, among the strikers and unionists.[76] Marrell McCollough reported that at one strike meeting, the unionists, seeking to broaden the appeal of their campaign, urged the Invaders to "drum up community support, against Police Brutality," and at another, he ominously detailed how one minister, "who is now sporting a beard . . . hollered 'Soul Power'" during his speech.[77] When the strikers marched through the city, the DIU, as well as the FBI, was there to watch and take photographs. As Ernest Withers had demonstrated with his photographic surveillance for the FBI, pictures were a valuable tool for helping intelligence officials identify their targets. Arkin appreciated the usefulness of pictures too. He often was the one photographing demonstrators for the DIU, and he carried a small black book with photographs of those under surveillance.[78] Because he was not undercover, his presence with a camera was in itself a form of intimidation against demonstrators. "Just the fact that someone was there taking pictures," he later remarked, "would and did have a psychological effect" on targets.[79] Arkin judged the photographs to be such an important tool that he wrote to his supervisor after photographing one march, "This bureau would like to encourage the building up of a larger photograph file of agitators and subversives, as this photographic evidence has proved invaluable."[80]

Given the DIU's sensitivity to any challenges to the norms and conventions that governed daily life in Memphis, it is not surprising that it made little distinction between avowed Black Power radicals and those promoting moderate reform goals. All such activists threatened to cause disruptions in Memphis. The DIU was deeply antagonistic to the NAACP, which had been at the forefront of the civil rights struggle in Memphis for many years. Its size, base in the middle-class and professional community, and national reputation made it a formidable foe under the expert leadership of executive secretary Maxine Smith, a tough, wily, and tireless advocate of civil rights. Smith was a Black Memphis native who first became involved in the NAACP in the late 1950s, when, upon returning to the city with her husband, Vasco, MSU, which was still an all-white university, rejected her application for graduate study despite her possessing degrees from Spelman College in Atlanta and Middlebury College in Vermont and having taught as an assistant professor at universities in Texas and Florida. She rose to the position of NAACP executive secretary in 1962 and in that role became a key advocate for Black equality in Memphis for decades.[81] In the years after 1968, Smith and the NAACP repeatedly clashed with the MPD over police brutality allegations, charges that, *Time* magazine noted, reflected the "Memphis police department's traditional policy of heavy-handedness toward Negroes, which ranges from routine rudeness to blatant brutality."[82] Smith's monthly reports regularly cataloged incidents in which police officers harassed, abused, intimidated, extorted, assaulted, and killed Black Memphians.[83] Her reports also revealed the NAACP's raw, tense relations with the MPD. In 1971, for example, Smith reported that "as a result of numerous calls to the NAACP office complaint was filed with the chief of police against the repeated use of the term 'n——' by a police inspector while being interviewed on a local radio station. The police chief's answer indicated that he could not decide which was worse a southern pronunciation of 'Negro' (which was not the case), or 'pigs' (allegedly used by the blacks referred to as 'n——s'). The police chief further stated that he was concerned about the bias and prejudice of the NAACP."[84]

The adversarial relationship between the NAACP and the MPD likely contributed to the decision by several NAACP leaders, including Maxine and Vasco Smith, to quietly furnish information to the FBI about the Memphis movement. Driven by a desire to demonstrate to William Lawrence and his FBI colleagues that the movement was peaceful, the activists hoped to secure a measure of security from MPD violence and abuse. "We thought it was for our own protection" to talk to the FBI, Maxine Smith recollected. Unlike Ernest Withers, who eagerly informed on the movement and accepted payment for his work, the Smiths were never paid and were not driven by animus against their colleagues or community. By cultivating ties with the federal officials, they saw an opportunity to mitigate police abuses and ultimately advance the movement's goals.[85]

Yet there is no evidence that their cooperation with the FBI yielded results. The bureau, though perhaps more professional than the MPD, was no more sympathetic to Black rights. The discussion with the Smiths served the bureau's interest in keeping track of the movement. The Smiths's reports provided FBI agents in Memphis with insights on the operation of the NAACP chapter, and during the sanitation strike, the reports kept them informed on the chapter's plans for actions. And the bureau did not persuade the MPD to curtail its use of force. Although the NAACP was moderate in comparison to the Invaders, the police considered it a "fairly militant group" and consistent threat given its size and power in Memphis.[86] The DIU sought to develop an "intelligence liason [*sic*]" in the group in the late 1960s. It is unclear whether it did so, though Marrell McCollough did infiltrate the NAACP Youth Group in 1968 and reported that it was preparing a list of grievances to present the board of education, including a request "that Negro History be taught in the schools."[87] Unlike the MPD's long history with the NAACP, the DIU had no inkling what to make of the newly formed Black Knights in 1969. Described by the *Commercial Appeal* as a "Negro self-help group," the Black Knights, among whose participants was Stax Records singer and composer Isaac Hayes, had appealing qualities, in the DIU's estimation. In one intelligence report, Eli Arkin approvingly noted that the group was "made up basically of adults, and men who have jobs." It met weekly at Clayborn Temple and sought to improve the Black community through nonviolent means. None of this inoculated it against the DIU's prying eyes. "It is the belief that the Black Knights are a potentially dangerous group," Arkin wrote in one report, "and the Intelligence Bureau for this reason keeps them under surveillance."[88]

The DIU's surveillance efforts occasionally took it far afield from monitoring meetings, observing marches, and arresting activists. The officers unwittingly validated the view of many Black activists that art and culture had the power to transform lives and empower a community. The ideas of the Black Arts movement, including the notion that music and film, poetry and literature, theater and sculpture, could instill pride in Black heritage and history and promote Black unity and strength, compelled the DIU to take notice of cultural developments. In 1969, an officer noted in an intelligence report that Stax recording artists Ollie & the Nightingales had released the new single "I've Got a Feeling," a follow-up to its hit "I Know I've Got a Sure Thing."[89] The officers also found the time in their busy schedules to view the Blaxploitation film *Up Tight*, whose music was scored by Isaac Hayes. The film took John Ford's *The Informer*, about the Irish Republican Army in the 1920s, and relocated it to the inner city of the United States and made it about an impending violent Black uprising. In the DIU's estimation, "the movie did advocate revolutionary ideas" and thus dramatized the fears that underlay the DIU's activities. The film gave the unit more reason to be vigilant.[90]

SURVEILLING THE MEMPHIS PEACE MOVEMENT

In the constellation of threats the Memphis Police Department organized itself to face in the late 1960s and 1970s, opposition to the Vietnam War and growing radicalism among high school and college students joined Black activism as causes for concern to authorities. The city's leadership filtered the surge of activism through a Cold War ideology that framed dissent as evidence of a broad, metastasizing radical movement that in some amorphous way was tied to international communism. Frank Holloman, the director of fire and police, gave voice to this view when he suggested that charges of police brutality against the MPD were part of a communist plot to undermine law enforcement.[91] Mayor Henry Loeb did, too, when he mistakenly thought *Look to the East,* an anticommunist tract that was distributed at a local high school, was, in fact, an effort to recruit students to work against the country. The neutralization of the Invaders, then, was but a small success in the larger struggle to ward off dangers that lurked throughout the city, a struggle that led the DIU to train its power and resources on the antiwar movement.[92]

Local groups, such as the Draft Resistance Union of Memphis (DRUM) and the MidSouth Citizens Dissatisfied with US Policy in Vietnam, and regional and national ones, including the Nashville-based Southern Student Organizing Committee, the Vietnam Veterans Against the War, and the Students for a Democratic Society, all organized in the city against the war. Because many of these organizations involved white students, Memphis leaders feared that their own children were being radicalized right under their noses in local high schools, at Southwestern, and at Memphis State. The *Memphis Press-Scimitar* both reflected and stoked white concern in two fear-inducing, provocatively titled 1968 articles, "U.S. Student Radicals Honor Red Leaders as Heroes and Vow to Destroy Capitalism" and "Communism Too Tame—Student Activists Adopt Nihilism and Anarchy as Pattern of Conquest." In overheated, hyperbolic language, the articles sought to raise the alarm about SDS: "Their power is explosive. They have disrupted dozens of universities, struck and closed Columbia. They have been in the forefront of the swirling maelstrom of violence that cut like a knife through the fabric of American Society."[93] The articles warned that the group was bent on destroying the American way of life, as SDS "direct[ed]" student protests, was a "catalyst" of the antiwar movement," and was the "diamond-hard point of the phalanx of university students who are dedicated to wreaking revolutionary changes in American society." Quoting J. Edgar Hoover's warning that it would be "'a grave mistake'" to "'dismiss the New Left, as some do, as a collection of simpletons, eccentrics, and jocular fools,'" the articles imbued SDS and other groups with a power and influence that exceeded their small numbers. Vigilance and watchfulness were required at all times to defuse the threat they posed.[94]

Memphis's political leadership fully backed such a response. Mayor Loeb urged the police to vigorously pursue antiwar activists, particularly when they sought to organize or distribute literature on high school campuses. When angry parents wrote Loeb to complain that the Memphis Draft Resistance and the Memphis Workshop in Nonviolence were, in one of Loeb's correspondent's words, trying "to confuse and pervert the minds of our children" by handing out flyers encouraging young men to apply for conscientious objector status or seek a deferment, Loeb demanded that the police investigate. Loeb fully concurred with the parents' sentiment. "I think the young people who are doing this, are at best misguided, and at worst are revolutionaries," he responded to one parent. "I thoroughly resent the immorality of asking some of our young people to fight for our country and risk their lives, while allowing others to hurt their efforts at home." Fulminating against antiwar students was easier than stopping them. As Frank Holloman gently replied to the mayor about his demand for an investigation of the literature distribution, "It has not been possible for any legal action to be taken in view of the fact that no violations of the law are indicated." But Holloman assured the mayor that police kept a close eye on antiwar activists through the work of the DIU.[95]

Thanks to its national reputation, SDS was a primary DIU target. In May 1968, shortly after the Columbia University takeover, fifteen Memphis State students—twelve white and three Black—formed the city's first SDS chapter, naming it after Larry Payne, the African American youth killed by police during a violence-marred demonstration during the previous spring's sanitation workers' strike. The DIU received information about the group's creation from an informant who attended the founding meeting, and the day after its creation, Eli Arkin sent a memo to his supervisor listing the names of all the individuals involved in the group, including a German instructor who may have served as a faculty advisor. The DIU kept the group in its sights in the succeeding months, aided, according to Arkin, by reports from informants in the chapter. It also relied on reports from undercover officer Marrell McCollough, who used his position as an MSU student and Invader to get close to students involved in SDS and feed information back to the intelligence unit. Because MSU had not approved SDS as an official student organization, the chapter met off campus, frequently at the Westminster Presbyterian Center near MSU, which was overseen by Rev. Richard Moon, who the police derisively described as someone who "projects himself in any leftist or liberal campaign."[96] *Memphis Press-Scimitar* reporter Kay Pittman Black, a frequent collaborator with the FBI and MPD, also fueled concerns about SDS. In one article, she quoted the fanciful statements of SDSer Ted Carter that more than one hundred students belonged to SDS chapters at MSU and Southwestern, suggesting that the group was a growing threat to Memphis.[97]

In its surveillance of leftist students at MSU, the DIU had an ally in school officials, who were anxious to control the student population and prevent the type of unrest that had roiled other campuses. MSU had had a taste of this discord with the 1966 antiwar skirmishes over the distribution of the *Logos* newspaper. It also faced growing demands from Black students through the Black Student Association (BSA), culminating in the arrest of more than one hundred students who were holding a sit-in in President Cecil C. Humphreys's office in April 1969. SDS was particularly worrisome to MSU administrators, who saw it as representing the potential for radicalism and violence on campus. Humphreys, whose political conservatism aligned with that of the city's political leadership, castigated SDS in a 1969 speech to the Southern Association of Colleges and Schools for promoting chaos, nihilism, and the "destruction of existing institutions." More broadly, he defined all student activism as a problem and expressed incomprehension of activists' beliefs and goals. "The only definite conclusion that I can draw," he declared, "is that students on college and school campuses are not 'like they used to be.'" He did not mean that as a compliment.[98]

Humphreys's skepticism of liberal activism and opposition to student protest pervaded his administration and made officials at the school receptive to DIU appeals for assistance. Over the course of several years, MSU administrators routinely provided intelligence officers with the personal information and educational records of students who had participated in protest actions or joined activist organizations, information that normally required a court order or search warrant to access. DIU officers frequently worked through the security office at MSU. Located in the main administration building on campus, security officers could readily access student files and provide the DIU with student transcripts and personal data, including social security numbers, next of kin, and car license plate numbers. If there were pictures of students available, either in a yearbook or a copy of the student's ID, they would provide that too. Information flowed from the DIU to MSU as well. Eli Arkin would identify for security officers students about whom the unit had gathered information, and as the unofficial photographer for the intelligence bureau, he showed them pictures he had taken of young people at demonstrations whom he suspected of being MSU students—both to alert campus officials and to learn their identities.[99] Arkin and other intelligence officers maintained a strong relationship with the director of the security office, William F. Youngson, and he proved a regular source of information on student activities. In one instance, Youngson contacted Arkin to notify him that the Human Relations Commission of the MSU Student Government had reserved a room in the University Center for a forum involving four panelists: a Southwestern student, an MSU assistant professor of sociology, and two priests, one from the MSU Newman Foundation and one from a local church. While the surviving documentation redacts the individuals' names as well as the subject of the forum, the mere fact that the security director found the event noteworthy enough to contact the DIU highlighted officials' sensitivity to any type of progressive activity and made it likely that the police would investigate those involved. In fact, as a matter of course, the security office informed the DIU whenever an organization that the DIU might have an interest in sought to hold an event on campus.[100]

Relations between the MPD and MSU extended beyond security officers and intelligence unit officials to also include the top leadership of both institutions. Beginning in the late 1960s, Cecil Humphreys, who in the 1940s had served as an FBI special agent, hosted an annual gathering in his home that brought together MSU vice presidents and the campus security director with MPD officials, including Frank Holloman, Eli Arkin, and the police chief. The meetings, which occurred near the start of each academic year and continued after Humphreys's retirement in 1972, focused on student activism, both nationally and in Memphis. As Arkin, who was the commanding officer of the intelligence unit, recalls, "We would sit around and just discuss basically . . . things that were trouble that had happened in other areas of the country . . . [and] and what their feeling was for the forthcoming year at Memphis State." With the intensification of antiwar organizing and the growing assertiveness of Black students on campus, there was plenty for the officials to discuss.[101]

DIU officials also routinely traded information with John D. Jones, a professor of education and the vice president for Student Affairs at Memphis State in the early 1970s.[102] A native of Lacy, Arkansas, he had earned his doctorate from the University of Mississippi and a master's degree in public health from the University of Alabama at Birmingham before arriving at MSU. As an administrator, Jones forged a relationship with Eli Arkin and other DIU officers. Undoubtedly among the vice presidents who attended the meetings at the president's house, Jones supplied his DIU contacts with information about students. In one instance, Arkin remembers having provided damaging information to Jones on a student group—possibly SDS—to undermine its bid for official status at MSU. Arkin is evasive in his testimony about the specifics of this interaction and his other conversations with Jones over the years. But he makes clear that Jones was a valuable source to the DIU given his role on campus. "He was well known on campus and he knew, being in the capacity he was, a lot of students."[103]

Undercover police officers who attended classes at Memphis State also were a ready source of information about campus activities. Eli Arkin insisted that a number of these officers were going to school for their own personal benefit and not as part of their assignment. But some officers clearly posed as students to create a more convincing persona. Marrell McCollough had done just that when he infiltrated the Invaders. Another, Byron "Gene" Townsend, a Vietnam veteran from Parsons, Tennessee, who operated most likely as "Agent 503," posed as a student to infiltrate several activist groups between 1969 and 1974.[104] Perhaps recognizing his value to the intelligence bureau as a veteran who would be able to quickly gain the trust of antiwar students, a recruiting officer recommended Townsend to Eli Arkin shortly after he joined the force in 1969. Townsend's transition from recruit to undercover officer was so fast that it was agreed that whenever his assignment ended, Townsend would take a new officer training class before going out on the street as a uniformed policeman.[105]

Once embedded at MSU, Townsend quickly became involved with peace and anti-draft activities. In the summer of 1969, a new series of weekly antiwar demonstrations organized by the Draft Resistance Union of Memphis and reminiscent of the silent peace vigils of 1967, took place at the Federal Building and First National Bank downtown. DRUM had caused consternation in Memphis with its opposition to the war and efforts to counsel draft-eligible men on their alternatives to military service. The prospect of antiwar organizing offended many. Reflecting a sentiment of many of her readers, a *Memphis Press-Scimitar* reporter, most likely Kay Pittman Black, contacted the Domestic Intelligence Unit after receiving DRUM literature in the mail and within thirty minutes had arranged to meet an officer and give him the material, presumably to support surveillance of the group.[106] Townsend was among the small group of protesters at the first DRUM demonstration. The weekly protests were modest, peaceful affairs. The forty or so people who participated read the names of Tennessee troops killed in action and marched along the sidewalk with placards that read "Food Not Napalm," "Up against the Wall Westmoreland," and "War Is Not Healthy for Children or Anything." Because the group only had six placards total, they took turns holding them and marching in front of the building. In addition to Townsend providing information from inside DRUM, DIU agents attended DRUM rallies, taking pictures of activists and producing reports that described the rallies and identified the participants. The FBI also tracked the group, relying on informant Ernest Withers's photographs of the activists associated with it.[107]

The discovery of a nexus between Black radicals and white activists in the city exacerbated MPD fears. Interracial alliances among leftists were neither unusual nor surprising in Memphis or anywhere else. But to law enforcement, such ties suggested a broad conspiracy of subversives who were scheming to destabilize the community and overturn the social order. The MPD knew Coby Smith, for instance, not merely because he was a cofounder of the Black Organizing Project and associated with the Invaders but because he had participated in antiwar demonstrations and was one of the few Black members of SSOC, a group the MPD and the FBI misidentified—or misunderstood—as a communist student group. Moreover, emerging links between SDS and the Invaders were a troubling possibility for the police and FBI alike, with the bureau concluding in 1969 that "a definite rapport and liaison has developed" between the two groups.[108] When FBI agent William Lawrence looked beyond SDS and the Invaders, he saw Black-white alliances as an emerging threat. "A loose 'united front,'" he wrote in 1969, "appears to be developing on the part of the DRUM movement . . . the SCLC loose affiliate . . . the Local 1733 of American Federation of State, County and Municipal Employees (AFSCME) faction, and the Tennessee Council on Human Relations faction headed by Baxton Bryant." Even his language—describing well-established civic and labor groups as "factions" forming a "united front"—betrayed a fear that these organizations were devious, dangerous, and allied with America's enemies.[109]

The specter of communist insurgency underlay Lawrence's concerns. He and his law enforcement peers subscribed to the commonly held view among southern whites that civil rights activists were communist dupes or collaborators and New Left students and antiwar protesters were revolutionaries in league with the country's adversaries. Memphis city leaders promoted this view as well, questioning the motives of civil rights protesters and conflating antiwar activism with communist sympathies. In 1970, for example, Mayor Henry Loeb labeled draft resisters as "scum" and "traitors" and warned one citizen that mass draft resistance would lead to "the Russians and Chinese taking over."[110]

Memphis authorities became especially alarmed when overtly communist organizations formed in the city in 1970. A group of white activists created a small chapter of the Young Workers Liberation League (YWLL), the successor organization to the W. E. B. Du Bois Clubs of America, the Communist Party's youth group. Perhaps a dozen people participated in the group, and they focused their efforts on labor organizing, opposing the war, and supporting civil rights campaigns. A small Communist Party chapter developed in Memphis as well, and it was active in civil rights efforts and in organizing support for the "Free Angela Davis" campaign, a global effort to get the activist released from jail. Two of the leftists, the married couple Mike Honey and Martha Allen, started the Memphis Community Bookstore and Center for Community Dialogue in the early 1970s, which became a meeting place for activists and the base for the regional office of the civil liberties organization the National Committee Against Repressive Legislation, which Honey ran.[111] Some of the activists involved with the YWLL and CP were drawn to the communist groups by an affinity for its ideology. With society beset by so many problems—war, white oppression, feckless political leaders—alternative systems and the possibility of radical reform or even revolution captivated many. For example, Mike Welch, a Memphis native who had gone to Southwestern for a time before dropping out to work in the movement full-time, initially activated over civil rights, but by 1969, his views had evolved and he was moving toward the CP.[112] His roommate, Nashville-native Allan Fuson, who had arrived in Memphis in 1969 to begin his alternative service as a conscientious objector, found socialist ideals and theories appealing and persuasive.[113] Others joined the YWLL or CP to connect with progressive whites in Memphis and were only marginally interested in communism itself. Dating back to her years as a Southwestern student in the late 1960s, Kathy Roop participated in SDS, the Memphis Welfare Rights Organization, and Citizens Opposed to Starvation Taxes, and she also worked as an organizer with the Distributive Workers of America. Initially galvanized by the war and civil rights, the YWLL and CP attracted her interest because "'they were the only ones standing up against racism.'"[114]

The YWLL and CP quickly drew law enforcement's attention. The possibility of resurgent communist organizing in Memphis, not two decades after William Lawrence had apprehended Junius Scales in the city, ensured FBI interest. The Memphis FBI gathered information from sources close to their targets. For instance, someone close to Mike Welch, possibly a family member or friend, told the bureau about his comings and goings from his mother's house in the summer of 1967.[115] Particularly significant was the spying done by Ernest Withers, who had befriended many of the young whites and whom they thought of as a father figure. Withers provided his FBI handler with a steady stream of information about the activists and their doings. The revelation that Withers was a paid informant who had spied on the activists was crushing to many. Kathy Roop suffered more than others from her association with

Withers. The photographer had provided the FBI with photos and information about her activities, and the circulation of this material disrupted her life for years. In the early 1970s, she was the victim of FBI and police harassment, as they monitored her activities and tracked her involvement in various organizations. In one incident, the police raided a party that she and another activist hosted to support the "Free Angela Davis" effort. In another, an assailant who Roop and her colleagues believed was either an informant or a white supremacist, destroyed her car with a grenade in an early-morning blast, and when the police arrived, they seemed disinclined to investigate, even suggesting that the car had caught fire on its own. The FBI and police campaign continued to reverberate in her life long after she had left Memphis and her participation in the YWLL and CP had ceased, the groundless surveillance prompting a federal agency to reject her for employment as a security risk.[116]

The MPD's intelligence unit also mobilized against the YWLL and CP and kept its surveillance regime in place until 1976, according to Capt. Patrick Ryan, who oversaw the intelligence bureau from 1973 until its dissolution in 1976.[117] The DIU viewed the young white activists as a threat not only because of their communist ties but because they were allied with the Invaders and had appeared at demonstrations with the group. Eli Arkin said the police saw the white activists as agitators and provocateurs who "were injecting themselves" into disputes in the city.[118] Through the early 1970s, the DIU maintained at least one paid informant inside the YWLL, and officers staked out the group's meetings at the Memphis Community Book Store, taking pictures of those coming and going from the building and investigating individuals associated with the group. Undercover officer Gene Townsend also infiltrated the organization. His association with activists at MSU in his guise as a student smoothed his path into the YWLL, and he remained involved with the group for several years. All of this surveillance, though, never yielded any evidence of wrongdoing or criminal activity by the YWLL. In the estimation of George Hutchinson, who became a deputy chief with oversight of the DIU starting in late 1973, the surveillance never produced any useful information. "The stuff that I read in regards to the Communist Party," he commented about the reports produced by Townsend and the informants, "I thought was really garbage."[119]

THE DISCOVERY OF POLICE SPYING IN MEMPHIS

Just as the intelligence unit discounted the differences among Black activist groups, lumping the Invaders and the NAACP together as a singular threat, it similarly ignored or was oblivious to distinctions between various organizational formations of white New Leftists. To a police department inclined to see all activists as disloyal or traitorous, New Leftists, like Black civil rights activists, needed to be monitored, tracked, investigated, and harassed in order to foil their plans and disrupt their plots. Gene Townsend, thanks to his cover as a Memphis State student, was central to the DIU's work. Friendly, affable, and easygoing, he readily connected with activist students and joined their organizations. When a chapter of the Vietnam Veterans Against the War emerged on campus, he was there. His involvement in the organization and his friendship with—and betrayal of—a student in the group ultimately led to the exposure of the MPD's surveillance activities and resulted in litigation, scandal, and the first agreement by a metropolitan police department anywhere in the country to cease all political surveillance work.

The VVAW, which started in 1967 in New York, distinguished itself from other war opponents by its members' service in Vietnam. The group garnered significant media attention—both positive and negative—and gained adherents around the country.[120] Eric Carter, a Memphis native and former marine, was one of the veterans who became involved in the MSU chapter. Its origins were in the coffee-fueled morning "bull" sessions Carter and his veteran friends regularly held in the student union. When conversation turned to the war, as it often did, nearly everyone opposed it because, Carter explained, "the things that were happening were not in our best interest."[121] The Memphis chapter was small, never numbering more than twenty or twenty-five, Carter recalls. But they made their presence felt by attending local antiwar demonstrations, where they carried placards announcing their status as veterans who opposed the war. "It wasn't the most, best organized group," Carter said, "but we did what we could locally." And the group gave the student veterans an outlet for their views beyond just sitting around talking about the war.[122]

Carter knew Gene Townsend as one of the veterans on campus who joined in conversations about the war and participated in the VVAW chapter. Although Townsend was a few years older than Carter, the two struck up a friendship and became, in Carter's recollection, "good buddies."[123] Carter's primary interest was the war, so he was surprised and a bit concerned that his friend participated in several other activist groups, including SDS and YWLL. His association with communists particularly worried Carter—"You shouldn't be doing that," he remembers cautioning Townsend.[124] But Townsend never raised suspicion that he was anything other than what he seemed, and his commitment to the VVAW appeared strong; at one point, he was among a group of VVAW activists arrested for leafleting. Throughout this time, though, he was feeding information to his MPD colleagues about the VVAW, including reporting on a strategy session with the VVAW attorneys after the leafleting arrest. The DIU may have had a particular interest in Carter himself because he had emerged as a campus leader. In addition to his work with the VVAW—the *Commercial Appeal* identified him as a regional director of the organization—he served as student government president in the 1973–74 school year. He made a positive impression on the MPD in this role by helping contain a streaking episode involving a large number of students. He remembers the police chief seeking him out afterward to thank him for helping control the situation, and Deputy Chief George Hutchinson later publicly praised him as a "fine student" and a "hell of a good guy" who "really knew how to keep students under control." But in the twisted logic that guided the police surveillance operation, Carter's prominence meant that this upstanding student leader was a target for any number of "bad actors" and thus needed to be watched. "You've got a young guy," Hutchinson explained, "who's a leader. And here's a group"—left vague and undefined by Hutchinson—"that we believe is planning some criminal activity. It could be this leader is going to be influenced the wrong way. So we had people watching his activities."[125]

Carter's friend Gene Townsend was watching the closest. But there wasn't much to see. Townsend's reports revealed nothing suspicious about his activities and certainly no evidence of criminal wrongdoing.[126] This hardly surprised Carter when he reflected on the spying many years later. "I didn't have any fear" of being spied on, he said, "because we weren't dangerous. As far as I was concerned, we weren't doing anything for which somebody ought to be alarmed." He also thought that Townsend may have tried to protect him by preventing his arrest at demonstrations and by never inviting him to SDS or YWLL meetings, where his appearance would have led to heightened MPD scrutiny and also put him on the FBI's radar. The two friends continued to work together in the VVAW until early 1975, when Townsend suddenly stopped attending class and dropped away from the group. Carter, confused and concerned about what had happened to his friend, soon learned from one of the communist activists that Townsend was a police officer. Hurt and disappointed, Carter went downtown to the police station in hopes of confronting Townsend. After waiting in the cafeteria and watching officers come and go, he spotted his friend: "Sure enough, here he comes, in uniform. And [I] said, 'you got to be shittin' me. How in the world—when did you do this?'" Apologizing profusely, Townsend responded, "'I've always been this. I've been part of a group called "Domestic Intelligence" . . . and I wasn't spying on you. We're friends. You weren't a target of ours, you're just . . . ancillary. We're friends.'" Carter accepted the apology, and the two remained friends. "Couple days later he came over to my house and had a beer. He came over two or three times." Once he had surfaced and given up his undercover identity, Townsend went into the uniformed patrol and continued his career at the MPD, eventually becoming a captain and serving for thirty-three years until his retirement in 2002. Although their friendship survived the revelation, at least until Carter graduated and moved away, the episode gnawed at Carter. On one level, his friend's betrayal saddened him: "It broke my heart that he lied to me all that time." But on another level, he was angry that the police had trained their surveillance weapons on him, a veteran who had served the country in war and was simply engaging in constitutionally protected political activities while pursuing his education. After he graduated, Carter recalled, "I get to thinking about this, and I said, 'bullshit.' . . . He's got to be reporting to somebody. There's got to be a file on this."[127]

Indeed, there was a file, and over two weeks in August 1976, Carter sent three letters to the department to request it. At one point, the MPD's legal advisor, Stephen Cohen, now a congressman representing Memphis's Ninth District in the House of Representatives, told Carter he needed to send a notarized letter before the police would consider his request. As the police deliberated, several officials handled Carter's file, including Eli Arkin, who said he only remembers seeing newspaper clippings about the streaking incident at MSU, and George Hutchinson, who said the file contained no evidence that Carter was involved in criminal activity. Clearly alarmed by this first ever request for a file from the secret intelligence unit, police leaders determined to conceal the file's contents even if they had to acknowledge its existence. In the first days of September 1976, before Cohen could render a legal opinion on whether Carter had a right to his file, Hutchinson ordered it destroyed, telling the press that he had done so because the file included informants' names—"sources who were giving us information about a criminal element we were trying to infiltrate." Left unsaid was that this "criminal element" was likely the VVAW, the only political organization in which Carter participated.[128]

The matter did not end there. On September 8, Cohen determined that the destruction of Carter's file was legal but urged the department to end the practice of keeping files on citizens. As the story that the police department had surveilled citizens and compiled files exploded in the press, MPD officials denied responsibility for authorizing the surveillance. Henry Lux, the police chief at the time Carter was under surveillance, said that approvals "came from a lower level than I was in." Jay Hubbard, who was police director in the early 1970s, said he was not involved but defended the work as an appropriate way to "defend the public" when the department faced those "with subversive if not outright revolutionary intents." Mayor Wyeth Chandler likewise denied knowledge, saying he had learned about the spying only from the newspapers.[129] But Chandler, an experienced and wily politician, undoubtedly recognized the danger the files posed to the department and to his leadership of the city. It was bad enough that the files' existence was now public knowledge, but untold damage could be done if their contents, replete as they were with surveillance photographs and undercover agents' reports, spilled into public view. He would not allow this to happen. Chandler quickly convened a meeting with the top leadership of the department, including Eli Arkin and Patrick Ryan from the intelligence bureau, and after a brief discussion ordered the files destroyed.[130]

The destruction prompted an ACLU lawsuit accusing the police of violating constitutional rights by spying on citizens for their political views. Although the crisis had started with his file, Carter did not want anything to do with the lawsuit, writing ACLU attorney Bruce Kramer, "I feel Mayor Chandler has successfully resolved the problem." Chandler, in fact, had contacted Carter at least once, worried that Carter would join the suit. But Carter's primary concern, as it was when he first sought his file, was to ensure he would be able to pursue his legal career. A law student in Houston at the time, he recalled telling Chandler, "Mayor, I'm trying to stay in law school and. . . . you guys are jamming me up."[131] The ACLU lawsuit thus proceeded without Carter. His absence from the case turned out not to matter. Deposition testimony from police officials and the unexpected discovery of documents that the police had failed to destroy painted a picture of a department with a long history of extensive spying and surveillance conducted with little oversight, dismissive if not unaware of constitutional concerns, and contemptuous of the leftists causes, from civil rights to antiwar, that animated Memphis activists. In 1978, worried about the possibility of an adverse court ruling, the city agreed to stop all political surveillance of protected constitutional activities, to prohibit the MPD or any other municipal agency from forming a unit to engage in political intelligence, and to ban the collection and maintenance of records and files on citizens. The agreement, formalized in a consent decree approved in federal district court, made Memphis the first city in the nation to agree to controls on police intelligence activities and made it a model for efforts to rein in Red Squads around the country.[132]

Until its discovery, the Memphis police department operated with impunity as it surveilled, harassed, and sought to undermine the work of activists in the city. Throughout the 1960s and 1970s, the police department's domestic intelligence operations, spearheaded by its Red Squad, used its vast powers to intimidate and abuse individuals and groups that dissented from the conservative, white supremacist status quo. While Memphis's Black civil rights activists initially took the brunt of this harassment, white activists emerged as targets of surveillance as social unrest intensified in Memphis over the war in Vietnam, the demands of organized labor, and the sharpening leftist critique of the capitalist order. Multiple fears gripped city officials: that the unrest that had roiled other communities that had experienced student activism would soon be visited upon Memphis; that communists were insidiously using the student movement to undermine the sociopolitical order; that white students and Black activists were collaborating to destroy the Memphis that they knew and loved. Driven by these fears, and with the firm support of the city's political leadership, the police moved to crack down on activism at Memphis State, local high schools, and wherever else it sprouted.

The ACLU lawsuit and resulting restraints on police surveillance distinguished Memphis from other locales where police spying operations went undetected or unchallenged. Police departments in communities around the country used, and often abused, their powers to target student activists and other leftists whom they considered subversive. Such conflating of dissent with subversion and radicalism revealed the fears of unrest that underlay surveillance programs. Like their federal and state counterparts, Red Squads saw civil rights and antiwar protesters as unpatriotic and under the control or influence of foreign forces whose ultimate goal was to destroy the nation's socioeconomic order. In southern cities like Memphis, the concerns took on a sharper edge given the existing white supremacist social structure. Any activism was perceived as threatening to the oppressive racial order that still prevailed in the region and therefore justified—necessitated, even—a strong police response. The Domestic Intelligence Unit in Memphis represented that city's response to the surge in activism. Two hundred miles to the east, the Nashville Police Department built its own surveillance infrastructure in response to the flourishing of activism there.

4

NASHVILLE

STUDENT NONVIOLENT COORDINATING COMMITTEE chairman Stokely Carmichael was a major national figure in early 1967. A staunch advocate of Black Power who alternately dazzled and frightened the national media with his erudite and sharply worded attacks on segregationists and their enablers, Carmichael led SNCC as it transformed itself from a biracial organization into an all-Black group that moved away from the integrationist, nonviolent ideals that had motivated the group at its founding in the wake of the 1960 sit-ins. His embrace of angry and aggrieved young African Americans who rejected Martin Luther King Jr.'s approach to civil rights made him a controversial figure and ensured that white southerners would be deeply worried were he to appear in their community. Such was the case in Nashville in April 1967, when Carmichael accepted an invitation from Vanderbilt University students to speak during a two-day symposium on campus along with other prominent national figures, including King, segregationist South Carolina senator Strom Thurmond, and Beat poet Allen Ginsberg.

The announcement that Carmichael would appear at the event caused a stir. Many whites reacted with shock, their response revealing their fear of him. The *Nashville Banner* newspaper editorialized against him, the American Legion post in the city called on the school to rescind his invitation, and the state coordinator for the John Birch Society suggested Carmichael should be tried for treason. Even the state legislature weighed in, with the Senate passing a resolution that scorned Carmichael as a "dangerous, unprincipled demagogue" who promotes anti-Americanism and spreads "racist poison" around the country. Backed by the university's leaders, however, the student organizers stood by their invitation, and the school and the city braced for his appearance. On April 8, over four thousand students—and more than seventy Nashville police officers—filled Memorial Gymnasium to hear Carmichael and the others.[1] Later that evening, after Carmichael had received a rousing ovation for a talk that skewered white liberals and the Black political establishment alike and that offered a vision of Black Power rooted in community improvement, a small dispute in a restaurant adjacent to the Fisk University campus spiraled into a four-day spasm of violence and confrontation between riot-clad police and primarily Black students that resulted in nearly a hundred arrests and tens of thousands of dollars in property damage.[2]

Federal investigators later determined that the aggressive response to the disturbance by police officers already on edge due to Carmichael's visit helped to turn a spontaneous and unplanned gathering of students into a wider conflict.[3] In the aftermath of the crisis, however, city officials laid the blame squarely on Carmichael and the city's activist community, accusing them of plotting the disorder and charging that Carmichael's incendiary rhetoric had lit the fuse to what amounted to a revolt. Information gleaned from police surveillance activity underlay these accusations. In the weeks leading up to Carmichael's appearance, the police, through an intelligence unit vested with broad autonomy, had kept close watch on activists in the city. Local SNCC members were an obvious target. But the police also singled out for surveillance white activists, particularly students associated with the Southern Student Organizing Committee. Intelligence officers believed that SSOC provided crucial logistical and financial support to SNCC and that the two groups were conspiring to plan a riot timed to coincide with Carmichael's visit. In their zeal to castigate Carmichael and other activists for the mayhem, the police revealed that they had monitored meetings, utilized informants, and collaborated with the FBI to gather information and undermine leftist activists.

The 1967 episode was not an isolated instance of police surveillance in Nashville. Since 1964, the police had operated a feared Red Squad that worked to monitor and disrupt activism in the city. While police officials claimed that they sought to exterminate extremism of all types, the intelligence unit's work overwhelmingly focused on groups and individuals that promoted civil rights and that allegedly had communist ties. Believing a nexus existed between

Black civil rights activists and white political radicals made the situation more urgent in the eyes of the police. When white students in Nashville founded SSOC in 1964, just days after the intelligence unit itself was created, the police department took note. As a white student group, SSOC was of concern to the police because it suggested a growing dissatisfaction among white youth with the political and social status quo. The revolt against authority that the Berkeley Free Speech Movement represented provided a stark example to authorities across the South of the disruption and chaos that could occur if they allowed student activism to grow unchecked. Moreover, as the white students' activism grew to encompass opposition to the war in Southeast Asia, the police feared the specter of anti-American, communist-tied white students making common cause with Black nationalists to destabilize the peace and prosperity that white Nashvillians prized.

Such fears fueled the rise of an intrusive surveillance program undertaken by the Nashville police that reached its apotheosis with Stokely Carmichael's 1967 visit. The crisis that followed his appearance and the police's surveillance-based accusations against him and other activists catapulted Nashville into the national headlines. But the violence and destruction also served to obscure the longer, broader history of police surveillance in the city. Nashville's Red Squad had emerged several years before the 1967 conflict and continued after the spotlight had turned elsewhere. Additionally, the unit's focus on SSOC made clear that the police saw risk in allowing a modestly sized organization of white students to operate unimpeded in Nashville. SSOC was not SNCC, let alone the more notorious Students for a Democratic Society. But police in Nashville were all too eager to see connections, real and imagined, among various groupings, heightening their fears that a full-fledged revolt was metastasizing on the city's campuses. The attention that the intelligence unit showered on these groups, though, was vastly disproportionate to their size or strength. As the local ACLU chapter leader put it, these groups "have limited financial resources and low membership lists. They certainly don't work together in any Communist conspiracy."[4] But it was their potential for disruption that galvanized the police to act. Aware of protests that had engulfed communities from Birmingham to Boston earlier in the 1960s, the Nashville police were determined to choke off a crisis before one emerged. That they failed to do so in 1967 only heightened their sense of urgency and provided justification for the intrusive surveillance regime they built to undercut student activism in the city.

THE "NASHVILLE WAY" AND THE NASHVILLE POLICE

Set in the gently rolling hills of the Tennessee central highlands and built around the winding Cumberland River, Nashville was a medium-sized, regionally oriented state capital in the mid-twentieth century. While important as the center of state government, Nashville's political significance did not extend to other realms, as its economy, social scene, and cultural cachet—despite its self-proclaimed title as "Music City U.S.A.," thanks to its connections to country music—suffered in comparison to other Mid-South cities such as Atlanta, Birmingham, and Memphis. Nashville, though, did not seem to be in a big hurry to catch up to its peers. On a reporting visit to the city in 1951, a New York journalist commented that he found people—white people, he meant—generally suspicious of change. "The true Nashvillian is more interested in living as his grandfather did than in having his city a model of civic progress." As one local told him, "We have always liked the way life was lived in Nashville, and there is a feeling here that what is called progress too often replaces something that was better."[5]

The city that Nashville had become owed much to its fortuitous geographic location. Easy access to the Cumberland River and the creation of the Louisville and Nashville Railroad in 1859 made Nashville a transit and distribution center for the region. It also made it a strategically valuable target for Union troops during the Civil War, and they captured the city in 1862. In the decades after the war, retail businesses and wholesalers leveraged the transportation infrastructure to expand into surrounding areas. Industries based on the region's natural resources, such as timber, coal, and cotton, also grew during these years and helped draw both white and Black migrants to the city in search of opportunity. Nashville's industrial economy, however, lagged behind its regional peers throughout the first half of the twentieth century. Despite periods of industrial growth, particularly around the world wars, the city was less nimble in moving to exploit its regional manufacturing advantages—

natural resources, a low-wage, anti-union environment—than other Mid-South cities, and by 1930, industry employed fewer than one-third of the city's workers. Unable to rely on industry to drive the economy meant that the city had to look elsewhere for growth. This proved fortuitous because it enabled the city to prosper by developing a diversified economy that built on long-standing strengths in service-oriented businesses. For instance, Nashville became a center of religious publishing, as Baptists, Methodists, and Presbyterians produced Bibles and schoolbooks in the city. And Nashville celebrated itself as the "Athens of the South" owing to the many institutions of higher education that served striving Black and white students alike. These included the overwhelmingly white Vanderbilt University, George Peabody College for Teachers, and Scarritt College and the historically Black Fisk University, Meharry Medical College, and Tennessee Agricultural & Industrial State (A&I) University. This well-developed higher education infrastructure fueled the city's educational renaissance and turned out knowledge workers to meet the demands of the postwar world. Thus, publishing and education, along with insurance, health care, retail, radio, and banking—the "Wall Street of the South" was another moniker the city embraced—compensated for a less highly developed industrial economy and provided sturdy foundations for growth in the post–World War II years.[6]

By 1950, nearly a half-million people called Nashville and surrounding Davidson County home, attracted by the prospect of stable employment and new opportunities in a postwar economy powered by the burgeoning service economy and facilitated by technological advances, such as the interstate highway system, which put Nashville at the crossroads of three major highways. African Americans made up an increasingly significant stream of the migrants making their way to the city; in 1960, Nashville's Black population stood at a record high 43 percent. As in many other southern cities in the era of Jim Crow, race starkly divided the urban landscape of Nashville. Whites remained in firm control of the downtown business district and also dominated the suburban communities that extended to the south and west of the city center, encompassing the Vanderbilt area and beyond, toward the affluent and exclusive enclave of Belle Meade. Although African Americans increasingly were moving to suburban areas south and east of downtown, North Nashville remained the historic home of the city's Black community. Poverty and blight shaped some parts of North Nashville, but more middle-class sections developed as Fisk, Meharry, and Tennessee A&I anchored many African American professionals to the area. Race similarly shaped the contours of daily life in the city. African Americans endured segregated and usually inferior public accommodations and found limited employment opportunities outside of Black-controlled institutions and businesses.[7] More opportunities existed in the political world thanks to the fractious nature of white politics. The political machine that ran the city in the early decades of the century, led from 1923 to 1938 by Mayor Hilary Howse, though not as totally controlling as Boss Crump's in Memphis, utilized inducements and coercion to cultivate the Black vote—promises of modest improvements to city services and paying poll taxes for Black supporters were joined to more aggressive efforts that deployed the police to get Black men from the saloon to the voting booth on Election Day.[8]

The franchise created limited space for Black advancement, including the election of two African Americans to the city council in 1951, without threatening white control of the city.[9] Moreover, the white elite maintained a firm grip on the levers of economic and political power in Nashville and believed that its enlightened leadership had ensured peaceful race relations that served the best interests of citizens of both races. Their high self-regard on matters of race came to be known as the "Nashville Way," a fusion of local pride and racial paternalism that emphasized civility, good manners, and especially, moderation as the keys to the city's racial success. These whites rejected extremism, whether in the form of Klan-inspired violence to enforce segregationist norms or direct action protests by civil rights activists aimed at toppling these very norms, as destabilizing and threatening, a blot on the image of the city they had cultivated. The moderate whites who embraced such views considered the absence of racial discord or conflict as a sign of racial progress and contentedness. African Americans, of course, would dissent from any suggestion that the outward appearances of racial peace and stability was indicative of progress on civil rights and racial justice concerns. At bottom, moderate whites were moderate only in their actions, not their views; they were segregationists who differed in style rather than substance from whites who committed acts of racial violence. They may have thought that segregation would one day disappear, but they were not about to rock the boat to speed that day's arrival. As one historian of the city summarized, "Moderation meant a more or less genuine sympathy for black advancement undergirded by deeply felt assumptions of black inferiority and white superiority." Mayor Beverly Briley put this more baldly in 1968, intertwining the most offensive of racial epithets with a paternalistic sense of superiority and care: "The 'n——s' think that I don't understand them, but I do."[10]

As the postwar era progressed, Nashville's fate became increasingly intertwined with that of the rest of Davidson County. Population growth in the county surpassed the city's, driven by cheap suburban housing and the allure of open spaces. Nashville, meanwhile, saw population growth slow and even reverse thanks to the white flight to the suburbs, and the city was unable to use annexation to add to its population and tax base because it lacked the necessary legislative support for such action. Davidson and its municipalities faced their own growth-induced challenges, as the infrastructure needs of the quickly growing county communities led to overcrowded roads, overworked sewer systems, and under-resourced fire and police services. With separate city and county governments facing different yet interconnected challenges, a push toward metropolitan consolidation gained strength in the 1950s and ultimately resulted in voters approving, in 1962, the merger of Nashville and Davidson County into a single metropolitan entity. The new government that took office in 1963 was led by Mayor Beverly Briley, the former head of the county government, who was a strong proponent of consolidation. The new entity covered more than five hundred square miles and infused many with the hope that a new era of economic growth and civic pride had dawned.[11]

Nashville boosters' optimism for the region's future depended on an ability to manage race relations in the city. But their capacity to do so faced a direct challenge from the emergence of the lunch counter sit-ins of 1960 and the subsequent years of rising civil rights agitation. The burgeoning movement, initiated and powered by Black college students in the city, exposed the simmering discontent among African Americans with segregationist norms and thereby threatened white Nashvillians' smug satisfaction about the supposed superiority of the Nashville Way. Additionally, the Black students' nonviolent direct action campaigns captured the imagination of white college students in Nashville and inspired them to join the cause.[12] As the sit-in movement morphed into a broader assault on segregationist barriers across the city in a campaign that civil rights leaders called "Operation Open City," white students became a visible component of the demonstrations and protests, including a bold interracial freedom march through downtown in March 1963.[13] Later that year, white students from Scarritt, Peabody, and Vanderbilt undertook a picketing drive against the segregated Campus Grill restaurant in their West End neighborhood that ultimately resulted in its desegregation, and in 1964, they conducted a "sip-in" at Morrison's Cafeteria, another segregationist holdout. The white students sought to formalize and expand their work on behalf of civil rights by creating the Joint University Council on Human Relations, and in April 1964, the group was the driving force behind the creation of the Southern Student Organizing Committee. Founded at an Easter weekend meeting on the Vanderbilt campus of white student activists from across the region, SSOC developed into the leading white progressive student organization in the South. SSOC was especially active in Nashville, where the group maintained its headquarters. SSOC's activities in the city not only threatened to further erode the stability that city leaders cherished but brought the group into conflict with a police department tasked with suppressing dissent.[14]

Like their counterparts in Memphis, the police in Nashville long had acted as a bulwark of the status quo, defending the city's image as a place of order, safety, and cleanliness. In 1942, when the war-fueled growth of the city's military population brought increased prostitution and a surge in venereal disease cases that risked sullying the carefully crafted image of the city its leaders had relentlessly promoted, the police force created its own vice squad as well as joined with the FBI to establish a special unit to enforce the May Act, which criminalized vice activities around military installations.[15] The police also served as guardians of the segregationist order. It had a fearsome reputation for brutality among African Americans, who understood that the smallest misstep could prompt a violent response from white officers. After an unpleasant encounter with the police, a Black Nashvillian captured this sentiment succinctly: "I knew I was in the right but I knew that the officer wanted an excuse to hit me or shoot me, so I kept quiet." The hiring of the city's first Black police officers in 1948, at least partly in response to a petition drive organized by a Black political organization, did not quell allegations of police abuse.[16]

With the merger of the city and county governments in 1963, the Nashville

Police Department and the Davidson County Sheriff's Office combined to form the new Metropolitan Nashville Police Department (MNPD), with jurisdiction over the entire area. The new department faced the immediate task of integrating two different work cultures, policies, and approaches to policing into one cohesive entity. Complicating the task was the fact that the Nashville Police Department was in turmoil at the time of the merger. Morale was low, discipline was poor, officers had been involved in bar fights and arrested for crimes ranging from bootlegging to conspiracy, and several of them faced indictments as the result of bribery investigations. To lead the new department, Mayor Beverly Briley named Hubert O. Kemp, a veteran of the Nashville force, as the first police chief of the metropolitan department. Kemp quickly set to work to raise morale and professionalize the department, yet relations with the Black community remained strained. Throughout 1963 and 1964, Black citizens lodged numerous complaints against officers in the department, ranging from harassment of motorists to unwarranted searches to hurling racial epithets at people. The police also faced accusations of heavy-handed and violent tactics in response to the civil rights demonstrations in April 1964.[17]

One step Kemp took was to assign increasing responsibility to an ambitious, up-and-coming young officer, John Sorace, who would go on to be the most important official in the development of the department's intelligence operations in the 1960s and 1970s. Sorace was a Brooklyn native who arrived in Nashville in 1959 to pursue a graduate degree in physics at Vanderbilt. While he occasionally wore a beard and frequented The Tulip Is Black, a beatnik coffeehouse—even working there for a week—he had a developing interest in law enforcement, which prompted him to approach the Davidson County Sheriff's Office about possible opportunities. Without experience, there was little he was qualified to do. However, he had asked about working with juvenile offenders, which led to his appointment to an unpaid position as a youth aid officer. The precise nature of his work in this position is unclear, but in at least one instance, he joined the questioning of an underage suspect who had alleged police abuse. Sorace enjoyed the work, and he began to drift away from his academic pursuits. By 1962, he had parlayed his volunteer assignment into a full-time position as an investigator with the sheriff's office and then transitioned to the new metropolitan force as a detective. His work investigating drug cases brought him to the attention of Kemp, who saw him as a bright and competent officer who could help him remake the department.[18]

Kemp's support fueled Sorace's rapid rise through the ranks. In mid-1963, he assigned Sorace to lead what one of the local newspapers, the *Nashville Tennessean,* called a "a super-secret investigation" into public corruption cases that exposed financial misdeeds in city offices. Among the investigative techniques he deployed were "the use of cameras and tape recorders," the other major daily newspaper, the *Nashville Banner,* reported.[19] Indeed, he frequently turned to technological devices during his nascent police career. Among officers, he was well known to have "a fondness for using tape recorders in interrogating witnesses," according to the *Tennessean.*[20] His technological savvy appealed to Kemp, who, as part of his modernization efforts, won Mayor Briley's support to create an Intelligence and Security Division within the department—a Red Squad. Kemp tapped the twenty-six-year-old Sorace to lead the new unit, declaring that he had the "education requirements, the temperament and the training for the job."[21] Sorace's quick ascent in the department—to lead the unit, Kemp promoted him to temporary lieutenant exactly one year after he joined the force as a patrolman—rankled others on the force, some of whom disparagingly called him "the Bug" in reference to his new intelligence role. Rumors spread that he was a federal agent sent to spy on police and city leaders. And two city councilmen charged that the selection of such a young, untested officer damaged morale in the department. His alliance with Kemp made him enemies as well among those who resisted Kemp's leadership. Sorace shrugged off such complaints, telling the Vanderbilt student newspaper that others were resentful of him because "I didn't operate like they did and carried a briefcase."[22] In the space of a year, Sorace had emerged as a center of power in the MNPD, with the strong support of both Kemp and Briley. As Briley later enthused, "John Sorace is the most brilliant young man I know. . . . I love that boy."[23]

Kemp ensured that the Intelligence Division would be well staffed. He authorized the transfer of two officers to the division at its founding and two more a few months later. Sorace personally selected these officers.[24] One was Robert Hill, a well-regarded African American officer who would become Sorace's most important collaborator in the Intelligence Division.[25] A former navy frogman and professional boxer who hailed from the town of Sparta, a hundred miles east of Nashville, Hill had joined the force in 1959, after studying political science at Fisk and Tennessee A&I. In 1964, a few weeks after the creation of the Intelligence Division, the local press celebrated his undercover work in breaking up a local marijuana ring. Hill, along with another officer, Benedict Cook, conspired with police leaders to fake their own firing from the force for "conduct unbecoming an officer," a move that persuaded the drug ringleaders that the two were no longer policemen and were committed to working with the drug operation. They even managed to convince their own families that they had lost their jobs. With their cover in place, the two officers joined the dealers to buy and sell marijuana, activity that other officers monitored and which led to the arrest of the ring's leaders. Hill's undercover work and the publicity it received enhanced his reputation in the department—he soon was promoted to sergeant—and before the year was over, Sorace had drafted him into the Intelligence Division.[26]

From its inception, the Intelligence and Security Division had wide-ranging investigative authority. Mayor Briley said the impetus for the creation of the division was a recommendation he had received from the National Association of Chiefs of Police. City leaders emphasized the unit's crime fighting potential. Strong budgetary support from Kemp enabled the division to acquire new technical tools and equipment to conduct surveillance and gather information in pursuit of criminals in the city and county. Sorace's enthusiasm for cameras, tape recorders, and listening devices lent a scientific sheen to the division's work.[27] The division held an expansive view of what constituted criminal activity. While Sorace and his team investigated organized crime, burglary rings, and petty corruption within the department, such as allegations of a traffic ticket fixing scheme, they also trained their sights on the individuals and groups that appeared to pose a threat to Nashville's cherished if fading reputation for racial tranquility, political moderation, and polite civic discourse. Such a perspective meant that groups or people espousing views outside the bounds of mainstream norms—"extremists," in the lexicon of the day—could face scrutiny from the Intelligence Division.[28]

A sensitivity to extremism suggested that political ideology did not play a role in the division's work—it pursued supposed threats across the political spectrum. Indeed, in 1965, the division won praise for its work surveilling Klan activity in the city, including a rally that was a point of embarrassment to city leaders. Sorace and his team quickly identified the rally's organizers and dispatched agents to attend the meeting, where they took "hundreds of photographs" that enabled them to identify many of the participants. The division's work helped stymie the Klan's efforts to build support in the area and prompted Mayor Briley to praise Sorace's team for "know[ing] more about members of the Klan here than some of the Klansmen."[29] The intelligence squad's response to the Klan, though, obscures the fact that it spent the vast majority of its time and effort investigating, monitoring, and thwarting the activities of social justice advocates, opponents of the war, and others on the political Left. In the years after its creation, intelligence officers spent little time worrying about the Klan not merely because the group was a shriveling, diminished entity but because they saw leftist activists as a greater threat to community peace and order. The dissenting views of civil rights activists and war opponents fell outside community norms and therefore constituted a challenge to the Nashville Way. Because more white students were joining activist groups and speaking out, they became targets for the Intelligence Division.

Civil rights were of particular interest to the Intelligence Division. The 1960 sit-ins had inaugurated years of protests against the continued segregation of public accommodations in Nashville, and the police had struggled to corral the movement and keep the peace. In some instances, the police unleashed violence against unarmed, peaceful demonstrators, including white students, such as during protests at segregated eateries in April and May 1964, which occurred shortly after the Intelligence Division's creation. In the aftermath of these protests, the department prioritized preparing for future unrest. To better understand and respond to community concerns, the department announced that it would conduct a study of the civil rights movement in Nashville since the 1930s, although there is no evidence that it ever produced a report. Additionally, Sorace and other officers traveled to a New York conference called "Community and Racial Crises" and a Boston gathering of police from across the country focused on the challenges that civil rights and civil disorders created for law enforcement. The consensus among the police at the Boston meeting was that metro police departments should form intelligence units to track groups in their cities, thus validating the creation of Nashville's squad. Reflecting an awareness that such work could tread close to infringing upon constitutional rights, the officers cautioned that these units "must not seek to destroy the right of association or violate the civil liberties of the members of the various groups and organizations" they monitor.[30]

Communists—or suspected communists—also drew the attention of the Intelligence Division. Like police officials and white city leaders around the region, those in Nashville readily associated civil rights with international communism, typically arguing that communists and fellow travelers had duped the local Black community to protest segregationist ordinances and customs. Mayor Briley, for instance, insisted that civil rights demonstrations like those Nashville had repeatedly experienced were part of a national conspiracy to destabilize the country, and he claimed that Sorace had photographic evidence that three communists had come to Nashville to lead protests in 1963. Such charges neatly weaved together fears of communist infiltration with the assumption that outside agitators were the cause of disorder and disruption. It did not take many communists or outsiders to stir trouble, which meant the community—and the police—must be ever vigilant. "There are very few real Communists in this country," Briley argued. "But they maneuver their way into influence in organizations. Just one in 10,000 persons can create a great deal of havoc." Fortunately for Nashville, Sorace's unit closely monitored these dangerous individuals. As Briley explained, the intelligence unit "had assembled an extensive file on Communists and their activities in demonstrations" in Nashville.[31]

As in Memphis, the Intelligence Division developed an elaborate record-keeping system to segregate most of the information it gathered from the regular police files. While the division's records contained innocuous material, such as newspaper and magazine clippings, they also included evidence of the unit's use of tactics that were unsavory and potentially illegal. Such contents provided motivation for separating these files from the department's central records. Warrantless surveillance, the reliance on informants, and the use of undercover officers to infiltrate activist groups drove Sorace and his team to shield the division's work from potential discovery. By maintaining control of its files, the division would limit the number of police officials with access to the records—and thus limit potential leaks—and, more important, would protect the files from the prying eyes of the courts or the press.[32] An unusual 1967 memo written by a sheriff officer from Jefferson County, Alabama, after a secret meeting he held with Sorace in a Nashville hotel room, highlighted the importance Sorace attached to ensuring the secrecy of the files. Jefferson County, where the city of Birmingham is located, was a frequent site of civil rights protests, and the sheriff's office had sought the meeting with Sorace to learn how Nashville's intelligence operation had worked to control protests there. In their discussion, Sorace told the visiting sheriff that his officers took great care to conceal the identities of its confidential informants, including using symbols rather than names when referring to them. Additionally, "certain very confidential matters are not filed in the regular file but are maintained by Captain Sorace as his own personal property," the sheriff wrote. Though Sorace denied the charge when the memo surfaced many years later, he acknowledged that he occasionally took files home to review. With its files protected and its sources and methods unknown to most in the department, the Intelligence Division operated outside the normal bounds of accountability. The division, Sorace told the Alabama sheriff, "was free from any interference or questioning by any superior officer . . . with the exception of the chief of police." The division's structure, sources, and secrecy were all key to its success. As Sorace put it, the memo approvingly notes, the intelligence squad "had been of great use to prevent the police department and mayor from being embarrassed, trapped, and unprepared when certain groups endeavored to promote causes."[33]

THE INTELLIGENCE DIVISION AND LEFTIST STUDENTS

The Intelligence Division received a dose of publicity for its 1965 investigation of the Klan—opposition to the Klan was a sure way for white elites to demonstrate their moderation on race issues—but otherwise operated outside the spotlight as it investigated radical political organizing. Mayor Briley alluded to the division's work in this area when he lauded it in 1966 for uncovering information about allegedly subversive local movements, thereby enabling the city "to ward off potential trouble before it starts."[34] The sources of such potential trouble were not hard to identify. The Student Nonviolent Coordinating Committee was an obvious source of concern given its reputation for protest activity and its increasingly aggressive stance toward the white power structure across the South. The group's turn toward Black Power in 1966, which catapulted Stokely Carmichael into the chair's position and led to a purge of whites from the group, marked SNCC as a dangerous and potentially disruptive presence wherever it appeared.[35] In Nashville, the group had supporters at Fisk and Tennessee A&I, and the rise of a city-wide chapter ensured that the Intelligence Division would keep a wary eye on the group.[36]

The Southern Student Organizing Committee was another seemingly subversive formation that merited observation. The group's orientation toward white students, which became more pronounced over time, particularly after SNCC turned away from interracialism, made it a unique threat to Nashville city leaders. While the group was active on predominantly white campuses in such places as Atlanta, Charlottesville, Gainesville, and Little Rock, its home was Nashville. From its headquarters in a house on Portland Avenue, it published newsletters and magazines, promoted the activism of white students throughout the region, organized actions in the city, and coordinated with other groups, including SNCC and the Southern Conference Educational Fund. SSOC had a long, intimate history with both organizations. SNCC was the group that several SSOC founders had joined when they first became involved in the movement, and the groups maintained close fraternal ties once the students created SSOC. SCEF, based in Louisville, Kentucky, and the successor organization to the Southern Conference on Human Welfare, provided funding and mentorship. The young white activists were particularly close to SCEF leaders Anne and Carl Braden, the battle-scarred veterans of the southern movement who had been fighting for civil rights since most of the white students were toddlers and who long had faced allegations of being communists or at least fellow travelers; Carl Braden was convicted of contempt of Congress for refusing to testify when called before the House Un-American Activities Committee.[37] The ties among these groups were not unusual; operating in often inhospitable if not downright hostile environments, they turned to one another for support and comfort. The mutual aid they provided each other, though, took on a sinister glow from the perspective of a police unit inclined to see such connections as evidence of conspiratorial intent.

If SSOC's association with SNCC and SCEF signaled to white officials that it was in league with Black radicals and communists, its involvement in activist causes in the city also invited scrutiny. SSOC activists joined interracial demonstrations against segregated facilities and businesses in Nashville and distinguished itself from other groups by promoting Black equality among whites. Its outreach to white Nashvillians extended to issues beyond civil rights. In 1966, for example, SSOC activists led an organizing campaign in the overwhelmingly white North Nashville neighborhood of Cheatham. The activists, several of whom moved into the neighborhood, sought to help residents campaign for economic improvements and expanded city services.[38] The group also sought to build opposition in Nashville to the Vietnam War, a position it had steadily come to embrace as the American role in the conflict grew. SSOC activists helped create the Nashville Committee for Alternatives to the War in Vietnam and the Draft Resistance Union of Metropolitan Nashville, and they joined or led teach-ins, anti-draft leafleting, and public protests. Two actions, in particular, drew a sharp police response. In July 1966, SSOC members Don Boner, Ed Hamlett, and Jody Palmour were among the seven antiwar activists who launched a planned five-day fast and vigil at the city's War Memorial Auditorium across from the state capitol in response to the bombing of Haiphong and Hanoi. At first, the police merely observed the vigil from a distance. But as it continued into a fourth day and drew visits from supporters, curious onlookers, and occasional hecklers, officers moved in to stop it. They arrested the fasters and a dozen others who had congregated there, dragging Palmour and several others down the auditorium stairs to awaiting police cars.[39] Then, in a particularly notorious action in March 1967, the group staged a protest when President Johnson came to Nashville to deliver a speech at the capitol. SSOC activists led more than two dozen demonstrators in a protest outside the statehouse as the president spoke inside to assembled dignitaries, and when he departed, one of the activists, Brian Heggen, brazenly threw himself in the road to try to block the president's departing limousine. The vehicle evasively drove around him, and he and two colleagues who tried to join him, Janet Dewart and Shirley Newton, were swiftly hauled off by the police.[40]

The overwhelming show of force for the president foreshadowed the department's response to Stokely Carmichael's visit to the city three weeks later. Just as with the president's appearance, police officials believed radical elements in Nashville were plotting a violent campaign to sow discord and chaos in the city and that Carmichael's appearance would be the catalyst for action. As a result, police leaders mobilized the department to respond to the slightest provocation. A disturbance at a restaurant adjacent to the Fisk campus on the night of Carmichael's talk that drew a large crowd of students thus propelled the police to action, as officers believed this was the beginning of a coordinated action to start a melee. The disturbance, in fact, had nothing to do with Carmichael's visit. But with riot police at the ready, police leaders sent them into action when the incident occurred, a move that researchers for the Kerner Commission concluded "triggered the general violence which followed.[41]

The Intelligence Division played a pivotal role in priming the department for action. For months leading up to the spring event at Vanderbilt, Sorace's officers had stepped up the surveillance of SNCC and SSOC amid concerns that they each were adopting more radical and extreme positions.[42] The extent of the Intelligence Division's efforts became apparent in the months after the unrest thanks to testimony Sorace gave before two congressional committees and during a federal trial in which SNCC accused city officials of conspiring to limit their rights of free speech and assembly. Sorace used these platforms to give the police version of the April events, a version based on the Intelligence Division's surveillance operations. Sorace claimed that the conflict was the result of a premeditated conspiracy crafted in secret meetings by hate-mongering, anti-American Black extremists and their communist-linked white allies, many from outside Nashville, who had duped and manipulated the local community into rioting. In his telling, the activists were a cancer on the community whose only interest was upsetting the city's delicate racial harmony and stirring dissent. "It has been most difficult to see in the last few years the work that the so-called civil rights groups, such as SNCC and SSOC, have done in the area of civil rights," he told the Senate Permanent Subcommittee on Investigations, led by John L. McClellan of Arkansas. They have "turned completely to anti-U.S. government work in terms of the draft, in terms of the war in Vietnam," he charged. "This is the central theme that occupies these groups' attention. . . . Not civil rights or human rights, but these anti–U.S. Government themes."[43] Sorace's appearances made him a minor celebrity in Nashville and won him plaudits from business elites and the influential, segregationist

Nashville Banner publisher James "Jimmy" Stahlman. But his public remarks also revealed the tactics the Intelligence Division had deployed against those it considered subversives and radicals—SNCC, especially, but also SSOC and SCEF. To an Intelligence Division steeped in Cold War paranoia and fear about the dangers that lurked within the polity, each group represented a dire threat to the community's well-being.

Sorace's unit maintained close and wide-ranging surveillance of activists in the city. It included gathering newspaper articles, flyers, newsletters, and other published material put out by activists or in which they were quoted. The assumption that SNCC and SSOC were in some fashion tied to communists meant that division officers also collected "all known communist publications."[44] But deciphering their meaning was another story. "We nonexperts in the field of communism, we local police officers attempting to understand this [faced a challenge]," Sorace told McClellan's subcommittee. Yet determining the specific differences between, say, Chinese Communists and Cuban Communists was less important than the mere fact that the activists were drawn to a foreign ideology, thus bolstering the charge that they were anti-American.[45]

Beyond the written word, intelligence officers tracked the activists' comings and goings, particularly their interactions with one another. Physical surveillance of SNCC and SSOC picked up in late 1966 and early 1967. The unit began monitoring SNCC meetings after receiving a tip that the group was targeting Nashville for violence. It extended its surveillance to SSOC meetings, concerned that the two groups were coordinating to cause disruptions in Nashville. The division also conducted surveillance of activists' homes and their churches, seeking to keep tabs on their movements across the city.[46] Such close monitoring was necessary because Sorace believed the activists were plotting in secret against the city. Indeed, he repeatedly accused the groups of secretive behavior, implying that their meetings, especially when held together, were a sign of their nefarious intent. The local activists were involved in "secret types of operations . . . and very probably, they were planning violence for our community," he charged at the federal trial. Vague as these concerns were, they prompted the Intelligence Division to cast its net broadly as it surveyed the activist landscape. In addition to SNCC and SSOC, the squad also focused on SCEF, the Students for a Democratic Society, the Revolutionary Action Movement, and the Nashville Committee for Alternatives to War in Vietnam, all for the purpose of exposing what Sorace told members of the McClellan subcommittee was the dangerous "pattern of . . . interlock between the various organizations."[47]

The officers who watched the activists' meetings frequently photographed the attendees as they arrived and departed. The pictures they took, usually surreptitiously, helped investigators connect the dots among organizations. When SSOC students attended an SNCC meeting or SCEF leaders joined an SSOC discussion, the pictures served as photographic evidence of their ill intent. Bob Russell, a member of the intelligence squad who joined Sorace and Hill at the McClellan subcommittee hearing, told the senators of surveilling several meetings prior to the April unrest. He produced photos taken of one meeting at the SSOC house and identified members of SSOC, SCEF, and SNCC in the pictures, including Don Boner, Brian Heggen, and Sherry Myers of SSOC; Robert Analavage, Carl Braden, and Margaret McSurely of SCEF; and Cooley Diaz, Willie Ricks, and George Washington Ware of SNCC. The police treated Braden's presence—who arrived after the others, suggesting to Russell that he did not want to be seen—as the key to understanding what was happening in the city. The intelligence officers concluded that Braden used SCEF to direct SSOC and SNCC toward violence. With SCEF serving as the "parent organization," the officers believed that the groups hatched "Operation Nashville" to train Black youth in martial arts and the use of weapons in order to attack white businesses and start a riot. Secret meetings, extremist rhetoric, communist involvement—all pointed to a conspiracy, and the police believed it had the photographic evidence to prove it. As Hill testified before the Senate Judiciary Committee headed by Mississippi's James Eastland, "We had quite a bit of subversive activities going on before the riots." Sorace was blunter: "These are people working together to perpetrate terrible things."[48]

The use of civilian informants was another critical element of the Intelligence Division's surveillance efforts. Sorace trumpeted the division's human intelligence sources as key to its successes in his congressional testimony while taking care to shield their identity, even when Senator Edward Kennedy pressed him on the subject during the Eastland committee hearing. In one example, he said a tip the department had received from an informant in 1966 alerted the police to SNCC's plans to target Nashville for violence. In another, informant reporting underlay Sorace's allegation that a federally funded summer program for Black youth was being used to teach children "hatred of the white man."[49] The Intelligence Division had an informant reporting on SSOC as well in 1967. Bill Doss, who had suddenly showed up at the SSOC office in the first half of the year, later said he was an "undercover operator" for the Intelligence Division whom officers had tasked to infiltrate SSOC in order to taint the group's reputation in the city. As part of this effort, he took publicity information the SSOC office had received about an upcoming talk at Vanderbilt by the Communist Party USA national youth director, Mike Zagarell, and delivered it to the office of the *Nashville Banner*. The paper, which was openly hostile to student activists, used the material as the basis for an article suggesting that SSOC itself was a communist group.[50]

Doss was neither a reliable nor an effective informant; he was not a trusted member of the leadership group in Nashville, and his involvement with the organization was brief. That the police depended on him for intelligence on SSOC meant that the information it received was likely distorted, misinterpreted, or flat-out inaccurate. The reliability of informants was a perpetual issue for intelligence units like Nashville's. As private citizens, the motives that drove informants to engage with law enforcement could range from the personal to the political, and handlers who did not carefully vet potential informants were taking chances. Informants were also prone to misunderstand discussions among activists with whom they did not share a long history and groups with which they had limited experience. Ideological disputes over seemingly arcane issues could confuse them, petty personal conflicts could seem more important than they were, and real differences among organizations could elude informants. Sorace and his team were unaware or unconcerned about such issues. They believed their informants had provided vital intelligence about the work and plans of activists in the city, particularly SNCC and the lead-up to the April 1967 disturbance. Hill, for example, claimed, that police were well prepared for SNCC to provoke violence because the intelligence squad "had been forewarned that something like this was in the mill. Our informants related to us that SNCC was organizing 'Operation Nashville.'"[51] The Kerner Commission researchers disagreed and pointedly disputed the informants' reporting. "Their intelligence informants," the report concluded, "had interpreted youthful bravado about 'tearing this town apart' as a developing plan for insurrection." The informants' misreading of the situation meant that the police were primed for violence, ready to respond in force to the slightest hint of trouble or unrest. Such criticism did not faze Sorace or shake his view of the importance of informants to police intelligence operations. In his opinion, the unrest proved the "value of intelligence."[52] "If there is anything that these riots are teaching the municipal police organizations," Sorace told Eastland's Judiciary Committee, "it is something that we very luckily had to begin with, and that is to build a very strong intelligence operation." As the Kerner researchers summarized his view, "He was very proud of his surveillance, informant, and infiltration procedures. He made it quite clear that efforts in these areas are being stepped up."[53]

Sorace's very public role during and after the crisis fueled his meteoric rise in the department and made him a star in Nashville. In December 1967, he was promoted to assistant police chief, with responsibility for the Bureau of Staff Services, which included oversight of the intelligence squad. He became a highly sought-after speaker among local civic organizations and frequently appeared in the local press. The *New York Times* also featured him in stories in 1967, including one with a photo.[54] Sorace shrewdly used appearances before sympathetic groups of business elites and civic boosters to rally support for the police and to shape the narrative about the threat Nashville faced. In particular, Sorace's characterization of Nashville activists as dangerous, devious extremists determined to unleash a violent assault on the city's way of life served to rationalize and legitimize aggressive police action, including intelligence work. In florid and vivid rhetoric, Sorace painted a picture of extremists running amok and threatening all that the city held dear. "What is going on in our country?" he asked in one speech, in language similar to Frank Holloman's words in Memphis after the sanitation strike and the King assassination.[55] He decried the civil rights movement, he told the Optimist Club two weeks after his appearance before the Judiciary Committee, as "a movement now causing riots, bloodshed, murder, and plunder throughout the land."[56] Communists, he explained to a group of Rotarians, had led the civil rights movement astray and turned the poor, minorities, and youth against the police. It was beyond doubt, he charged, that communists had infiltrated or led activist groups in a concerted effort to destroy the country. Not only SSOC and SCEF but Chinese-inspired communist groups such as the Progressive Labor Party and "violent, secret organizations" such as the Revolutionary Action Movement and the Deacons of Defense had joined together with the objective of destabilizing and ultimately overthrowing the government.[57]

In increasingly dire language, Sorace evoked a vision of chaos and destruction that awaited Nashville if it did not mobilize to confront this existential threat. Lest his listeners think they were secure in central Tennessee, immune from the disruptions that plagued the big cities and college town of the West and North, he predicted the April disturbances were just a taste of things to come. The "potential for what can happen is frightening," he warned in one talk. "It's quite clear these terrorist groups aren't interested in civil rights. What they want is anarchy."[58] Sorace tailored his remarks to each audience. To the annual meeting of the Tennessee Electric Cooperative, he highlighted the possibility of infrastructure damage, telling the power administrators that "it would be easy for an anarchist group to paralyze a city such as Nashville that is dependent on electrical power." To the proper, upper-crust white women of the Robert Taft Republican Women's Club, he cited the potential for violence and death in Nashville because the city's location made it a convenient meeting place for radicals from around the region. The April events "are just the beginning," he told the women. "The next phase will be stark-naked sabotage. . . . They will kill indiscriminately." And they won't need many people to achieve their diabolical ends, he told Rotarians. "It would take less than one-tenth of the men in this room right now to work a few hours to cripple Nashville and throw it into a state of panic."[59]

Sorace's dire warnings of the apocalypse approaching Nashville were a strategic effort to use public fears of radical violence to build support for law enforcement. The police, Sorace repeatedly said, lacked the personnel, resources, and funding to adequately protect the city from the grave threat that activists posed. He implored his listeners for support: "It is time that everybody woke up and not just pay lip service [to backing the police]."[60] Moreover, Sorace's scaremongering and overheated, dramatic rhetoric served to justify aggressive policing against activists in Nashville, including the Intelligence

Division's work. Sorace claimed that the division was judicious and restrained in its surveillance operations. He distinguished between what he called "optical" surveillance, such as photography, which the department utilized, and "electronic" surveillance, such as wiretaps and listening devices, which he claimed the Intelligence Division did not. The absence of publicly available police records from the era makes it difficult to assess his claim. It certainly is plausible that the police did not routinely use electronic surveillance because a court order was required to deploy listening devices. Moreover, given how off base were their views about what transpired at "secret" meetings, it was clear they were not listening to the discussions. In one instance, what intelligence officers thought was a secret meeting at the Methodist Board of Evangelism to plot a riot was, in fact, a staid business meeting of the SCEF board. Bishop Charles Golden, who hosted the meeting, told the McClellan subcommittee that people noticed the police car stationed outside and thought they might be eavesdropping. But, he said, "if they had listening devices, they would know it didn't have anything to do with the riots."[61]

However, it seemed to be an open secret in Nashville that the police commonly used wiretaps and other listening devices to surveil activists. A reporter for the *Nashville Tennessean* told the Kerner Commission researchers that police intelligence operations used a "panel truck" with surveillance equipment that included "sensitive audio pick-up equipment" and "snooping devices."[62] Others whom the researchers interviewed spoke "with alarm about the widespread use of illegal surveillance devices used in monitoring the conversations of many of those involved in the disturbance."[63] The use of such devices would not have been unusual for a division led by Sorace. Sorace was a technology enthusiast who throughout his career had sought to incorporate the latest and newest technical tools into the department's surveillance and crime fighting arsenal. As a young officer, he was known to have surreptitiously recorded conversations during investigations when he first joined the department—hence, his nickname the Bug among other officers—and later in his career, as head of the Department's Technical Services Bureau, oversaw the introduction of a new computer system to the department.[64] In an era in which law enforcement around the country used electronic surveillance methods against perceived radicals and subversives, it would have been unusual if Nashville's intelligence squad bucked this trend, especially given its leader's favorable disposition toward these tools. The Kerner Commission researchers discovered as well only limited and scattered opposition to electronic surveillance and that any concern dissipated after the events of early April. "Wire-tapping has not yet become a public issue in Nashville," they wrote in their report, "but our judgement of the current climate of opinion is that the police would be supported by most whites, and Negroes as well, on the grounds that any *means* are legitimate if it aids in running the 'rascals' out of town." Although they found that before the crisis there had been "mounting concern within city circles concerning the use of illegal information gathering devices by the intelligence division," the researchers concluded that "the disturbance vindicated the use of such devices because of the 'demonstrated danger' of SNCC radicals." The unrest "convinced the Mayor that there were Communists at work here."[65]

Not everyone accepted Sorace's characterization of the situation in Nashville. The activist community, certainly, dissented from its portrayal as communist infused and violence prone. African Americans argued that the police were the problem, too quick to resort to force and uninterested in improving relations with the Black community. Many laid the blame on Sorace. Z. Alexander Looby, the longtime city councilman and Black community leader, remarked in 1968: "I've been in Nashville for the past 42 years. My people think less of the police department today than ever before. Chief Sorace is a big contributing factor to this atmosphere."[66] Others chided Sorace for grandstanding. The Kerner Commission researchers accused Sorace of playing up the unrest, saying he "has been able to further his own career through nationally televised exposés."[67] The *Nashville Tennessean*, the voice of white moderation on civil rights led by editor and former Kennedy man John Seigenthaler, was a persistent critic of Sorace. The paper accused him of red-baiting and gave voice to those uneasy with the methods of the Intelligence Division. Calling him "an amateur Red chaser," the paper editorialized in 1967 that "it is doubtful that Mr. Sorace, only about five years out of college and the coffee houses, would know a Communist if he saw one, although how he comes by some of his information might in itself make an interesting congressional hearing." After his explosive testimony before the McClellan subcommittee, the *Tennessean* slammed Sorace for reorienting the department toward political investigations through the dubiously legal tactics of the Intelligence Division. Sorace had steered the department "from steady, firm, enforcement of the law to preparation for war" against putative radicals and communists, the paper said. "If the Mayor's idea of local law enforcement is a police force trained for political inquisition, snooping into the private affairs of local citizens and institutions, and creating a climate of suspicion, . . . then Captain Sorace is his man."[68]

Sorace *was* Briley's man. The mayor, along with the police chief and most of city council, strongly backed him. As the Kerner Commission recognized, Sorace also drew support from across the white community. The *Nashville Banner* both reflected and drove this support. Parting ways with the *Tennessean*, as he often did, publisher Jimmy Stahlman gave Sorace his full-throated support. Stahlman represented the view that Nashville faced an existential threat from white radicals and Black extremists that required an innovative and aggressive police response. If foreign-inspired or controlled activists were conspiring to start a violent revolution, then the police were justified in using whatever means were necessary to protect the city. In essence, the police had to fight fire with fire. In such a formulation, national security was a local issue, and as Stahlman argued, "the first lines of defense today are the local police departments."[69] Nashville had been well served, Stahlman said, by its "alert intelligence department" composed of "trained, trustworthy and dedicated" public servants who carefully sifted the evidence to identify and pursue "individuals and organizations whose purpose is to cause chaos in city life." Stahlman believed Sorace deserved much of the credit for keeping the threats to the city at bay. As he put it, "Because of its intelligence unit organized [and] directed by Asst. Chief John Sorace, Nashville has always been prepared to meet trouble."[70] Briley shared Stahlman's enthusiasm for Sorace, later reflecting that he "was shrewd as hell, he was smart, and he knew what he was doing."[71]

STRENGTHENING THE SURVEILLANCE INFRASTRUCTURE IN NASHVILLE

Police department intelligence units like Nashville's were critical components of the larger national effort to contain and control, disrupt and dismantle, activism deemed threatening to the community and the country. Red Squads benefited from the development of a national infrastructure that helped sustain and advance local intelligence operations. The rise of a nongovernmental association of intelligence units and the creation of federal policies to channel new resources to police departments were important aspects of this infrastructure. Their effect can be seen in Nashville, where the Intelligence Division expanded its work and gained new tools in its battle against suspected subversives.

Shortly after its creation in 1964, the MNPD's Intelligence Division became enmeshed in a national network of metropolitan police intelligence units that came together in the blandly named Law Enforcement Intelligence Unit (LEIU). Founded in 1956 by police intelligence officers on the West Coast as a clearinghouse to help coordinate the fight against organized crime, the LEIU grew by 1965 to include representatives from more than 150 police offices around the country. By connecting intelligence units across the country, the LEIU allowed for the "exchange of confidential information not available through police channels."[72] The LEIU functioned as a central repository of information—memorialized in files it maintained—on organized crime figures gathered from intelligence units. As a private group, it was not under the purview of any governmental authority and thus operated without meaningful oversight. One critical study of the LEIU said its structure "combines aspects of the professional association, the fraternal society, and the private country club." It was a situation that was ripe for abuse. As social activism and protests surged in the 1960s, the LEIU came to reflect the new orientation of many of its member police departments by broadening its focus beyond organized crime to include suspected political radicals. LEIU files and gatherings increasingly focused on individuals engaged in constitutionally protected activities rather than on those involved in criminal enterprises.[73] The MNPD intelligence unit, whose creation in 1964 occurred as the LEIU reoriented toward social activists and political dissenters, was the first such unit in the state to join the LEIU. Sorace was an enthusiastic participant in the organization. In 1966, he arranged for the MNPD to host an LEIU meeting in the city, which included a workshop on riots and subversive activities and a screening of a film on the 1965 Watts uprising. Sorace also quickly moved into a leadership position in the group, just as he had done in the MNPD. In 1966, he was elected vice chairman and then chairman of the Central Zone of the LEIU. In his 1967 congressional testimony, he credited the LEIU with bolstering the Nashville Red Squad's anti-subversive work.[74]

At the federal level, the emergence of the Law Enforcement Assistance Administration (LEAA) in 1968 was a boon to local law enforcement. Authorized by the Omnibus Crime Control and Safe Streets Act of 1968, the LEAA offered federal grants to local and state law enforcement agencies to modernize equipment, conduct training exercises, and conduct research. Importantly, the federal funding came in the form of block grants to state-level planning agencies that, in turn, distributed the funds to localities at their own discretion. The LEAA thus established a bureaucracy for the distribution of federal funds for police departments. It also created an opening for federal agencies to influence local policing. Through coordination with the LEAA, defense and intelligence agencies began to act in the area of local law enforcement. Army and CIA trainers, for example, made presentations on bomb disposal, recordkeeping, and street surveillance to local police in Montgomery, Alabama; Washington, DC; and New York. Additionally, federal funds could now be directed to local policing and could introduce to the streets of American cities various tools and tactics borrowed from the military's war in Southeast Asia, the first steps toward the militarization of local policing. And LEAA funding enabled police departments to enhance their surveillance capabilities by organizing intelligence units and deploying new digital tools in their work. In one critic's words, the LEAA was a "funding mechanism for local police . . . to set up and operate intelligence divisions" to acquire crime protection hardware and techniques. In short, LEAA funds served to institutionalize police departments' surveillance infrastructure.[75]

In Tennessee, the state moved quickly to create administrative units to take advantage of the newly available federal funds. Through the Tennessee Law Enforcement Planning Commission and the Tennessee Law Enforcement Planning Agency, the state distributed funds to police departments in the state.[76] The MNPD welcomed the infusion of funds, not merely for the budgetary support it provided but for its facilitation of the surveillance work it already was doing. Moreover, the technological focus of the LEAA funding fit well with John Sorace's interest in acquiring the latest computer hardware to support the police department's work. The creation of the Intelligence Division, with its mandate to collect information on individuals and groups, encouraged Sorace to use emerging computer technologies in the development of its recordkeeping system. This effort came to fruition after the department gained access to federal funds through the LEAA. By the early 1970s, Sorace, now assistant chief for technical services, with oversight of the department's technology, had led the MNPD in winning three LEAA grants to modernize its computer system and connect it to federal criminal databases. In 1971, the MNPD unveiled a new records system that ran on two UNIVAC mainframe computers. The new system particularly benefited the Intelligence Division, which would "be able to store and retrieve data in the computer privately," the *Nashville Tennessean* reported. Sorace and department leaders framed these acquisitions as a mechanism for making the police department more efficient in its work while downplaying any threat they posed to civil liberties. Sorace disputed the characterization of the computers as "big brother" that would spy on citizens, telling the *Tennessean*, "computers don't have any more information in them about a citizen than a conventional paper file would have."[77] But the secretive nature of the files, the restrictions limiting access to them to a few officials, and the vague definition of who could be targeted for surveillance, and thus have a file created on them, left a great deal unknown and invested significant authority in unelected and publicly unaccountable police officials such as John Sorace. What Sorace portrayed as a positive development—only intelligence officers would have access to records about "known rabble rousers"—was a frightening scenario. Facilitated by LEAA funds, the computer system opened the door to limitless surveillance over which there was no oversight. As the police chief, Hugh Mott, put it in 1972, "The limitations of this system are only confined by the imagination of the men operating it."[78]

The MNPD also relied on the FBI to strengthen its intelligence capabilities. J. Edgar Hoover's animus toward activists of all types made the bureau an important ally to police departments around the nation. In Nashville, the April 1967 disturbance and the growing number of white students involved in activism earned the bureau's attention and ensured that the FBI agents would bolster the work of the local Red Squad. They did so by sharing intelligence with their local counterparts, a function that Hoover touted in his testimony before the Kerner Commission as a key form of support the bureau offered police in their fight against violent extremists.[79] The bureau deployed its own network of confidential sources in Nashville as it did elsewhere, and it readily shared its informants' findings with the MNPD. The Red Squad learned from the bureau, for instance, that white activist Sherry Myers, who was involved in SSOC and had participated in antiwar activity dating back to 1965, was a "particularly close associate of Carl and Anne Braden."[80] The MNPD's Red Squad especially welcomed the FBI's input on the non-Nashville residents whom Sorace blamed for stirring the discontent in the city. Sorace's view that "outside agitators" were the source of the city's problems dovetailed with the bureau's narrative, relentlessly promoted by Hoover, that communists had infiltrated, inspired, and led civil rights and social activism in communities throughout the land. Sorace told the McClellan subcommittee that the police maintained "intimate communication" with the FBI and that the relationship was vital because the FBI "kept us informed on people and individuals and others who [we] would have no way of knowing of where they are from and who they are when they come into our city if they are considered potentially dangerous." With the bureau's help in identifying potential troublemakers "from out of town . . . we would develop surveillance photographs."[81] The intelligence unit also provided information to the bureau. "Our files are open to them," Sorace explained to the Judiciary Committee. "We give all information that we feel they are interested in to them, and we deal with them almost daily."[82] The Red Squad and FBI agents thus routinely collaborated in Nashville to keep activists under surveillance. This intergovernmental cooperation and use of state power reflected authorities' fears about the ability of social and political activists to cause havoc.

SSOC formed a part of the activist threat that the Intelligence Division sought to counter. Its composition as a white student group made it conspicuous in Nashville and made the group vulnerable to harassment by other whites who considered the activists "race traitors." The SSOC house, for instance, was vandalized several times, and the activists fielded occasional bomb threats. The police, though, seemed uninterested in investigating the threats or even protecting the group. In May 1967, when several thugs threw beer bottles and a cement block at the house, breaking several windows, the police did not respond immediately, and the next night they made only a cursory appearance when the activists reported that eight threatening-looking men were parked across the street from the house. The following summer, when the activists had decamped for a meeting in Mississippi, thieves broke into the empty house and stole a typewriter, bank statements, canceled checks, and the mailing list, raising suspicions that the Red Squad was behind the break-in.[83] Sorace's enmity toward the group was well known. He considered the activists un-American and likely communists intent on harming the community. The Kerner Commission researchers captured Sorace's distaste for SSOC when, after the April 1967 violence, they wrote, "Captain Sorace noted that SSOC is certainly not doing anything to restore good feeling in Nashville . . . and is deliberately lying and distorting the events for their own ulterior, selfish purposes." To the SSOC students, Sorace was a dangerous tool of the establishment who used the Intelligence Division to undermine the group. As SSOC's David Nolan put it in the *New South Student*, the group's monthly magazine, Sorace was not like "the old breed of Bull Connor rednecks, but the new breed of button-down fascists."[84]

After the tumult and controversy surrounding the 1967 unrest passed, the Intelligence Division kept a lower profile but continued its surveillance of political and social activism in Nashville. Robert Hill took over the reins of the Intelligence Division as Sorace advanced up the ranks in the department. Hill had been in the division since its earliest days and was a close ally of Sorace, at least until the two had a falling out in the early 1970s.[85] Well versed in the division's activities, Hill oversaw the work of seven officers as they continued to surveil and monitor those they considered a threat to the social order of Nashville. In 1969, Hill told the *Tennessean* that "the surveillance of subversive groups . . . will continue on a major scale" even as the division's portfolio expanded to include a new focus on criminal activity.[86] That criminal intelligence was considered new to the division's work in 1969 was revealing given that a focus on criminal activity was part of the rationale for the division's creation in 1964. But ordinary criminal activities had never preoccupied the division's time. Investigations of civil rights proponents, student demonstrators, and Vietnam War opponents defined the division's agenda and won it administrative support and plaudits from city's boosters. Hill remained in charge of intelligence until 1973, when Kenneth Reasonover, a captain in the Homicide

Division who previously had worked with intelligence, took over leadership of the group upon Hill's move to the personnel office in a leadership shuffle.[87]

Gradually, though, the division's focus shifted as student activism receded with the end of the Vietnam War and congressional investigations and media exposés in the early 1970s revealed the vast network of domestic surveillance perpetrated by the FBI and other federal agencies. Mundane criminal matters, such as prostitution stings, drug busts, and investigations of illicit firearms sales, replaced surveillance of suspected subversives as the focus of the Intelligence Division.[88] Yet unlike in Memphis, there was never a public reckoning in Nashville over the police department's surveillance campaigns against political and social activists. In Memphis, the assassination of Martin Luther King Jr. brought intense scrutiny of the city's police force and highlighted the abusive and harsh tactics it had long deployed against civil rights, labor, and student activists. The subsequent revelation that the police had maintained files on citizens fueled outrage and led to the lawsuit that compelled the city to reform its surveillance practices. The situation was quite different in Nashville, where the police never received a similar level of criticism over their tactics. Police files were perhaps the one issue that could ignite protests against the department's surveillance practice. The Intelligence Division appeared to appreciate the sensitivity of its files and worked to keep them out of public view or simply stonewalled when calls emerged to release them. In 1975, when the *Tennessean* reported that the Intelligence Division had files on 230 individuals and groups, a police official dismissed the files as a relic of an earlier time and framed the intelligence work of the era as a necessary public safety measure to monitor what the newspaper called "organizations that caused trouble during the 1960s," thereby tarring all activists with the broad brush of extremism. In the police official's words, the department created files on "subversive groups or people who advocate the violent overthrow of the U.S. or local government." When a new group, the Coalition for the Protection of Political Rights, formed to demand the opening of the files to those named in them and "an immediate halt to all police spying on Nashville political groups and on the political activities of individual citizens," city officials circled the wagons. Neither the police chief nor the Metro Council would meet with the group, and the mayor falsely said that he was unaware of the group's demands. The Metro government attorney told the group that the police department would neither end its surveillance practices nor open its files to the public. While the coalition managed to hold a series of public meetings, it could not sustain the effort in the face of complete city resistance. Despite threatening a lawsuit, a tact that Memphis citizens would pursue the next year, none materialized in Nashville, and the issue, though not the Intelligence Division, faded away.[89]

John Sorace was the police official most readily identified with the Intelligence Division, and his work creating, building, and promoting the division helped advance his career within the MNPD. Over the course of the 1970s and 1980s, he served as one of the department's assistant chiefs, with oversight of a number of areas, most notably technical services. His interest in computers and his unabashed enthusiasm for deploying technology to enhance police work, generally, and to improve surveillance capabilities, in particular, made him the department's leading technologist. It also prompted him, in the mid-1970s, to found a computer consulting business to provide technical and software support to police departments across the country. This led to the entanglement of his personal and public roles, as he at one point was supplying support for the same computer system the MNPD had purchased. He later faced complaints from city officials for mismanaging the department's computer systems, including overpaying for hardware, executing no-bid contracts for services, and misplacing or losing thousands of dollars in computer equipment. In 1988, an internal audit found that computers purchased in 1984 were sitting unused as the department continued to rely on the computer system that Sorace had prevailed on the department to purchase back in 1971. In 1992, Sorace accepted a buyout and left the department. Free from the public scrutiny that came with high-profile police work, he devoted himself to his consulting business, Intelamation Security and Investigations.[90]

Sorace's role as a leader of the Metropolitan Nashville Police Department's Red Squad went unmentioned in the coverage of his retirement from the force. Yet while the domestic intelligence operations of the 1960s were a distant memory in 1992, they were a central concern and preoccupation of Nashville police leaders at the time. Sorace was in the middle of it all. Under his leadership, the police developed a feared intelligence unit that aggressively pursued activists across the city. The unrest that followed Stokely Carmichael's appearance in Nashville, much of it provoked by the police, distracted attention from the role that Sorace's Red Squad played in trying to thwart activism in the city. Determined to counter activism wherever it emerged, the police unit surveilled and harassed white student activists in addition to the Black students who had formed the bedrock of the city's civil rights community. SSOC's rise from the city's white institutions put it in the sights of Sorace and his peers, who saw the group both as a source of support for the Black activists and as a dangerous beacon for other white students attracted to its positions of dissent and opposition to community norms.

The rise of SSOC as expression of white student discontent suggested to Sorace's team that a Berkeley-style revolt was brewing in the city and thereby justified intrusive and vigorous surveillance of the group and its members. In this, the Nashville Red Squad shared a similar attitude and orientation toward white student activism as the police in Memphis, state-level intelligence agencies in the region, and the FBI. The surveillance operations conducted across all levels of government and directed at white students in the South exposed authorities' concern that they faced a future of campus upheaval and student dissent unless they responded forcefully. By working to repress student activism in the city, the Nashville Red Squad unintentionally revealed that the politically conservative, segregationist social order needed constant reinforcement. While their concerns about a leftist assault emanating from the campuses may have been overblown, their reaction demonstrated that student activists, in Nashville and elsewhere, exerted a power that belied their numbers. The potential for white-led revolt compelled the police to see themselves as defenders of the city's order and exposed the shaky foundation on which that order rested. Anxious that white student activism raised the troubling specter of generational revolt, the Intelligence Division considered white activists like those in SSOC a threat that, if left unaddressed, risked the destruction of the sociopolitical order that had entrenched white supremacy and white elite power.

CONCLUSION

ON OCTOBER 1, 1969, nearly four months after SSOC broke up amid internal disagreements and factional discord, an unwelcome delivery arrived at the former SSOC office in Nashville: a subpoena that commanded several SSOC activists to appear before the Senate Internal Security Subcommittee. Led by its powerful chairman, the ardent segregationist, James O. Eastland of Mississippi, the subcommittee investigated student activists around the country as part of a campaign to expose the supposedly anti-American and communist underpinnings of the civil rights and anti–Vietnam War movements. The subpoena instructed the activists to bring with them what amounted to most of the group's files: "Records, financial and otherwise. . . . Correspondence and copies thereof, bank statements, checkbooks and/or stubs. . . . Membership lists, rosters and records, and . . . all other documents and records of the said S.S.O.C."[1]

The subcommittee's interest in SSOC, even after it ceased to exist, reflected the deep suspicion that policymakers and security officials harbored about student activists in the 1960s. SSOC was one threat among many, but it stood out in the South for its focus on white students. Campus administrators and law enforcement in the region worried that the group would stir discontent among other students and threaten the calm cherished by civic leaders, thereby justifying efforts to stop the group.

More generally, authorities at all levels of government, from federal national security officials to local Red Squads, moved aggressively against white student activists in the South. Such activists were especially conspicuous. Despite their small numbers, they stood out in a region where dissent and activism among white students was unusual, at least before the civil rights revolution of the era and the outrage sparked by the expanding American war in Southeast Asia. With the white supremacist order already under attack from African Americans, white students' outspoken opposition to segregation and the war risked further destabilizing the status quo. The seeming collapse of authority on campuses elsewhere as students rebelled against established norms and business-as-usual policies that limited students' rights and accommodated an often racist status quo heightened officials fears of student activism.

Led by the FBI, federal authorities designed and implemented programs to discredit and hinder the work of white New Leftists in the South, making it an important counterpart to the federal campaign against white students in the North and Black activists everywhere. The centerpiece of the bureau's efforts was COINTELPRO–New Left, one of the dozen counterintelligence programs the bureau developed under J. Edgar Hoover's leadership. G-men around the region responded to the bureau's demand for actionable intelligence on white activists by deploying informants to spy on students, spreading rumors and disinformation to sow discord among the activists, and hatching plans to disrupt activists' personal lives. Students could find themselves in the crosshairs of federal officials for any number of supposed offenses. Trivial and fleeting actions, such as subscribing to a leftist publication or attending a teach-in on the war, took on heightened significance to authorities on the lookout for signs of discontent and disruption. In this context, students who engaged in overt and direct protest activity faced especially sharp responses. The bureau's files are filled with page after page of surveillance information about students who had the temerity to exercise their constitutional rights in an environment where these rights were contingent on support of the status quo.

State investigative agencies complemented the work of federal officials to surveil and disrupt white student activism in the South. States across the region launched campaigns against student activists operating within their borders. Civil rights activism was a particular concern given the challenge the Jim Crow order faced from the African American–led movement of the era. As white student activists joined with their Black peers to demand racial reforms on their campuses and in their communities, officials responded by using the powers of the state to monitor and disrupt the students' activities. With the surge of antiwar sentiment, these efforts intensified. The Mississippi

State Sovereignty Commission was the most notorious of the state investigative agencies, but other states, including Alabama, Florida, Georgia, Louisiana, Oklahoma, South Carolina, Tennessee, and Texas, also operated units to thwart student activism in their states. The work of state-run domestic security operations against white New Leftists highlighted the states' repressive mission and illustrates how little room for dissent existed in the region.

Police Red Squads, the investigative units within city police departments, provided another layer of surveillance of white activists in the South. The work of Red Squads in Memphis and Nashville exemplified how domestic intelligence units within police departments operated with impunity as they sought to crush student activism. While their work often prioritized surveilling and harassing Black activists, white students emerged as targets as they advocated for civil rights and spearheaded opposition to the war. Police leaders, with support from the political leaders in both cities, considered white activists to be anti-American radicals bent on the destruction of the social order. They readily saw white activists as communist sympathizers and fellow travelers, if not outright communists themselves. Understood in this way, activism against the war took on an existential hue; students were not just opposing a foreign policy objective but threatening the entire sociopolitical order. That locally oriented activism in Tennessee came to represent a potent threat to national security highlights official sensitivity to dissent and exposes authorities' deep unease about the durability of a social order built on white supremacy and elite political and economic power.

The web of surveillance that government authorities stitched together to circumscribe white student activism in the South reveals several important points about the history of the era's social movements—and the reaction to them. First, the surveillance operations complicate and enhance the narrative of the movements of the 1960s. In most histories of the era, white students in the South appear as opponents of the causes that animated young people elsewhere in the country, if they appear in such works at all. But many white students, in fact, were active participants in these movements. Though fewer in number than in other parts of the country, their race made them highly visible in the South. The counterintelligence operations deployed against them show that authorities perceived them as constituting a real threat to the social order and make clear that the drive against dissent waged by national security and police operatives targeted whites in the South in addition to northern New Leftists and Black activists throughout the country. Second, it highlights two interrelated points: the persistence of white student activism and the shrinking of space for this activism in the South. Surveillance drives disrupted but did not end student activism. Despite the personal and professional costs exacted by surveillance operations, student activists in the South continued to express their support for the social and political causes that mattered to them. The rise of surveillance campaigns were themselves testimony to the enduring activism of white southern students. Yet these surveillance drives demonstrated how little space, how little tolerance, there was for dissent. Campus administrators, city leaders, and law enforcement officials collaborated to identify, malign, harass, and intimidate student activists. Fearful that the protests that had engulfed campuses elsewhere would spread to their communities, they moved to extinguish dissent in their communities before it could threaten the status quo.

The sharp response that white student activism provoked from authorities reveals a third key point: the instability of the existing sociopolitical order. The status quo was so unstable that it required continuous support and shoring up. Jim Crow and segregation laws were under attack from all sides. The war had called into question the basic tenets of American foreign policy and fueled a growing distrust of authorities. College students, in particular, had become especially distrustful and disillusioned, with many rejecting traditional lines of authority and the conventions and norms of their parents' generation. Like a failing dam, the social order seemed to authorities to be on the brink of collapse, and their drive to repress student activism was a desperate effort to plug the holes and repair the fissures in the social order. Consequently, no threat was too small, no organization too obscure, to merit official attention. The coming together of a handful of activists at the University of Oklahoma or the questioning of the war by veterans who attended Memphis State University fueled the paranoia of state actors, who readily interpreted such developments as harbingers of things to come unless they swiftly moved against the students. SSOC's emergence was an even more ominous development because it was a region-wide organization that could threaten the social order on several fronts at once.

Lastly, the surveillance of white student activists in the South reveals the breadth and depth of efforts to control and suppress dissent. Officials turned the full power and resources of the state against students. They spied on their meetings, launched disinformation campaigns against them, deployed informants to infiltrate their organizations, disrupted their activities, and sought to discredit them among other students. Their efforts were extensive, pervasive, and sustained. Yet they were remarkably fruitless in identifying evidence of subversion on the part of students. Repeatedly, Red Squads, state investigators, and federal agents produced evidence not of disloyalty but of political engagement, of students exercising their rights to assemble, to express their views, and to voice dissent in the country's best tradition. Moreover, numerous students came under suspicion for mundane and ordinary activities that authorities interpreted as signs of dissent. In a climate in which political and law enforcement leadership sanctioned spying as a useful tool for rooting out subversives, there was no off-ramp, no incentive for authorities to stop the surveillance. FBI field offices and police intelligence units preserved vital budget lines and aligned themselves with the priorities of their superiors by pressing ahead with surveillance operations. To try to change paths and stop surveilling was to court criticism and pushback, as the Knoxville, Tennessee, FBI office experienced when Hoover chastised the agents for proposing to end its reporting on white New Leftists because they had not been active in the area recently. Rather than exonerating white students of charges of radicalism and disloyalty, the lack of evidence of extremism and subversion became evidence itself, a sign that authorities needed to redouble their efforts to uncover the extremism lurking on the region's campuses.

While the FBI and the rest of the domestic security apparatus searched for evidence of subversion and dissent among white students in the South, this book has focused on documenting evidence of the often secret surveillance campaigns authorities directed against students. My work, along with that of other scholars, has helped uncover and expose the surveillance that activists endured. But there remains much still to learn. Despite the voluminous COINTELPRO records, not all of the bureau's files have survived or received public disclosure. The Mississippi State Sovereignty Commission's files are such a celebrated source because they are so unique. No other state has preserved or made available the files of their investigative agencies. And the documentation that offers a window on the activities of the Memphis and Nashville Red Squads is not available for other police department intelligence units. Scholars continue to face a challenge to account for the work of these public agencies because the records are so hard to access. As intelligence scholar Amy Zegart has written, a "deep-seated culture of secrecy . . . pervades intelligence agencies."[2] These agencies simply have no incentive to search for, locate, or preserve evidence of what often was illegal spying on the citizens they were supposed to protect. And when evidence of records does emerge, they have done their best to stonewall and erect barriers to access. The Freedom of Information Act process is a tool agencies, including the FBI, have used to delay release of information about their surveillance work and to obfuscate through redactions when they eventually release information. Additionally, they have made it a costly endeavor for scholars to obtain records, despite "fee reductions" available for those conducting academic research. In my own case, it took more than five years and considerable expense to pry from the bureau the records on the Southern Student Organizing Committee that inform part of this study, and even then I cannot be certain that I have received all relevant documents. Time, cost, and secrecy have continued to prevent a full accounting of the surveillance of the civil rights era.

In the decades since the law enforcement surveillance campaigns that are the focus of this book took place, technological advances and the growing interconnectedness of people and markets have made surveillance increasingly commonplace across all sectors of society as well as heightened public sensitivity to violations of privacy and security that have resulted. This surveillance is seemingly everywhere, providing governments, businesses, and criminals with the ability to monitor our most intimate communications as well as our most mundane transactions.[3] Law enforcement and national security agencies—in the United States and abroad—have used new tools of surveillance to pursue age-old agendas of monitoring political opponents, suppressing dissent, and harassing and controlling racial and ethnic minorities. Examples of such activities abound: the National Security Agency's post-9/11 program that swept up Americans' cell phone data as part of its counterterrorism operations; police departments' surveillance of demonstrators at major political gatherings, such as the Republican National Convention in New York in 2004, and of the daily routines of ordinary citizens and activists alike in cities as varied as Los Angeles, New Orleans, and New York; the Chinese Communist Party's use of advanced surveillance technologies to enforce COVID lockdowns and quarantines and to round up and detain members of the Uighur minority as part of a campaign to decimate their culture and destroy their identity; and the rush by governments around the world to deploy the technology developed by the Israeli firm NSO that allows them to hack into cell phones undetected, a tool they have used to track journalists, political opponents, and human rights advocates.[4] In Memphis, in an echo of its actions a half-century earlier, police in the 2010s surveilled and ran intelligence operations against perceived opponents. This time, their targets were Black Lives Matter and environmental activists rather than students who opposed the Vietnam War and supported civil rights.[5]

The routinization of surveillance does not auger well for the future. As the public becomes inured to the loss of privacy that accompanies the widespread use of surveillance in our daily lives, law enforcement will face less resistance to its use of new technologies to surveil putative extremists and radicals. Citizens who speak out, whether online or in the streets, in opposition to government policies or in support of unpopular causes, will invite police scrutiny and surveillance. Now, as in the past, law enforcement will characterize their work as being designed to promote public safety. Officials will attest to their respect and reverence for political dissent and mouth shibboleths about democracy and citizen engagement. But their actions, if history is a guide, will serve to criminalize dissent and political disagreements. Activists can expect the prying eyes of law enforcement to monitor their actions and the ever-expanding arsenal of surveillance tools to be deployed against them. The result will be to discourage people from engaging with the issues of the day if they hold views that fall outside the mainstream. Individuals will think twice before joining a protest or sharing dissenting views. The effect will be chilling. What the Church Committee concluded in 1976 about the damage caused by the government's surveillance activities in the 1960s remains true today: "The most basic harm was to the values of privacy and freedom which our Constitution seeks to protect and which intelligence activity infringed on a broad scale."[6]

NOTES

INTRODUCTION

1. Silkwood's family ultimately reached a $1.3 million settlement with Kerr-McGee, the company that ran the plant where she worked. Coverage of Silkwood's death was voluminous and continued for years. Examples include David Burnham, "Death of Plutonium Worker Questioned by Union Official," *New York Times*, November 19, 1974, 28; Jack Taylor, "Key Answers Still Mystery in Death Case," *Sunday Oklahoman* (Oklahoma City), December 8, 1974, 1; "Plutonium Incident Possibly Contrived," *Dallas Morning News*, January 7, 1975, 1; Vivian Vahlberg, "The Karen Silkwood Story Won't Die," *Sunday Oklahoman*, April 6, 1975, 15; B. J. Phillips, "The Case of Karen Silkwood: The Mysterious Death of a Nuclear Plant Worker," *Ms.*, April 1975, 59–66; Howard Kohn, "Karen Silkwood: The Case of the Activist's Death," *Rolling Stone*, January 13, 1977, https://www.rollingstone.com/culture/culture-news/karen-silkwood-the-case-of-the-activists-death-52287; Jill Friedlander, "Anti-Nuclear Power Protestors Rally in Memory of Silkwood," *Harvard Crimson*, November 20, 1978, https://www.thecrimson.com/article/1978/11/20/anti-nuclear-power-protesters-rally-in-memory; "Nation: Poisoned by Plutonium," *Time*, March 19, 1979, https://content.time.com/time/subscriber/article/0,33009,947011-1,00.html; "The Karen Silkwood Story," *PBS Frontline*, https://www.pbs.org/wgbh/pages/frontline/shows/reaction/interact/silkwood.html, first published in *Los Alamos Science* 23, November 23, 1995; Jennifer Latson, "The Nuclear-Safety Activist Whose Mysterious Death Inspired a Movie," *Time*, November 13, 2014, https://time.com/3574931/karen-silkwood.

2. U.S. House of Representatives, *Problems in the Accounting For and Safeguarding of Special Nuclear Materials: Hearings before the Subcommittee on Energy and Environment of the Committee on Small Business*, 94th Cong. (1976), 312. Srouji's book is Jacque Srouji, *Critical Mass: Nuclear Power, the Alternative to Energy Famine* (Nashville: Aurora Publications, 1977). She wrote the book after first publishing articles in a local Nashville magazine that focused on nuclear power and the Tennessee Valley Authority. Jacque Srouji, "Now Let Us All Praise Nuclear Power . . . ," *Nashville!* January 1975, 19–23, 42–45; Jacque Srouji, "How Safe Is Nuclear Power?" *Nashville!* February 1975, 36–39, 46–49, 64–66. On Srouji's connection to the Silkwood case, see the House hearings cited earlier, especially the testimony of Srouji (242–63) and Seigenthaler (315–50); "Editor Fired for Alleged FBI Ties," *Boston Globe*, May 8, 1976, 2; "F.B.I. Bars Data on Ties to a Nashville Journalist," *New York*

Times, May 21, 1976, 11; "A Special Relationship," *Time*, May 24, 1976, 81; "Reporter-Informant for FBI Threatens Agents' Exposure," *Pittsburgh Post-Gazette*, May 28, 1976, 2; Sanford J. Ungar, "Among the Piranhas: A Journalist and the F.B.I.," *Columbia Journalism Review*, September–October 1976, 19–26; Irvin Muchnick, "The Bizarre Career of Jacque Srouji, Alias Lelia Hassan," *More*, October 1976, 26–30; Ken Brannon, "Why Srouji Was Fired," *Nashville!* October 1976, 37–39, 84, 86–88, 90; Ken Brannon, "Was Jacque Srouji Really a Spy for the FBI?" pt. 2, *Nashville!* November 1976, 44–46, 86–89, 91–94. The *Nashville Tennessean* extensively covered the Srouji case and the fallout from it. Articles from the newspaper as well as other related material can be found in the John Seigenthaler Papers, 1927–2014, Vanderbilt University Special Collections & Archives, Nashville (hereafter cited as Seigenthaler Papers). Also see Richard Rashke, *The Killing of Karen Silkwood: The Story behind the Kerr-McGee Plutonium Case* (Boston: Houghton Mifflin, 1981).

3. Srouji variously reported both years as her start date at the *Banner*. See, for example, "Personnel Record," October 7, 1968; and "Personnel Record," September 30, 1975, both in box 32, folder "Tennessean–Srouji, Jacque–Personnel Records–1976," Seigenthaler Papers.

4. Howard Zinn, *SNCC: The New Abolitionists* (Boston: Beacon Press, 1965), 19–23; Powledge, *Free at Last*, 203–10; Howell Raines, *My Soul Is Rested: Movement Days in the Deep South Remembered* (New York: Putnam, 1977), 98–100; Morris, *Origins of the Civil Rights Movement*, 174–78, 205–13; Henry Hampton, *Voices of Freedom: An Oral History of the Civil Rights Movement from the 1950s through the 1980s* (New York: Bantam Books, 1990), 53–61, 65–67; Taylor Branch, *Parting the Waters: America in the King Years, 1954–1963* (New York: Simon and Schuster, 1988), 260–64, 278–80, 295, 345, 379–80; James Forman, *The Making of Black Revolutionaries: A Personal Account* (New York: Macmillan, 1972), 145–57; David Halberstam, *The Children* (New York: Ballantine, 1998); John Lewis, *Walking with the Wind: A Memoir of the Movement* (New York: Simon and Schuster, 1998); Benjamin Houston, *The Nashville Way: Racial Etiquette and the Struggle for Social Justice in a Southern City* (Athens: University of Georgia Press, 2012), 82–163.

5. Gregg L. Michel, *Struggle for a Better South: The Southern Student Organizing Committee, 1964–1969* (New York: Palgrave Macmillan, 2004).

6. Ungar, "Among the Piranhas"; Muchnick, "Bizarre Career of Jacque Srouji"; Brannon, "Why Srouji Was Fired."

7. John M. Crewdson, untitled teletype of article for Times News Service, May 28, 1976, box 31, folder "Tennessean–Srouji–Chronological–1976 May 5–1976 May 10," Seigenthaler Papers.

8. See, for example, Ward Churchill and Jim Vander Wall, *Agents of Repression: The FBI's Secret Wars against the Black Panther Party and the American Indian Movement*, corrected ed. (1988; reprint, Boston: South End Press, 1990); Alice Echols, *Daring to Be Bad: Radical Feminism in America, 1967–1975* (Minneapolis: University of Minnesota Press, 1989); Frank Donner, *Protectors of Privilege: Red Squads and Police Repression in Urban America* (Berkeley: University of California Press, 1990); David Montejano, *Quixote's Soldiers: A Local History of the Chicano Movement, 1966–1981* (Austin: University of Texas Press, 2010); Seth Rosenfeld, *Subversives: The FBI's War on Student Radicals, and Reagan's Rise to Power* (New York: Farrar, Straus and Giroux, 2012); Max Felker-Kantor, *Policing Los Angeles: Race, Resistance, and the Rise of the LAPD* (Chapel Hill: University of North Carolina Press, 2018); Johanna Fernández, *The Young Lords: A Radical History* (Chapel Hill: University of North Carolina Press, 2020); Simon Balto, *Occupied Territory: Policing Black Chicago from Red Summer to Black Power* (Chapel Hill: University of North Carolina Press, 2020).

9. *Gibson v. Florida Legislative Investigative Committee*, 372 U.S. 539 (1963), 557.

10. Select Committee to Study Government Operations with Respect to Intelligence Activities, S. Rep. No. 94-755, 6 bks. (1976), bk. 2, 291 (hereafter cited as *Church Committee Report*).

11. Athan G. Theoharis, *Spying on Americans: Political Surveillance from Hoover to the Huston Plan* (Philadelphia: Temple University Press, 1978); David J. Garrow, *The FBI and Martin Luther King, Jr.: From "Solo" to Memphis* (New York: Norton, 1981); Kenneth O'Reilly, *Racial Matters: The FBI's Secret File on Black America, 1960–1972* (New York: Free Press, 1989). Other important studies include Nelson Blackstock, *COINTELPRO: The FBI's Secret War on Political Freedom*, 3rd ed. (1975; reprint, New York: Anchor Foundation, 1988); Frank J. Donner, *The Age of Surveillance: The Aims and Methods of America's Political Intelligence System* (New York: Knopf, 1980); David Cunningham, *There's Something Happening Here: The New Left, the Klan, and FBI Counterintelligence* (Berkeley: University of California Press, 2004).

12. Angus Mackenzie, *Secrets: The CIA's War at Home* (Berkeley: University of California Press, 1997); John Prados, *The Family Jewels: The CIA, Secrecy, and Presidential Power* (Austin: University of Texas Press, 2013).

13. Donner, *Protectors of Privilege*. Also see Frank Donner, "Spies on Campus," *Playboy* 15, March 1968, 107ff., which explores similar topics as those he writes about in his book on Red Squads.

14. Sarah Rowe-Sims, "The Mississippi State Sovereignty Commission: An Agency History," *Journal of Mississippi History* 61 (1999): 29–58; Yasuhiro Katagiri, *The Mississippi State Sovereignty Commission: Civil Rights and States' Rights* (Jackson: University Press of Mississippi, 2001); Jenny Irons, *Reconstituting Whiteness: The Mississippi State Sovereignty Commission* (Nashville: Vanderbilt University Press, 2010). Sarah Eppler Janda's *Prairie Power: Student Activism, Counterculture, and Backlash in Oklahoma, 1962–1972* (Norman: University of Oklahoma Press, 2018) is a rare work that focuses on investigative agencies in a state other than Mississippi.

15. Doug Rossinow, "Historiographical Reflections," in *Rebellion in Black & White*, ed. Robert Cohen and David J. Snyder (Baltimore: Johns Hopkins University Press, 2013), 310.

16. Personal email from law enforcement operative to author, October 1, 2021.

17. Trevor Griffey, "History Declassified: Using U.S. Government Intelligence Documents to Write Left History," *Left History* 16, no. 1 (2012): 115.

18. Richard M. Gutman, "Combatting Defendants' Obstructionism in the Discovery Process," *University of Detroit Journal of Urban Law* 55, no. 4 (1978): 983–1003; Paul G. Chevigny, "Politics and Law in the Control of Local Surveillance," *Cornell Law Review* 69, no. 4 (1984): 735–83; Leonard N. Moore, *Black Rage in New Orleans: Police Brutality and African American Activism from World War II to Hurricane Katrina* (Baton Rouge: Louisiana State University Press, 2010); Simon Ezra Balto, "'Occupied Territory': Police Repression and Black Resistance in Postwar Milwaukee, 1950–1980," *Journal of African American History* 98, no. 2 (2013): 229–52; David Ponton III, "A Protracted War for Order: Police Violence in the Twentieth Century United States," *History Compass* 16, no. 6 (2018): 1–12; Felker-Kantor, *Policing Los Angeles*; Andrew S. Baer, *Beyond the Usual Beating: The Jon Burge Police Torture Scandal and Social Movements for Police Accountability in Chicago* (Chicago: University of Chicago Press, 2020).

19. Beverly Gage, "Stormy Weather," *Chronicle of Higher Education (Chronicle Review)* 63, no. 19, January 13, 2017, B14.

1. FEDERAL SURVEILLANCE

1. O'Reilly, *Racial Matters*, 310–16; Beverly Gage, *G-Man: J. Edgar Hoover and the Making of the American Century* (New York: Viking, 2022), 604–6, 690–92.

2. John Edgar Hoover, "An Open Letter to College Students," September 21, 1970, with cover letter, folder "Campus Unrest [3 of 8]," box 20, Subject File 1, White House Central Files: Staff Member & Office Files: Daniel Patrick Moynihan, Richard Nixon Presidential Library and Museum, Yorba Linda, CA, accessed July 2, 2018, https://www.nixonlibrary.gov/sites/default/files/virtuallibrary/documents/ju110/58.pdf, 2. Among the newspapers that published Hoover's letter were the *Atlanta Constitution* ("Hoover Pinpoints Extremist Strategies," September 21, 1970, 7A), the *Orlando Sentinel* ("How Campus Riots Are Born—Hoover Lists Radical Ploys," September 21, 1970, 6A), the *Miami Herald* ("Look Critically at Society, but Avoid Extremism, Students Told," September 21, 1970, 9C), the *Charlotte Observer* ("FBI's Hoover Warns Students about Radicals' Ploys," September 21, 1970, 1A), the *Nashville Tennessean* ("Hoover Lists 8 Extremist Ploys," September 21, 1970, 36), the *Jackson Clarion-Ledger* ("Hoover Writes Open Letter to Students," October 2, 1970, 4A), and the *Memphis Commercial Appeal* ("Hoover Warns Students, Expresses Confidence," October 4, 1970, sec. 6, 3).

3. The most significant of these investigations was the one conducted in 1975 by a newly created Senate committee chaired by Idaho's Frank Church. The Senate Select Committee to Study Governmental Operations with Respect to Intelligence Activities was charged with investigating illegal activities among the nation's intelligence agencies and making recommendations for reform. Over fifteen months, the committee conducted more than 800 interviews, held twenty-one days of public hearings, and led 250 executive hearings. The committee's final report, which had six different parts and was supported by seven volumes of hearings, was a stinging rebuke of FBI, CIA, and other intelligence agencies for their cavalier and flagrant disregard for the constitutionally protected rights of Americans, and it presented nearly 200 specific recommendations for reform. U.S. Senate, *Select Committee to Study Government Operations with Respect to Intelligence Activities*, 94 Cong., 1st sess., *Hearings*, 7 vols. (Washington, DC, 1976); *Senate Reports*, 94 Cong., 2nd sess., no. 755: *Final Report of the Select Committee to Study Government Operations with Respect to Intelligence Activities*, 6 vols. (Washington, DC, 1976). The committee also drew on the work of the presidentially appointed U.S. Commission on CIA Activities within the United States, known as the Rockefeller Commission because Vice President Nelson Rockefeller headed it. While historians consider the report issued by the commission to be a whitewash due to administrative interference with its work, it did provide valuable information that informed the Church Committee's reports. *Report to the President by the Commission on CIA Activities within the United States* (Washington, DC: Government Printing Office, 1975).

4. Revelations about CIA domestic intelligence operations first came to light in an explosive article by Seymour Hersh in the *New York Times* in 1974 that detailed an internal agency review of its files that identified numerous instances of spying, break-ins, and other activities that were illegal or violated the agency's charter. The review, which resulted in a nearly seven hundred–page collection of reports from each of the agency's directorates, came to be known as the "Family Jewels" and led to the creation of the Church Committee and the Rockefeller Commission the following year.

Seymour Hersh, "Huge CIA Operation Reported in U.S. against Anti-War Forces, Other Dissidents in Nixon Years," *New York Times*, December 22, 1974, 1. The "Family Jewels" were finally released to the public in 2007 thanks to the efforts of the National Security Archive, which now hosts a digital copy of the documents. "Memorandum for Executive Committee, CIA Management Committee, Subject: "Family Jewels," May 16, 1973, https://nsarchive2.gwu.edu/NSAEBB/NSAEBB222/family_jewels_full_ocr.pdf. Works that discuss the CIA's counterintelligence activities include Robert Justin Goldstein, *Political Repression in Modern America from 1870 to the Present* (Cambridge, MA: Schenkman Publishing, 1978), 454–57, 477–79; Donner, *Age of Surveillance*, 268–77; Mackenzie, *Secrets;* Hugh Wilford, *The Mighty Wurlitzer: How the CIA Played America* (Cambridge: Harvard University Press, 2008); Tity De Vries, "The 1967 Central Intelligence Agency Scandal: Catalyst in a Transforming Relationship between State and People, *Journal of American History* 98, no. 4 (2012): 1075–1092; Prados, *Family Jewels;* Tyler Russell Rollins, "Domestic Surveillance in the United States: World War II to Vietnam" (PhD diss., University of Colorado, 2016), 104–16, 177–200. On staffing within the CHAOS program, see *Report to the President by the Commission on CIA Activities within the United States*, 130, 136; Prados, *Family Jewels*, 49–50.

5. "Memorandum for Executive Committee, CIA Management Committee, Subject: "Family Jewels," 173; *Report to the President by the Commission on CIA Activities within the United States*, 134; *Church Committee Report*, bk. 3 (Supplementary Detailed Staff Reports of Intelligence Activities and the Rights of Americans), 696; Prado, *Family Jewels*, 46. The Church Committee's discussion of CIA domestic activities includes *Church Committee Report*, bk. 3, 703–4, 721–23.

6. Rockefeller Commission, 138–41; *Church Committee Report*, bk. 3, 703–4.

7. Rockefeller Commission, 138–41; *Church Committee Report*, bk. 3, 703–4, 716.

8. *Church Committee Report*, bk. 3, 716.

9. The Church Committee offered examples of CIA actions in its report but tended not to identify the campuses where the agency worked. Nor did the committee provide a discrete volume of supporting documentation and testimony regarding the CIA's stateside surveillance.

10. *Church Committee Report*, bk. 2 (Intelligence Activities and the Rights of Americans), 98; *Church Committee Report*, bk. 3, 694, 711–12.

11. *Church Committee Report*, bk. 3, 711.

12. Donner, *Age of Surveillance*, 294.

13. All quotations from U.S. Senate, *Subcommittee on Constitutional Rights, Committee on the Judiciary, Army Surveillance of Civilians: A Documentary Analysis* (Washington, DC: U.S. Government Printing Office, 1972), iv–v; U.S. Senate, *Subcommittee on Constitutional Rights of the Committee on the Judiciary: Federal Data Banks, Computers and the Bill of Rights: Hearings*, 92nd Cong., 2 pts. (1971) (hereafter cited as Ervin Subcommittee Hearings). Pyle was a former army captain who taught at the army's intelligence school in Maryland. He left the army 1969 and began graduate work at Columbia University. His initial article, in the *Washington Monthly* in January 1970, along with a follow-up piece six months later set off a firestorm and led to the investigation undertaken by Ervin's Subcommittee on Constitutional Rights. Christopher H. Pyle, "CONUS Intelligence: The Army Watches Civilian Politics," *Washington Monthly* (January 1970): 4–16; Christopher H. Pyle, "CONUS Revisited: The Army Covers Up," *Washington Monthly* (July 1970): 49–58; "Ex-Officer Says Army Spies on Civilian Activists," *New York Times*, January 16, 1970, 26; Richard Halloran, "Army

Spied on 18,000 Civilians in 2-Year Operation," *New York Times*, January 18, 1971, 1, 22. Also see Christopher H. Pyle, "The Domestic Intelligence Community," in *Uncle Sam Is Watching You: Highlights from the Hearings of the Senate Subcommittee on Constitutional Rights* (Washington, DC: Public Affairs Press, 1971), 41–60; and Christopher H. Pyle, "Military Intelligence Overkill," in *Uncle Sam Is Watching You*, 74–147. Secondary works that consider military intelligence in this era include Joan M. Jensen, *Military Surveillance of Civilians in America* (Morristown, NJ: General Learning Press, 1975); Joan M. Jensen, *Army Surveillance in America, 1775–1980* (New Haven, CT: Yale University Press, 1991), 230–67; Donner, *Age of Surveillance*, 287–320; and Katherine A. Scott, *Reining in the State: Civil Society and Congress in the Vietnam and Watergate Eras* (Lawrence: University Press of Kansas, 2013), 50–73, 82–90.

14. *Church Committee Report*, bk. 3, 787–89, 794–804; Ervin Subcommittee Hearings, 147–277; Donner, *Age of Surveillance*, 294–314.

15. Ervin Subcommittee Hearings, pt. 1, 251, 259; *Church Committee Report*, bk. 3, 815–16. The Ervin subcommittee hearing transcript offers two different spellings for the name of the fictitious PO box owner.

16. Ervin Subcommittee Hearings, pt. 1, 160, 267–68; Goldstein, *Political Repression in Modern America*, 458. Goldstein does not indicate his source on the Fort Sam Houston files.

17. Ervin Subcommittee Hearings, pt. 1, 191–92, pt. 2, 266–68; Donner, *Age of Surveillance*, 295–300.

18. Ervin Subcommittee Hearings, pt. 2 (Relating to Departments of Army, Defense, and Justice), 1488; Ervin Subcommittee Hearings, pt. 1, 196–198, 273–74; Donner, *Age of Surveillance*, 305–7. Donner includes a variation of this quotation, though his source for it is unclear.

19. Ervin Subcommittee Hearings, pt. 2, 1484–85.

20. Pyle, "CONUS Intelligence," 9; Ervin Subcommittee Hearings, pt. 1, 971. Stein mistakenly called the group the Southern Students [*sic*] Organizing Committee. Ervin Subcommittee Hearings, pt. 1, 264–65 (Stein's full testimony is at 244–77). Also see Ralph M. Stein, "Expansion of Counterintelligence," in *Uncle Sam Is Watching You: Highlights from the Hearings of the Senate Subcommittee on Constitutional Rights*, 148–71. Washington, DC: Public Affairs Press, 1971.

21. Ervin Subcommittee Hearings, pt. 1, 189; Janda, *Prairie Power*, 77.

22. Ervin Subcommittee Hearings, pt. 2, 1457–58.

23. *Church Committee Report*, bk. 3, 815–16. For an overview of the coffeehouse movement, see David L. Parsons, *Dangerous Grounds: Antiwar Coffeehouses and Military Dissent in the Vietnam Era* (Chapel Hill: University of North Carolina Press, 2017).

24. Donner, *Age of Surveillance*, 305; U.S. Senate, *Army Surveillance of Civilians*, 96. On the army's efforts to conceal its domestic intelligence activities in the face of journalistic and congressional scrutiny, see Pyle, "CONUS Revisited."

25. U.S. Senate, Army Surveillance of Civilians, 96–97.

26. Donner, "Spies on Campus," 118; Hoover, "Open Letter to College Students," 4.

27. Director, FBI, to Special Agent in Charge (SAC), Albany, Church Committee Hearings, vol. 6 (Federal Bureau of Investigations), 612–13. Note that, alphabetically, Albany was the first of the fifty-nine field offices. Hence, memos sent to all field offices started with the ones to Albany.

28. Hoover, "Open Letter to College Students," 3.

29. That the bureau used the same "hate" label for a program focused on civil rights and Black empowerment groups as it did for its work against the Klan illuminates the low regard in which it held civil rights activists. Studies that focus on COINTELPRO include Theoharis, *Spying on Americans;* Donner, *Age of Surveillance,* 177–240; Ward Churchill and Jim Vander Wall, *The COINTELPRO Papers: Documents from the FBI's Secret Wars against Domestic Dissent* (Boston, MA: South End Press, 1990); and Athan G. Theoharis, *The FBI and American Democracy: A Brief Critical History* (Lawrence: University Press of Kansas, 2004). Discussion of COINTELPRO–New Left can be found in Donner, *Age of Surveillance,* 232–40; Churchill and Vander Wall, *COINTELPRO Papers,* 165–226; David Cunningham, "State versus Social Movement: FBI Counterintelligence against the New Left," in *States, Parties, and Social Movements,* ed. Jack A. Goldstone (Cambridge: Cambridge University Press, 2003), 45–77; and Cunningham, *There's Something Happening Here.* For works that focus on specific COINTELPROs, see Blackstock, *COINTELPRO,* which examines the campaign against the Social Workers Party; O'Reilly, *Racial Matters;* and Garrow, *FBI and Martin Luther King, Jr.,* on the bureau's assault on civil rights activists; Churchill and Vander Wall, *Agents of Repression: The FBI's Secret Wars against the Black Panther Party and the American Indian Movement,* on the work against these two notable groups; David Cunningham, *Klansville, U.S.A.: The Rise and Fall of the Civil Rights–Era Ku Klux Klan* (New York: Oxford University Press, 2013), regarding the drive against the Klan; and Fernández, *Young Lords,* 165–76, 350, 373–74, which briefly considers the campaign against Puerto Rican activists.

30. Among the many studies of the FBI, particularly useful and insightful works include Sanford J. Ungar, *FBI* (Boston: Little, Brown, 1975); Kenneth O'Reilly, *Hoover and the Un-Americans: The FBI, HUAC, and the Red Menace* (Philadelphia: Temple University Press, 1983); Richard Gid Powers, *Broken: The Troubled Past and Uncertain Future of the FBI* (New York: Free Press, 2004); Theoharis, *FBI & American Democracy;* Douglas M. Charles, *J. Edgar Hoover and the Anti-Interventionists: FBI Political Surveillance and the Rise of the Domestic Security State, 1939–1945* (Columbus: Ohio State University Press, 2007); Rhodri Jeffreys-Jones, *The FBI: A History* (New Haven, CT: Yale University Press, 2007). Also see Gage, *G-Man.*

31. Powers, *Broken,* 237–38 (Hoover to Cutler, January 16, 1958, 237). Hoover made similar remarks in testimony before the House Un-American Activities Committee. *U.S. House, Committee on Un-American Activities: Hearings on H.R. 1884 and H.R. 2122, Bills to Curb or Outlaw the Communist Party of the United States, Part 2: Testimony of J. Edgar Hoover, Director, Federal Bureau of Investigation,* 80th Cong. (March 26, 1947), 33–50, esp. 37–38.

32. FBI agents officially were known as "special agents," and the agent who headed each field office was the "special agent in charge," or SAC (in Washington, DC, and New York City, the field offices were led instead by "assistant directors in charge"). Communications from the field offices to headquarters typically were attributed to the SAC regardless of which agent actually authored a memo or document. Athan G. Theoharis et al., *The FBI: A Comprehensive Reference Guide* (Phoenix: Oryx Press, 1999), 217.

33. SAC, Atlanta, to Director, FBI (HQ 100-442367-1), July 10, 1964, and Director, FBI, to SAC, Memphis (HQ 100-442367-2), July 28, 1964, Records of the Federal Bureau of Investigation, Freedom of Information Act releases to author (hereafter cited as FBI Records). The date of the New York memo was June 30, 1964, not July 30, 1964, as mistakenly indicated in the July 10 memo

from the Atlanta office. Although the author has not been able to locate this document, the June 30 date is noted in other bureau communications, such as Director, FBI, to SAC, Memphis (HQ 100-442367-2), July 28, 1964; and SAC, Memphis, to Director, FBI (HQ 100-442367-3), September 25, 1964, FBI Records. As FBI intelligence operations progressed, Hoover and his leadership team established a filing system that served to segregate into secret files the information it gathered in order to conceal the illegal and political nature of its domestic security work. These files would expand exponentially with the advent of the COINTELPROs. All FBI records had a unique record, or serial, number typically in the format (xxx-xxxxxx-xx). The first number is the classification number, which corresponds to the same number used in the Department of Justice system and relates to particular federal crimes. Classification 100, Domestic Security, was used for the vast majority of files connected to the New Left. The second number is the individual case number that an office assigns to a case. The third number is the document number in the case file. Crucially, FBI records often carried more than one serial because both headquarters and the field offices assigned their own numbers to a case. When citing FBI records with multiple serial numbers, I use the number assigned by FBI Headquarters in Washington and indicate this with "HQ" before the serial number. For all its complexity, the bureau's filing system contained numerous inconsistencies. Serials, for example, sometimes contained four sets of number rather than three. And some documents only have two numbers—the classification and case numbers but not the document number. On the FBI filing system, see Ann Mari Buitrago and Leon Andrew Immerman, *Are You Now or Have You Ever Been in the FBI Files? How to Secure and Interpret Your FBI Files* (New York: Grove Press, 1981); and Gerald K. Haines and David A. Langbart, *Unlocking the Files of the FBI: A Guide to Its Records and Classification System* (Wilmington, DE: Scholarly Resources, 1993). Cominfil began in 1960 with an explicit focus on the Communist Party. By 1964, it had expanded to include civil rights groups, a program known as "Communist Influence in Racial Matters." O'Reilly, *Hoover and the Un-Americans*, 198–99; O'Reilly, *Racial Matters*, 138–41; Powers, *Broken*, 236–37. On SCEF and the Bradens, see Catherine Fosl, *Subversive Southerner: Anne Braden and the Struggle for Racial Justice in the Cold War South* (New York: Palgrave Macmillan, 2002).

34. SAC, Memphis, to Director, FBI (HQ 100-442367-3), September 25, 1964; and Director, FBI, to SAC, Memphis (HQ 100-442367-3), October 14, 1964, FBI Records. Note that the two documents cited here have the same serial number, which the bureau sometimes assigned when the two documents are related, another inconsistency in the filing system. Memos to the field offices from the director were not always written by Hoover. William Sullivan and other top bureau officials often penned memos sent out from the director. David Cunningham, "The Patterning of Repression: FBI Counterintelligence and the New Left," *Social Forces* 82, no. 1 (2003): 213; Cunningham, *There's Something Happening Here*, 81–82.

35. SAC, Memphis, report, *Communist Infiltration: Southern Student Organizing Committee* (HQ 100-442367-8), January 8, 1965; and Director, FBI, to SAC (HQ 100-442367-10), Memphis, January 28, 1965, FBI Records.

36. SAC, Memphis, to Director, FBI (HQ 100-442367-22), August 30, 1965, FBI Records.

37. SAC, Little Rock, Letterhead Memorandum (HQ 100-442367-25), November 18, 1965; SAC, Oklahoma City to Director, FBI (HQ 100-442367-26), November 23, 1965; SAC, San Antonio, Letterhead Memorandum (HQ 100-442367-28), December 4, 1965; SAC, Little Rock, Letterhead Mem-

orandum (HQ 100-442367-29), December 9, 1965; and, SAC, Memphis, Letterhead Memorandum (HQ 100-442367-31), February 17, 1966, all in FBI Records.

38. SAC, Memphis, to Director, FBI (HQ 100-442367-32), June 2, 1966; and Director, FBI, to SAC, Memphis (HQ 100-442367-32), June 14, 1966, FBI Records. Hoover's concern about embarrassment if the bureau was found to be working covertly on college campuses was not misplaced as the scandal that erupted a few months later over the CIA's clandestine funding of the National Student Association made clear.

39. SAC, Memphis, to Director, FBI (HQ 100-442367-42), October, 26, 1966, and Director, FBI, to SAC, Memphis (HQ 100-442367-42), November 14, 1966, FBI Records. On the Peace Fast, see SAC, Memphis, Letterhead Memorandum (HQ 100-442367), July 13, 1966; and Memphis, teletypes (HQ 100-442367-34 to 100-442367-40), July 3–8, 1966, FBI Records; "5-Day Fast over War in 3rd Day," *Nashville Tennessean*, July 6, 1966, 3; Jerry Thompson, "20 War Protesters Arrested," *Nashville Tennessean*, July 8, 1966, 1; "Demonstrators End Fast Early," *Nashville Tennessean*, July 9, 1966, 20; "Seven Fast for Peace," *Southern Patriot*, August 1966, 2.

40. SAC, Memphis, Letterhead Memorandum cover sheet (HQ 100-442367-43), November 16, 1966; and SAC, Memphis, Letterhead Memorandum (HQ 100-442367-43), November 16, 1966, FBI Records.

41. SAC, Richmond, Letterhead Memorandum (HQ 100-442367-48), December 29, 1966; SAC, Little Rock, Letterhead Memorandum cover sheet (HQ 100-442367-52), January 5, 1967; SAC, Little Rock, Letterhead Memorandum (HQ 100-442367-52), January 5, 1967; SAC, Detroit, to Director, FBI (HQ 100-442367-53), January 5, 1967; SAC, Boston, to Director, FBI (HQ 100-442367-55), January 17, 1967; and SAC, New York, to Director, FBI (HQ 100-442367-57), January 23, 1967, all in FBI Records.

42. SAC, Richmond, Letterhead Memorandum cover sheet (HQ 100-442367-59), February 16, 1967; and SAC, Richmond, Letterhead Memorandum (HQ 100-442367-59), February 16, 1967, FBI Records. The bureau was also the recipient of surveillance information gathered by other agencies. For instance, the 111th Military Intelligence Group in Fayetteville, North Carolina, informed the Charlotte FBI office about antiwar protest by SSOC activists near Fort Bragg. SAC, Charlotte, Letterhead Memorandum (HQ 100-442367-359), November 18, 1968, FBI Records.

43. SAC, Memphis, Letterhead Memorandum cover sheet (HQ 100-442367), March 15, 1967; SAC, Memphis, Letterhead Memorandum (HQ 100-442367), March 15, 1967; [unknown author] to Mr. [Cartha] DeLoach (HQ 100-442367], March 14, 1967, FBI Records.

44. The agents' reports on SSOC are filled with redactions in the place of names and personal information on the students the bureau investigated. SAC, Miami, Letterhead Memorandum (HQ 100-442367-70), March 31, 1967; SAC, Atlanta, Letterhead Memorandum (HQ 100-442367-[??]), April 15, 1967; FBI, Atlanta, to FBI, Washington, DC, teletype (HQ 100-442367[??]), May 20, 1967; SAC, Atlanta, Letterhead Memorandum (HQ 100-442367-[??]), October 17, 1967; and SAC, Little Rock, Letterhead Memorandum (HQ 100-442367-98), October 25, 1967, all in FBI Records.

45. C. D. Brennan to W. C. Sullivan (HQ 100-442367-91), September 1, 1967, FBI Records.

46. Director, FBI, to SACs (HQ 100-442367-116), December 15, 1967, FBI Records. The SACs that received the memo from the director's office were in field offices spread across eleven southern states: Memphis, Atlanta, Birmingham, Charlotte, Columbia, Jackson, Jacksonville, Knox-

ville, Little Rock, Louisville, Miami, Mobile, New Orleans, Norfolk, Richmond, Savannah, and Tampa.

47. Director, FBI to SACs (HQ 100-442367-116), December 15, 1967, FBI Records.

48. *Church Committee Report*, bk. 3, 255–56, 485–86.

49. SAC, Jackson, to Director, FBI (HQ 100-442367-133), January 8, 1968; SAC, Little Rock, to Director, FBI (HQ 100-442367-132), January 10, 1968; and SAC, Charlotte, to Director, FBI (HQ 100-442367-150), January 15, 1968, FBI Records.

50. The individual's name is redacted in the FBI files. SAC, Mobile, to Director, FBI (HQ 100-442367-135), January 12, 1968, FBI Records.

51. SAC, Richmond, to Director, FBI (HQ 100-442367-143), January 12, 1968, FBI Records. For other examples of school officials' involvement in FBI surveillance, see SAC, Columbia, to Director, FBI (HQ 100-442367-134), January 11, 1968, SAC, Richmond, to Director, FBI (HQ 100-442367-143), January 12, 1968; and SAC, Jacksonville, to Director, FBI (HQ 100-442367-148), January 15, 1968, FBI Records.

52. SAC, New Orleans, to Director, FBI (HQ 100-442367-146), January 18, 1968; and SAC, Miami, to Director, FBI (HQ 100-442367-152), January 12, 1968, FBI Records.

53. SAC, Memphis, report, *Southern Student Organizing Committee (SSOC* (HQ 100-442367-130), January 5, 1968, FBI Records.

54. Ibid. Agents also gained access to the group's savings account at First Federal Savings and Loan Association in Nashville.

55. Ibid. See 60–62 on the reading list.

56. Ibid.

57. SAC, Memphis, Letterhead Memorandum cover sheet; and SAC, Memphis, Letterhead Memorandum, both in (HQ 100-442367-212), April 24, 1968, FBI Records.

58. SAC, Miami, report, *Southern Student Organizing Committee (SSOC)* (HQ 100-442367-187), March 15, 1968; FBI, Miami, to Director, Teletype (HQ 100-442367-195), March 16, 1968; SAC, Little Rock, Letterhead Memorandum (HQ 100-442367-199), March 21, 1968; SAC, Charlotte, SAC, Memphis, report, *Southern Student Organizing Committee (SSOC)* (HQ 100-442367-203), April 8, 1968; and FBI, Atlanta, to Director and Memphis, teletype (HQ 100-442367-224), May 2, 1968, all in FBI Records.

59. Cunningham, *There's Something Happening Here*, 50. The precise number of COINTELPRO actions against New Left targets cannot be definitively determined, but Powers writes that there were exactly 291 actions, and Cunningham says there were more than 400. Powers, *Broken*, 279–80; Cunningham, *There's Something Happening Here*, 49–50.

60. On Sullivan, see Ungar, *FBI*, 295–314; Powers, *Broken*, 250–58; William C. Sullivan, with Bill Brown, *The Bureau: My Thirty Years in Hoover's FBI* (New York: Norton, 1979). On the King letter, see Garrow, *FBI and Martin Luther King, Jr.*, esp. 121–35; David J. Garrow, *Bearing the Cross: Martin Luther King, Jr., and the Southern Christian Leadership Conference* (New York: Vintage, 1986), 372–74; O'Reilly, *Racial Matters*, 142–45; Taylor Branch, *Pillar of Fire: America in the King Years, 1963–1965* (New York: Simon and Schuster, 1998), 527–29; and Beverly Gage, "I Have a [Redacted]: Would the F.B.I.'s Smear Campaign against Martin Luther King Jr. Work Today?" *New York Times Magazine*, November 16, 2014, 15. Perhaps unsurprisingly, Sullivan's memoir reveals how delusional he was regarding his own culpability for bureau malfeasance, including the King letter, despite the

fact it was found in his own files. Sullivan, *Bureau*, 142; Donner, *Age of Surveillance*, 216–17; and Gage, *G-Man*, 584–85, 608–9.

61. Sullivan, *Bureau*, 148.

62. C. D. Brennan to W. C. Sullivan, May 9, 1968, in Church Committee Hearings, 6:393–94. Clarence Kelley, who headed the FBI in the mid-1970s, echoed Brennan's memo in a press release in 1973 when COINTELPRO–New Left came to light. In seeking to rationalize the Bureau's actions, Kelley aptly captured the fearful, distorted view of the New Left that permeated the FBI, declaring it "a hard-core revolutionary movement" that wanted "to bring the government to its knees through the use of force and violence." Clarence M. Kelley and James Kirkpatrick Davis, *Kelley: The Story of an FBI Director* (Kansas City: Andrews, McMeel & Parker, 1987), 172. Sanford Unger includes a slightly different version of Kelley's remarks. Unger, *FBI*, 470–71.

63. Director, FBI, to SAC, Albany (HQ 449698), May 10, 1968, COINTELPRO–New Left–HQ, pt. 1, *FBI Records: The Vault*, https://vault.fbi.gov/cointel-pro/new-left (hereafter cited as FBI Vault); FBI Headquarters to all SACs, May 23, 1968, in *Church Committee Report*, bk. 3, 24. Cunningham, *There's Something Happening Here*, 50, 92–93, 277–78.

64. *Church Committee Report*, bk. 3, 508.

65. Director, FBI, to SAC, Albany, July 6, 1968, in Church Committee Hearings, 6:395–96; also see *Church Committee Report*, bk. 3 26.

66. "SAC Letter," July 23, 1968, in Church Committee Hearings, 6:684.

67. Director, FBI, to SAC, Albany, October 9, 1968, in Church Committee Hearings, 6:613.

68. SAC Letter No. 68-21, April 2, 1968, in *Church Committee Report*, bk. 3, 507.

69. Director, FBI, to SAC, Albany, October 28, 1968, in Church Committee Hearings, 6:669.

70. SAC, Memphis, to Director, FBI (HQ 100-4491-15), June 22, 1967, FBI Records. Also see SAC, Memphis, to Director, FBI (HQ 100-442367-335), October 18, 1968; SAC, Memphis, to Director, FBI (HQ 100-442367-388), January 21, 1969; SAC, Memphis, to Director, FBI (HQ 100-442367-407), February 3, 1969; and Director, FBI, to SAC, Memphis (HQ 100-442367-412), February 13, 1969, all in FBI Records.

71. Congressional investigators found that reliance on confidential sources constituted the third most used counterintelligence tool of the FBI in domestic security cases. *Church Committee Report*, bk. 3, 229.

72. SAC, Richmond, to Director, FBI (HQ 100-449698-41-1), May 29, 1968, Records of the Federal Bureau of Investigation, Freedom of Information Act releases, generously shared with the author by Christina Greene (hereafter cited as FBI Records–Greene); SAC, Charlotte, to Director, FBI (HQ 100-442367-405), January 30, 1969, FBI Records.

73. *Church Committee Report*, bk. 3, 228.

74. Ibid., 255–59, 485–86; SAC, Richmond, to Director, FBI (HQ 100-449698-41-3), July 2, 1968, FBI Records–Greene; SAC, Charlotte, to Director (HQ 100-449698-8-3), FBI, July 2, 1968, COINTELPRO–New Left–Charlotte, FBI Vault.

75. SAC, Charlotte, to Director (HQ 100-449698-8-3), FBI July 2, 1968, COINTELPRO–New Left–Charlotte, FBI Vault; SAC, Jackson, to Director, FBI (HQ 100-449698-54-8), December 4, 1968; SAC, Birmingham, to Director, FBI (HQ 100-442367-291), September 13, 1968; SAC, Richmond, report, *Southern Student Organizing Committee (SSOC)* (HQ 100-442367-301), September 23, 1968, all in FBI Records.

76. Ken Lawrence, phone conversation with author, March 1, 2023; interview with David Doggett by the author, Philadelphia, PA, August 30, 1994; A. L. Hopkins to Director Erle Johnston Jr., May 26, 1964, 1-100-0-1-1-1-1; Charles E. Snodgrass to Col. T. B. Birdsong and Chief A. D. Morgan, August 22, 1967, 1-100-0-3-2-1-1; W. Webb Burke to Hon. G. V. Montgomery, 1-100-0-6-1-1-1, all in ser. 2515: Mississippi State Sovereignty Commission Records, 1956–2002, Mississippi Department of Archives and History; Ken Lawrence, "Beware of This Man," *Southern Patriot*, April 30, 1974.

77. SAC, Little Rock, report, *Southern Student Organizing Committee (SSOC)* (HQ 100-442367-292), September 13, 1968; FBI, Little Rock, to Director, teletype (HQ 100-442367-320), October 12, 1968; and SAC, Jackson, report, *Southern Student Organizing Committee (SSOC)*, November 25, 1968; and various reports on interviews with SSOC activists by Jackson FBI agents, August 13 to November 25, 1968 (HQ 100-442367-361), all in FBI Records.

78. SAC, Richmond, to Director, FBI (HQ 100-449698-41-4), November 5, 1968; Director, FBI, to SAC, Richmond (HQ 100-449698-41-4), November 18, 1968; SAC, Richmond, to Director, FBI (HQ 100-449698-41-5), November 19, 1968; and Director, FBI, to SAC, Richmond (HQ 100-449698-41-5), November 27, 1968, all in FBI Records–Greene.

79. SAC, Jackson to Director, FBI (HQ 100-449698), March 27, 1970, FBI Records–Greene.

80. *Church Committee Report*, bk. 3, 36.

81. SAC, Jackson, to Director, FBI (HQ 100-449698-54-6), October 2, 1968, FBI Records–Greene.

82. Director, FBI, to SAC, Jackson (HQ 100-449698-54-6), October 18, 1968, FBI Records–Greene.

83. SAC, Jackson, to Director, FBI (HQ 100-449698-54-6), October 2, 1968; and Director, FBI, to SAC, Jackson (HQ 100-449698-54-6), October 18, 1968, FBI Records–Greene; Robert Hessen, "Campus or Battleground? Columbia Is a Warning to All American Universities," *Barron's National Business & Financial Weekly*, May 20, 1968, 1, 10, 12, 15; James Kirkpatrick Davis, *Assault on the Left: The FBI and the Sixties Antiwar Movement* (Westport, CT: Praeger Publishers, 1997), 90–91.

84. SAC, Jackson, to Director, FBI (HQ 100-449698-54-7), November 21, 1968, FBI Records–Greene. The articles ran between November 19 and 26. "Campus or Battleground?" is featured in the November 21 column.

85. SAC, Jackson, to Director, FBI (HQ 100-449698-54-8), December 4, 1968, FBI Records–Greene.

86. SAC, Jackson, to Director, FBI, February 11, 1969, in Church Committee Hearings, 6:807–8; Director, FBI, to SAC, Jackson, February 26, 1969, in Church Committee Hearings, 6:804–6.

87. Hessen, "Campus or Battleground," 1.

88. Director, FBI, to SAC, Albany, July 6, 1968, in Church Committee Hearings, 6:395–96; also see *Church Committee Report*, bk. 3, 26.

89. SAC, Jackson, to Director, FBI (HQ 100-449698-54-1), May 29, 1968, FBI Records–Greene.

90. Director, FBI, to SAC, Jackson (HQ 100-449698-54-1), June 7, 1968, FBI Records–Greene.

91. "Mississippi Belle Says 'Goodbye to All That,'" *Southern Patriot*, March 1969, 4; SAC, Jackson, to Director, FBI (100-449698-54-10), May 28, 1969, FBI Records–Greene. The name of the individual to whom the letter was sent is redacted. Although Carpenter's name is also redacted, her identity was easily deduced by reference to her Natchez background, which was well known and had received coverage elsewhere.

92. Director, FBI, to SAC, Jackson (HQ 100-449698-54-10), June 16, 1969; and SAC, Jackson, to Director, FBI (HQ 100-449698), July 25, 1969, both in FBI Records–Greene.

93. Director, FBI, to SAC, Albany, October 9, 1968, in Church Committee Hearings, 6:612–13; and Director, FBI, to SAC, Albany, July 6, 1968, in Church Committee Hearings, 6:395–96; also see *Church Committee Report*, bk. 3, 26.

94. SAC, Memphis, Letterhead Memorandum (HQ 100-442367-293), September 11, 1968, FBI Records.

95. Jackson to Director, Memphis and New Orleans, teletype (HQ 100-442367-318), October 13, 1968, FBI Records.

96. Director, FBI, to SAC, Albany, October 9, 1968, in Church Committee Hearings, 6:612.

97. C. D. Brennan to W. C. Sullivan (HQ 100-449698), October 7, 1968, COINTELPRO–New Left–HQ, pt. 1, FBI Vault.

98. SAC, Little Rock, to Director, FBI (HQ 100-449698-25-7), October 14, 1968, FBI Records–Greene.

99. Director, FBI, to SAC, Little Rock (HQ 100-449698-25-7), October 17, 1968, FBI Records–Greene.

100. Director, FBI, to SAC, Albany, July 6, 1968, in Church Committee Hearings, 6:395–96; also see *Church Committee Report*, bk. 3, 26.

101. SAC, Memphis, to Director, FBI, June 28, 1968 (100-449698-28-2), FBI Vault.

102. SAC, Richmond, to Director, FBI (HQ 100-449698-41-6), January 11, 1969; and SAC, Richmond, to Director, FBI (HQ 100-449698-41-7), April 22, 1969, FBI Records–Greene.

103. SAC, Little Rock, to Director, FBI (HQ 100-449698-25-8), December 18, 1968, FBI Records–Greene; C. D. Brennan to W. C. Sullivan (HQ 100-449698), January 29, 1969, COINTELPRO–New Left–HQ, pt. 1, FBI Vault.

104. SAC, Little Rock, to Director, FBI (HQ 100-449698-25-9), August 20, 1968; SAC, Little Rock, to Director, FBI (HQ 100-449698-25-6), September 18, 1968; and SAC, Little Rock, to Director, FBI (HQ 100-449698-25-8), December 18, 1968, all in FBI Records–Greene.

105. SAC, San Antonio, to Director, FBI (HQ 100-449698-45-45), March 12, 1969, COINTELPRO–New Left–San Antonio, FBI Vault. Hoover, in his memo approving the mailing of the letter, instructed the agents to add a sentence explaining why the author sought to remain anonymous: "As I consider [name redacted] to be a friend and wish to maintain that friendship, I am remaining anonymous with the hope that you can take effective action as a concerned parent." Director, FBI, to SAC, San Antonio (HQ 100-449698-45-45), March 24, 1969, COINTELPRO–New Left–San Antonio, FBI Vault.

106. Director, FBI, to SAC, Albany, July 6, 1968, in Church Committee Hearings, 6:395–96; also see *Church Committee Report*, bk. 3, 26.

107. SAC, Columbia, to Director, FBI (HQ 100-449698), July 31, 1969; SAC, Columbia, to Director, FBI (HQ 100-449698), August 6, 1969; SAC, Columbia, to Director, FBI (HQ 100-449698-66-7), August 7, 1969; SAC, Columbia, to Director, FBI (HQ 100-449698-66-9), September 29, 1969; and SAC, Columbia, to Director, FBI (HQ 100-449698-66-1), December 29, 1969, all in FBI Records–Greene.

108. SAC, Columbia, to Director, FBI (HQ 100-449698-66-10), October 8, 1969; and Director, FBI, to SAC, Columbia (HQ 100-449698-66-10), October 20, 1969, both in FBI Records–Greene.

109. SAC, Richmond, to Director, FBI (HQ 100-449698-41-8), June 26, 1969; Director, FBI, to SAC, Richmond (HQ 100-449698-41-8), July 7, 1969; SAC, Richmond, to Director, FBI (HQ 100-449698-41-9), August 7, 1969; SAC, Richmond, to Director, FBI (HQ 100-449698), November 10, 1969; Director, FBI, to SAC, Richmond (HQ 100-449698-41-4), November 18, 1969; SAC, Richmond, to Director, FBI (HQ 100-449698-41-10), December 31, 1969; SAC, Richmond, to Director, FBI (HQ 100-449698-41-11), January 12, 1970; and Director, FBI, to SAC, Richmond (HQ 100-449698-41-10), January 19, 1970, all in FBI Records–Greene.

110. SAC, Knoxville, to Director, FBI (HQ 100-449698-24-7), June 24, 1969; and Director, FBI, to SAC, Knoxville (HQ 100-449698-24-7), July 8, 1969, FBI Records–Greene; SAC, Knoxville, to Director, FBI (HQ 100-449698-24-9), July 17, 1970, COINTELPRO–New Left–Knoxville, FBI Vault.

111. The FBI memo ending the COINTELPRO programs is Director, FBI, to SAC, Albany, April 28, 1971, COINTELPRO–New Left–HQ, pt. 5 (Sub A), FBI Vault. Among works that cover the Media break-in and the end of COINTELPRO are Blackstock, *COINTELPRO;* Powers, *Broken*, 307–9; Betty Medsger, *The Burglary: The Discovery of J. Edgar Hoover's Secret FBI* (New York: Vintage, 2014).

2. STATE SURVEILLANCE

1. Kenneth W. Fairly to Rex P. Armistead, Webb Burke, and Col. Julian Ervin, June 11, 1969, 2-158-4-20-1-1-1; and David Davidson to Kenneth W. Fairly, June 9, 1969, 2-158-4-20-2-1-1 to 2-158-4-20-8-1-1, both in Mississippi State Sovereignty Commission Records, 1956–2002, Mississippi Department of Archives and History (hereafter cited as MSSC). Davidson had traveled to Mt. Beulah with a friend, Bob Head, who does not appear to have been an informer because his name does not appear elsewhere in the Sovereignty Commission.

2. "Final Files of Segregation-Era Snooping Agency Unsealed," *Tampa Bay Times*, August 25, 2005, https://www.tampabay.com/archive/2005/08/04/final-files-of-segregation-era-snooping-agency-unsealed.

3. On some of the state surveillance programs, see Jeff Woods, *Black Struggle, Red Scare: Segregation and Anti-Communism in the South, 1948–1968* (Baton Rouge.: Louisiana State University Press, 2003), 93–103; Christopher Paul Lehman, "Civil Rights in the Twilight: The End of the Civil Rights Movement Era in 1973," *Journal of Black Studies* 36, no. 3 (2006): 419–21; Aaron D. Purcell, "Seeing Red in the Bluegrass: The Kentucky Un-American Activities Committee and Conservatism in the Late 1960s," *Register of the Kentucky Historical Society* 117, no. 1 (Winter 2019): 57–93; Dewey Dykes, "The Arkansas State Sovereignty Commission," *Encyclopedia of Arkansas*, last updated June 16, 2023, https://encyclopediaofarkansas.net/entries/arkansas-state-sovereignty-commission-6490; Michael Pierce, "Odell Smith, Teamsters Local 878, and Civil Rights Unionism in Little Rock, 1943–1965," *Journal of Southern History* 84, no. 4 (2018): 947–48; Stacy Braukman, *Communists and Perverts under the Palms: The Johns Committee in Florida, 1956–1965* (Gainesville: University Press of Florida, 2012); Emma Pettit, "The Inquisition," *Chronicle of Higher Education* 69, no. 4, October 14, 2022, https://www.chronicle.com/article/the-inquisition; Emma Pettit, "'Private Little Hell,'" *Chronicle of Higher Education* 69, no. 8, December 9, 2022, https://www.chronicle.com/article/private-little-hell; Sarah Eppler Janda, "'Even Mild Protest Is Not Generally Considered to Be Very Patriotic': Surveillance Culture and the Rise of the 'Sooner CIA,'" *Western Historical Quarterly* 48, no. 4 (2017): 1–22.

4. Dewey F. Bartlett, Memorandum for: The Adjutant General, Oklahoma Military Department Commissioner, Department of Public Safety Director, State Bureau of Investigation, June 5, 1968, in Kenneth Kottka and Earl Mitchell v. Dewey F. Bartlett et al. (hereafter cited as Kottka case file), generously shared with the author by Stephen Jones; U.S. Senate, *Subcommittee on Constitutional Rights of the Committee on the Judiciary: Federal Data Banks, Computers and the Bill of Rights: Hearings*, 92nd Cong., 2 pts. (1971), 172; Janda, "'Even Mild Protest,'" 1–5, 11; Landry Brewer, "Maurice Halperin: From Sooner Subversive to Soviet Spy," *Chronicles of Oklahoma* 96, no. 2 (2018): 161–64.

5. Janda, "'Even Mild Protest,'" 1–6; Janda, *Prairie Power*, 68–71.

6. Partial Transcript of NBC News Program "First Tuesday" Broadcast December 1, 1970, As Part of Plaintiffs Response to Defendants Motion for Summary Judgment, ca. January 1971, Kottka case file, 24; Mike Flanagan, "Secret Bartlett Agency 'Watching' Sooners," *Tulsa Daily World*, July 11, 1970, A-1, A-4; Janda, "'Even Mild Protest,'" 16–17.

7. Deposition of James J. DeFrates, January 5, 1971, Kottka case file, 24; Application for Grant, Discretionary Funds FY70, Under Title I, Omnibus Crime Control and Safe Streets Act of 1968, submitted by State of Oklahoma, Office of Interagency Coordination, April 21, 1970, revised June 5, 1970, and June 10, 1970, Kottka case file, 1.

8. Application for Grant, Discretionary Funds FY70, Under Title I, Omnibus Crime Control and Safe Streets Act of 1968, Kottka case file, 1; "Bartlett Bars Intelligence Information," *Elk City Daily News*, September 10, 1970, Oklahoma Clipping Bureau, Kottka case file.

9. Janda, "'Even Mild Protest,'" 5–6; Janda, *Prairie Power*, 78–80.

10. Throughout its existence the OIC employed four or five people, including DeFrates. In his 1971 deposition in the ACLU lawsuit, DeFrates named George Wallingford, Sybil Hood, and Helen Tristol as working for the OIC, though he does not identify their positions or their duties. However, the application for federal funds named existing positions as Director, Assistant Director, Steno Clerk, and Clerk Typist. Deposition of James J. DeFrates, 14–15. Application for Grant, Discretionary Funds FY70, Under Title I, Omnibus Crime Control and Safe Streets Act of 1968, 2.

11. Janda, "'Even Mild Protest,'" 6–7; Janda, *Prairie Power*, 80–81.

12. Affidavit of J. Herbert Holloman in Support of Plaintiffs [*sic*] Response to Defendants [*sic*] Motion for Summary Judgment, December 22, 1970, Kottka case file; Janda, "'Even Mild Protest,'" 6–7; Janda, *Prairie Power*, 131–32.

13. Flanagan, "Secret Bartlett Agency 'Watching' Sooners," A-1, A-4; "Bartlett Bars Intelligence Information"; Deposition of James J. DeFrates, 26; Martin Waldron, "Oklahoma Suit Challenges Secret Files on Activists," *New York Times*, November 1, 1970, 48; Janda, "'Even Mild Protest,'" 11.

14. Waldron, "Oklahoma Suit Challenges Secret Files on Activists," 48. The precise number of files the OIC maintained cannot be determined because they later were destroyed. In 1970, DeFrates provided wildly inconsistent figures for the number of incident reports the OIC had collected. In an application for federal funds in June 1970 he said there were 5,465 incident reports. Six months later, in a television interview, he estimated the OIC had collected approximately 10,000 reports. Application for Grant, Discretionary Funds FY70, Under Title I, Omnibus Crime Control and Safe Streets Act of 1968, 8, and Partial Transcript of NBC News Program "First Tuesday" Broadcast December 1, 1970, as part of Plaintiffs Response to Defendants Motion for Summary Judgment, ca. January 1971, 24, both in Kottka case file.

15. Deposition of James J. DeFrates, 27–30, 33, 43.

16. Application for Grant, Discretionary Funds FY70, Under Title I, Omnibus Crime Control and Safe Streets Act of 1968, 1, 8; Flanagan, "Secret Bartlett Agency 'Watching' Sooners," A-1, A-4; Waldron, "Oklahoma Suit Challenges Secret Files on Activists," 48.

17. Application for Grant, Discretionary Funds FY70, Under Title I, Omnibus Crime Control and Safe Streets Act of 1968, 6.

18. The news clippings attached to the application were divided into two groups: sixteen about "Unrest on campus" and twenty-four about "Unrest in Cities." Application for Grant, Discretionary Funds FY70, Under Title I, Omnibus Crime Control and Safe Streets Act of 1968 (quotations from "Index").

19. Application for Grant, Discretionary Funds FY70, Under Title I, Omnibus Crime Control and Safe Streets Act of 1968, 7.

20. In its award notification announcement for the grant to support office and personnel, the LEAA noted that "this grant is being made in coordination with another LEAA grant that will enable OIC to purchase communications equipment." The amount of the other award is not included in the surviving award documentation. However, a *New York Times* article about the OIC after its existence became public noted that the "agency received $29,953 in Federal funds" after it applied for a LEAA grant. It is thus probable that the communications-related LEAA grant totaled $11,606. If accurate, these grants brought the OIC's combined funding from state and federal sources to nearly $57,000 for the 1971 fiscal year. Law Enforcement Assistance Administration Grant Award, Discretionary Grant Project Summary, June 24, 1970, Kottka case file; Waldron, "Oklahoma Suit Challenges Secret Files on Activists," 48.

21. Flanagan, "Secret Bartlett Agency 'Watching' Sooners," A-1, A-4.

22. Partial Transcript of NBC News Program "First Tuesday" Broadcast December 1, 1970, as part of Plaintiffs Response to Defendants Motion for Summary Judgment, ca. January 1971, 24–30; Janda, "'Even Mild Protest,'" 16–17.

23. Kenneth Kottka Affidavit, September 28, 1970, and Earl Mitchell Affidavit, September 29, 1970, both in Kottka case file.

24. Verified Complaint, September 16, 1970, 6, 7, Kottka case file; Janda, "'Even Mild Protest,'" 20. Jones later gained national prominence for representing Timothy McVeigh, who was convicted for the 1995 bombing of the Alfred P. Murrah Federal Building in Oklahoma City. "About Stephen Jones," accessed August 12, 2021, https://stephenjoneslaw.com/about-stephen-jones; Stephen Jones and Peter Israel, *Others Unknown: Timothy McVeigh and the Oklahoma City Bombing Conspiracy* (New York: PublicAffairs, 1998); Jeffrey Toobin, *Homegrown: Timothy McVeigh and the Rise of Right-Wing Extremism* (New York: Simon and Schuster, 2023).

25. Pre-Trial Memorandum, n.d., Kottka case file.

26. Waldron, "Oklahoma Suit Challenges Secret Files on Activists," 48; Janda, "'Even Mild Protest,'" 20–21.

27. On the Orangeburg Massacre, see Jack Nelson and Jack Bass, *The Orangeburg Massacre* (New York: World Publishing, 1970); Cleveland Sellers with Robert Terrell, *The River of No Return; the Autobiography of a Black Militant and the Life and Death of SNCC* (New York: Morrow, 1973).

28. Report of the Committee to Investigate Communist Activities in South Carolina, 1971, https://dc.statelibrary.sc.gov/handle/10827/32083, 1, 5.

29. *1969 Legislative Manual, 98th General Assembly of South Carolina* (Columbia, 1969), 208, https://dc.statelibrary.sc.gov/handle/10827/35905; Chief J. P. Strom, "Statewide Agency in South Carolina Aids Enforcement," *FBI Law Enforcement Bulletin* (June 1958): 3–6, 21.

30. Nelson and Bass, *Orangeburg Massacre*, 32; Sandi MeGahee, "'J. Edgar Hoover of South Carolina' Praised at Event," *Greenwood (SC) Index-Journal*, August 9, 1979, 1; Strom, "Statewide Agency in South Carolina Aids Enforcement"; Mike Livingston, "Longtime SLED Chief Strom Dies," *The State* (Columbia, SC), December 15, 1987, 1A, 13A; John Batteiger, "'Chief' Strom Was 47th Sheriff," *Columbia (SC) Record*, December 15, 1987, 1A, 16A; "Pete Strom Had Key Role in Stormy Times," *The State*, in *Congressional Record Daily Edition*, 100th Cong., 2nd sess., 1987, 134, pt. 35: S2678, https://congressional-proquest-com.libweb.lib.utsa.edu/congressional /docview/t17.d18.9e42f02183d29209?accountid=7122.

31. "Pete Strom Had Key Role in Stormy Times"; Nelson and Bass, *Orangeburg Massacre*, 32–33; Livingston, "Longtime SLED Chief Strom Dies"; Batteiger, "'Chief' Strom Was 47th Sheriff"; "J. P. Strom—Innovative, Evenhanded Lawman," *Columbia Record*, December 15, 1987, 18A.

32. Michel, *Struggle for a Better South*, 148–52; Gregg L. Michel, "It Even Happened Here: Student Activism at Furman University, 1967–1970," *South Carolina Historical Magazine* 109, no. 1 (2008): 38–57; *New South Student* 5, no. 6 (December 1968); South Carolina Southern Student Organizing Committee, "Newsletter #1," ca. March 1969, and "The Shaft: Clemson, SC, SSOC Newsletter," 1969, both in box 17, Boyte Family Papers, 1941–2018, David M. Rubenstein Rare Book & Manuscript Library, Duke University, Durham, NC; "GI's March at U of SC," *Phoenix* 1, no. 5 (January 1969). In March 1969, SSOC held its first statewide conference at USC's Westminster Center. Eddie Chen, "Cuba, Draft Discussed: First SSOC State Meeting," *The Gamecock*, March 14, 1969, 6.

33. Ginny Carroll, "Picketers Interrupt Ceremony," *The Gamecock*, April 28, 1967, 1; Nelson and Bass, *Orangeburg Massacre*, 32–33.

34. Donald Janson, "Antiwar Coffeehouses Delight G.I.'s but Not Army," *New York Times*, August 12, 1968, 1, 41; "Students and Soldiers Protest Closing of Antiwar Coffeehouse," *New York Times*, January 19, 1970, 4; Claudia Smith Brinson, "UFO Coffeehouse Typified Clash of Wills in the 1960s," *The State*, September 28, 1988, 1, 10–11; Fred Gardner, "Hollywood Confidential: Part I," *Viet Nam Generation Journal & Newsletter* 3, no. 3 (November 1991), http://www2.iath.virginia.edu/sixties /HTML_docs/Texts/Narrative/Gardner_Hollywood_1.html; William Shepard McAninch, "ESSAY: The UFO," *South Carolina Law Review* 46, no. 2 (1995): 363–79; Henry H. Lesesne, *A History of the University of South Carolina, 1940–2000* (Columbia: University of South Carolina Press, 2001), 212–13; Andrew H. Myers, *Black, White & Olive Drab: Racial Integration at Fort Jackson, South Carolina and the Civil Rights Movement* (Charlottesville: University of Virginia Press, 2006), 201–3; *Garnet and Black* (1971), 47–49; Andrew Grose, "Voices of Southern Protest during the Vietnam War Era: The University of South Carolina as a Case Study," *Peace & Change* 32, no. 2 (April 2007): 153–67; Ashley Elizabeth Miles, "The GI Coffeehouse Movement, 1968–1982: Class-Based Activism in the Vietnam War" (Master's thesis: Auburn University, 2020), 20–23, 32–33, 36–37; Parsons, *Dangerous Grounds*, 79–87; David L. Parsons, "How Coffeehouses Fueled the Vietnam Peace Movement," *New York Times*, January 9, 2018.

35. "'I Was on Their Radar Because They Needed Somebody on Their Radar,'" *University of South Carolina News & Events*, April 27, 2020, https://www.sc.edu/uofsc/posts/2020/05/months_of

_may_brett_bursey.php#.YT9qlS1h1TZ; interview with Brett Bursey by the author, Peak, SC, March 11, 1995; interview with Brett Bursey by the author, Columbia, SC (telephone), May 19, 2021; Pat Muthig and Ed Chen, "White Awareness Week Starts," *The Gamecock*, February 4, 1969, 1; Jim Wannamaker, "Seven Students Arrested after Scuffle with Police," *The Gamecock*, May 6, 1969, 1: Carl Stepp, "Students Welcome President," *The Gamecock*, May 6, 1969, 1; Jim Wannamaker, "SCYRM Wants 'War' Brought to Horseshoe," *The Gamecock*, September 15, 1969, 1.

36. Mike Krochmalny, "Confederate Flag Burned on Campus," *The Gamecock*, February 14, 1969, 1; Michel, *Struggle for a Better South*, 196–97.

37. Interviews with Brett Bursey by the author, March 11, 1995 and May 19 and September 21, 2021; *Garnet and Black* (1971), 47–49; Lesesne, *History of the University of South Carolina*, 212–21.

38. Claudia Smith Brinson, "A Villain and a Hero, but Which Was Which," *The State*, September 29, 1988, 1, 14–15. Barbara Herbert, a USC student who worked closely with both Weatherford and Bursey in AWARE, later wrote that Weatherford had been arrested for dealing acid in the summer of 1969 and had gone to work for SLED in exchange for having the charges dropped. Barbara Herbert, "Jack Weatherford," in Paul Cowan, Nick Egleson, and Nat Hentoff, with Barbara Herbert and Robert Wall, *State Secrets: Police Surveillance in America* (New York: Holt, Rinehart and Winston, 1974), 228–29. Bursey and others, however, have surmised that Weatherford began working for SLED to help win the release of his younger brother, David, who was serving time for housebreaking. In May 1970, his brother's sentence was suspended and he was released from custody. Brinson, "Villain and a Hero," September 29, 1988, 15; Bursey interview, May 19, 2021. Despite the lack of clarity around the genesis of his undercover work, state officials made clear that he was not an informant but a "salaried undercover police agent." *Jack M. Weatherford, etc., et al., Petitioners, v. Brett Allen Bursey, Respondent*, Proceedings, in the Supreme Court of the United States, December 7, 1976 (Washington, DC: Hoover Reporting Company, 1976), 3, 15, 40, 42.

39. *South Carolina v. Brett Bursey*, transcript of Malicious Mischief Trial for Damage Done to Richland County SC Draft Board Office in March 1970 (July 30, 1970), 50–51, generously shared with the author by Brett Bursey; Brinson, Villain and a Hero," 15. Barbara Herbert wrote that Weatherford had been involved in shutting down the coffeehouse, though she inaccurately labeled him an informant rather than a SLED employee. Herbert, "Jack Weatherford," 227–36; Myers, *Black, White & Olive Drab*, 203.

40. *SC v. Bursey* transcript, 35, 57; Brinson, "Villain and a Hero," 1, 14–15.

41. "Law Enforcement Officials Visit Commons Room, Monday: Gasque," *The Gamecock*, October 14, 1970, 1. Greg Merrick was another undercover agent who likely was based on campus. *Weatherford et al. v. Bursey*, Proceedings, 40; Bursey interview, September 21, 2021.

42. "Protests over 'UFO' Closing—Outtakes," WLTX-TV News, January 16, 1970, Local Television Newsfilm Collection, Moving Image Research Collections, University of South Carolina Libraries, https://digital.tcl.sc.edu/digital/collection/localtvnews/id/291.

43. "'I Was on Their Radar.'"

44. "Bursey's Guilt Not Yet Proved," *The Gamecock*, December 8, 1969, 2; Pat Steele, "Former Student Told Campus Closed to Him," *The Gamecock*, December 8, 1969, 1; Bursey interview, May 19, 2021.

45. Jack Rosenthal, "Antiwar Groups Are Planning New, Peaceful Demonstrations," *New York*

Times, February 8, 1970, 3; "Let's Revive Peace Movement," *The Gamecock*, March 16, 1970, 2; "USC-Mobe Quiet during Anti-Draft Week," *The Gamecock*, March 18, 1970, 1.

46. *SC v. Bursey* transcript, 53, 112–13.

47. The Berrigan brothers were part of the Catonsville Nine who raided the draft office in Catonsville, Maryland, and seized draft records which they proceeded to burn in the parking lot. The activists were tried, convicted, and sentenced to prison for the action. Daniel Berrigan, *The Trial of the Catonsville Nine* (Boston: Beacon Press, 1970); Shawn Francis Peters, *The Catonsville Nine: A Story of Faith and Resistance in the Vietnam Era* (Oxford: Oxford University Press, 2012). Between January and September 1970, there had been more than two hundred such incidents at draft offices around the country. David E. Rosenbaum, "Attacks Slow Up Draft Procedure," *New York Times*, September 8, 1970, 5.

48. Bursey interview, September 21, 2021.

49. Brett Bursey, "Letter from the Underground: 'A Pig by Any Other Name,'" *The Gamecock*, April 28, 1971, 1–3; author phone conversation with C. Rauch Wise, August 30, 2021; Bursey interview, September 21, 2021; The State of South Carolina, County of Richland, "Indictment-Two Counts, Brett Allen Bursey and Jack M. Weatherford," April 2, 1970, in the author's possession; David W. Bledsoe, "Bursey Convicted; Agent Uncovered," *The State*, July 28, 1970, 1A, 12A; "'I Was on Their Radar'";" *SC v. Bursey* transcript, 35–53, 112–17; Brinson, "Villain and a Hero," 14.

50. The State of South Carolina, County of Richland, "Indictment-Two Counts," Brett Allen Bursey and Jack M. Weatherford," April 2, 1970; "Two Students Charged during Anti-Draft Week," *The Gamecock*, March 23, 1970, 1; "Police Action Dangerous" (letter from Barbara Herbert for Aware to Mr. Wannamaker), *The Gamecock*, March 23, 1970; "Grand Jury Indicts Former USC Student," *The State*, April 14, 1970, 1; "Bursey, Weatherford Indicted Monday," *The Gamecock*, April 15, 1970, 1; Bursey, "Letter from the Underground," *The Gamecock*, April 28, 1971; *Weatherford v. Bursey*, Proceedings, 5; *Bursey v. Weatherford*, 528 F.2d 483; (1975 U.S. App.); *Weatherford v. Bursey*, 429 US 545 (1977); "'I Was on Their Radar'"; Bursey interview, March 11, 1995.

51. *Weatherford v. Bursey*, Proceedings, 56–57; *Bursey v. Weatherford*, 528 F.2d 483; (1975 U.S. App.); *Weatherford v. Bursey*, 429 US 545 (1977); Brinson, "Villain and a Hero." Merrick was out of the country and unavailable to testify. It is unclear if Strom had sent him away or encouraged him to travel in order to preserve his viability as an agent once it became clear that Weatherford would testify. *Weatherford v. Bursey*, Proceedings, 40–41, 53.

52. Bursey interview, September 21, 2021; Bursey, "Letter from the Underground," *The Gamecock*, April 28, 1971, 2.

53. Bursey, "Letter from the Underground," *The Gamecock*, April 28, 1971, 2.

54. *SC v. Bursey* Transcript, 118, 126; author phone conversation with C. Rauch Wise, August 30, 2021; *Bursey v. Weatherford*, 528 F.2d 483; (1975 U.S. App.); Bursey, "Letter from the Underground," *The Gamecock*, April 28, 1971, 2; Bledsoe, "Bursey Convicted; Agent Uncovered." Weatherford testified that Bursey had planned to bomb the draft board office and was conducting a dry run on the night of the incident. But Bursey testified that while Molotov cocktails briefly came up in conversation they never considered using them and took no steps to make them. *SC v. Bursey* Transcript, 37–40, 112–13; Ginny Carroll, "Foard Attacks USC Activists," *The State*, August 18, 1970, 1B, 5B; Brinson, "UFO Coffeehouse," 10A.

55. *Weatherford v. Bursey*, 429 US 545 (1977), 545, 562. For discussion of the legal significance of the Supreme Court's decision, see Scott M. Beller, "Government Agents and the Sixth Amendment Reconsidered," *Chicago-Kent Law Review* 54, no. 1 (1977): 239–53; David R. Lurie, "Sixth Amendment Implications of Informant Participation in Defense Meetings," *Fordham Law Review* 58 (1990): 795–822; Bursey interview, May 19, 2021; Lesesne, *History of the University of South Carolina*, 211–21; Andrew Grose, "Voices of Southern Protest during the Vietnam War Era: The University of South Carolina as a Case Study," *Peace & Change* 32, no. 2 (April 2007): 153–67.

56. His home also was broken into and his house seriously damaged by fire the month after the trial, though he believes such incidents were the product of his work on drug cases rather than student activism. Weatherford left SLED's payroll in September 1970 but remained a student at USC and earned his master's degree in sociology in 1972. Perhaps seeking a change of scenery in the aftermath of his exposure as a SLED agent as well as reflecting new academic interest, he moved to Southern California, where he earned a master's degree in anthropology from the University of California, San Diego, in 1973 and a doctorate in 1977. He went on to a distinguished career as an anthropologist, teaching for many years at Macalester College in St. Paul, Minnesota. His academic work has focused on Bolivia, the Amazon, and, most notably, Genghis Khan and Mongolia. To my knowledge, he has never publicly addressed his work for SLED. My attempts to contact him went unanswered. "SLED Agent's House Damaged by Blaze," *The State*, August 22, 1970, 12; Claudia Smith Brinson, "Villain and a Hero," 1, 14–15; "Jack Weatherford," Macalaster College, Department of Anthropology, accessed May 26, 2021, https://www.macalester.edu/anthropology/facultystaff/jackweatherford; Jack McIver Weatherford, "Family Culture, Behavior, and Emotion in a Working-Class German Town" (PhD diss., University of California, San Diego, 1977); Jack Weatherford, "A Scholarly Quest to Understand Genghis Khan," *Chronicle of Higher Education* 46, no. 32, April 14, 2000, B10.

57. Weatherford, quoted in Brett Bursey, "Letter from the Underground: 'A Pig by Any Other Name,'" *The Gamecock*, April 28, 1971, 1–3.

58. Weatherford v. Bursey, Proceedings, 40.

59. Lee Bandy, "FBI Files Tell of Work against USC Left, UFO," *The State*, December 16, 1977, 1A, 11A.

60. Winter quoted in Katagiri, *Mississippi State Sovereignty Commission*, 229; also see Charles C. Bolton, "William F. Winter: The Politician as Historian," *Southern Quarterly* 54, no. 1 (Fall 2016): 108–9.

61. In addition to Katagiri's *Mississippi State Sovereignty Commission*, the only other book-length scholarly treatment of the organization is Irons's, *Reconstitution Whiteness*. More narrowly drawn works on the commission's history, including the controversy and litigation about the preservation and public release of its files, include Rowe-Sims, "The Mississippi State Sovereignty Commission, 29–58; Lisa K. Speer, "Fresh Focus: Mississippi's 'Spy Files': The State Sovereignty Commission Records Controversy, 1977–1999," *Provenance, Journal of the Society of Georgia Archivists* 17, no. 1 (1999): 101–17; Christopher Paul Lehman, "Civil Rights in the Twilight: The End of the Civil Rights Movement Era in 1973," *Journal of Black Studies* 36, no. 3 (January 2006): 415–28); and Calvin Trillin, *Jackson, 1964: And Other Dispatches from Fifty Years of Reporting on Race in America* (New York: Random House, 2016), 253–75 (originally published as "State Secrets," *New Yorker*, May 29, 1995, 54–64). Erle Johnston, the director of the commission from 1963 to 1968, published his recollections of his

time with the commission in a 1990 memoir. While the book contains some useful information on the commission's history and actions, it is a largely self-serving and exculpatory account in which he portrays himself as a racial moderate—for Mississippi—who sought to temper some of the commission's worst excesses. Ultimately, his account is an effort to rewrite the past and rehabilitate his own reputation by soft-pedaling the commission's activities and portraying it not as the threatening force it was but merely as a troubleshooting and problem-solving agency. Such a portrayal rings hollow. Erle Johnston, *Mississippi's Defiant Years, 1953–1973: An Interpretive Documentary with Personal Experiences* (Forest, MS: Lake Harbor Publishers, 1990).

62. House Bill No. 880, "An Act Creating the State Sovereignty Commission, Prescribing the Membership Thereof, the Method by Which They Are to Be Selected and Their Terms of Service, Describing Its Authority, Duties and Powers; and for Related Purposes," Regular Session, 1956, 99-211-0-1-1-1 to 99-211-0-1-3-1-1, 2, MSSC; Katagiri, *Mississippi State Sovereignty Commission*, 5–8.

63. Katagiri, *Mississippi State Sovereignty Commission*, 9–11, 33–34, 45, 62–69; Irons, *Reconstituting Whiteness*, 94.

64. Erle Johnston, interview by Orley B. Caudill, July 30, 1980, Mississippi Oral History Project, Center for Oral History and Cultural Heritage, McCain Library and Archives, University of Southern Mississippi, Hattiesburg (hereafter cited as COHCH), 85, https://usm.access.preservica.com/uncategorized/IO_46deba19-6595-414a-ac32-8cfd3cc81686; "Hopkins Becomes Fourth Sovereignty Commission Investigator," *Jackson Clarion-Ledger*, June 18, 1960; and "Hopkins to Serve on Agency Staff," *Memphis Commercial Appeal*, June 20, 1960, 8-15-0-1-1-1-1, MSSC; Katagiri, *Mississippi State Sovereignty Commission*, 69; Rowe-Sims, "Mississippi State Sovereignty Commission," 30–31; Irons, *Reconstituting Whiteness*, 99.

65. "Investigative Report, Oxford, Ohio and Jackson, Mississippi," June 26, 1964, box 135, folder 10, ser. 2, sub-ser. 9, Sovereignty Commission, Paul B. Johnson Family Papers, McCain Library and Archives, University Libraries, University of Southern Mississippi, Hattiesburg; Johnston interview, July 30, 1980, 79–80; Katagiri, *Mississippi State Sovereignty Commission*, 162–63.

66. "Report of Operator #79, Re: Special Report," Jackson, Mississippi, Wednesday, May 13, 1964, 9-32-0-2-1-1-1 and 9-32-0-2-2-1-1, MSSC; "New Ferment Stirs the Campus," *Southern Patriot*, April 1964, 2-158-2-4-1-1-1, MSSC; List of White Community Project workers, August 9, 1964, 6-44-0-13-11-1-1, MSSC; Johnston interview, July 30, 1980, 79–80; Michel, *Struggle for a Better South*, 64–74.

67. Johnston, *Mississippi's Defiant Years*, 383.

68. Jo Freeman, "The Berkeley Free Speech Movement and the Mississippi Sovereignty Commission," *Left History* 8, no. 2 (2003). 135–44, 137. Freeman, a veteran of the Berkeley movement, had traveled to Mississippi in the summer of 1966 to work on a voter registration drive by the Southern Christian Leadership Conference. In August, the *Jackson Daily News* ran a long editorial, accompanied by several photos of Freeman, "exposing" her work as an activist in Berkeley who had come to Mississippi to stir up trouble. As the editorial declared in its title, Freeman was a "Professional agitator [who] hits all major trouble spots." The opening of the Sovereignty Commission's records allowed Freeman to trace the source of the editorial through the Commission back to Edgar Downing, among other sources. On this episode, also see Director Erle Johnston to File, Subject: Edgar Downing, August 11, 1966, 9-37-0-1-1-1-1; Director Erle Johnston to File, Subject: Jo Freeman, white, female, about twenty-five years old, August 11, 1966, 9-37-0-4-1-1-1; Director Erle Johnston to File,

Subject, Jimmy Ward, Editor, *Jackson Daily News,* August 11, 1966, 9-37-0-3-1-1-1; "Professional Agitator Hits All Major Trouble Spots," *Jackson Daily News,* August 18, 1966, 97-37-0-17-1-1-1, all in MSSC.

69. A. L. Hopkins, Investigator, to Erle Johnston Jr., director, Sovereignty Commission, August 9, 1965, 2-36-2-53-1-1-1; and A. L. Hopkins, Investigator, to Erle Johnston Jr., director, State Sovereignty Commission, May 4, 1967, 2-44-2-9-1-1-1, MSSC.

70. Tom Scarbrough, investigator, "Pike County," December 10, 1964, 2-36-2-42-1-1-1 to 2-36-2-42-2-1-1, MSSC.

71. The commission often accounted for disbursements to Downing on purchase orders for his services as well as for photo development of the pictures he provided. On payments to Downing, see, for instance, Director, Sovereignty Commission, to File, Subject: Edgar Downing, P.O. Box 981, Long Beach, CA, December 17, 1964, 3-30A-1-80-1-1-1; Director Erle Johnston to File, Subject: Edgar Downing, August 11, 1966, 9-37-0-1-1-1-1; Director Erle Johnston to File, Subject: Edgar Downing, October 28, 1966, 9-37-0-7-1-1-1, all in MSSC.

72. Director, Sovereignty Commission, to File, Subject: Edgar Downing, P.O. Box 981, Long Beach, CA, December 17, 1964, 3-30A-1-80-1-1-1, MSSC.

73. Edgar Downing to Earl [*sic*] Johnston, February 28, 1965, 2-158-3-13-1-1-1 to 2-158-3-13-4-1-1-1, MSSC; Jacob Carpenter and Claire Goodman, "Black Alumni Forcing a Reckoning at Houston Schools," *Houston Chronicle,* June 22, 2022, 1A, 13A, https://www.pressreader.com/usa/houston-chronicle/20200622/281492163575078; Michael F. Cusack Jr., "A Letter from the Rector and Headmaster," Saint Thomas' Episcopal Church, ca. June 2020, https://stthomashouston.org/a-letter-from-the-rector-and-headmaster.

74. Tom Scarbrough, Investigator, to Honorable Erle Johnston Jr., Director, Subject: Edgar Downing, March 9, 1965, 2-36-2-46-1-1-1; Edgar Downing to Mr. Johnston, March 16, 1965, 99-28-0-34-1-1-1; Edgar Downing to Mr. Earl [*sic*] Johnston, March 20, 1965, 99-28-0-37-1-1-1, MSSC. The correct description of the Houston meeting actually appears in a report that Downing drafted in 1967 on SSOC; see Untitled Report, 2-158-3-14-7-1-1 to 2-158-3-14-8-1-1, MSSC.

75. Director Erle Johnston to File, Subject: Edgar Downing, April 24, 1967, 9-37-0-13-1-1-1; Edgar Downing to Mr. Earl [*sic*] Johnston Jr., April 26, 1967, 9-37-0-12-1-1-1; Rep. William M. Tuck to Edgar Downing, April 18, 1967, 9-37-0-12-2-1-1; Untitled Report, 2-158-3-14-7-1-1 to 2-158-3-14-57-1-1, all in MSSC.

76. Director, Sovereignty Commission, to File, Subject: Southern Student Organizing Committee, April 4, 1967, 2-158-1-14-1-1-1, MSSC.

77. Director, Sovereignty Commission, to the Honorable Paul B. Johnson, Governor, Subject: Report of Principal Activities and Policies from January 1, 1964, through August 31, 1964, September 1, 1964, 99-208-0-9-3-1-1; John S. Kochtitzky Jr. to the Southern Student Organizing Committee, July 12, 1965, 99-86-0-39-1-1-1; Erle Johnston Jr. to File, Subject: John S. Kochtitzky Jr., August 19, 1965, 99-86-0-36-1-1-1, all in MSSC; Katagiri, *Mississippi State Sovereignty Commission,* 160–61.

78. Erle Johnston Jr. to Mr. Ernest Cochrane, Subject: John S. Kochtitzky Jr., August 19, 1965, 99-86-0-9-1-1-1. Cochrane may have been an FBI official in Mississippi. "Ernest Cochrane Obituary," Legacy.com, published by *Clarion Ledger* on November 5, 2013, https://www.legacy.com/us/obituaries/clarionledger/name/ernest-cochrane-obituary?pid=167872899.

79. Smith later said that he participated in this subterfuge because he thought it would be a good story to find communists working in the civil rights and leftist movements of the era: "I had vi-

sions of a Pulitzer Prize or something if I did really find that this linkage existed." But Smith's earlier collaboration with the commission on news stories renders such an explanation dubious. Michael Smith, interview by Reid Derr, n.d. [ca. 1993], COHCH, accessed March 9, 2022, https://usm.access.preservica.com/uncategorized/IO_4dd67815-afe9-45a2-a3e7-90348f8bded3, 12; Erle Johnston, interview by Yasuhiro Katagiri, August 13, 1993, COHCH, https://usm.access.preservica.com/uncategorized/IO_8b604cc1-109d-410c-9eff-4dd5ec3c63f2, 25–26; Director, Sovereignty Commission [Erle Johnston Jr.], to File, Subject: Michael C. "Mike" Smith, January 24, 1967, 7-0-10-25-1-1-1; Director, Sovereignty Commission [Erle Johnston Jr.], to File, Subject: Ted Seaver, November 14, 1966, 2-156-0-56-1-1-1; Director, Sovereignty Commission, to Honorable Herman Glazier, Executive Assistant, Office of the Governor, April 24, 1967, 3-17A-2-15-1-1-1; Mike Smith, "Mississippi Reports Least Integration in the South," *Jackson Clarion-Ledger–Jackson Daily News*, April 24, 1967, 3-17A-2-15-1-1-1; purchase order, January 16, 1967, 97-12-0-99-1-1-1; purchase order, February 5 [1967?], 97-13-0-256-1-1-1; Reconciliation Report, February 29, 1968, 97-3-0-7-1-1-1, all in MSSC. On Smith's subscription letters, see MSSC Records classification group 99-138.

80. Investigator A. L. Hopkins to Director Erle Johnston Jr., State Sovereignty Commission, Subject: Organization of the Southern Student Organizing Committee, etc., April 14, 1967, 2-158-3-2-1-1-1 to 2-158-3-2-7-1-1, 2; Director, Sovereignty Commission, to File, Subject: Southern Student Organizing Committee, Students for a Democratic Society, National Student Association, March 9, 1967, 2-158-1-13-1-1-1; Director, Sovereignty Commission, to File, Subject: Southern Student Organizing Committee, April 4, 1967, 2-158-1-14-1-1-1, all in MSSC; Johnston interview, July 30, 1980.

81. Minutes, State Sovereignty Commission, August 8, 1966, box 139, folder 3, Paul B. Johnson Family Papers, quoted in Katagiri, *Mississippi State Sovereignty Commission*, 197–98.

82. Newspaper clippings, ca. October 1968, 6-46-0-4-1-1-1; Director, Sovereignty Commission, to File, Subject: Millsaps Students, June 20, 1967, 3-11-0-26-1-1-1, MSSC.

83. Director, Sovereignty Commission, to File, Subject: Millsaps Students, June 20, 1967, 3-11-0-26-1-1-1. The style of the report on the march matches that of Downing's report on SSOC. Both are handwritten, single-spaced documents, with similar formatting. Untitled report on march, ca. June 1967, 3-11-0-32-1-1-1 to 3-11-0-32-18-1-1; photos of the marchers located in 3-11-0-25, 3-11-0-28, and 3-11-0-29, MSSC.

84. *The Kudzu*, 1, no. 1, September 18, 1968, 6-46-0-1-1-1-1; newspaper clippings, *Jackson Clarion-Ledger* and *Memphis Commercial Appeal*, ca. October 10–11, 1968, 6-46-0-4-1-1-1; H. A. Gusack to Mr. Webb Burke, Director, Subject: Debriefing on Confidential Source of Information (CSI-1-8), on August 15, 1969, 99-135-0-10-1-1-1 to 99-135-0-10-5-1-1, MSSC. The commission's collection of *The Kudzu* is located in classifications 6-46 and 99-172. On *The Kudzu*, see *Southern Patriot*, December 1968; David Doggett, "*The Kudzu* Story: Underground in Mississippi," *Southern Exposure* 2, no. 4 (1975): 86–95; David Doggett, "*The Kudzu:* Birth and Death in Underground Mississippi," in *Voices from the Underground: Insider Histories of the Vietnam Era Underground Press*, ed. Ken Wachsberger (Tempe, AZ: Mica Press, 1993), 1:213–32; Stephen Flinn Young, "*The Kudzu:* Sixties Generational Revolt—Even in Mississippi," *Southern Quarterly* 34, no. 3 (1996): 122–36; Donald Cunnigen, "Standing at the Gates: The Civil Rights Movement and Liberal White Mississippi Students," *Journal of Mississippi History* 62, no. 1 (2000): 1–19.

85. Untitled memo, April 8, 1969, 2-152-0-45-1-1-1; untitled memo, April 10 and 12, 1969,

2-152-0-46-1-1-1; untitled memo, April 14, 1969, 2-152-0-47-1-1-1; *The Kudzu*, April 5, 1969, 99-172-0-1-2-1-1; *The Kudzu*, April 24, 1969, 99-172-0-2-6-1-1 and 99-172-0-2-10-1-1, MSSC. *The Kudzu* later published a photograph of five men at the April Jubilee who it said were informants, including one who was an FBI agent. *The Kudzu*, October 29, 1969, 99-172-0-8-2-1-2, all in MSSC. The author thanks Jane Adams for bringing to his attention the surveillance operations related to the Jubilee.

86. Director, Sovereignty Commission, to the Honorable John Bell Williams, governor of Mississippi, February 5, 1970, 7-0-11-189-4-1-1, MSSC; Katagiri, *Mississippi State Sovereignty Commission*, 202–10.

87. See, for example, H. A. Gusack to Mr. Webb Burke, Director, Mississippi State Sovereignty Commission, Subject: 1.78 pounds of marijuana delivered through the U.S. Mail to an unidentified post office box at the University of Mississippi Post Office, Oxford, MS, April 29, 1969, 99-135-0-2-1-1-1, MSSC.

88. Director, State Sovereignty Commission, to the Honorable John Bell Williams, Subject: Report of Principal Activities—January 1968 through December 1971, January 5, 1970, 99-208-0-8-1-1-1. Erle Johnston resigned as director of the Sovereignty Commission in July 1968. "'Webb' Burke, Veteran of Highway Patrol, FBI," *Jackson Clarion-Ledger*, June 20, 1987, 2B, https://www.newspapers.com/image/185680269; Edgar Fortenberry biography, n.d., 99-208-0-2-1-1-1; James M. Mohead biography, n.d., 99-208-0-3-1-1-1; C. Fulton Tutor biography, n.d., 99-208-0-4-1-1-1, all in MSSC. Two of the previous investigators, Virgil Downing and Tom Scarbrough, had recently died. The third, Andy Hopkins, had been battling cancer for a number of years. "Highway Patrol Leader Dies," *Greenwood Commonwealth*, March 29, 1968, 1, https://www.newspapers.com/clip/11970080/tom-scarbrough-dies-p1; "Andy Hopkins Dies, Funeral Set Tuesday," *Jackson Clarion-Ledger*, September 7, 1971, https://www.newspapers.com/image/181069269; Katagiri, *Mississippi State Sovereignty Commission*, 147, 208–9.

89. "Report of Activities and Accomplishments, Mississippi State Sovereignty Commission, 1968–1971," ca. 1971, 99-208-0-7-23-1-1, MSSC.

90. [H. A. Gusack], Security Consultants, Inc., to Mr. Webb Burke, Director, Mississippi State Sovereignty Commission, Subject: Semi-Annual Report of Activities of Charles Lamar Neill Jr., Confidential Source of Information at the University of Mississippi, Oxford, ca. July 1969, 99-135-0-5-1-1-1; "Charles Lamar Neill, Jr.," *Northside Sun* (Jackson, MS), October 24, 2002, 19, https://www.newspapers.com/clip/25619913/2002-obit-charles-lamar-neill-jr/#. On the commission's use of private detective agencies, see Katagiri, *Mississippi State Sovereignty Commission*, 148–49. Erle Johnston remembers that the commission employed several detective agencies for the express purpose of handling informants in order to keep such activity off the state's accounting books. The agency the commission used most regularly during Johnston's tenure as director between 1963 and 1968 was Day Detectives. Johnston interview, August 13, 1993, 23.

91. [H. A. Gusack], Security Consultants, Inc., to Mr. Webb Burke, Director, Mississippi State Sovereignty Commission, Subject: Semi-Annual Report of Activities of Charles Lamar Neill Jr., Confidential Source of Information at the University of Mississippi, Oxford, ca., July 1969, 99-135-0-5-1-1-1 to 99-135-0-15-1-1-1; H. A. Gusack to Mr. Webb Burke, Director, Mississippi State Sovereignty Commission, Subject: Telephonic Contact from Confidential Source of Information

(CSI-1-C-8), April 21, 1969, 99-135-0-1-1-1-1; H. A. Gusack to Mr. Webb Burke, director, Mississippi State Sovereignty Commission, Subject: 1.78 pounds of marijuana delivered through the U.S. Mail to an unidentified post office box at the University of Mississippi Post Office, Oxford, April 29, 1969, 99-135-0-2-1-1-1; L. T. Rogers Jr., Director of Operations, to Webb Burke, Subject: Projected student demonstrations to be held on the campus of the University of Mississippi on October 15, 1969, in protest to the Vietnam War, 99-135-0-9-1-1-1, all in MSSC. Gusack identifies Neill by name in his report on activities in the first half of 1969. In subsequent reports, the Ole Miss informant is identified by the code name CSI-1-C-8. While the MSSC had other student informers at Ole Miss, Neill was the only one identified as working for Security Consultants. Neill later said that he did not realize his reports were being sent to the Sovereignty Commission. While plausible, it seems unlikely given that his father was in attendance at the detective agency's first meeting with the governor and the commission's staff, after which Neill was recruited to work for Security Consultants. Jerry Mitchell, "School Bears Name Linked to Agency," *Jackson Clarion-Ledger*, January 28, 1990, 3I; James Dickerson, *Dixie's Dirty Secret: The True Story of How Government, the Media, and the Mob Conspired to Combat Integration and the Vietnam Antiwar Movement* (Armonk, NY: M. E. Sharpe, 1998), 185.

92. [H. A. Gusack], Security Consultants, Inc., to Mr. Webb Burke, Director, Mississippi State Sovereignty Commission, Subject: Semi-Annual Report of Activities of Charles Lamar Neill Jr., Confidential Source of Information at the University of Mississippi, Oxford, ca., July 1969, 99-135-0-5-14-1-1, MSSC. The commission targeted the ACLU for surveillance during Burke's tenure as director. In 1970, it paid a Jackson resident named Eddie Sandifer, who went by the alias Ronnie Davis, to attend and report on an ACLU meeting held at Millsaps. W. Webb Burke, director to File, Subject: Ronnie Davis, May 18, 1970, 97-89-0-96-3-1-1; "Report from Ronnie Davis," May 1970, 3-11-0-38-1-1-1, MSSC.

93. Fulton Tutor, Investigator, to Director, State Sovereignty Commission, February 25, 1970, 3-10-0-23-1-1-1; Fulton Tutor, Investigator, to Director, State Sovereignty Commission, May 6, 1970, 3-10-0-25-1-1-1; Fulton Tutor, "Weekly Report," May 23, 1970, 3-10-0-26-1-1-1; Webb Burke to Col. Julian M. Ervin, Mississippi National Guard, January 29, 1969, 3-10-0-18-1-1-1; Carroll Jackson and Mary Stowers Abbott, "Taylor Titles Viet Nam War 'Enigma'; Some Students Dissent," *Mississippi State University Reflector*, December 18, 1969, 3-10-0-16-1-1-1, all in MSSC.

94. Pat Coughlin, "Sovereignty Commission Promotes Bigotry," *Mississippi State University Reflector*, December 6, 1968, 99-64-0-21-1-1-1.

95. Director, Sovereignty Commission, to File, Subject: "News Article Entitled 'Sovereignty Commission Promotes Bigotry' in Mississippi State University School Paper by Pat Coughlin," December 12, 1968, 99-64-0-20-1-1-1 to 99-64-0-20-2-1-1, MSSC.

96. W. Webb Burke to Pat Coughlin, December 13, 1968, 99-64-0-19-1-1-1, MSSC. This was not the first time a commission director had aggressively responded to what it considered objectionable statements by Mississippi State students in the press. In 1966, Erle Johnston reached out to the Mississippi State president to ask him to respond to an article implying that activist students were trying to disrupt campus. The president, Johnston wrote to Governor Paul Johnson's special assistant, "will correct certain misrepresentations in this letter and reassure the Governor that a close watch is being made of any students with rebellious ideas. Any flareups will be dealt with under strict disciplinary policies." Director, Sovereignty Commission, to Honorable Frank Barber, Special

Assistant to the Governor, Subject: Mississippi State University, December 30, 1966, 3-10-0-6-1-1-1, MSSC; Evan Richardson, "MSU Student Sees Organized Efforts to Embarrass Officials," *Jackson Clarion-Ledger*, December 21, 1966, 3-10-0-8-1-1-1, MSSC.

97. Director Erle Johnston hosted Eli Howell, his counterpart in the newly created Alabama Sovereignty Commission, on a visit to the office to acquaint him with how the Mississippi agency worked: "He wanted to see our filing system, how reports are made, and learn all the functions in connection with investigation, research, and public relations." Director, Sovereignty Commission, to File, Subject: Eli Howell, director, Alabama Sovereignty Commission, March 16, 1964, 99-25-0-6-1-1-1, MSSC.

98. For instance, see Erle Johnston Jr. to Honorable Eli Howell, May 19, 1964, 99-25-0-4-1-1-1; and W. Webb Burke to Henry A. Sibley, February 18, 1969, 3-22A-3-14-1-1-1, MSSC.

99. Alabama Legislative Commission to Preserve the Peace, *S.A.I. Report: Confidential* 1, no. 1 (January 1967): 13-8-1-12-1-1-1 to 13-8-1-12-9-1-1, 1, 6, MSSC.

100. Interstate Sovereignty Association, ca. 1968, 99-83-0-2-1-1-1 to 99-83-0-2-3-1-1, MSSC; Katagiri, *Mississippi State Sovereignty Commission*, 217–18.

101. Johnston interview, July 30, 1980, 83; Johnston, *Mississippi's Defiant Years*, 230–31; Katagiri, *Mississippi State Sovereignty Commission*, 211.

102. Johnston interview, July 30, 1980, 88.

3. MEMPHIS

1. Eric Carter, interview by author, July 11, 2018, Houston; Joseph Weiler, "Police Order Burning of File on Vietnam War Protester," *Memphis Commercial Appeal*, September 8, 1976, 25.

2. *Kendrick v. Chandler*, case no.76-449, box 2 (accession no. 021-84-0116), RG 21—Records of the District Courts of the United States, Civil Case Files, 1972–78, Memphis, TN, National Archives at Atlanta. The case file includes the complaint, affidavits, motions, documents, deposition transcripts, and judicial orders, all of which inform this chapter. The city's two daily newspapers, the *Commercial Appeal* and the *Memphis Press-Scimitar*, extensively reported on the police spying and the ACLU lawsuit. This coverage included Weiler, "Police Order Burning of File on Vietnam War Protester"; Joseph Weiler, "File Burning Draws Mayor's Attention," *Memphis Commercial Appeal*, September 9, 1976, 1, 10; "Why the Fire?" (editorial), *Memphis Commercial Appeal*, September 9, 1976, 4; "Court Order Too Late; Police Burn Intelligence Files," *Memphis Press-Scimitar*, September 11, 1976, 1; "ACLU Suit Hits Police—Council Action Asked," *Memphis Commercial Appeal*, September 15, 1976, 31; Kay Pittman Black, "Surveillance Curbs Hit Memphis Police," *Memphis Press-Scimitar*, September 13, 1978, 1; Otis L. Sanford, "ACLU Lawsuit Opens Door on Police Intelligence Gathering," *Memphis Commercial Appeal*, September 14, 1978, 9. Also see Bruce Kramer, "Surveillance of Protected First Amendment Activities: Kendricks [*sic*] v. Memphis Police Department," September 14, 1978 (published by American Civil Liberties Union Foundation); "Domestic Intelligence Reform[:] A Court Order against a Red Squad," *First Principles* 4, no. 2 (October 1978): 1–3; *The Police Threat to Political Liberty: Discoveries and Actions of the American Friends Service Committee Program on Government Surveillance and Citizens' Rights* (Philadelphia: American Friends Service Committee, 1979), 77.

3. "Bucket brigade" quotation from Eli H. Arkin deposition, February 16, 1977, 322, *Kendrick v. Chandler;* "just old newspapers" quotation from "Court Order Too Late; Police Burn Intelligence Files." Also see "Intelligence Unit Dissolved; Files Are Burned," *Memphis Commercial Appeal,* September 11, 1976, 1, 3; and Kramer, "Surveillance of Protected First Amendment Activities," 2.

4. "Intelligence Unit Dissolved; Files Are Burned."

5. Because it was the site of Martin Luther King Jr.'s assassination during the 1968 sanitation workers' strike, Memphis is one of the few locales to which historians have devoted attention to Red Squads. But these studies, by concentrating on the iconic and tragic events of 1968, obscure the deep roots of police repression in Memphis as well as sever the 1968 intelligence work from the years of expanded surveillance that followed. Garrow, *FBI and Martin Luther King, Jr.;* O'Reilly, *Racial Matters;* Gerald D. McKnight, "The 1968 Memphis Sanitation Strike and the FBI: A Case Study in Urban Surveillance," *South Atlantic Quarterly* 83, no. 2 (Spring 1984): 138–56; Gerald D. McKnight, "A Harvest of Hate: The FBI's War against Black Youth—Domestic Intelligence in Memphis, Tennessee," *South Atlantic Quarterly* 86, no. 1 (Winter 1987): 1–21; Gerald McKnight, *The Last Crusade: Martin Luther King, Jr., the FBI, and the Poor People's Campaign* (Boulder, CO: Westview Press, 1998). Some works do give attention to police surveillance in Memphis. Michael Honey has shown that the police department was an effective tool of economic and political power in Memphis, as its abusive practices served to contain labor militancy and damage biracial industrial union drives between the 1930s and 1960s. Laurie Green concurs that police harassment and brutality were routine throughout these decades and highlights the ways in which African Americans maneuvered to advance reformist goals and combat the "plantation mentality" despite concerted police resistance. And Marc Perrusquia, in his deeply researched book exposing the famed civil rights photographer Ernest Withers as an FBI informant, highlights the numerous and varied targets of FBI surveillance in Memphis during the 1960s and 1970s, ranging from the African American leadership of the civil rights movement to the white students who participated in antiwar demonstrations. None of these authors, however, take the MPD as the focal point of their work. Michael K. Honey, *Southern Labor and Black Civil Rights: Organizing Memphis Workers* (Urbana: University of Illinois Press, 1993); Michael K. Honey, *Black Workers Remember an Oral History of Segregation, Unionism, and the Freedom Struggle* (Berkeley: University of California Press, 1999); Michael K. Honey, *Going Down Jericho Road: The Memphis Strike, Martin Luther King's Last Campaign* (New York: Norton, 2007); Laurie Boush Green, *Battling the Plantation Mentality: Memphis and the Black Freedom Struggle* (Chapel Hill: University of North Carolina Press, 2007); Marc Perrusquia, *A Spy in Canaan: How the FBI Used a Famous Photographer to Infiltrate the Civil Rights Movement* (Brooklyn: Melville House, 2018). Perrusquia's book grew out of a series of articles on Withers that he wrote for the *Memphis Commercial Appeal.* See, for instance, Marc Perrusquia, "Double Exposure—Ernest Withers, Whose Camera Captured Civil Rights History, Also Provided FBI with an Insider's View of Volatile Period," *Memphis Commercial Appeal,* September 12, 2010, V1; and Marc Perrusquia, "'Pictures Tell the Story,'" *Memphis Commercial Appeal,* July 7, 2013, V1.

6. Peter Taylor, *A Summons to Memphis* (New York: Knopf, 1986), 26. For background on Memphis, see Robert Alan Sigafoos, *Cotton Row to Beale Street: A Business History of Memphis* (Memphis: Memphis State University Press, 1979); Roger Biles, *Memphis in the Great Depression* (Knoxville: University of Tennessee Press, 1986); Kathleen C. Berkeley, *Like a Plague of Locusts: From an Antebellum*

Town to a New South City, Memphis, Tennessee, 1850–1880 (New York: Garland, 1991); Preston Lauterbach, *Beale Street Dynasty: Sex, Song, and the Struggle for the Soul of Memphis* (New York: Norton, 2015). On the Memphis Race Riot, see Hannah Rosen, *Terror in the Heart of Freedom: Citizenship, Sexual Violence, and the Meaning of Race in the Postemancipation South* (Chapel Hill: University of North Carolina Press, 2009); Stephen V. Ash, *A Massacre in Memphis: The Race Riot That Shook the Nation One Year after the Civil War* (New York: Hill and Wang, 2013). Works that treat Memphis's economic development and industrial transformation include Sigafoos, *Cotton Row to Beale Street;* Honey, *Southern Labor and Black Civil Rights;* Jefferson Cowie, *Capital Moves: RCA's Seventy-Year Quest for Cheap Labor* (Ithaca, NY: Cornell University Press, 1999); and Wanda Rushing, *Memphis and the Paradox of Place: Globalization in the American South* (Chapel Hill: University of North Carolina Press, 2009). Crump was a native of nearby Holly Springs, Mississippi, who moved to Memphis in the 1890s and built the region's most prominent insurance and real estate firm. Elected mayor in 1909, he served only a few years before being recalled from office in a dispute with Prohibitionists. Despite this setback, he was elected a county trustee in 1916, a position from which he came to dominate city politics. See David M. Tucker, *Memphis since Crump: Bossism, Blacks, and Civic Reformers, 1948–1968* (Knoxville: University of Tennessee Press, 1980), 17–59; Biles, *Memphis in the Great Depression*, 27–40; G. Wayne Dowdy, *Mayor Crump Don't Like It: Machine Politics in Memphis* (Jackson: University Press of Mississippi, 2006).

7. Biles, *Memphis in the Great Depression*, 40–45, 123 (quotation originally appeared in *Memphis Press-Scimitar*, April 3, 1944); Otis Sanford, *From Boss Crump to King Willie: How Race Changed Memphis Politics* (Knoxville: University of Tennessee Press, 2017), 19–26; Jason Jordan, "'We'll Have No Race Trouble Here': Racial Politics and Memphis's Reign of Terror," in *An Unseen Light: Black Struggles for Freedom in Memphis, Tennessee*, ed. Aram Goudsouzian and Charles W. McKinney Jr. (Lexington: University Press of Kentucky, 2018), 130–49. When the wealthy Black businessman and Republican leader Robert Church Jr. broke with Crump politically, Crump retaliated by forcing him to sell off property to pay back taxes and ultimately spurred Church to abandon Memphis altogether. While Church had condemned the city's racial violence and police brutality, Crump did not move against the prominent Black businessman until Church posed a political threat to the machine's dominance. In 1938, Church refused to endorse the Crump machine's candidate for governor, Congressman Walter Chandler, later mayor of Memphis and the father of Wyeth Chandler, who was mayor during the surveillance crisis in the 1970s. Church also threw his support behind Wendell Wilkie's 1940 presidential bid, further angering Crump. Honey, *Southern Labor and Black Civil Rights: Organizing Memphis Workers*, 166–67; Green, *Battling the Plantation Mentality*, 32–33; Darius Young, "'The Saving of Black America's Body and White America's Soul': The Lynching of Ell Persons and the Rise of Black Activism in Memphis," in *An Unseen Light: Black Struggles for Freedom in Memphis, Tennessee*, ed. Aram Goudsouzian and Charles W. McKinney Jr. (Lexington: University Press of Kentucky, 2018), 50–57; Jordan, "'We'll Have No Race Trouble Here,'" 132.

8. Crump, quoted in Tucker, *Memphis since Crump*, 57.

9. Boyle, quoted in Green, *Battling the Plantation Mentality*, 39; also see Jordan, "'We'll Have No Race Trouble Here.'"

10. While a few Black officers had served on the force in the early twentieth century, by the 1930s the department was once again all-white. Not until 1948, in response to growing public concern among both Blacks and whites over allegations of police brutality, were African Americans

again appointed to the force, when nine officers took to the street. But their powers were limited: they were not allowed to carry weapons, could not arrest whites, and were assigned only to the Beale Street corridor. Among these first recruits was Ernest Withers, who later gained fame as a civil rights photographer and, more recently, notoriety for being an FBI informant. Green, *Battling the Plantation Mentality*, 106–10; Perrusquia, *Spy in Canaan*, 107–8; Simon Hosken, "Policing the Blues: Remembering the Desegregation of Law Enforcement in West Memphis, Arkansas," *Arkansas Historical Quarterly* 72, no. 2 (Summer 2013): 135.

11. On the "John Gaston Turban," see Sanford, *From Boss Crump to King Willie*, 163. Bunche, quoted in Honey, *Southern Labor and Black Civil Rights*, 49–50. On the Memphis police and the Black community, see Biles, *Memphis in the Great Depression*, 37–40; Honey, *Southern Labor and Black Civil Rights;* Honey, *Black Workers Remember*, 19–36; G. Wayne Dowdy, *Crusades for Freedom: Memphis and the Political Transformation of the American South* (Jackson: University Press of Mississippi, 2010), 12–14; and Jordan, "'We'll Have No Race Trouble Here.'" On the furor that erupted over Mayor Edmund Orgill's abortive effort to appoint a Black trustee to the board that oversaw John Gaston Hospital in 1956, see Elizabeth Gritter, "A Matter of Black and White: Edmund Orgill, J. E. Walker, and the John Gaston Hospital Controversy in Memphis, Tennessee, in 1956," *Tennessee Historical Quarterly* 78, no. 3 (2019): 168–93.

12. George quoted in Honey, *Southern Labor and Black Civil Rights*, 165–73; Green, *Battling the Plantation Mentality*, 29–33, 38–41, 222–23; Jordan, "'We'll Have No Race Trouble Here.'"

13. On political developments and the weakening of Crump machine, see Dowdy, *Crusades for Freedom*; Tucker, *Memphis since Crump*, 40–95. On the civil rights struggle and labor unionism in the decades prior to the sanitation strike, see Honey, *Southern Labor and Black Civil Rights;* Honey, *Black Workers Remember;* Green, *Battling the Plantation Mentality;* and Dowdy, *Crusades for Freedom.*

14. In 1963, the United States Supreme Court rejected the city's plan to gradually desegregate city parks and required their immediate desegregation. *Watson v. City of Memphis*, 373 U.S. 526 (1963). Dowdy, *Crusades for Freedom;* Green, *Battling the Plantation Mentality*, 198–275; Honey, *Going Down Jericho Road*, 40–45; Stephen R. Haynes, *The Last Segregated Hour: The Memphis Kneel-Ins and the Campaign for Southern Church Desegregation* (New York: Oxford University Press, 2012); Shirletta J. Kinchen, *Black Power in the Bluff City: African American Youth and Student Activism in Memphis, 1965–1975* (Knoxville: University of Tennessee Press, 2016), 18–36; Steven A. Knowlton, "'Since I Was a Citizen, I Had the Right to Attend the Library': The Key Role of the Public Library in the Civil Rights Movement in Memphis," in *An Unseen Light: Black Struggles for Freedom in Memphis, Tennessee*, ed. Aram Goudsouzian and Charles W. McKinney Jr., 203–27 (Lexington: University Press of Kentucky, 2018). Rev. James Lawson, whose workshops on nonviolence helped spark the sit-in movement in the South, moved to Memphis in 1962 and played an important role in the growing civil rights movement in the city. Honey, *Going Down Jericho Road*, 77–82.

15. The Inspectional Bureau likely was in business by 1965. Police lieutenant Eli H. Arkin, who worked for nearly a decade on intelligence matters in the MPD, testified in his deposition in *Kendrick v. Chandler* that it was his understanding that the bureau was created two years before he started working for it in 1967. Marc Perrusquia mentions in passing that the MPD established an intelligence branch even earlier, in 1963. Perrusquia, *Spy in Canaan*, 214.

16. Letterhead Memorandum, Re: "Logos," Memphis, TN, March 11, 1966 (100-4284-1), 33; and SA [Special Agent] William H. Lawrence to SAC [Special Agent in Charge] [Memphis], May 26,

1966 (100-4284-102), 1–2, both located in the collection of Ernest Withers FBI case files obtained and generously shared with the author by Marc Perrusquia as a result of the settlement of *Memphis Publishing Company and Marc Perrusquia v. the Federal Bureau of Investigation,* 10cv01878, U.S. District Court for the District of Columbia (hereafter cited as Withers-FBI). In his book *Spy in Canaan,* Perrusquia details the long, arduous, and contentious process that eventually resulted in the FBI's releasing some, though by no means all, Withers-related materials in its possession. On Logos, also see Perrusquia, *Spy in Canaan,* 194–95, 211–12.

17. Editorial, *Tiger Rag* (Memphis State University), May 4, 1966; Letterhead Memorandum, re: "Logos," Memphis, TN, May 6, 1966, box 4, folder 26, Cecil C. Humphreys Collection, University Archives, Special Collections Department, University Libraries, University of Memphis; editorial ("Freedom Is for Learning—Not Campus Violence"), *Memphis Press-Scimitar,* May 4, 1966, 10; and editorial ("Handful of Nobodies"), *Memphis Commercial Appeal,* ca. May 4, 1966, 6, both located in box 12, folder 94-2, ser. 2—Documents and Artifacts File, Memphis Search for Meaning Committee Records, University Archives, Special Collections Department, University Libraries, University of Memphis (hereafter cited as MSM Records).

18. Arkin deposition, December 14, 1976, 32–43; and December 15, 1976, 95–98. Ernest Withers also surveilled the vigils for the FBI. Letterhead Memorandum, re: Demonstrations Protesting United States Policy in Vietnam, Memphis, June 22, 1967 (100-4491-14), 1; and Letterhead Memorandum, re: Demonstrations Protesting United States Policy in Vietnam, Memphis, June 28, 1967 (100-4491-19), 1, Withers-FBI.

19. Arkin deposition, December 15, 1976, 109; *Investigation of the Assassination of Martin Luther King, Jr.: Hearings before the Select Committee on Assassinations of the U.S. House of Representatives* (hereafter cited as HSCA), vol. 4, 95th Cong. (1978) (testimony of Edward Redditt and Frank C. Holloman); HSCA, vol. 6 (testimony of Marrell McCollough and William H. Lawrence); Honey, *Going Down Jericho Road,* 145, 164, 201–10, 217–18; "Police Reports on Suspicious Cars," February 15, 1968–March 18, 1968, box 5, folder "Civil Disorders–Sanitation Strike–Suspicious Car List–1968," ser. 3—Memphis Fire and Police Division, Frank Holloman Collection, Memphis and Shelby County Room, Memphis Public Libraries.

20. Lt. E. H. Arkin, *Civil Disorders, Memphis, Tennessee (February 12, through April 16, 1968), A Report Submitted to Mr. Frank Holloman, Director of Fire and Police,* 2, 83, n.d., box 3, folders 88–89, Kenneth Lawrence Beaudoin Papers, University Archives, Special Collections Department, University Libraries, University of Memphis.

21. Kinchen, *Black Power in the Bluff City,* 56.

22. Kinchen, *Black Power in the Bluff City,* 52–61. The Black Organizing Project was founded by two native Memphians, Coby Vernon Smith and Charles Laverne Cabbage. Smith, one of the first two Black students to attend Southwestern, had gone to Atlanta after graduation hoping to work in the movement, and that is where he met Cabbage, who recently had graduated from Morehouse, where he had become radicalized. The two struck up a friendship and together conceptualized the BOP, which they returned to Memphis to create in mid-1967. Their goal, Smith later said, was "to teach awareness of what it was to be black and live in America and . . . what it meant to be black and live in Memphis." They encapsulated their views in "The Black Organizing Project: Where We Go from Here" in early 1968. It was an eight-point program inspired by and infused with the spirit of Black Power that called for African Americans to exert authority over their own education, establish

Black policing in their community, and control resources designed to improve Black lives. Kinchen, *Black Power in the Bluff City*, 50; Honey, *Going Down Jericho Road*, 227–39; Perrusquia, *Spy in Canaan*, 233–42; Coby Vernon Smith, interview by author, July 18, 2018.

23. Arkin deposition, December 15, 1976, 77–78; HSCA, vol. 6 (testimony of Calvin L. Taylor Jr., John B. Smith, and Charles Laverne Cabbage); Honey, *Going Down Jericho Road*, 280. On the FBI campaign against the Invaders, see McKnight, "Harvest of Hate." Anthony C. Sircausa shows that the FBI's efforts to disrupt the Invaders and the strike involved the use of at least one informant, James Elmore Phillips. It's unclear precisely when Phillips began to cooperate with the FBI, as his name appears as one of the Invaders in a lengthy memo on the group that the Memphis FBI office sent to headquarters and other bureau offices. Anthony C. Siracusa, "Nonviolence, Black Power, and the Surveillance State in Memphis's War on Poverty," in *An Unseen Light: Black Struggles for Freedom in Memphis, Tennessee*, ed. Aram Goudsouzian and Charles W. McKinney Jr. (Lexington: University Press of Kentucky, 2018), 279–305; Letterhead Memorandum, re: Black Organizing Project, Racial Matters, May 6, 1968 (157-1067-36), FBI Memphis Field Office File, The Invaders, in the author's possession.

24. "Appendix, Invaders: Also Known as: Black Organizing Project," box 11, folder "Intelligence Division–1969," ser. 3, Holloman Papers. It is unclear to what document this appendix was attached, though the language used to describe the Invaders was standard phrasing that the FBI also deployed in its descriptions of the group, suggesting that the two law enforcement agencies borrowed the phrasing from one another. See, for instance, "Re: INVADERS, also known as Black Organizing Project," May 27, 1970 (157-1067-1863), Withers-FBI; and Letterhead Memorandum, re: Potential for Racial Violence, July 2, 1970 (157-1067-1936a), 8, Withers-FBI.

25. *Report of the National Advisory Commission on Civil Disorders* (New York: Bantam Books, 1968), 487; Legal Development Division, *History of Police Intelligence Operations, 1880–1975* (final draft) (Gaithersburg, MD: International Association of Chiefs of Police, 1976), 86–87; *Police Threat to Political Liberty*, 10–12, 14–16.

26. *Police Threat to Political Liberty*, 15; Chevigny, "Politics and Law in the Control of Local Surveillance," 736–37; Legal Development Division, *History of Police Intelligence Operations*, 87–88; Donner, *Protectors of Privilege*, 77–79.

27. "Biographical Sketch of Frank C. Holloman," box 128, folder 8, ser. 3, Papers of Henry Loeb III, Memphis and Shelby County Room, Memphis Public Libraries; HSCA, vol. 4 (testimony of Frank C. Holloman), 236–38; untitled document on J. Edgar Hoover, box 3, folder "General, 1964–1976," ser. 1: FBI, 1937–64, Holloman Collection; McKnight, *Last Crusade*, 46–47; Gage, *G-Man*, 661.

28. On Loeb, see Jackson Baker, "Profile of Henry Loeb," pt. 1, *Memphis* (January 1980), 25–33; Tucker, *Memphis since Crump*; Honey, *Going Down Jericho Road*; Dowdy, *Crusades for Freedom*; and Sanford, *From Boss Crump to King Willie*.

29. HSCA, vol. 4 (testimony of Frank C. Holloman), 244.

30. W. E. Routt, assistant chief, Staff Services Division, to H. E. Lux, chief of police, May 20, 1969, located in Selected Expurgated Documents Produced in Discovery, *Kendrick v. Chandler* (hereafter cited as "Expurgated Documents"); Deposition of George H. Hutchinson, October 5, 1976, 59, *Kendrick v. Chandler*; Deposition of Patrick Timothy Ryan Sr., November 17, 1976, 24–25, *Kendrick v. Chandler*; Arkin deposition, December 14, 1976, 66–68. It is unclear precisely when the shift of intelligence operations from the Inspectional Bureau to the Domestic Intelligence Unit occurred. In files that survived the destruction of the MPD records, references to the Inspectional Bureau

disappear by the fall of 1968. But the nomenclature used within the MPD remained in flux; there was a striking lack of consistency in how the intelligence unit was identified, with some documents referring, for example, to an "Intelligence Bureau." No matter the name, the key point is that the MPD had set up an autonomous and secret branch to conduct its intelligence operations.

31. Hutchinson deposition, October 5, 1976, 46–47; HSCA, vol. 6 (testimony of William H. Lawrence), 541.

32. Hutchinson deposition, October 5, 1976, 93, 97.

33. Ryan deposition, December 13, 1976, 264.

34. Hutchinson deposition, November 16, 1976, 75–76.

35. Arkin deposition, December 14, 1976, 38–39.

36. Ryan deposition, November 17, 1976, 57–58; and December 13, 1976, 196.

37. McKnight, "Harvest of Hate," 8–9; Kinchen, *Black Power in the Bluff City*, 108–9.

38. Lt. E. H. Arkin to Capt. J. G. Ray, "Summary of the Plans of the Black Extremists in the United States of America (Taken from Newspapers, and Sources Known to This Bureau)," May 22, 1968, Expurgated Documents.

39. Frank Holloman, "The Badge Speaks: Introduction," ca. October 1968; and "Film Transparency Slide Directory," ca. October 1968, box 2, folder "The Badge Speaks–1968," ser. 3, Holloman Collection; Honey, *Going Down Jericho Road*, 265–66.

40. *Time*, August 16, 1968, 23.

41. HSCA, vol. 6 (testimony of William H. Lawrence), 539, 546; Arkin deposition, August 11, 1977, 489–99, 503; Ryan deposition, December 14, 1976, 351–54; Perrusquia, *Spy in Canaan*, 8–9, 81–82, 214–15; Marc Perrusquia, "In the Shadows—William H. Lawrence, Whose FBI Work Focused on Memphis, Led a Cadre of Informants Including Photographer Ernest Withers," *Memphis Commercial Appeal*, December 19, 2010, V1.

42. Arkin deposition, August 11, 1977, 489–524; HSCA, vol. 6 (testimony of William H. Lawrence), 540–41; Letterhead Memorandum, Re: Black Organizing Project, Racial Matters, May 6, 1968 (157-1067-36), FBI Memphis Field Office File, The Invaders, in the author's possession; Perrusquia, *Spy in Canaan*, 215.

43. Chandler, quoted in Kinchen, *Black Power in the Bluff City*, 104.

44. H. E. Lux to John Buckley, "Militant Black Power Advocates in Memphis Active in OEO projects under WOPC," September 26, 1968, Expurgated Documents; McKnight, "Harvest of Hate," 9–13; Kinchen, *Black Power in the Bluff City*, 83–115; Siracusa, "Nonviolence, Black Power, and the Surveillance State in Memphis's War on Poverty."

45. HSCA, vol. 6 (testimony of William H. Lawrence), 541; M. A. Sample, Detective, Intelligence Bureau, to Don H. Smith, Inspector, "Monthly Report of Intelligence Bureau for Month of May, 1969," June 5, 1969, Expurgated Documents; Honey, *Going Down Jericho Road*, 499–500; Kinchen, *Black Power in the Bluff City*, 111–12. Perrusquia, *Spy in Canaan*, 235–36, 249–52.

46. Capt. J. G. Ray to Inspector G. P. Tines, February 16, 1968, box 5, folder "Civil Disorders–Sanitation Strike–Suspicious Car List–1968," ser. 3, Holloman Collection.

47. Smith interview; E. H. Arkin, Lt., to Inspector G. T. Tines, "Activities, Intelligence Bureau for September 1968," October 18, 1968, Expurgated Documents; Arkin deposition, February 14, 1977, 176–85; February 15, 1977, 237–39; February 16, 1977, 290–94; and August 11, 1977, 441–42.

48. There is no clear accounting of the number of officers assigned to infiltrate the Invaders because records have not survived. Also note that some sources misspell McCollough's name as *McCullough*.

49. Eli Arkin testified that the 500-series code names were chosen randomly. "Why not?" he said. "No rhyme or reason." Arkin deposition, February 16, 1977, 292. McCollough's daughter, Leta McCollough Seletzky, provides a compassionate telling of her father's journey from the Mississippi Delta to the Memphis Police Department's intelligence unit in *The Kneeling Man: My Father's Life as a Black Spy Who Witnessed the Assassination of Martin Luther King Jr.* (Berkeley, CA: Counterpoint, 2023), 22–75, 83–89, 101–16. For more on McCollough, see "It's Mace," *Memphis Commercial Appeal*, December 8, 1967, 29 (thanks to Leta McCollough Seletzky for calling this photo spread to my attention); HSCA, vol. 6 (testimony of Marrell McCollough), 412–43; Honey, *Going Down Jericho Road*, 405; Perrusquia, *Spy in Canaan*, 14–17, 33; Leta McCollough Seletzky, "The Man in the Picture: How I Came to Terms with My Father's Secret CIA Past," *O, The Oprah Magazine*, May 2018, http://www.oprah.com/inspiration/leta-mccollough-on-learning-to-accept-her-fathers-secret-cia-past.

50. Frank Kallaher, interviewed by Joan Beifuss, John Beifuss, Carol Lynn Yellin, and David Yellin, March 7, 1970, 33–34, ser. 1 of 5, container 19, ser. 3—Audiotape File, MSM Records.

51. McCollough's presence at the scene of the murders plays an important role in conspiracy theories—all unproven and based on innuendo and unfounded allegations—that implicate the government in King's assassination.

52. HSCA, vol. 6 (testimony of Marrell McCollough), 439–41; SA William H. Lawrence to SAC [Special Agent in Charge], September 18, 1968, and Inspector G. P. Tines, Inspectional Bureau, to Lt. E. H. Arkin, Intelligence Bureau, Subject: Activities of Invaders, September 10, 1968 (both 157-1067-452), Withers-FBI; McKnight, "Harvest of Hate," 9–13; Kinchen, *Black Power in the Bluff City*, 108–9; McCollough Seletzky, *Kneeling Man*, 150–51, 157–58.

53. Lt. O. B. Holcomb to Inspector G. P. Tines, "Report from Agent 500 for 10–3–68," October 4, 1968; and Detective Jerry C. Davis to Inspector G. P. Tines, "Report Agent 500," October 7, 1968, Expurgated Documents.

54. McCollough's identity was known to the FBI, as his name appeared in FBI reports, contradicting the conclusion of the House Select Committee on Assassination's final report that no one in the bureau knew McCollough was a police officer. HSCA, *Final Report of the Select Committee to Study Government Operations with Respect to Intelligence Activities*, 411–12.

55. McKnight, *Harvest of Hate*, 6, 12.

56. Arkin deposition, December 15, 1976, 127–33.

57. McCollough makes this point in a letter he wrote many years later to his daughter. McCollough Seletzky, "Man in the Picture." Also see McCollough Seletzky, *Kneeling Man*, 172–76.

58. HSCA, vol. 6 (testimony of Charles Laverne Cabbage), 515–16; HSCA, vol. 6 (testimony of John B. Smith), 486–87.

59. McCollough, for instance, was among the DIU officers who observed an antiwar demonstration in August 1969 in downtown Memphis. SAC, Memphis, to Director, FBI, August 25, 1969 (100-4630-63), Withers-FBI; Letterhead Memorandum, Re: Peace Caravan, 1969, American Friends Service Committee, Information Concerning Draft Resistance Union of Memphis (DRUM), August 25, 1969 (100-4630-62), Withers-FBI. McCollough Seletzky, *Kneeling Man*, 176–80, 194–214, 226–32.

60. Marc Perrusquia, handwritten notes on Donald Clarence Pigford police personnel file, in the author's possession; Smith interview; SA William H. Lawrence to SAC [Memphis], April 15, 1969 (100-4579-44), Withers-FBI; Arkin deposition, August 11, 1977, 408–22.

61. SA Howell S. Lowe to SAC [Memphis], June 4, 1970 (157-1067-1869).

62. Kinchen, *Black Power in the Bluff City*, 112.

63. Letterhead Memorandum, Re: Invaders, August 26, 1969 (157-1067-1502A), 3, Withers-FBI.

64. HSCA, vol. 6 (testimony of Marrell McCollough), 415; McCollough Seletzky, *Kneeling Man*, 135, 150.

65. Arkin deposition, August 12, 1977, 558–59.

66. E. H. Arkin, Lt., to Inspector G. T. [*sic*] Tines, "Activities, Intelligence Bureau for September 1968," October 18, 1968, Expurgated Documents.

67. Arkin deposition, August 12, 1977, 564, 657.

68. On the FBI files, see, for instance, Buitrago and Immerman, *Are You Now or Have You Ever Been in the FBI Files;* Haines and Langbart, *Unlocking the Files of the FBI.*

69. Eli Arkin discusses the DIU's files at several points in his deposition: December 15, 1976, 124–26; February 16, 1977, 290–94; and August 12, 1977, 557–58, 657–69. Kenneth O'Reilly, interview by Marc Perrusquia, March 18, 2013, in Perrusquia, *Spy in Canaan*, 12–13.

70. Arkin deposition, August 11, 1977, 476–478.

71. Arkin deposition, February 15, 1977, 237–38.

72. Ryan deposition, December 13, 1976, 147–49, 156, 163–65, 168.

73. Examples include a memo by Lieutenant Arkin conveying information that "Max" had reported on an NAACP Youth Group meeting he attended in 1968 (Lt. E. H. Arkin to Capt. J. G. Ray, "Information from 'Max,'" May 17, 1968, Expurgated Documents); an October 1968 intelligence report attributed to information provided by Agent 500 (Detective Jerry C. Davis to Inspector G. P. Tines, "Report Agent 500," October 7, 1968, Expurgated Documents); and a September 1968 Arkin memo on Invader activities that repeatedly identifies McCollough by his name (Lt. E. H. Arkin, Intelligence Bureau, to Inspector G. P. Tines, Inspectional Bureau, "Activities of Invaders, 9–10–68," September 11, 1968, located in SA William H. Lawrence to SAC [Memphis], September 18, 1968, 157-1067-452, Withers-FBI).

74. Detective J. C. Davis to Inspector Don H. Smith, "Dr. [name redacted]," September 16, 1969, Expurgated Documents. The doctor's name was redacted in the *Kendrick v. Chandler* case files.

75. Davis had also been asked to research the Memphis Search for Meaning Committee but reported that he had been unable to find anything on the two-month old group. J. C. Davis, Detective, to W. E. Routt, Assistant Chief, "Investigation of [redacted] & Memphis Search for Meaning Committee," July 8, 1968, Expurgated Documents; Arkin deposition, August 11, 1977, 507–8.

76. E. H. Arkin, Lt., to Inspector G. T. [*sic*] Tines, "Activities, Intelligence Bureau for September 1968," October 18, 1968, Expurgated Documents.

77. Detective Jerry C. Davis to Inspector G. P. Tines, "Report Agent 500," October 7, 1968; Lt. O. B. Holcomb to Inspector G. P. Tines, "Report from Agent 500 for 10–3–68," October 4, 1968, both in Expurgated Documents.

78. Marc Perrusquia, email to author, August 11, 2018; the author thanks Perrusquia for sharing the photos from Arkin's book.

79. Arkin deposition, August 11, 1977, 455.

80. E. H. Arkin, Lt., to Inspector G. P. Tines, "Activities, Intelligence Bureau, for September 1968," October 18, 1968, Expurgated Documents, *Kendrick v. Chandler.* Also see Lt. O. B. Holcomb to Inspector G. P. Tines, "Black Power Group at JGH [John Gaston Hospital]," October 3, 1968; and Lt. E. H. Arkin to Inspector G. P. Tines, "Hospital Strike Demonstration March, Saturday, 10–26–68," October 28, 1968, both in Expurgated Documents. There is no evidence that the MPD's intelligence unit utilized electronic surveillance in its work, despite the growing availability of the technology and its routine use by the FBI in its COINTTELRPO campaign. This was more a function of the intelligence bureau's technological ignorance than a concerted decision to avoid such methods. Eli Arkin said the bureau had the equipment to take movies of demonstrators but rarely did because none of the officers were skilled at doing so. Similarly, when the bureau used a grant to acquire advanced electronic equipment, much of it was never unboxed, Arkin said, because "we had no one in our outfit that knew anything about it, how to work it, how to use it, or anything else, and no training was afforded to anyone." Arkin deposition, August 11, 1977, 452–53; and February 15, 1977, 247.

81. The Maxine A. Smith NAACP Collection (Finding Aid), 2004, 2–3, Memphis and Shelby County Room, Memphis Public Libraries; Kinchen, *Black Power in the Bluff City,* 19–23; Sherry L. Hoppe and Bruce W. Speck, *Maxine Smith's Unwilling Pupils: Lessons Learned in Memphis's Civil Rights Classroom* (Knoxville: University of Tennessee Press, 2007). On Smith and the 1969 Black Monday school protest, see James David Conway, "Moderated Militants in the Age of Black Power: The Memphis NAACP, 1968–1975" (PhD diss., University of Memphis, 2015); James Conway, "Beyond 1968: The 1969 Black Monday Protest in Memphis," in *An Unseen Light: Black Struggles for Freedom in Memphis, Tennessee,* ed. Aram Goudsouzian and Charles W. McKinney Jr. (Lexington: University Press of Kentucky, 2018), 306–29. Laurie Sugarmon also was rejected by MSU at the same time as Smith. Sugarmon, who later became MSU's first Black faculty member, and her husband, Russell, along with Maxine and Vasco Smith, played central roles in the freedom movement in Memphis. Honey, *Going Down Jericho Road,* 39–40.

82. *Time,* August 16, 1968, 23.

83. Reports of Executive Secretary, Maxine A. Smith–NAACP Collection, Memphis and Shelby County Room, Memphis Public Libraries.

84. Report of Executive Secretary, January 6–February 2, 1971, box 1, folder 11, Smith-NAACP Collection.

85. David Garrow first revealed that the Smiths and others had cooperated with the FBI in his 1981 book *The FBI and Martin Luther King, Jr.* The Smiths later unsuccessfully sued Garrow for libel when he referred to them as "informers" in a radio program. To label the Smith informers is to paint with too broad a brush, to suggest a kinship of sorts between those like the Smiths, who spoke with law enforcement—sometimes merely in response to innocuous questions—to protect the movement, and Withers and others, who engaged in systematic and regular spying and received compensation for their efforts. Garrow, *FBI and Martin Luther King, Jr.,* 295–96, *Turner v. Garrow,* Case no. 83-2076, U.S. District Court, Western District of Tennessee, May 21, 1986, *Media Law Reporter* 12: 2314–2320; McKnight, *Last Crusade,* 31–32, 151; Honey, *Black Workers Remember: An Oral History of Segregation, Unionism, and the Freedom Struggle,* 166; Perrusquia, *Spy in Canaan,* 197–99.

86. E. H. Arkin, Lt., to Inspector G. P. Tines, "Activities, Intelligence Bureau for September 1968," October 18, 1968, Expurgated Documents.

87. Lt. E. H. Arkin to Capt. J. G. Ray, "Information from 'Max,'" May 17, 1968, Expurgated Documents.

88. Robert Kellett, "Curfew Canceled on Blacks' Plea; Incidents Continue," *Memphis Commercial Appeal*, October 21, 1971, 1; Arkin to Tines, "Activities, Intelligence Bureau for September 1968."

89. M. A. Sample, Detective, Intelligence Bureau, to Don H. Smith, Inspector, "Monthly Report of Intelligence Bureau for Month of May, 1969," June 5, 1969; "Ollie and the Nightingales," Stax Records website, accessed October 19, 2018, https://www.staxrecords.com/pages/ollie-the-nightingales.

90. Mary Sample, Detective, Intelligence Bureau, to Don H. Smith, Inspector, "Monthly Report Intelligence Bureau, for Month of January 1969," February 6, 1969, Expurgated Documents; "Uptight," IMBd.com, accessed October 19, 2018, https://www.imdb.com/title/tt0063748; Kevin Hagopian, "The Informer," New York State Writers Institute, SUNY, accessed October 19, 2018, https://www.albany.edu/writers-inst/webpages4/filmnotes/fns99n10.html.

91. "Brutality Claims Linked to Communist Plot," July 13, 1969, *Memphis Press-Scimitar*, located in box 26, folder 46, ser. 3, MSM Records.

92. *Look to the East*, October 1969; Henry Loeb to Frank Holloman, March 16, 1970; and Frank C. Holloman to Henry Loeb, March 18, 1970, all in box 105, folder 2, ser. 3, Loeb Papers.

93. Richard Starnes, "U.S. Student Radicals Honor Red Leaders as Heroes and Vow to Destroy Capitalism," *Memphis Press-Scimitar*, June 12, 1968, 12.

94. Richard Starnes, "Communism Too Tame—Student Activists Adopt Nihilism and Anarchy as Pattern of Conquest," *Memphis Press-Scimitar*, June 13, 1968, 10.

95. "Up Tight with the Draft?" ca. 1970; Mrs. R. J. Flaniken to Mayor Loeb, February 24, 1970; Henry Loeb to Mrs. R. J. Flaniken, February 27, 1970; and Frank C. Holloman to Henry Loeb, March 4, 1970, all in box 128, folder 5, ser. 3, Loeb Papers.

96. Lt. E. H. Arkin to Capt. J. G. Ray, "Students for a Democratic Society (SDS) Organizational Meeting MSU 5/16/68," May 17, 1968; E. H. Arkin, Lt., to Inspector G. T. [*sic*] Tines, "Activities, Intelligence Bureau for September 1968," October 18, 1968; Mary Sample, Det., Intelligence Bureau, to Don H. Smith, Inspector, "Monthly Report Intelligence Bureau, for Month of January 1969," February 6, 1969, all in Expurgated Documents; Arkin deposition, August 11, 1977, 451–52; McCollough Seletzky, *Kneeling Man*, 115–16, 145–47, 163–70. For an overview of Richard Moon's work during the strike, see Amanda Campbell, "'The Chaplain of the New Left': Reverend Richard Moon's Community of Influence and the 1968 Memphis Sanitation Workers' Strike," *QuaesitUM Undergraduate Research Journal* (Spring 2020): 21–36. The MSU Student Government Association twice voted not to recognize SDS as an official student group. Jack Lorenzini, "'We Didn't Reject the System, the System Rejected Us': The SDS Failure to Obtain a Charter at Memphis State University, 1968–1970," *West Tennessee Historical Society Papers* 62 (2009): 25–43.

97. Kay Pittman Black, "Student Society Has 2 Active Chapters in City," *Memphis Press-Scimitar*, November 15, 1968, 1, located in box 128, folder 1, ser. 3, Loeb Papers. FBI documents identify a source at the *Memphis Press Scimitar* who likely was Black, but the name is redacted, leaving open the possibility that other journalists worked with the bureau. See, for example, SAC, Memphis, to Director, FBI (HQ 100-4491-31), July 11, 1967, Withers-FBI. On Pittman Black, see Perrusquia, *Spy in Canaan*, 238–41.

98. Cecil C. Humphreys, "Speech to Southern Association of Colleges and Schools," December

3, 1969, box 11, folder 32, ser. 2, MSM Records, 2, 5, 6. On the MSU sit-in, see Kinchen, *Black Power in the Bluff City*, 143–73. On the emergence of the Black Student Association and its role in the sanitation strike, see Jack Lorenzini, "United by a Cause: Student Activists and the Memphis Sanitation Strike of 1968," *Tennessee Historical Quarterly* 78, no. 4 (2019): 266–91.

99. Arkin deposition, December 14, 1976, 46–48; February 15, 1977, 260–64; and August 12, 1977, 540–42, 555; Ryan deposition, December 13, 1976, 214–15.

100. Lt. E. H. Arkin to Inspector G.P. Tines, "Forum at the University Center, Memphis State University, 7 P.M. this date, 11–13–68," November 13, 1968, Expurgated Documents. Youngson was identified as chief of security in SA William H. Lawrence to SAC [Memphis], July 21, 1967 (100-4394-60A), 3.

101. Arkin deposition, February 15, 1977, 262; and August 15, 1977, 532–44; "C. C. Humphreys Dies; Led U of M Growth Era," *Memphis Commercial Appeal*, June 15, 1995, A7.

102. Jones's name was inadvertently left unredacted in one place in Arkin's lengthy deposition. Arkin deposition, August 12, 1977, 547.

103. Jones later left MSU for the University of Alabama at Birmingham, where he also served in administrative roles. John D. Jones obituary, Dignity Memorial, accessed July 21, 2018, https://www.dignitymemorial.com/obituaries/pelham-al/john-jones-4517043; *DeSoto*, vol. 59 (1971), 62; *DeSoto*, 1972, n.p.; *DeSoto*, 1973, 111; *DeSoto*, vol. 64 (1974), 1976, 51; all located in University Archives, Special Collections Department, University Libraries, University of Memphis; Arkin deposition, August 12, 1977, 546–49.

104. Arkin deposition, February 15, 1977, 243–44, 263–64; and August 12, 1977, 534–35; Perrusquia, *Spy in Canaan*, 215–16. While definitive evidence does not exist that Townsend was "Agent 503," Arkin said in his deposition that it was "a logical assumption" that was his identity given that he was not Agents 500, 501, or 502. Arkin deposition, August 11, 1977, 425.

105. Shirley Downing, "Hour's Wait, Mayor's 'Chat' Delay Access to Public Records," *Memphis Commercial Appeal*, October 13, 1976, 15; Marc Perrusquia, "'They Were Watching'—'It's Just Like the Movies,' Former '70s Activist Recalls. 'You Could Spot Them a Mile Away,'" *Memphis Commercial Appeal*, December 19, 2010, V3; Arkin deposition, February 15, 1977, 243–45.

106. Patrolman H. A. Embrey to Inspector Don H. Smith, "DRUM," August 5, 1969, Expurgated Documents.

107. The protests were supported, in part, by "Peace Caravan 1969," a project sponsored by the Philadelphia-based Quaker pacifist organization American Friends Service Committee. Lt. E. H. Arkin to Inspector Don H. Smith, "Peace Caravan 1969 Anti Viet Nam War," July 3, 1969; and Lt. E. H. Arkin to Inspector Don H. Smith, "Peace Caravan, 1969 American Friends Service Committee (AFSC)," July 10, 1969, Expurgated Documents; Arkin deposition, August 12, 1977, 638–39. On the FBI's surveillance, see, for example, Letterhead Memorandum, Peace Caravan, 1969, American Friends Service Committee Information Concern Draft Resistance Union of Memphis (DRUM) Selective Service Act, Internal Security–Miscellaneous, August 8, 1969 (100-400-1333); and Letterhead Memorandum, Peace Caravan, 1969, American Friends Service Committee Information Concern Draft Resistance Union of Memphis (DRUM) Selective Service Act, Internal Security–Miscellaneous, August 15, 1969 (100-400-1344), Withers-FBI.

108. Perrusquia, *Spy in Canaan*, 236–37; SA William H. Lawrence to SAC [Memphis], November 29, 1966 (100-4394-1), Withers-FBI. Two of the Invaders identified by the FBI as having

ties to SDS leaders were, in fact, MPD undercover officers Marrell McCollough and Donald Pigford. SAC, Memphis, to Director, FBI; and Letterhead Memorandum "Re: Invaders," March 3, 1969 (157-8460-21), Withers-FBI.

109. SA William H. Lawrence to SAC [Memphis], September 26, 1969 (100-4000-1400), Withers-FBI.

110. Jean Gifford to Henry Loeb, April 3, 1970; Betty Gifford (Mrs. Charles) to Henry Loeb, April 4, 1970; and Henry Loeb to Mrs. Charles Gifford (Betty), April 8, 1970, all in box 128, folder 5, ser. 3, Loeb Papers.

111. Michael Honey, email message to author, November 8, 2018. In 1970, Allen and Honey faced the unusual charge of embracery—trying to corruptly influence a jury—for protesting the prosecution of the "Black Six," African American activists who had organized a 1968 protest after King's assassination. "SCEF Couple Charged with Embracery" and "A Free Press Issue," *Southern Patriot*, January 1970; "Embracery Case to Be Heard," *Southern Patriot*, November 1970, 4.

112. Michel, *Struggle for a Better South*, 135, 213.

113. Perrusquia, *Spy in Canaan*, 223.

114. Perrusquia, *Spy in Canaan*, 225–30; Informant Report, Received from ME 338-E [Ernest Withers] by SA Howell S. Lowe, September 26, 1973 (dictated October 2, 1973; transcribed October 5, 1973; authenticated by Informant October 9, 1973), "International Night and Party Sponsored by Memphis Communist Party Chapter" (100-4708-623), Withers-FBI. Local 19 of the Distributive Workers of America had suffered abuse and attacks during the red scare of the 1940s and 1950s. Honey, *Southern Labor and Black Civil Rights*, 263–71.

115. SAC, Memphis, to Director, FBI (HQ 100-4491-31), July 11, 1967, Withers-FBI.

116. The surveillance materials prevented Roop from securing a federal position as an industrial hygienist in the National Institute for Occupational Safety and Health in the 1980s on the grounds that her participation in a communist organization many years earlier made her a security risk. Withers's exposure as an informant left her angry and betrayed. "This man has ruined my life," she told Marc Perrusquia. "Betrayal? Betrayal isn't even the word. I have been scarred for life." Perrusquia, *Spy in Canaan*, 225–30; Michael Honey, "Some Comments on FBI/MPD Surveillance," August 7, 2018, in author's possession; "Angela Davis Benefit Raided," *Memphis Tri-State Defender*, February 20, 1971; Mike Honey, "Bomb Shakes Activists," *Memphis Tri-State Defender*, May 1, 1971, 2; Mike Honey, "Activists' Car Is Bombed," *Southern Patriot*, May 1971, 3. The author thanks Michael Honey for pointing him to these articles.

117. Ryan's oversight of the DIU coincided with a departmental reorganization in which domestic intelligence, criminal intelligence, and interstate theft were brought together in the newly formed Special Investigations bureau, which Ryan led. The DIU, though, retained its autonomy as a distinct and separate unit, walled off from the others, in this new structure. Ryan deposition, December 13, 1976, 101–13, 124–25.

118. The MPD officers who were deposed as part of the *Kendrick v. Chandler* suit typically conflated the YWLL and the Communist Party, using those terms interchangeably.

119. Ryan deposition, December 14, 1976, 331–55; Arkin deposition, February 14, 1977, 191–204; and August 11, 1977, 430–31; Hutchinson deposition, November 16, 1976, 38–41; Perrusquia, *Spy in Canaan*, 221.

120. On the VVAW, see David Cortright, *Soldiers in Revolt: The American Military Today* (Garden City, NY: Anchor Press–Doubleday, 1975), 80–83; Richard Stacewicz, *Winter Soldiers: An Oral History of Vietnam Veterans Against the War* (New York: Twayne Publishers, 1997); Gerald Nicosia, *Home to War: A History of the Vietnam Veterans' Movement* (2001; reprint, New York: Carroll & Graf, 2004); Tom Wells, *The War Within: America's Battle over Vietnam,* (1994; reprint, New York: Henry Holt, 1996), 492–96.

121. Weiler, "Police Order Burning of File on Vietnam War Protestor"; Carter interview.

122. Carter interview.

123. Although an ACLU summary of the *Kendrick v. Chandler* litigation in 1978 indicated the two were roommates, Carter said that was never the case. Townsend, in fact, was married and took Carter to his home on one occasion. Carter remembers being surprised to learn his friend of more than a year was married. Carter interview; Kramer, "Surveillance of Protected First Amendment Activities," 2.

124. Carter interview.

125. Ibid.; Weiler, "Police Order Burning of File on Vietnam War Protester"; James Cole, "File Was Destroyed to Protect Undercover Men, Police Claim," *Memphis Commercial Appeal,* September 10, 1976 "Intelligence Unit Dissolved; Files are Burned"; Arkin deposition, February 15, 1977, 254–57; and August 12, 1977, 536.

126. Weiler, "Police Order Burning of File on Vietnam War Protester"; Cole, "File Was Destroyed to Protect Undercover Men, Police Claim."

127. Carter interview; Weiler, "File Burning Draws Mayor's Attention"; Arkin deposition, August 12, 1977, 536–37. When the story of the police files broke in the local press, Carter told the *Memphis Commercial Appeal* that he had learned that the MPD had a file on him from his friend Jerry Davis, a detective in the DIU whom he presumably knew as a police officer taking classes at Memphis State. "'He started talking about my private life and said they had pictures of me—so many that they'd stopped printing them. They were just filing the negatives.'" When reached by the newspaper for comment, Davis denied knowing anything about Carter's file. It is curious, to say the least, that Davis would betray the secrecy of the intelligence unit to divulge information about its files to a subject even if he was a friend. Weiler, "Police Order Burning of File on Vietnam War Protester."

128. Carter interview; Hutchinson deposition, October 5, 1976, 94–95; Arkin deposition, February 16, 1977, 331–36; and August 12, 1977, 537; Weiler, "Police Order Burning of File on Vietnam War Protester"; Weiler, "File Burning Draws Mayor's Attention"; Cole, "File Was Destroyed to Protect Undercover Men, Police Claim."

129. "Weiler, "File Burning Draws Mayor's Attention."

130. Arkin deposition, February 16, 1977, 315–21; "Complaint," September 14, 1976, *Kendrick v. Chandler;* Bruce Kramer, interviewed by author, July 17, 2018, Memphis; Clifford Pierce, interview by author, July 18, 2018, Memphis.

131. Carter letter, September 15, 1976, quoted in Hutchinson deposition, November 15, 1976, 83; Carter interview.

132. "Order, Judgment and Decree," September 14, 1978, *Kendrick v. Chandler;* Black, "Surveillance Curbs Hit Memphis Police"; "Domestic Intelligence Reform," 1–3; Chevigny, "Politics and Law in the Control of Local Surveillance," 751–60.

4. NASHVILLE

1. "'Impact' Slates Carmichael," *Nashville Tennessean*, March 18, 1967, 14; "Carmichael Still to Speak," *Nashville Tennessean*, March 24, 1967, 1, 9; "Vanderbilt Will Survive," *Nashville Tennessean*, March 27, 1967, 8; "Negroes Urged by Carmichael to Scorn Law," *Nashville Tennessean*, April 5, 1967, 40; "Carmichael Talk Stand Draws Fire," *Nashville Tennessean*, April 6, 1967, 24; John Haile, "Senate Protest Won't Halt Impact Talk," *Nashville Tennessean*, April 7, 1967, 1, 7; Tom Ingram, "Carmichael Accuses Negroes of Yielding to 'White Lies,'" *Nashville Tennessean*, April 7, 1967, 7; Houston, *Nashville Way*, 168–70.

2. The violence and conflict were the subject of a report produced by researchers for the National Advisory Commission on Civil Disorders, better known as the Kerner Commission, which President Johnson had convened after urban unrest had occurred across the country in 1967. "Nashville, Tennessee: Description of City and Chronology of Disorders" (draft), January 8, 1968, City Analyses 1967, box 3, National Advisory Commission on Civil Disorders, LBJ Presidential Library, Austin, TX (hereafter cited as NACCD). For a cogent discussion of the unrest, see Houston, *Nashville Way*, 164–75. Also insightful, if less detailed, is Clayborne Carson, *In Struggle: SNCC and the Black Awakening of the 1960s* (Cambridge: Harvard University Press, 1981), 245–48.

3. "Nashville, Tennessee," NACCD; *Field Research Report, Civil Disturbances in Nashville, Tennessee, Spring 1967*, pt. 1, Narrative, February 1968, box E71, Records of the National Advisory Commission on Civil Disorders (Embargoed Series), LBJ Presidential Library, Austin, TX (hereafter cited as RNACCD-ES).

4. Pat Harris, "Sorace: Portrait of a Cop," *Nashville Magazine*, November 1968, 11–15.

5. Rufus Jarman, "Nashville," *Saturday Evening Post*, October 27, 1951, 22.

6. Don H. Doyle, *Nashville in the New South, 1880–1930* (Knoxville: University of Tennessee Press, 1985), 14–15, 19–32, 41–58, 183, 188–232; Don H. Doyle, *Nashville since the 1920s* (Knoxville: University of Tennessee Press, 1985), 108, 159; John Egerton, *Nashville: The Faces of Two Centuries, 1970–1980* (Nashville: PlusMedia, 1979), 237; Houston, *Nashville Way*, 27–28. The city enjoyed an industrial revival during the World War II years. The self-styled "Inner Citadel" of the country, as the *Tennessean* newspaper labeled Nashville in a slogan that ran on the front page throughout the war, welcomed the new economic opportunities war provided. This included the Vultee Aircraft plant, which produced bombers; the Nashville Bridge Company, which turned to producing small naval vessels; the Tennessee Enamel Company, which made shells; the Allen Manufacturing Company, which made stoves; and textile firms, which began producing uniforms. Although these developments did not put Nashville in the same league as Detroit or even Mobile, they did spur significant growth in the city. Doyle, *Nashville since the 1920s*, 110–15; Robert G. Spinney, "Municipal Government in Nashville, Tennessee, 1938–1951: World War II and the Growth of the Public Sector," *Journal of Southern History* 61, no. 1 (1995): 81–83. Also see Egerton, *Nashville*, 237.

7. Egerton, *Nashville*, 242–43, 250; Doyle, *Nashville in the New South, 1880–1930*, 109–20; Doyle, *Nashville since the 1920s*, 30–42; Houston, *Nashville Way*, 23–27.

8. Doyle, *Nashville in the New South*, 165–77; Yollette Trigg Jones, "The Black Community, Politics, and Race Relations in the 'Iris City': Nashville, Tennessee, 1870–1954" (PhD diss., Duke University, 1985), 1–82; Houston, *Nashville Way*, 30–31. While Black migration to Nashville continued

despite the challenges and insults African Americans faced in the segregated city, others chose to leave Nashville instead. This was nothing new, as Nashville Blacks had been a part of the wave of migrants who had departed the South starting in the World War I era. They were drawn north not just by opportunity but by the belief, confirmed by long experience, that they would never be treated fairly by white leaders. As the city's Black newspaper, the *Nashville Globe*, reported in 1917, African Americans who had departed the city did so "to escape the oppression that is so prevalent in official circles. The black man knows he has no redress and it is better for him to leave than to be subjected to the indignities that are his daily portion." Quoted in "The Flight into Egypt," *The Crisis* 14, no. 3 (July 1917), 136; and Jones, "Black Community, Politics, and Race Relations," 190.

9. On the 1951 election, see Spinney, "Municipal Government in Nashville," 105–6; Jones, "Black Community, Politics, and Race Relations," 326–37.

10. Houston, *Nashville Way*, 4; *Field Research Report, Civil Disturbances in Nashville*, pt. 2, Appendixes, C38, February 1968, box E71, RNACCD-ES.

11. Egerton, *Nashville*, 260–64; Doyle, *Nashville since the 1920s*, 191–218, 273; Spinney, "Municipal Government in Nashville,"; Houston, *Nashville Way*, 134–37. Briley, a tax lawyer who in 1932 became the youngest person admitted to the Tennessee Bar, went on to serve in the navy and then unsuccessfully sought election to the county legislature on a "GI Joe" ticket in 1946, before scoring a startling upset over the county political machine to win election as county judge in 1950, making him the top elected official in Davidson. Briley held this position until he was elected mayor of the new metropolitan government in late 1962 and took office in the spring of 1963. Doyle, *Nashville since the 1920s*, 214–15; Spinney, "Municipal Government in Nashville," 98–99, 104–7.

12. On the Nashville movement, see Zinn, *SNCC*, 19–23; Fred Powledge, *Free at Last? The Civil Rights Movement and the People Who Made It* (Boston: Little, Brown, 1991), 203–10; Howell Raines, *My Soul Is Rested: Movement Days in the Deep South Remembered* (New York: Putnam, 1977), 98–100; Aldon D. Morris, *The Origins of the Civil Rights Movement: Black Communities Organizing for Change* (New York: Free Press, 1984), 174–78, 205–13; Hampton, *Voices of Freedom*, 53–61, 65–67; Branch, *Parting the Waters*, 260–64, 278–80, 295, 345, 379–80; Forman, *Making of Black Revolutionaries*, 145–57; Houston, *Nashville Way*, 82–163; Halberstam, *The Children;* Lewis, *Walking with the Wind*, 67–117.

13. *Nashville Banner* clipping, ca. March 23, 1963, Southern Student Organizing Committee Records, Albert and Shirley Small Special Collections Library, University of Virginia, Charlottesville.

14. Michel, *Struggle for a Better South*, 25–39; Houston, *Nashville Way*, 156–57.

15. Spinney, "Municipal Government in Nashville, Tennessee," 85–87.

16. Josephine Taylor, Harry Walker, and Lewis W. Jones, "Forms of Segregation and Discrimination in Nashville, Tennessee," n.d., quoted in Houston, *Nashville Way*, 20. On the hiring of the first Black officers, see Egerton, *Nashville*, 251; Jones, "Black Community, Politics, and Race Relations," 311; Houston, *Nashville Way*.

17. Jerry Thompson, "Job for Metro: A Better Nashville Police Force," *Nashville Tennessean*, February 10, 1963, 1B, 3B; Jim Squires, "Power Struggle Racks Metro Police Department," *Nashville Tennessean*, November 27, 1966, 1B, 3B; "Chief H. O. Kemp Papers," Chief H. O. Kemp Papers, Metropolitan Government Archives of Nashville–Davidson County, Nashville (hereafter cited as Kemp Papers). Complaints of police brutality are collected in Police Brutality Complaints, 1967–68, box

12, folder 2, Kemp Papers; despite the folder's title, most complaints were from 1963 and 1964. On the April 1964 demonstrations, see "Metropolitan Council Public Safety Sub-Committee," June 1, 1964, box 5, folder 4; and "Metropolitan Council Public Safety Sub-Committee," June 15, 1964, box 5, folder 4, Kemp Papers. On bribery investigations, see Squires, "Power Struggle Racks Metro Police Department," 1B, 3B.

18. "Putt Probe 'Welcome,' Jett Says," *Nashville Banner*, February 23, 1962; "Lt. Sorace to Aid on Police Book," *Nashville Banner*, February 26, 1966; Larry Brinton, "Lt. Sorace Launches New Police Programs," *Nashville Banner*, August 24, 1966; and "Sorace, 3 Other Metro Policemen Promoted," *Nashville Banner*, January 16, 1967, all in *Nashville Banner* Clippings Files, *Nashville Banner* Archives, Nashville Public Library (hereafter cited as NBCF); Jim Squires, "New Police Unit Formed," *Nashville Tennessean*, April 2, 1964, NBCF (note that the NBCF also includes articles from the *Nashville Tennessean*); Squires, "Power Struggle Racks Metro Police Department," 1B, 3B; Harris, "Sorace," 11–15.

19. Larry Brinton, "Top-Secret Metro Probe Nears End," *Nashville Tennessean*, August 8, 1963, NBCF; Larry Brinton, "City Officials Suspects in Loans Racket," *Nashville Banner*, August 10, 1963, NBCF. Also see Jack Hurst, "Metro Worker under Probe as Loan Shark," *Nashville Tennessean*, August 10, 1963, 1, 7; "Jury to Probe License Case," *Nashville Tennessean*, March 8, 1964, 10A; and Sam McPherson, "Public Works Man Draws Suspension," *Nashville Banner*, August 13, 1963, NBCF.

20. Squires, "Power Struggle Racks Metro Police Department," 1B, 3B; also see "Jury to Probe License Case," *Nashville Tennessean*, March 8, 1964, 10A.

21. Jim Squires, "New Police Unit Formed," *Nashville Tennessean*, April 2, 1964, NBCF; also see Larry Brinton, "Councilmen Blast Sorace Promotion," *Nashville Banner*, April 1, 1964, NBCF.

22. Brinton, "Councilmen Blast Sorace Promotion"; Squires, "New Police Unit Formed"; Squires, "Power Struggle Racks Metro Police Department," 1B, 3B. Sorace interview with *Vanderbilt Hustler*, quoted in "Sorace, 3 Other Metro Policemen Promoted."

23. Craven Crowell, "St. John to Be Next Police Chief?" *Nashville Tennessean*, June 27, 1969.

24. A December 1964 *Tennessean* article notes that Officers Brode Pruitt and Kenneth Reasonover worked under Sorace (Reasonover would later lead the Intelligence Division); it is uncertain if they were the first two officers brought into the division. "7 Held, Questioned in Thefts, Blackmail," *Nashville Tennessean*, December 5, 1964, 2. Also see Frank Gibson, "60s Police Spy Operation Told," *Nashville Tennessean*, July 9, 1978, NBCF.

25. Hill's first name appears in newspapers throughout the 1960s and 1970s as *Robert*, *Bobbie*, *Bobby*, and *Robbie*.

26. "3 Officers Face Conduct Probes," *Nashville Banner*, March 16, 1964, NBCF; "Two Suspended Officers Resign," *Nashville Banner*, March 17, 1964, NBCF; "Four Metro Policemen Promoted," *Nashville Banner*, February 15, 1967, NBCF; Dick Battle, "Sorace Seeks Support, Raps School 'Distortions,'" *Nashville Banner*, August 22, 1967, NBCF; Neil Terrell, "Sorace's New Post Best for Metro Police: Hill," *Nashville Banner*, December 13, 1967, NBCF; Robert Glass, "Capt. Hill Named to Head Mayor's Office Security," *Nashville Banner*, December 1, 1973, NBCF; "3 Policemen Suspended," *Nashville Tennessean*, March 16, 1964, NBCF; "2 Police Resign after Suspensions," *Nashville Tennessean*, March 17, 1964, NBCF; Wayne Whitt, "2 Officers 'Quit' under Cloud, Shine as Ringbusters, *Nashville Tennessean*, May 23, 1964, 5; "Kemp to Create Narcotics Division," *Nashville Tennessean*,

May 24, 1964, 6A; Jim Squires, "Police Hike City's Largest," *Nashville Tennessean,* December 16, 1964, 1, 17; "VU Cagers Honor Police Lt. Hill," *Nashville Tennessean,* January 27, 1968, 24.

27. Squires, "New Police Unit Formed"; Jim Squires, "Dragon Got Police Escort," *Nashville Tennessean,* November 28, 1965, 2B.

28. "'Fixing' Probe Covers 1965 Traffic Tickets," *Nashville Tennessean,* February 12, 1966, 1; Jerry Thompson, "Numbers Raids Net 6 Arrests," *Nashville Tennessean,* December 3, 1966, 1.

29. Wayne Whitt, "Briley: Police Not in KKK," *Nashville Tennessean,* October 21, 1965, 5; Squires, "Dragon Got Police Escort," 2B; Houston, *Nashville Way,* 166–67; Harris, "Sorace," 13.

30. Wayne Whitt, "Rights History Guide Planned," *Nashville Tennessean,* December 4, 1964, 16; Wayne Whitt, "Action Urged in Race Crisis," *Nashville Tennessean,* December 6, 1964, 8A; Wayne Whitt, "3 from Metro at Police Meet," *Nashville Tennessean,* May 13, 1965, 48. On the April and May protests, see interview with Archie Eugene Allen by Kathy Bennett, Nashville, March 31 and September 30, 2003, Civil Rights Collection of the Nashville Public Library, ser. 3: The Civil Rights Oral History Collection; Houston, *Nashville Way,* 153–58.

31. "Communist Effort Here Revealed," *Nashville Banner,* February 1, 1965, NBCF.

32. Brinton, "Lt. Sorace Launches New Police Programs."

33. Gibson, "60s Police Spy Operation Told"; Frank Gibson and Kathleen Gallagher, "Unaware of Police Spy Files: Briley," *Nashville Tennessean,* July 10, 1978. Also see John Brittingham, "Sorace Denies Keeping Files at Home," *Nashville Banner,* July 10, 1978, NBCF.

34. Jacque Stubbel, "Briley Cites Police for Uncovering Subversives," *Nashville Banner,* October 28, 1966, NBCF.

35. On SNCC and Black Power, see Stokely Carmichael and Charles V. Hamilton, *Black Power: The Politics of Liberation in America* (New York: Vintage Books, 1967); Carson, *In Struggle,* 191–243; William Van Deburg, *New Day in Babylon: The Black Power Movement and American Culture, 1965–1975* (Chicago: University of Chicago Press, 1992); Peniel E. Joseph, *Waiting for the Midnight Hour: Black Power in America* (New York: Henry Holt, 2006).

36. Carson, *In Struggle,* 245–46.

37. Michel, *Struggle for a Better South,* 14, 77–81. On the Braden and SCEF, see Linda Reed, *Simple Decency & Common Sense: The Southern Conference Movement, 1938–1963* (Bloomington: Indiana University Press, 1991); Fosl, *Subversive Southerner.*

38. Michel, *Struggle for a Better South,* 125–26.

39. "5-Day Fast over War in 3rd Day," *Nashville Tennessean,* July 6, 1966, 3; Jerry Thompson, "20 War Protesters Arrested," *Nashville Tennessean,* July 8, 1966, 1; "Demonstrators End Fast Early," *Nashville Tennessean,* July 9, 1966, 20; "Seven Fast for Peace," *Southern Patriot,* August 1966, 2; Gregg L. Michel, "We'll Take Our Stand: The Southern Student Organizing Committee and the Radicalization of White Southern Students, 1964–1969" (PhD diss., University of Virginia, 1999), 337–42.

40. Craven Crowell, "Police Book 3 Protestors," *Nashville Tennessean,* March 16, 1967, 1, 6; Bill Preston, "President's Talk Here Disappoints Anti-War Group," *Nashville Tennessean,* March 17, 1967, 29; Michel, *Struggle for a Better South,* 104, 144–45, 147.

41. Field Research Report, Civil Disturbances in Nashville, pt. 1: Narrative, 6, 30, RNACCD-ES.

42. In 1966, Sorace was appointed to lead the Bureau of Inspectional Services, which oversaw the Intelligence Division. Robert Hill replaced Sorace as the new operational commander of

the Intelligence Division. Shortly thereafter, Hill was promoted from sergeant to lieutenant. Jerry Thompson, "Duke Resigns Police Post," *Nashville Tennessean*, August 23, 1966, 1, 3; Nellie Kenyon, "Riot 'Cocktails' Shown in Court," *Nashville Tennessean*, June 1, 1967, 1, 4; Brinton, "Lt. Sorace Launches New Police Programs"; "Four Metro Policemen Promoted"; "It Seems Everybody But Mr. Davis Knew It Was Coming," *Nashville Banner*, August 9, 1967, NBCF.

43. U.S. Senate, *Permanent Subcommittee on Investigations of the Committee on Government Operations: Hearings*, 90th Cong., pt. 2 (1967) (hereafter cited as McClellan Subcommittee Hearings), 638–708; U.S. Senate, *Committee on the Judiciary: Hearings on H.R. 421 to Amend Title 18 of the United States Code to Prohibit Travel or Use of Any Facility in Interstate or Foreign Commerce with the Intent to Incite a Riot or Other Violent Civil Disturbance, and for Other Purposes*, 90th Cong., pt. 1 (1967) (hereafter cited as Eastland Committee Hearings), 135–72, 216–24.

44. Sorace, quoted in memo from Jefferson County, AL, sheriff regarding Nashville's intelligence squad. Gibson, "60s Police Spy Operation Told."

45. McClellan Subcommittee Hearings, 699.

46. Doug Looney, "Mob Assailed Police during April Riots Here: FBI Agent," *Nashville Banner*, May 29, 1967, NBCF; Nellie Kenyon, "Riot Described by FBI Agent," *Nashville Tennessean*, May 30, 1967, 1, 2.

47. Looney, "Mob Assailed Police during April Riots"; McClellan Subcommittee Hearings, 659.

48. Looney, "Mob Assailed Police during April Riots Here"; "Sorace Tells Probe Panel," *Nashville Banner*, August 3, 1967, NBCF; Frank Van Der Linden, "Sorace's Charge of 'Hate White' Teaching Jolts Senate Hearing," *Nashville Banner*, August 4, 1967, NBCF; Frank Van Der Linden, "Communist Link Cited," *Nashville Banner*, November 21, 1967, NBCF; Edmund Willingham, "Sorace: OEO Funds Aid Riots," *Nashville Tennessean*, August 4, 1967, NBCF; Edmund Willingham, "Role in Riot Laid to Brooks," *Nashville Tennessean*, November 22, 1967, NBCF; McClellan Subcommittee Hearings, 686–90; Eastland Committee Hearings, 141.

49. Kenyon, "Riot Described by FBI Agent," 1, 2; "Sorace Tells Probe Panel," *Nashville Banner*, August 3, 1967, NBCF; Eastland Committee Hearings, 137, 218–25, 347–50. Sorace's sensational charges stirred significant controversy in Nashville and received extensive coverage in the papers.

50. Doss outed himself as an informant at a public meeting in August 1967 over the fate of the liberation school that Sorace had alleged was teaching hate. LHM, "National Mobilization Committee to End the War in Vietnam Information Concerning (Internal Security)" (104-10063-10315), October 24, 1967, *House Select Committee on Assassinations*, December 15, 2017, document release, National Archives, document ID 32346867, https://www.archives.gov/files/research/jfk/releases/docid-32346867.pdf; and National Archives, "JFK Assassination Records—2018 Additional Documents Release," last reviewed on December 15, 2022, https://www.archives.gov/research/jfk/release; Bill Kovach, "MAC Cancels School Support," *Nashville Banner*, August 18, 1967, NBCF; David Nolan, email to author, March 8, 2021.

51. Eastland Committee Hearings, 137; "Sorace Tells Probe Panel," *Nashville Banner*, August 3, 1967, NBCF.

52. *Field Research Report, Civil Disturbances in Nashville*, pt. 1: Narrative, 29, and pt. 2: Appendixes, C41, RNACCD-ES.

53. Eastland Committee Hearings, 161; *Field Research Report, Civil Disturbances in Nashville*, pt. 2: Appendixes, C41, RNACCD-ES.

54. John Herbers, "Police Official Says Negroes in Nashville Teach Hatred in Name of Liberation," *New York Times*, August 4, 1967, 1, 12; "Senate Panel Told of Push by Negroes," *New York Times*, November 22, 1967, 9.

55. "Cities Must Be Prepared for Violence," *Nashville Banner*, September 15, 1967, NBCF; Frank Holloman, "The Badge Speaks: Introduction," ca. October 1968, ser. 3—Memphis Fire and Police Division, Holloman Collection.

56. Jacque Srouji, "Rights Not Reason for Riots: Sorace," *Nashville Banner*, August 18, 1967, NBCF.

57. "Cities Must Be Prepared for Violence."

58. Jacque Srouji, "New Guerilla Groups Formed, Sorace Warns," *Nashville Banner*, October 4, 1967, NBCF.

59. Frances Meeker, "Writer Sees U.S., Soviet Vietnam Deal," *Nashville Banner*, October 23, 1968, NBCF; Behway K. Sparkes, "Stark-Naked Terrorism Next Step, Sorace Says," *Nashville Banner*, September 18, 1967, NBCF; "Cities Must Be Prepared for Violence."

60. Behway K. Sparkes, "Crime Increase Here Can Be Cut, Sorace Says," *Nashville Banner*, July 26, 1968, NBCF.

61. Edmund Willingham, "Role of Riot Laid to Brooks," *Nashville Tennessean*, November 22, 1967, NBCF.

62. Field Research Report, Civil Disturbances in Nashville, pt. 2, Appendixes, C66, RNACCD-ES.

63. Field Research Report, Civil Disturbances in Nashville, pt. 1, Narrative, 37.

64. Brinton, "City Officials Suspects in Loans Racket"; Dick Battle, "Computer Revolutionizes Crime Fight," *Nashville Banner*, October 29, 1971, NBCF; Dick Battle, "Metro Police Complete FBI Information Hookup," *Nashville Banner*, February 18, 1972, NBCF; "Jury to Probe License Case," *Nashville Tennessean*, March 8, 1964, 10A; Squires, "Power Struggle Racks Metro Police Department."

65. Field Research Report, Civil Disturbances in Nashville, pt. 1, Narrative, 33–34 39.

66. "Mr. Sorace's Influence Divides the Community," *Nashville Tennessean*, February 22, 1968, NBCF.

67. Field Research Report, Civil Disturbances in Nashville, pt. 1, Narrative, 34.

68. "Capt. John Sorace and Red Menace," *Nashville Tennessean*, November 19, 1967, NBCF; "Mayor Leads Police Force in a Doubtful Direction," *Nashville Tennessean*, December 8, 1967, 20.

69. "Able Metro Police Work Protected the City," *Nashville Banner*, November 9, 1967, NBCF.

70. "Strong Intelligence Unit in Police Department," *Nashville Banner*, June 24, 1969, NBCF.

71. Gibson and Gallagher, "Unaware of Police Spy Files."

72. LEIU Report to Members, April 24, 1978, 1, quoted in *The Police Threat to Political Liberty*, 82.

73. *Police Threat to Political Liberty*, 81–95. Also see Legal Development Division, *History of Police Intelligence Operations*, 59; Donner, *Protectors of Privilege*, 79–85

74. McClellan Subcommittee Hearings, 661–62; "Top Intelligence Officers Arrive for 3-Day Meeting," *Nashville Banner*, October 26, 1966, NBCF; Stubbel, "Briley Cites Police for Uncovering Subversives"; Harris, "Sorace," 13.

75. *Police Threat to Political Liberty*, 14–16; Legal Development Division, *History of Police Intelligence Operations*, 87–88; Chevigny, "Politics and Law in the Control of Local Surveillance," 736–37;

Michael W. Flamm, *Law and Order: Street Crime, Civil Unrest, and the Crisis of Liberalism in the 1960s* (New York: Columbia University Press, 2005), 52–54; Naomi Murakawa, *The First Civil Right: How Liberals Built Prison in America* (Oxford: Oxford University Press, 2014), 71–73, 79–90; Elizabeth Kai Hinton, *From the War on Poverty to the War on Crime: The Making of Mass Incarceration in America* (Cambridge: Harvard University Press, 2016), 142–45. Hinton argues that the LEAA played a key role in federalizing local law enforcement and creating a carceral state in which the tools of surveillance, aggressive patrolling, and punitive sentencing policies resulted in "the criminalization of urban social problems." Hinton, *From the War on Poverty to the War on Crime,* 26.

76. "Governor Announces Appointments to Law Enforcement Planning Commission," press release, October 16, 1968, box 26, folder 5; "Development of New Courses for Tennessee Law Enforcement Training Academy," 1967, box 26, folder 5; meeting minutes, Tennessee Law Enforcement Planning Commission, February 7, 1969, box 26, folder 7; and newsletter, Tennessee Law Enforcement Planning Agency, 1, no. 1 (September 1969), box 27, folder 1, all in Governor Buford Ellington (Second Term) Papers, 1967–71, Tennessee State Library and Archives, Nashville.

77. Squires, "Power Struggle Racks Metro Police Department"; Tom Gillem, "Police Get $1.4 Million Computers," *Nashville Tennessean,* July 6, 1971, NBCF; Brinton, "City Officials Suspects in Loans Racket"; Dick Battle, "Local Police Head into Computer Age," *Nashville Banner,* July 3, 1970, NBCF; Battle, "Computer Revolutionizes Crime Fight."

78. Gillem, "Police Get $1.4 Million Computers"; Battle, "Metro Police Complete FBI Information Hookup."

79. "Proceedings, National Advisory Commission on Civil Disorders," August 1, 1967, ser. 1, box 1 (July 29–August 9, 1967), NACCD, 61.

80. Letterhead Memorandum, April 15, 1967, "Re: Civil Disturbances, Nashville, Tennessee, April 8–11, 1967; Racial Matters," in ser. 59, box 4, NACCD.

81. McClellan Committee Hearings, 700, 661.

82. Eastland Committee Hearings, 217.

83. *New South Student* 4, no. 4 (May 1967); Mike [Welch] to Ed Hamlett, July 12, 1968, Ed Hamlett White Folks Project Collection, McCain Library and Archives, University Libraries, University of Southern Mississippi, Hattiesburg.

84. Letterhead Memorandum, April 15, 1967, "Re: Civil Disturbances, Nashville, Tennessee, April 8–11, 1967; Racial Matters" in ser. 59, box 4, NACCD, 17 (appendix); *New South Student* 4, no. 7 (December 1967): 1. Eugene "Bull" Connor was the Commissioner of Public Safety for Birmingham, Alabama, off and on between 1937 and 1963.

85. Hill made lieutenant in 1967 and then was promoted to captain in 1972. The source of contention between Hill and Sorace is unclear, though Hill claimed Sorace and others were "trying to destroy my character in my neighborhood . . . my rapport with people." The tension boiled over in early 1972, when Hill brought a shotgun into headquarters in search of Sorace. The episode led to a thirty-day suspension but did not derail his promotion later in the year to captain. "Four Metro Policemen Promoted"; Bill Hance, "Four Officers Promoted to Rank of Captain, Two Shifted by Mott," *Nashville Banner,* July 19, 1972, NBCF; George Watson Jr., "Police Lieutenant Suspended," *Nashville Tennessean,* March 28, 1972, NBCF; Dwight Lewis, "Police Suspension a Threat: NAACP," *Nashville Tennessean,* March 31, 1972, NBCF.

86. "Intelligence Unit Expansion Slated," *Nashville Tennessean*, September 23, 1969, NBCF; McClellan Subcommittee Hearings, 638.

87. Gene Baker, "Mott Reassigns 17 Captains in Shakeup," *Nashville Banner*, February 9, 1973, NBCF; Kenneth Jost, "Police Revamp Moves Stoner Off Vice Squad," *Nashville Tennessean*, February 10, 1973, 1, 6; Kirk Loggins, "Reasonover Leaving after 32 Years," *Nashville Tennessean*, November 8, 1984, 7B.

88. See, for instance, George Watson Jr., "Police Probe Arms Traffic," *Nashville Tennessean*, February 28, 1974, 22; Randy Hilman, "16 Arrested as Suspects in Drug Bust," *Nashville Tennessean*, July 1, 1983, 1B, 4B.

89. Alan Carmichael, "Police 'Keeping' Subversive Files Closed," *Nashville Tennessean*, October 16, 1975, 79; "Coalition Holding Protest of 'Metro Police Spying,'" *Nashville Tennessean*, November 10, 1975, 19; "Fulton Got Spying Complaints prior to Media, Group Claims," *Nashville Tennessean*, November 17, 1975, 19; "Coalition Moves to Block Police 'Spying' on Citizens," *Nashville Tennessean*, November 24, 1975, 17; George Watson Jr., "Surveillance to Go On," *Nashville Tennessean*, January 13, 1976, 10. As discussed earlier in this chapter, the files received public attention once more in 1978, thanks to the discovery of the memo from the Jefferson County, Alabama, sheriff about his meeting a decade earlier with Sorace. The issue that drew scrutiny was the allegation that Sorace and other intelligence officers had taken the files home for periods of time to avoid potential subpoenas. The existence of the files themselves—the legality or morality of creating a record of citizens involved in constitutionally protected activities—was not questioned. Gibson, "60s Police Spy Operation Told"; Gibson and Gallagher, "Unaware of Police Spy Files"; Brittingham, "Sorace Denies Keeping Files at Home."

90. Marsha Vande Berg, "Sorace Computer Firm Supplied Colorado Needs," *Nashville Tennessean*, October 18, 1979, NBCF. Sorace's business, initially named Intelamation Sciences, Inc., was created in 1975 and appeared to leverage his expertise with police computer systems to market his company. In 1975, Colorado awarded Intelamation a contract for $167,000 to help the Colorado Bureau of Investigation operate its computer system, the same one the Nashville police used. Battle, "Metro Police Complete FBI Information Hookup"; Tam Gordon, "Report Hits Police Purchase Practices," *Nashville Banner*, April 24, 1987, NBCF; Mike Pigott and Tam Gordon, "Police Computers Lie Idle for a Year," *Nashville Banner*, June 20, 1988, NBCF; Mike Pigott and Jim Molpus, "Salvos Continuing over Sorace Audit," *Nashville Banner*, August 11, 1988, NBCF; Tom Gordon and Mike Pigott, "Sorace Discipline, New Audit Ordered," *Nashville Banner*, August 12, 1988, NBCF; Gail McKnight, "Audit Raises Credibility Question: Boner," *Nashville Banner*, August 13, 1988, NBCF; Tam Gordon, "Sorace Loses 3 Vacation Days," *Nashville Banner*, August 17, 1988, NBCF; Sharon Curtis-Flair, "Boner Makes More Changes in Metro Police Department," *Nashville Banner*, September 8, 1989, NBCF; Steve Majchrzak, "Sorace Requests Buyout," *Nashville Banner*, May 14, 1992; Marsha Vande Berg, "Sorace Computer Firm Supplied Colorado Needs," *Nashville Tennessean*, October 18, 1978, NBCF; Alan Bostick, "Police Reply to Audit's Criticisms," *Nashville Tennessean*, April 25, 1987, 1B, 2B; Jerry McCaskill, "Audit 90% Wrong, Sorace Declares," *Nashville Tennessean*, August 11, 1988, 1A, 4A; McKnight, "Audit Places Sorace under a Cloud," 1A, 8A; "Mr. Sorace Shouldn't Take All the Blame for Audit," *Nashville Tennessean*, August 14, 1988, 4G; Jerry McCaskill, "Sorace Gets Three-Day Suspension," *Nashville Tennessean*, August 17, 1988, 1A, 2A; Brad Schmitt, "3 Assistant Chiefs

May Get Buyout Offer," *Nashville Tennessean,* April 22, 1992, NBCF; Brad Schmitt, "New Police Computer Output: $1 Million on Trade-In," *Nashville Tennessean,* July 15, 1993, NBCF.

CONCLUSION

1. The subpoena apparently did not reach many of its intended recipients because they no longer frequented the SSOC house—or even remained in Nashville—after the group's collapse. At least one of the activists did receive the subpoena, and he ignored it. Subpoena of Joe Bogle, Subcommittee on Internal Security [Subcommittee to Investigate the Administration of the Internal Security Act and Other Internal Security Laws] of the Committee on the Judiciary, United States Senate, October 1, 1969, in the author's possession. Joe Bogle, interview by author, November 12, 1994.

2. Amy B. Zegart, "Universities Must Not Ignore Intelligence Research," *Chronicle of Higher Education* 53, no. 45, July 13, 2007, B9.

3. For a trenchant critique of the ubiquity of surveillance, see Shoshana Zuboff, *The Age of Surveillance Capitalism: The Fight for a Human Future at the New Frontier of Power* (New York: PublicAffairs, 2019).

4. On the NSA's cell phone surveillance program, see Glenn Greenwald, "NSA Collecting Phone Records of Millions of Verizon Customers Daily," *The Guardian,* June 5, 2013, https://www.theguardian.com/world/2013/jun/06/nsa-phone-records-verizon-court-order; Marshall Curtis Erwin and Edward C. Liu, "NSA Surveillance Leaks: Background and Issues for Congress," Congressional Research Service, July 2, 2013; and Charlie Savage and Jonathan Weisman, "N.S.A. Collection of Bulk Call Data Is Ruled Illegal," *New York Times,* May 7, 2015, A1, A8. On the Republican National Convention, see Jim Dwyer, "City Police Spied Broadly before G.O.P. Convention," *New York Times,* March 25, 2007, https://www.nytimes.com/2007/03/25/nyregion/25infiltrate.html; and Jim Dwyer, "Police Surveillance before Convention Was Larger than Previously Disclosed," *New York Times,* April 3, 2007, https://www.nytimes.com/2007/04/03/nyregion/03police.html. On police surveillance nationally, see, for instance, Matthew Feeney, "The Police Know What You're Doing," *New York Times,* October 24, 2017, A23; Ali Watkins, "A City under Surveillance in the Shadow of 9/11," *New York Times,* September 9, 2021, A1, A14; David W. Brown, "The Revolution Will Be Televised, Archived & Analyzed," *Stand* (American Civil Liberties Union) (Summer 2017): 18–23. On COVID lockdowns and quarantines in China, see Paul Mozur, Raymond Zhong, and Aaron Krolik, "In Coronavirus Fight, China Gives Citizens a Color Code, with Red Flags," *New York Times,* March 1, 2020, https://www.nytimes.com/2020/03/01/business/china-coronavirus-surveillance.html; and Brian Spegele, "China's Surveillance State Pushes Deeper into Citizens' Lives," *Wall Street Journal,* October 19, 2022, https://www.wsj.com/articles/xi-china-surveillance-covid-11666187151. On the Uighurs, see Chris Buckley and Paul Mozur, "How China Uses High Tech Surveillance to Subdue Minorities," *New York Times,* May 22, 2019, https://www.nytimes.com/2019/05/22/world/asia/china-surveillance-xinjiang.html; and Johana Bhuiyan, "'There's Cameras Everywhere': Testimonies Detail Far-Reaching Surveillance of Uyghurs in China," *The Guardian,* September 30, 2021, https://www.theguardian.com/world/2021/sep/30/uyghur-tribunal-testimony-surveillance-china. On NSO and its Pegasus program, see Ronen Bergman and Mark Mazzetti, "The Battle for the World's Most

Powerful Cyberweapon," *New York Times Magazine*, January 28, 2022 (updated January 31, 2022), https://www.nytimes.com/2022/01/28/magazine/nso-group-israel-spyware.html; Ronan Farrow, "How Democracies Spy on Their Citizens," *New Yorker* 98, no. 10 (April 25–May 5, 2022): 36–47, https://www.newyorker.com/magazine/2022/04/25/how-democracies-spy-on-their-citizens; Natalie Kitroeff and Ronen Bergman, "Spying by Mexico Raises Fears of 'Military State,'" *New York Times*, March 8, 2023, A1, A9; Natalie Kitroeff and Ronen Bergman, "How Mexico Became the Biggest User of the World's Most Notorious Spy Tool," *New York Times*, April 19, 2023, A1, A9; and Natalie Kitroeff and Ronen Bergman, "Spying Scandal in Mexico Goes Right to the Top," *New York Times*, May 23, 2023, A1, A6.

5. *Elaine Blanchard et al. v. City of Memphis*, February 22, 2017, http://www.aclu-tn.org/wp-content/uploads/2017/03/Blanchard-v-Memphis-Complaint.pdf; "ACLU of Tennessee Joins Lawsuit Challenging Memphis Police Spying on Political Groups; City's Surveillance Policies Violate 1978 Consent Decree," March 2, 2017, https://www.aclu.org/news/aclu-tennessee-joins-lawsuit-challenging-memphis-police-spying-political-groups; Bill Dries, "Police Documents Show Protest Spreadsheet and Fear of 'Radicals,'" *Memphis Daily News*, July 31, 2018, https://www.memphisdailynews.com/news/2018/jul/31/police-documents-show-protest-spreadsheet-and-fear-of-radicals; Daniel Connolly, "ACLU Wins Favorable Ruling from Judge in Advance of Memphis Police Spying Trial," *Memphis Commercial Appeal*, August 10, 2018, https://www.commercialappeal.com/story/news/2018/08/10/aclu-wins-favorable-ruling-judge-advance-memphis-police-spying-trial/964215002; Jamiles Lartey, "Memphis Police Accused of Using Fake Accounts to Surveil Black Activists," *The Guardian*, August 1, 2018, https://www.theguardian.com/us-news/2018/aug/01/memphis-police-black-lives-matter-activists?CMP=share_btn_fb; Ryan Poe, "The 9:01: 'Blacklist' Trial Shows Memphis Police Wasted Precious Time, Resources," *Memphis Commercial Appeal*, August 23, 2018, https://www.commercialappeal.com/story/news/local/the-901/2018/08/23/9-01-blacklist-trial-shows-memphis-police-blew-time-resources/1039004002; *Blanchard et al. v. City of Memphis, Tennessee*, Opinion and Order, Case. No. 2:17-cv-2120-JPM-egb, in the author's possession.

6. Final Report of the Select Committee to Study Government Operations with Respect to Intelligence Activities, bk. 2 (Intelligence Activities and the Rights of Americans), S. Rep. No. 94–755, 6 bks. (1976), 15.

BIBLIOGRAPHY

MANUSCRIPT COLLECTIONS

Albert and Shirley Small Special Collections Library, University of Virginia, Charlottesville
- Southern Student Organizing Committee Records

David M. Rubenstein Rare Book & Manuscript Library, Duke University, Durham, NC
- Boyte Family Papers, 1941–2018

LBJ Presidential Library, Austin, TX
- National Advisory Commission on Civil Disorders
- Records of the National Advisory Commission on Civil Disorders (Embargoed Series)

McCain Library and Archives, University Libraries, University of Southern Mississippi, Hattiesburg
- Ed Hamlett White Folks Project Collection
- Paul B. Johnson Family Papers

Memphis and Shelby County Room, Memphis Public Libraries
- Frank Holloman Collection
- Maxine A. Smith—NAACP Collection
- Papers of Henry Loeb III

Metropolitan Government Archives of Nashville-Davidson County, Nashville, TN
- Chief H. O. Kemp Papers

Mississippi Department of Archives and History, Jackson
- Mississippi State Sovereignty Commission Records, 1956–2002

Nashville Public Library
- Civil Rights Collection of the Nashville Public Library, ser. 3: Civil Rights Oral History Collection
- *Nashville Banner* Archives

Tennessee State Library and Archives, Nashville
- Governor Buford Ellington (Second Term) Papers, 1967–71

University Archives, Special Collections Department, University Libraries, University of Memphis

Cecil C. Humphreys Collection

DeSoto (Memphis State University yearbook)

Kenneth Lawrence Beaudoin Papers

Memphis Search for Meaning Committee Records

Vanderbilt University Special Collections & Archives, Nashville, TN,

John Seigenthaler Papers, 1927–2014

PERIODICALS

Atlanta Constitution

Boston Globe

Charlotte Observer

Chronicle of Higher Education

Columbia Journalism Review

Columbia (SC) Record

Congressional Record Daily Edition

Dallas Morning News

FBI Law Enforcement Bulletin

The Gamecock (University of South Carolina)

Greenwood (SC) Index-Journal

The Guardian

Harvard Crimson

Houston Chronicle

Jackson Clarion-Ledger

Jackson Daily News

The Kudzu

Memphis Commercial Appeal

Memphis Daily News

Memphis Press-Scimitar

Memphis Tri-State Defender

Miami Herald

More

Ms.

Nashville!

Nashville Banner

Nashville Magazine
Nashville Tennessean
New York Times
New Yorker
Northside Sun (Jackson, MS)
Orlando Sentinel
Pittsburgh Post-Gazette
Playboy
Rolling Stone
Saturday Evening Post
Southern Exposure
Southern Patriot
Stand
The State (Columbia, SC)
Sunday Oklahoman (Oklahoma City)
Tampa Bay Times
Tiger Rag (Memphis State University)
Time
Tulsa Daily World
Wall Street Journal
Washington Monthly
Washington Post

U.S. GOVERNMENT RECORDS

FBI Records: The Vault, https://vault.fbi.gov.

Investigation of the Assassination of Martin Luther King, Jr.: Hearings before the Select Committee on Assassinations of the U.S. House of Representatives, 95th Cong. (1978).

Memphis Publishing Co. and Marc Perrusquia v. the Federal Bureau of Investigation, 10cv01878, U.S. District Court for the District of Columbia, shared with the author by Marc Perrusquia.

National Archives. *House Select Committee on Assassinations*, December 15, 2017, document release, https://www.archives.gov/research/jfk/release.

———. "JFK Assassination Records—2018 Additional Documents Release," https://www.archives.gov/research/jfk/release.

Records of the Federal Bureau of Investigation. Freedom of Information Act releases, shared with the author by Christina Greene.

———. Freedom of Information Act releases, to author.

Report to the President by the Commission on CIA Activities within the United States. Washington, DC: Government Printing Office, 1975.

U.S. House of Representatives. *Problems in the Accounting for and Safeguarding of Special Nuclear Materials: Hearings before the Subcommittee on Energy and Environment of the Committee on Small Business,* 94th Cong. (1976).

U.S. Senate. *Committee on the Judiciary: Hearings on H.R. 421 to Amend Title 18 of the United States Code to Prohibit Travel or Use of Any Facility in Interstate or Foreign Commerce with the Intent to Incite a Riot or Other Violent Civil Disturbance, and for Other Purposes* 90th Cong., pt. 1 (1967).

———. *Permanent Subcommittee on Investigations of the Committee on Government Operations: Hearings* 90th Cong., pt. 2 (1967).

———. *Select Committee to Study Government Operations with Respect to Intelligence Activities* S. Rep. No 94-775 (6 bks., 1976).

———. *Select Committee to Study Government Operations with Respect to Intelligence Activities: Hearings* 94th Cong., 7 vols. (1976).

———. *Subcommittee on Constitutional Rights of the Committee on the Judiciary: Army Surveillance of Civilians: A Documentary Analysis.* Washington, DC: U.S. Government Printing Office, 1972.

———. *Subcommittee on Constitutional Rights of the Committee on the Judiciary: Federal Data Banks, Computers and the Bill of Rights: Hearings* 92nd Cong. 2 pts. (1971).

COURT RECORDS AND LEGAL PROCEEDINGS

Bursey v. Weatherford, 528 F.2d 483 (1975 U.S. App.).

Elaine Blanchard et al. v. City of Memphis, February 22, 2017. http://www.aclu-tn.org/wp-content/uploads/2017/03/Blanchard-v-Memphis-Complaint.pdf.

Gibson v. Florida Legislative Investigative Committee, 372 U.S. 539 (1963).

Jack M. Weatherford, etc., et al., Petitioners, v. Brett Allen Bursey, Respondent, Proceedings, in the Supreme Court of the United States, December 7, 1976. Washington, DC: Hoover Reporting Company, 1976.

Kenneth Kottka and Earl Mitchell vs. Dewey F. Bartlett et al. Shared with the author by Stephen Jones.

Kendrick v. Chandler. Case no. 76-449, box 2 (accession no. 021-84-0116). RG 21—Records of the District Courts of the United States, Civil Case Files, 1972–78. Memphis, TN, National Archives at Atlanta.

South Carolina v. Brett Bursey. Transcript of Malicious Mischief Trial for Damage Done to

Richland County (SC) Draft Board Office in March 1970 (July 30, 1970). Generously shared with the author by Brett Bursey.

State of South Carolina, County of Richland. "Indictment–Two Counts," [Brett Allen Bursey and Jack M. Weatherford], April 2, 1970. In the author's possession.

Turner v. Garrow. Case no. 83-2076, U.S. District Court, Western District of Tennessee, May 21, 1986, *Media Law Reporter* 12: 2314-2320

Weatherford v. Bursey, 429 US 545 (1977).

INTERVIEWS—CONDUCTED BY AUTHOR

Joe Bogle. November 12, 1994. Alcoa, TN

Brett Bursey. March 11, 1995. Peak, SC

———. May 19, 2021. Columbia, SC (Zoom)

———. September 21, 2021. Columbia, SC (Zoom)

Eric Carter. July 11, 2018. Houston

David Doggett. August 30, 1994. Philadelphia

Bruce Kramer. July 17, 2018. Memphis

Ken Lawrence. March 1, 2023. Phone conversation with author

Clifford Pierce. July 18, 2018. Memphis

Coby Vernon Smith. July 18, 2018. Memphis

C. Rauch Wise, August 30, 2021. Phone conversation with author

INTERVIEWS—ORAL HISTORY COLLECTIONS

Mississippi Oral History Project, Center for Oral History and Cultural Heritage, McCain Library and Archives, University of Southern Mississippi

Erle Johnston, interview by Orley B. Caudill, July 30, 1980, https://usm.access.preservica.com/uncategorized/IO_46deba19-6595-414a-ac32-8cfd3cc81686

Erle Johnston, interview by Yasuhiro Katagiri, August 13, 1993, https://usm.access.preservica.com/uncategorized/IO_8b604cc1-109d-410c-9eff-4dd5ec3c63f2

Michael Smith, interview by Reid Derr, n.d. [ca. 1993], https://usm.access.preservica.com/uncategorized/IO_4dd67815-afe9-45a2-a3e7-90348f8bded3

The Civil Rights Collection of the Nashville Public Library, ser. 3: The Civil Rights Oral History Collection

Archie Eugene Allen, interview by Kathy Bennett, March 31 and September 30, 2003

MISCELLANEOUS—OTHER

1969 Legislative Manual. 98th General Assembly of South Carolina. Columbia, SC, 1969.

Garnet and Black. Yearbook. University of South Carolina, 1971.

"I Was on Their Radar Because They Needed Somebody on Their Radar." *University of South Carolina News & Events.* April 27, 2020. https://www.sc.edu/uofsc/posts/2020/05/months_of_may_brett_bursey.php#.YT9qlS1h1TZ.

Local Television Newsfilm Collection, Moving Image Research Collections, University of South Carolina Libraries. https://digital.tcl.sc.edu/digital/collection/localtvnews/id/291.

Stax Records. "Ollie & the Nightingales." Accessed October 19, 2018. https://www.staxrecords.com/pages/ollie-the-nightingales.

The Invaders. Film, 2016.

"The Karen Silkwood Story." *PBS Frontline.* https://www.pbs.org/wgbh/pages/frontline/shows/reaction/interact/silkwood.html.

Dassin, Jules, dir. *Uptight.* Cleveland, OH: Marlukin, 1968. IMDB. https://www.imdb.com/title/tt0063748.

Honey, Michael. "Some Comments on FBI/MPD Surveillance." August 7, 2018, in author's possession.

———. Email correspondence with author. November 8, 2018.

Nolan, David. Email correspondence with author. March 8, 2021.

Report of the Committee to Investigate Communist Activities in South Carolina. 1971. https://dc.statelibrary.sc.gov/handle/10827/35905.

BOOKS, ARTICLES, AND OTHER WORKS

Agyepong, Tera. "In the Belly of the Beast: Black Policemen Combat Police Brutality in Chicago, 1968–1983." *Journal of African American History* 98, no. 2 (2013): 253–76.

Ash, Stephen V. *A Massacre in Memphis: The Race Riot That Shook the Nation One Year after the Civil War.* New York: Hill and Wang, 2013.

Bach, Damon Randolph. "A Hard Rain Fell: SDS and Why It Failed." *Journal for the Study of Radicalism* 4, no. 2 (2010): 167–69.

Baer, Andrew S. *Beyond the Usual Beating: The Jon Burge Police Torture Scandal and Social Movements for Police Accountability in Chicago.* Chicago: University of Chicago Press, 2020.

Baker, Jackson. "Profile of Henry Loeb." Part 1. *Memphis* (January 1980): 25–33.

Balko, Radley. *Rise of the Warrior Cop: The Militarization of America's Police Forces.* First edition. New York: PublicAffairs, 2013.

Balto, Simon Ezra. *Occupied Territory: Policing Black Chicago from Red Summer to Black Power.* Chapel Hill: University of North Carolina Press, 2020.

———. "'Occupied Territory': Police Repression and Black Resistance in Postwar Milwaukee, 1950–1980." *Journal of African American History* 98, no. 2 (2013): 229–52.

Barber, David. *A Hard Rain Fell: SDS and Why It Failed.* Jackson: University Press of Mississippi, 2008.

Batvinis, Raymond J. *The Origins of FBI Counterintelligence.* Modern War Studies. Lawrence: University Press of Kansas, 2007.

Beller, Scott M. "Government Agents and the Sixth Amendment Reconsidered." *Chicago-Kent Law Review* 54, no. 1 (1977): 239–53.

Berkeley, Kathleen C. *Like a Plague of Locusts: From an Antebellum Town to a New South City, Memphis, Tennessee, 1850–1880.* New York: Garland Pub., 1991.

Berrigan, Daniel. *The Trial of the Catonsville Nine.* 1970. Reprint, New York: Fordham University Press, 2004.

Biles, Roger. *Memphis in the Great Depression.* Knoxville: University of Tennessee Press, 1986.

Blackstock, Nelson. *COINTELPRO: The FBI's Secret War on Political Freedom.* 3rd ed. 1975. Reprint, New York: Anchor Foundation, 1988.

Bolton, Charles C. "William F. Winter: The Politician as Historian." *Southern Quarterly* 54, no. 1 (Fall 2016): 97–115.

Bond, Beverly G., and Janann Sherman. *Memphis In Black and White.* Charleston, SC: Arcadia Publishing, 2003.

Bond, Beverly Greene, and Susan Eva O'Donovan, eds. *Remembering the Memphis Massacre: An American Story.* Athens: University of Georgia Press, 2020.

Branch, Taylor. *Parting the Waters: America in the King Years, 1954–1963.* New York: Simon and Schuster, 1988.

———. *Pillar of Fire: America in the King Years, 1963–1965.* New York: Simon and Schuster, 1998.

Braukman, Stacy. *Communists and Perverts under the Palms: The Johns Committee in Florida, 1956–1965.* Gainesville: University Press of Florida, 2012.

Brewer, Landry. "Maurice Halperin: From Sooner Subversive to Soviet Spy." *Chronicles of Oklahoma* 96, no. 2 (2018): 156–77.

Buitrago, Ann Mari, and Leon Andrew Immerman. *Are You Now or Have You Ever Been in the FBI Files? How to Secure and Interpret Your FBI Files.* New York : Grove Press, 1981.

Burlingham, Bo. "Paranoia in Power." *Harper's*, October 1, 1974.

Burrough, Bryan. "'Broken': Not Your Father's FBI." *New York Times*, October 24, 2004, sec. Sunday Book Review. https://www.nytimes.com/2004/10/24/books/review/broken-not-your-fathers-fbi.html?mcubz=2&_r=0.

———. "Chasing Radicals (and Breaking the Rule of Law): Tim Weiner's 'Enemies' and F.B.I. Counterintelligence." *New York Times*, March 14, 2012. https://www.nytimes.com/2012/03/15/books/tim-weiners-enemies-and-fbi-counterintelligence.html.

———. *Days of Rage: America's Radical Underground, the FBI, and the Forgotten Age of Revolutionary Violence*. New York: Penguin Press, 2015.

Campbell, Amanda. "'The Chaplain of the New Left': Reverend Richard Moon's Community of Influence and the 1968 Memphis Sanitation Workers' Strike." *QuaesitUM Undergraduate Research Journal*, no. Spring (2020): 21–36.

Carmack, Margaret Williams. "Segregating the Police: Race and the Reality of Being a Black Police Officer in Postwar Memphis." *Southern Studies: An Interdisciplinary Journal of the South* 26, no. 1 (2019): 47–74.

Carmichael, Stokely, and Charles V. Hamilton. *Black Power: The Politics of Liberation in America*. New York: Vintage Books, 1967.

Carson, Clayborne. *In Struggle: SNCC and the Black Awakening of the 1960s*. Cambridge: Harvard University Press, 1981.

Charles, Douglas M. *J. Edgar Hoover and the Anti-Interventionists: FBI Political Surveillance and the Rise of the Domestic Security State, 1939–1945*. Columbus: Ohio State University Press, 2007.

Charns, Alexander. *Cloak and Gavel: FBI Wiretaps, Bugs, Informers, and the Supreme Court*. Urbana: University of Illinois Press, 1992.

Chevigny, Paul G. "Politics and Law in the Control of Local Surveillance." *Cornell Law Review* 69, no. 4 (1984): 735–83.

Chism, Jonathan. *Saints in the Struggle: Church of God in Christ Activists in the Memphis Civil Rights Movement, 1954–1968*. Lanham, MD: Lexington Books, 2019.

Churchill, Ward, and Jim Vander Wall. *Agents of Repression: The FBI's Secret Wars against the Black Panther Party and the American Indian Movement*. Corrected ed. 1988. Reprint, Boston: South End Press, 1990.

———. *The COINTELPRO Papers: Documents from the FBI's Secret Wars against Dissent in the United States*. Boston: South End Press, 1990.

Cohen, Robert. "G-Men in Georgia: The FBI and the Segregationist Riot at the University of Georgia, 1961." *Georgia Historical Quarterly* 83, no. 3 (Fall 1999): 508–38.

Conway, James David. "Beyond 1968: The 1969 Black Monday Protest in Memphis." In *An Unseen Light: Black Struggles for Freedom in Memphis, Tennessee*, edited by Aram Goudsouzian and Charles W. McKinney Jr., 306–29. Lexington: University Press of Kentucky, 2018.

———. "Moderated Militants in the Age of Black Power: The Memphis NAACP, 1968–1975." PhD diss., University of Memphis, 2015.

Cortright, David. *Soldiers in Revolt: The American Military Today*. Garden City, NY: Anchor Press / Doubleday, 1975.

Cowie, Jefferson. *Capital Moves: RCA's Seventy-Year Quest for Cheap Labor*. Ithaca, NY: Cornell University Press, 1999.

Crespino, Joseph. *In Search of Another Country: Mississippi and the Conservative Counterrevolution*. Politics and Society in Twentieth-Century America. Princeton, NJ: Princeton University Press, 2007.

Cunningham, David. *Klansville, U.S.A.: The Rise and Fall of the Civil Rights–Era Ku Klux Klan*. New York: Oxford University Press, 2013.

———. "The Patterning of Repression: FBI Counterintelligence and the New Left." *Social Forces* 82, no. 1 (2003): 209–40.

———. "State versus Social Movement: FBI Counterintelligence against the New Left." In *States, Parties, and Social Movements*, edited by Jack A. Goldstone, 45–77. Cambridge: Cambridge University Press, 2003.

———. *There's Something Happening Here: The New Left, the Klan, and FBI Counterintelligence*. Berkeley: University of California Press, 2004.

Cunnigen, Donald. "Standing at the Gates: The Civil Rights Movement and Liberal White Mississippi Students." *Journal of Mississippi History* 62, no. 1 (2000): 1–19.

Daniels, Jonathan. "He Suits Memphis." *Saturday Evening Post*, June 10, 1939.

Davis, James Kirkpatrick. *Spying on America the FBI's Domestic Counterintelligence Program*. New York: Praeger, 1992.

Delmez, Kathryn E., ed. *We Shall Overcome: Press Photographs of Nashville during the Civil Rights Era*. Nashville: Vanderbilt University Press, 2018.

Delong, Amy. "Change from the Inside Out: The Contribution of Memphis Catholics in Civil Rights Activism, 1961–1968." *Tennessee Historical Quarterly* 67, no. 2 (2008): 124–47.

Dickerson, James. *Dixie's Dirty Secret: The True Story of How Government, the Media, and the Mob Conspired to Combat Integration and the Vietnam Antiwar Movement*. Armonk, NY: M. E. Sharpe, 1998.

Doggett, David. "*The Kudzu*: Birth and Death in Underground Mississippi." In *Voices from the Underground: Insider Histories of the Vietnam Era Underground Press*, edited by Ken Wachsberger, 1:213–32. Tempe, AZ: Mica Press, 1993.

———. "*The Kudzu* Story: Underground in Mississippi." *Southern Exposure* 2, no. 4 (1975): 86–95.

Donner, Frank J. *The Age of Surveillance: The Aims and Methods of America's Political Intelligence System*. New York: Knopf, 1980.

———. *Protectors of Privilege: Red Squads and Police Repression in Urban America*. Berkeley: University of California Press, 1990.

———. "Spies on Campus." *Playboy*, March 1968.

Dowdy, G. Wayne. *Crusades for Freedom: Memphis and the Political Transformation of the American South*. Jackson: University Press of Mississippi, 2010.

———. *Mayor Crump Don't Like It: Machine Politics in Memphis*. Jackson: University Press of Mississippi, 2006.

Doyle, Don Harrison. *Nashville in the New South, 1880–1930*. Knoxville: University of Tennessee Press, 1985.

———. *Nashville since the 1920s.* Knoxville: University of Tennessee Press, 1985.

Drabble, John. "Fighting Black Power–New Left Coalitions: Covert FBI Media Campaigns and American Cultural Discourse, 1967–1971." *European Journal of American Culture* 27, no. 2 (June 2008): 65–91.

Dykes, Dewey. "Encyclopedia of Arkansas." Encyclopedia of Arkansas. Accessed February 14, 2023. https://encyclopediaofarkansas.net/entries/arkansas-state-sovereignty-commission-6490.

Echols, Alice. *Daring to Be Bad: Radical Feminism in America, 1967–1975.* Minneapolis: University of Minnesota Press, 1989.

Eckstein, Arthur M. *Bad Moon Rising: How the Weather Underground Beat the FBI and Lost the Revolution.* New Haven, CT: Yale University Press, 2016.

Egerton, John, ed. *Nashville: An American Self-Portrait.* Nashville: Beaten Biscuit Press, 2001.

———. *Nashville: The Faces of Two Centuries, 1870–1980.* Nashville: PlusMedia, 1979.

Elliff, John T. *The Reform of FBI Intelligence Operations.* 1979. Reprint, Princeton: Princeton University Press, 2016.

Estes, Steve. *I Am a Man! Race, Manhood, and the Civil Rights Movement.* Chapel Hill: University of North Carolina Press, 2005.

Federal Bureau of Investigation. Counterterrorism Division. "Black Identity Extremists Likely Motivated to Target Law Enforcement Officers, Intelligence Assessment," August 3, 2017.

Felker-Kantor, Max. *Policing Los Angeles: Race, Resistance, and the Rise of the LAPD.* Justice, Power, and Politics. Chapel Hill: University of North Carolina Press, 2018.

Fernández, Johanna. *The Young Lords: A Radical History.* Chapel Hill: University of North Carolina Press, 2020.

Flamm, Michael W. *Law and Order: Street Crime, Civil Unrest, and the Crisis of Liberalism in the 1960s.* New York: Columbia University Press, 2005.

"The Flight into Egypt." *The Crisis* 14, no. 3 (July 1917).

Forman, James. *The Making of Black Revolutionaries; a Personal Account.* New York: Macmillan, 1972.

Fosl, Catherine. *Subversive Southerner: Anne Braden and the Struggle for Racial Justice in the Cold War South.* New York: Palgrave Macmillan, 2002.

Freeman, Jo. "The Berkeley Free Speech Movement and the Mississippi Sovereignty Commission." *Left History* 8, no. 2 (2003): 135–44.

Friedly, Michael, with David Gallen, eds. *Martin Luther King, Jr.: The FBI File.* New York: Carroll & Graf, 1993.

Gage, Beverly. "Behind the Bureau." *The Nation,* September 10, 2012.

———. *G-Man: J. Edgar Hoover and the Making of the American Century.* New York: Viking, 2022.

———. "I Have a [Redacted]: Would the F.B.I.'s Smear Campaign against Martin Luther King Jr. Work Today?" *New York Times Magazine,* November 16, 2014.

———. "Stormy Weather." *Chronicle of Higher Education (Chronicle Review)* 63, no. 19, January 13, 2017, B14.

Gardner, Fred. "Hollywood Confidential: Part I." *Viet Nam Generation Journal & Newsletter* 3, no. 3 (November 1991). http://www2.iath.virginia.edu/sixties/HTML_docs/Texts/Narrative/Gardner_Hollywood_1.html.

Garrow, David J. *Bearing the Cross: Martin Luther King, Jr., and the Southern Christian Leadership Conference.* New York: Vintage, 1986.

———. *The FBI and Martin Luther King, Jr.: From "Solo" to Memphis.* New York: Norton, 1981.

———. "The Troubling Legacy of Martin Luther King." *Standpoint,* May 30, 2019. https://standpointmag.co.uk/issues/june-2019/the-troubling-legacy-of-martin-luther-king.

German, Mike. *Disrupt, Discredit, and Divide: How the New FBI Damages Democracy.* New York: New Press, 2019.

Goldstein, Robert Justin. *Political Repression in Modern America from 1870 to the Present.* Cambridge: Schenkman, 1978.

Gotham, Kevin. "Domestic Security for the American State: The FBI, Covert Repression, and Democratic Legitimacy." *JPMS: Journal of Political and Military Sociology* 22, no. 2 (1994): 203–22.

Goudsouzian, Aram, and Charles W. McKinney Jr., eds. *An Unseen Light: Black Struggles for Freedom in Memphis, Tennessee.* Lexington: University Press of Kentucky, 2018.

Goulden, Joseph. "The Cops Hit the Jackpot." In *Policing America,* edited by Anthony Platt and Lynn Cooper, 31–49. Englewood Cliffs, NJ: Prentice Hall, 1974.

Green, Laurie Boush. *Battling the Plantation Mentality: Memphis and the Black Freedom Struggle.* Chapel Hill: University of North Carolina Press, 2007.

———. "The Rural-Urban Matrix in the 1950s South: Rethinking Racial Justice Struggles in Memphis." In *From the Grassroots to the Supreme Court:* Brown v. Board of Education *and American Democracy,* edited by Peter F. Lau, 270–99. Durham, NC: Duke University Press, 2004.

———. "Saving Babies in Memphis: The Politics of Race, Health, and Hunger during the War on Poverty." In *The War on Poverty: A New Grassroots History, 1964–1980,* edited by Lisa Gayle Hazirjian and Annelise Orleck, 133–58. Athens: University of Georgia Press, 2011.

Greenberg, Ivan. *Surveillance in America: Critical Analysis of the FBI, 1920 to the Present.* Lanham, MD: Lexington Books, 2012.

Gritter, Elizabeth. "A Matter of Black and White: Edmund Orgill, J. E. Walker, and the John Gaston Hospital Controversy in Memphis, Tennessee, in 1956." *Tennessee Historical Quarterly* 78, no. 3 (2019): 168–93.

———. *River of Hope: Black Politics and the Memphis Freedom Movement, 1865—1954*. Lexington: University Press of Kentucky, 2014.

Grose, Andrew. "Voices of Southern Protest during the Vietnam War Era: The University of South Carolina as a Case Study." *Peace & Change* 32, no. 2 (April 2007): 153–67.

Gutman, Richard M. "Combatting Defendants' Obstructionism in the Discovery Process." *University of Detroit Journal of Urban Law* 55, no. 4 (1978): 983–1003.

Hagopian, Kevin. "Film Notes." *The Informer*. New York State Writers Institute. Accessed October 19, 2018. https://www.albany.edu/writers-inst/webpages4/filmnotes/fns99n10.html.

Haines, Gerald K., and David A. Langbart. *Unlocking the Files of the FBI: A Guide to Its Records and Classification System*. Wilmington, DE: Scholarly Resources, 1993.

Halberstam, David. *The Children*. New York: Ballantine, 1998.

Hampton, Henry. *Voices of Freedom: An Oral History of the Civil Rights Movement from the 1950s through the 1980s*. New York: Bantam Books, 1990.

Hart, Benjamin. "Two MLK Scholars Discuss Explosive, Disputed FBI Files on the Civil-Rights Icon." Intelligencer. *New York*, June 30, 2019. http://nymag.com/intelligencer/2019/06/martin-luther-king-fbi-files.html.

Haynes, Stephen R. *The Last Segregated Hour: The Memphis Kneel-Ins and the Campaign for Southern Church Desegregation*. New York: Oxford University Press, 2012.

Herbert, Barbara. "Jack Weatherford." In *State Secrets: Police Surveillance in America*, edited by Paul Cowan, Nick Egleson, and Nat Hentoff, with Barbara Herbert and Robert Wall, 227–36. New York: Holt, Rinehart and Winston, 1974.

Hinton, Elizabeth Kai. *From the War on Poverty to the War on Crime: The Making of Mass Incarceration in America*. Cambridge: Harvard University Press, 2016.

Holland, Max. *Leak: Why Mark Felt Became Deep Throat*. Lawrence: University Press of Kansas, 2012.

Honey, Michael K. *Black Workers Remember: An Oral History of Segregation, Unionism, and the Freedom Struggle*. Berkeley: University of California Press, 1999.

———. *Going Down Jericho Road: The Memphis Strike, Martin Luther King's Last Campaign*. New York: Norton, 2007.

———. "Martin Luther King, Jr., the Crisis of the Black Working Class, and the Memphis Sanitation Strike." In *Southern Labor in Transition, 1940–1995*, edited by Robert H. Zieger, 146–75. Knoxville: University of Tennessee Press, 1997.

———. *Southern Labor and Black Civil Rights: Organizing Memphis Workers*. Urbana: University of Illinois Press, 1993.

Honey, Michael K., and David H. Ciscel. "Race and Labor in Memphis since the King Assassination." In *Life and Labor in the New South*, edited by Robert H. Zieger, 236–57. Gainesville: University Press of Florida, 2012.

Hoppe, Sherry L., and Bruce W. Speck. *Maxine Smith's Unwilling Pupils: Lessons Learned in Memphis's Civil Rights Classroom*. Knoxville: University of Tennessee Press, 2007.

Hosken, Simon. "Policing the Blues: Remembering the Desegregation of Law Enforcement in West Memphis, Arkansas." *Arkansas Historical Quarterly* 72, no. 2 (Summer 2013): 120–38.

Houston, Benjamin. *The Nashville Way: Racial Etiquette and the Struggle for Social Justice in a Southern City.* Athens: University of Georgia Press, 2012.

Hrach, Thomas J. "Insults for Sale: The 1957 Memphis Newspaper Boycott." *Tennessee Historical Quarterly* 72, no. 1 (Spring 2013): 28–49.

Irons, Jenny. *Reconstituting Whiteness: The Mississippi State Sovereignty Commission.* Nashville: Vanderbilt University Press, 2010.

Jackson, Kenneth T. "Memphis, Tennessee: The Rise and Fall of Main Street." In *American Places: Encounters with History,* edited by William E. Leuchtenburg, 169–83. New York: Oxford University Press, 2000.

Janda, Sarah Eppler. "'Even Mild Protest Is Not Generally Considered to Be Very Patriotic': Surveillance Culture and the Rise of the 'Sooner CIA.'" *Western Historical Quarterly* 48, no. 4 (2017): 393–414.

———. *Prairie Power: Student Activism, Counterculture, and Backlash in Oklahoma, 1962–1972.* Norman: University of Oklahoma Press, 2018.

Jeffreys-Jones, Rhodri. *The FBI: A History.* New Haven, CT: Yale University Press, 2007.

Jensen, Joan M. *Army Surveillance in America, 1775–1980.* New Haven, CT: Yale University Press, 1991.

———. *Military Surveillance of Civilians in America.* Morristown, NJ: General Learning Press, 1975.

Johnston, Earle. *Mississippi's Defiant Years, 1953–1973: An Interpretive Documentary with Personal Experiences.* Forest, MS: Lake Harbor Publishers, 1990.

Jones, Stephen, and Peter Israel. *Others Unknown: Timothy McVeigh and the Oklahoma City Bombing Conspiracy.* New York: PublicAffairs, 1998.

Jones, Yollette Trigg. "The Black Community, Politics, and Race Relations in the 'Iris City': Nashville, Tennessee, 1870–1954." PhD diss., Duke University, 1985.

Jordan, Jason. "'We'll Have No Race Trouble Here': Racial Politics and Memphis's Reign of Terror." In *An Unseen Light: Black Struggles for Freedom in Memphis, Tennessee,* edited by Aram Goudsouzian and Charles W. McKinney Jr., 130–49. Lexington: University Press of Kentucky, 2018.

Joseph, Peniel E. *Waiting for the Midnight Hour: Black Power in America.* New York: Henry Holt, 2006.

Katagiri, Yasuhiro. *The Mississippi State Sovereignty Commission: Civil Rights and States' Rights.* Jackson: University Press of Mississippi, 2001.

Keller, William W. *The Liberals and J. Edgar Hoover: Rise and Fall of a Domestic Intelligence State.* Princeton: Princeton University Press, 1989.

Kelley, Clarence M., and James Kirkpatrick Davis. *Kelley: The Story of an FBI Director.* Kansas City: Andrews, McMeel & Parker, 1987.

Kinchen, Shirletta J. "Beauty and the Black Student Revolt: Black Student Activism at Memphis State and the Politics of Campus 'Beauty Spaces.'" In *Unseen Light: Black Struggles for Freedom in Memphis, Tennessee*, edited by Aram Goudsouzian and Charles W. McKinney Jr., 330–47. Lexington: University Press of Kentucky, 2018.

———. *Black Power in the Bluff City: African American Youth and Student Activism in Memphis, 1965–1975*. Knoxville: University of Tennessee Press, 2016.

Knowlton, Steven A. "'Since I Was a Citizen, I Had the Right to Attend the Library': The Key Role of the Public Library in the Civil Rights Movement in Memphis." In *An Unseen Light: Black Struggles for Freedom in Memphis, Tennessee*, edited by Aram Goudsouzian and Charles W. McKinney Jr., 203–27. Lexington: University Press of Kentucky, 2018.

Lanier, Robert A. "When Henry Wallace Came To Memphis: A Research Note on Race and Politics in the Post–World War II Era." *Tennessee Historical Quarterly* 74, no. 4 (Winter 2015): 298–311.

Lauterbach, Preston. *Bluff City: The Secret Life of Photographer Ernest Withers*. New York: Norton, 2019.

———. *The Chitlin' Circuit and the Road to Rock 'n' Roll*. New York: Norton, 2011.

Legal Development Division, *History of Police Intelligence Operations, 1880–1975* (final draft). Gaithersburg, MD: International Association of Chiefs of Police, 1976.

Lehman, Christopher Paul. "Civil Rights in the Twilight: The End of the Civil Rights Movement Era in 1973." *Journal of Black Studies* 36, no. 3 (2006): 415–28.

Lesesne, Henry H. *A History of the University of South Carolina, 1940–2000*. Columbia: University of South Carolina Press, 2001.

Lewis, John. *Walking with the Wind: A Memoir of the Movement*. New York: Simon and Schuster, 1998.

Little, Kimberly K. "'You Must Be from the North': Southern White Women in the Civil Rights Movement, Memphis, Tennessee, 1955–1971." PhD diss., Ohio University, 2004.

———. *You Must Be from the North: Southern White Women in the Memphis Civil Rights Movement*. Jackson: University Press of Mississippi, 2009.

Lorenzini, Jack. "United by a Cause: Student Activists and the Memphis Sanitation Strike of 1968." *Tennessee Historical Quarterly* 78, no. 4 (2019): 266–91.

———. "'We Didn't Reject the System, the System Rejected Us': The SDS Failure to Obtain a Charter at Memphis State University, 1968–1970." *West Tennessee Historical Society Papers* 62 (December 2008): 25–43.

Lovett, Bobby L. *The Civil Rights Movement in Tennessee: A Narrative History*. Knoxville: University of Tennessee Press, 2005.

Luckett, Robert E. *Joe T. Patterson and the White South's Dilemma: Evolving Resistance to Black Advancement*. Jackson: University of Mississippi Press, 2015.

Mackenzie, Angus. *Secrets: The CIA's War at Home*. Berkeley: University of California Press, 1997.

McAninch, William Shepard. "ESSAY: The UFO." *South Carolina Law Review* 46, no. 2 (1995): 363–79.

McCollough Seletzky, Leta. *The Kneeling Man: My Father's Life as a Black Spy Who Witnessed the Assassination of Martin Luther King Jr.* Berkeley, CA: Counterpoint, 2023.

———. "The Man in the Picture: How I Came to Terms with My Father's Secret CIA Past." *O, The Oprah Magazine*, May 2018. http://www.oprah.com/inspiration/leta-mccollough-on-learning-to-accept-her-fathers-secret-cia-past.

McKnight, Gerald D. "A Harvest of Hate: The FBI's War against Black Youth—Domestic Intelligence in Memphis, Tennessee." *South Atlantic Quarterly* 86, no. 1 (Winter 1987): 1–21.

———. *The Last Crusade: Martin Luther King, Jr., the FBI, and the Poor People's Campaign.* Boulder, CO: Westview Press, 1998.

———. "The 1968 Memphis Sanitation Strike and the FBI: A Case Study in Urban Surveillance." *South Atlantic Quarterly* 83, no. 2 (Spring 1984): 138–56.

Medsger, Betty. *The Burglary: The Discovery of J. Edgar Hoover's Secret FBI.* New York: Knopf, 2014.

Michel, Gregg L. "Surveilling the Memphis Movement: Police Spying in Memphis, 1968–1976." *Journal of Southern History* 87, no. 4 (November 2021): 673–710.

———. "It Even Happened Here: Student Activism at Furman University, 1967–1970." *South Carolina Historical Magazine* 109, no. 1 (2008): 38–57.

———. *Struggle for a Better South: The Southern Student Organizing Committee, 1964–1969.* New York: Palgrave Macmillan, 2004.

———. "'We'll Take Our Stand': The Southern Student Organizing Committee and the Radicalization of White Southern Students, 1964–1969." PhD diss., University of Virginia, 1999.

Miles, Ashley Elizabeth. "The GI Coffeehouse Movement, 1968–1972: Class-Based Activism in the Vietnam War." Master's thesis, Auburn University, 2020.

Montejano, David. *Quixote's Soldiers: A Local History of the Chicano Movement, 1966–1981.* Austin: University of Texas Press, 2010.

Moore, Leonard N. *Black Rage in New Orleans: Police Brutality and African American Activism from World War II to Hurricane Katrina.* Baton Rouge: Louisiana State University Press, 2010.

Morgan, Lynda J. "Undue Process: Reconstruction Legacies of Violence, Democracy, and Race." *Reviews in American History* 43, no. 3 (September 2015): 512–21.

Morgan, Richard E. *Domestic Intelligence: Monitoring Dissent in America.* Austin: University of Texas Press, 1980.

Morris, Aldon D. *The Origins of the Civil Rights Movement: Black Communities Organizing for Change.* New York: Free Press, 1984.

Murakawa, Naomi. *The First Civil Right: How Liberals Built Prison in America.* Oxford: Oxford University Press, 2014.

Murch, Donna. "A Historian's Claims about Martin Luther King Are Shocking—and

Irresponsible." *The Guardian*, June 8, 2019. https://www.theguardian.com/commentisfree/2019/jun/08/martin-luther-king-david-garrow-essay-claims.

Murray, Gail Schmunk. "Taming the War on Poverty: Memphis as a Case Study." *Journal of Urban History* 43, no. 1 (2017): 70–90.

Myers, Andrew H. *Black, White & Olive Drab: Racial Integration at Fort Jackson, South Carolina and the Civil Rights Movement*. Charlottesville: University of Virginia Press, 2006.

Nelson, Jack, and Jack Bass. *The Orangeburg Massacre*. New York: World Publishing, 1970.

Nicosia, Gerald. *Home to War: A History of the Vietnam Veterans' Movement*. 2001. Reprint, New York: Carroll & Graf, 2004.

O'Daniel, Patrick. *Crusaders, Gangsters, and Whiskey: Prohibition in Memphis*. Jackson: University Press of Mississippi, 2018.

Olmsted, Kathryn S. *Challenging the Secret Government: The Post-Watergate Investigations of the CIA and FBI*. Chapel Hill: University of North Carolina Press, 1996.

O'Reilly, Kenneth. *Hoover and the Un-Americans: The FBI, HUAC, and the Red Menace*. Philadelphia: Temple University Press, 1983.

———. *Racial Matters: The FBI's Secret File on Black America, 1960–1972*. New York: Free Press, 1989.

Palmer, Charles Steven. "Economics, Grievances, Protective-Employee Unionization, and the 1978 Memphis Fire and Police Strikes." *Essays in Economic & Business History* 22 (January 2004): 183–97.

———. "'I'm Tired of Feeling like a Garbage Man': Labor, Politics, Business, and the 1978 Memphis Fire and Police Strikes." PhD diss., University of Mississippi, 2002.

Parsons, David L. *Dangerous Grounds: Antiwar Coffeehouses and Military Dissent in the Vietnam Era*. Chapel Hill: University of North Carolina Press, 2017.

Payne, Cril. *Deep Cover: An FBI Agent Infiltrates the Radical Underground*. New York: Newsweek Books, 1979.

Perrusquia, Marc. *A Spy in Canaan: How the FBI Used a Famous Photographer to Infiltrate the Civil Rights Movement*. Brooklyn: Melville House, 2018.

Peters, Shawn Francis. *The Catonsville Nine: A Story of Faith and Resistance in the Vietnam Era*. Oxford: Oxford University Press, 2012.

Pettit, Emma. "The Inquisition." *Chronicle of Higher Education* 69, no. 4 (October 11, 2022). https://www.chronicle.com/article/the-inquisition.

———. "'Private Little Hell.'" *Chronicle of Higher Education* 69, no. 8 (November 28, 2022). https://www.chronicle.com/article/private-little-hell.

Pierce, Michael. "Odell Smith, Teamsters Local 878, and Civil Rights Unionism in Little Rock, 1943–1965." *Journal of Southern History* 84, no. 4 (2018): 925–58.

Pinto, Vince. "Weapons for the Homefront." In *Policing America*, edited by Anthony Platt and Lynn Cooper, 80–90. Englewood Cliffs, NJ: Prentice Hall, 1974.

Pohlmann, Marcus D., and Michael P. Kirby. *Racial Politics at the Crossroads: Memphis Elects Dr. W. W. Herenton*. Knoxville: University of Tennessee Press, 1996.

The Police Threat to Political Liberty: Discoveries and Actions of the American Friends Service Committee Program on Government Surveillance and Citizens' Rights. Philadelphia: American Friends Service Committee, 1979.

Ponton, David, III. "A Protracted War for Order: Police Violence in the Twentieth Century United States." *History Compass* 16, no. 6 (2018): 1–12.

Powers, Richard Gid. *Broken: The Troubled Past and Uncertain Future of the FBI*. New York: Free Press, 2004.

Powledge, Fred. *Free at Last? The Civil Rights Movement and the People Who Made It*. Boston: Little, Brown, 1991.

Prados, John. *The Family Jewels: The CIA, Secrecy, and Presidential Power*. Austin: University of Texas Press, 2013.

Prater, Tammy M. "'To Share in All the Blessings of Our Freedom': The Concerned Women of Memphis and Shelby County and the Embodiment of Great Society Ideology." *Southern Historian* 30 (Spring 2009): 37–49.

Purcell, Aaron D. "Seeing Red in the Bluegrass: The Kentucky Un-American Activities Committee and Conservatism in the Late 1960s." *Register of the Kentucky Historical Society* 117, no. 1 (Winter 2019): 57–93.

Pyle, Christopher H. "The Domestic Intelligence Community." In *Uncle Sam Is Watching You: Highlights from the Hearings of the Senate Subcommittee on Constitutional Rights*, 41–60. Washington, DC: Public Affairs Press, 1971.

———. "Military Intelligence Overkill." In *Uncle Sam Is Watching You: Highlights from the Hearings of the Senate Subcommittee on Constitutional Rights*, 74–147. Washington, DC: Public Affairs Press, 1971.

Raines, Howell. *My Soul Is Rested: Movement Days in the Deep South Remembered*. New York: Putnam, 1977.

Ransby, Barbara. "A Black Feminist's Response to Attacks on Martin Luther King Jr.'s Legacy." *New York Times*, June 3, 2019. https://www.nytimes.com/2019/06/03/opinion/martin-luther-king-fbi.html.

Rashke, Richard. *The Killing of Karen Silkwood: The Story behind the Kerr-McGee Plutonium Case*. Boston: Houghton Mifflin, 1981.

Reed, Linda. *Simple Decency & Common Sense: The Southern Conference Movement, 1938–1963*. Bloomington: Indiana University Press, 1991

Rollins, Tyler Russell. "Domestic Surveillance in the United States: World War II to Vietnam." PhD diss., University of Colorado Boulder, 2016. http://search.proquest.com/pqdtglobal/docview/1834960631/abstract/58F369B3F9D843CBPO/1.

Rosen, Hannah. *Terror in the Heart of Freedom: Citizenship, Sexual Violence, and the Meaning of Race in the Postemancipation South*. Chapel Hill: University of North Carolina Press, 2009.

Rosenfeld, Seth. *Subversives: The FBI's War on Student Radicals, and Reagan's Rise to Power*. New York: Farrar, Straus and Giroux, 2012.

Rosenfeld, Susan. "Tim Weiner's 'Enemies' Wears Its Anti-FBI Agenda on Its Sleeve." *History News Network* (blog), April 16, 2012. http://hnn.us/article/145631.

Rossinow, Doug. "Historiographical Reflections." In *Rebellion in Black and White: Southern Student Activism in the 1960s*, edited by Robert Cohen and David J. Snyder, 307–12. Baltimore: Johns Hopkins University Press, 2013.

Rowe-Sims, Sarah. "The Mississippi State Sovereignty Commission: An Agency History." *Journal of Mississippi History* 61 (1999): 29–58.

Rushing, Wanda. *Memphis and the Paradox of Place: Globalization in the American South.* Chapel Hill: University of North Carolina Press, 2009.

Sanford, Otis. *From Boss Crump to King Willie: How Race Changed Memphis Politics.* Knoxville: University of Tennessee Press, 2017.

Schuessler, Jennifer. "His Martin Luther King Biography Was a Classic. His Latest King Piece Is Causing a Furor." *New York Times*, June 4, 2019. https://www.nytimes.com/2019/06/04/arts/king-fbi-tapes-david-garrow.html.

Schwarz, Frederick A. O., and Aziz Z. Huq. *Unchecked and Unbalanced: Presidential Power in a Time of Terror.* New York: New Press, 2007.

Scott, Katherine A. *Reining in the State: Civil Society and Congress in the Vietnam and Watergate Eras.* Lawrence: University Press of Kansas, 2013.

Sellers, Cleveland L., Jr., with Robert Terrell. *The River of No Return: The Autobiography of a Black Militant and the Life and Death of SNCC.* New York: Morrow, 1973.

Seo, Sarah A. *Policing the Open Road: How Cars Transformed American Freedom.* Cambridge: Harvard University Press, 2019.

Sigafoos, Robert Alan. *Cotton Row to Beale Street: A Business History of Memphis.* Memphis: Memphis State University Press, 1979.

Silver, Christopher. "The Changing Face of Neighborhoods in Memphis and Richmond, 1940–1985." In *Shades of the Sunbelt: Essays on Ethnicity, Race, and the Urban South*, edited by Randall M. Miller and George E. Pozzetta, 93–126. New York: Greenwood Press, 1988.

Siracusa, Anthony C. *Nonviolence before King: The Politics of Being and the Black Freedom Struggle.* Chapel Hill: University of North Carolina Press, 2021.

———. "Nonviolence, Black Power, and the Surveillance State in Memphis's War on Poverty." In *An Unseen Light: Black Struggles for Freedom in Memphis, Tennessee*, edited by Aram Goudsouzian and Charles Wesley McKinney, 279–305. Lexington: University Press of Kentucky, 2018.

Smist, Frank John. *Congress Oversees the United States Intelligence Community, 1947–1989.* Knoxville: University of Tennessee Press, 1990.

Sokol, Jason. *There Goes My Everything: White Southerners in the Age of Civil Rights, 1945–1975.* New York: Knopf, 2006.

Sorrels, William Wright. *The Exciting Years: The Cecil C. Humphreys Presidency of Memphis State University, 1960–1972.* Memphis: Memphis State University Press, 1987.

Speer, Lisa K. "Fresh Focus: Mississippi's 'Spy Files': The State Sovereignty Commission Records Controversy, 1977–1999." *Provenance, Journal of the Society of Georgia Archivists* 17, no. 1 (1999): 101–17.

Spinney, Robert G. "Municipal Government in Nashville, Tennessee, 1938–1951: World War II and the Growth of the Public Sector." *Journal of Southern History* 61, no. 1 (1995): 77–112.

Sprayberry, Gary S. "Student Radicalism and the Antiwar Movement at the University of Alabama." In *Rebellion in Black and White: Southern Student Activism in the 1960s*, edited by Robert Cohen and David J. Snyder, 148–70. Baltimore: Johns Hopkins University Press, 2013.

Srouji, Jacque. *Critical Mass: Nuclear Power, the Alternative to Energy Famine.* Nashville: Aurora Publications, 1977.

Stacewicz, Richard. *Winter Soldiers: An Oral History of Vietnam Veterans Against the War.* New York: Twayne Publishers, 1997.

Stein, Ralph M. "Expansion of Counterintelligence." In *Uncle Sam Is Watching You: Highlights from the Hearings of the Senate Subcommittee on Constitutional Rights*, 148–71. Washington, DC: Public Affairs Press, 1971.

Strub, Whitney. "Black and White and Banned All Over: Race, Censorship and Obscenity in Postwar Memphis." *Journal of Social History* 40, no. 3 (2007): 685–715.

Sullivan, William C. *The Bureau: My Thirty Years in Hoover's FBI.* New York: Norton, 1979.

Taylor, Peter. *A Summons to Memphis.* New York: Knopf, 1986.

Theoharis, Athan G., et al. *The FBI: A Comprehensive Reference Guide.* Phoenix, Ariz.: Oryx Press, 1999.

Theoharis, Athan G. *From the Secret Files of J. Edgar Hoover.* Chicago: I. R. Dee, 1991.

———. "In-House Cover-Up: Researching FBI Files." In *Beyond the Hiss Case: The FBI, Congress, and the Cold War*, edited by Athan G. Theoharis, 20–77. Philadelphia: Temple University Press, 1982.

———. *Spying on Americans: Political Surveillance from Hoover to the Huston Plan.* Philadelphia: Temple University Press, 1978.

Toobin, Jeffrey. *Homegrown: Timothy McVeigh and the Rise of Right-Wing Extremism.* New York: Simon and Schuster, 2023.

Trillin, Calvin. "State Secrets." In *Jackson, 1964: And Other Dispatches from Fifty Years of Reporting on Race in America*, 253–75. New York: Random House, 2016.

Tucker, David M. *Memphis since Crump: Bossism, Blacks, and Civic Reformers, 1948–1968.* Knoxville: University of Tennessee Press, 1980.

Turner, Jeffrey A. "The Rise of Black and White Student Protest in Nashville." In *Rebellion in Black and White: Southern Student Activism in the 1960s*, edited by Robert Cohen and David J. Snyder, 129–47. Baltimore: Johns Hopkins University Press, 2013.

Ungar, Sanford J. *FBI.* Boston: Little, Brown, 1975.

Van Deburg, William. *New Day in Babylon: The Black Power Movement and American Culture, 1965–1975.* Chicago: University of Chicago Press, 1992.

Vaughn, Sandra. "Memphis: Heart of the Mid-South." In *In Search of the New South: The Black Urban Experience in the 1970s and 1980s,* edited by Robert D. Bullard, 98–120. Tuscaloosa: University of Alabama Press, 1989.

Vries, Tity de. "The 1967 Central Intelligence Agency Scandal: Catalyst in a Transforming Relationship between State and People." *Journal of American History* 98, no. 4 (2012): 1075–92.

Watters, Pat, and Stephen Gillers, eds. *Investigating the FBI.* Garden City, NY: Doubleday, 1971.

Weatherford, Jack McIver. "Family Culture, Behavior, and Emotion in a Working-Class German Town." PhD diss, University of California, San Diego, 1977.

Webb, Lee. "Repression—a New 'Growth Industry.'" In *Policing America,* edited by Anthony Platt and Lynn Cooper, 77–79. Englewood Cliffs, NJ: Prentice Hall, 1974.

Weiner, Tim. *Enemies: A History of the FBI.* New York: Random House, 2012.

Wells, Tom. *The War Within: America's Battle over Vietnam.* 1994. Reprint, New York: Henry Holt, 1996.

Wilford, Hugh. *The Mighty Wurlitzer: How the CIA Played America.* Cambridge: Harvard University Press, 2008.

Woods, Jeff. *Black Struggle, Red Scare: Segregation and Anti-Communism in the South, 1948–1968.* Baton Rouge: Louisiana State University Press, 2004.

Wright, Sharon D. *Race, Power, and Political Emergence in Memphis.* Garland Studies on Race and Politics. New York: Garland, 2000.

Young, Darius J. *Robert R. Church Jr. and the African American Political Struggle.* Gainesville: University Press of Florida, 2019.

———. "'The Saving of Black America's Body and White America's Soul': The Lynching of Ell Persons and the Rise of Black Activism in Memphis." In *An Unseen Light: Black Struggles for Freedom in Memphis, Tennessee,* edited by Aram Goudsouzian and Charles W. McKinney Jr., 39–60. Lexington: University Press of Kentucky, 2018.

Young, Stephen Flinn. "*The Kudzu:* Sixties Generational Revolt—Even in Mississippi." *Southern Quarterly* 34, no. 3 (1996): 122–36.

Zinn, Howard. *SNCC: The New Abolitionists.* Boston: Beacon Press, 1965.

Zuboff, Shoshana. *The Age of Surveillance Capitalism: The Fight for a Human Future at the New Frontier of Power.* New York: PublicAffairs, 2019.

INDEX